Haynes

Volvo 940
Service and Repair Manual

John S. Mead

Models covered

(3249-192-6AG1)

Volvo 940 Saloon and Estate, including special/limited editions
2.0 litre (1986 cc) & 2.3 litre (2316 cc) 8-valve petrol engines

Does not cover 16-valve petrol engine (B204/B234), nor Diesel engines

---

© Haynes Publishing 2003

A book in the **Haynes Service and Repair Manual Series**

All rights reserved. No part of this book may be reproduced or transmitted in any form or by any means, electronic or mechanical, including photocopying, recording or by any information storage or retrieval system, without permission in writing from the copyright holder.

ISBN **1 85960 249 5**

British Library Cataloguing in Publication Data
A catalogue record for this book is available from the British Library.

ABCDE
FGHIJ
K

Printed in the USA

Haynes Publishing
Sparkford, Yeovil, Somerset BA22 7JJ, England

Haynes North America, Inc
861 Lawrence Drive, Newbury Park, California 91320, USA

Editions Haynes
4, Rue de l'Abreuvoir
92415 COURBEVOIE CEDEX, France

Haynes Publishing Nordiska AB
Box 1504, 751 45 UPPSALA, Sweden

Contents

LIVING WITH YOUR VOLVO 940

Introduction	Page	0•4
Safety First!	Page	0•5

Roadside Repairs

Introduction	Page	0•6
If your car won't start	Page	0•6
Jump starting	Page	0•7
Wheel changing	Page	0•8
Identifying leaks	Page	0•9
Towing	Page	0•9

Weekly Checks

Introduction	Page	0•10
Underbonnet check points	Page	0•10
Engine oil level	Page	0•11
Coolant level	Page	0•11
Screen washer fluid level	Page	0•12
Brake fluid level	Page	0•12
Power steering fluid level	Page	0•13
Wiper blades	Page	0•13
Tyre condition and pressure	Page	0•14
Bulbs and fuses	Page	0•15
Battery	Page	0•15

Lubricants, fluids and tyre pressures

	Page	0•16

MAINTENANCE

Routine Maintenance and Servicing

	Page	1•1
Maintenance schedule	Page	1•3
Maintenance procedures	Page	1•5

Contents

REPAIRS & OVERHAUL

Engine and Associated Systems
In-car engine repair procedures	Page 2A•1
Engine removal and overhaul procedures	Page 2B•1
Cooling, heating and air conditioning systems	Page 3•1
Fuel and exhaust systems	Page 4A•1
Emission control systems	Page 4B•1
Starting and charging systems	Page 5A•1
Ignition systems	Page 5B•1

Transmission
Clutch	Page 6•1
Manual transmission and overdrive	Page 7A•1
Automatic transmission	Page 7B•1
Propeller shaft and rear axle	Page 8•1

Brakes and Suspension
Braking system	Page 9•1
Suspension and steering	Page 10•1

Body Equipment
Bodywork and fittings	Page 11•1
Body electrical systems	Page 12•1

Wiring Diagrams
	Page 12•13

REFERENCE

Dimensions and weights	Page REF•1
Conversion factors	Page REF•2
Buying spare parts	Page REF•3
Vehicle identification	Page REF•3
General repair procedures	Page REF•4
Jacking and vehicle support	Page REF•5
Radio/cassette anti-theft system - precaution	Page REF•5
Tools and working facilities	Page REF•6
MOT test checks	Page REF•8
Fault finding	Page REF•12
Glossary of technical terms	Page REF•20

Index
	Page REF•25

Introduction

The Volvo 940 Saloon and Estate models were introduced in 1991 as a replacement for the 740 series.

The engine used in the 940 range is a fuel-injected, in-line, four-cylinder unit of 2.0 or 2.3 litre capacity. Both normally-aspirated and turbocharged versions are available. The engines feature a comprehensive engine management system with extensive emission control equipment.

Manual and automatic transmissions are available across the range. The manual transmission may be 5-speed, or 4-speed plus overdrive. The automatic transmission is a 4-speed, or 3-speed plus overdrive unit. Drive is taken to the rear wheels via a traditional live rear axle.

Braking is by discs all round, the handbrake acting on separate drums on the rear wheels. Anti-lock braking (ABS) is also available together with power-assisted steering on all models.

A wide range of standard and optional equipment is available within the 940 range to suit most tastes.

Provided that regular servicing is carried out in accordance with the manufacturer's recommendations, the Volvo 940 will provide the enviable reliability for which this marque is famous. The engine compartment is spacious and most of the items requiring frequent attention are easily accessible.

Volvo 940 Estate

The Volvo 940 Team

Haynes manuals are produced by dedicated and enthusiastic people working in close co-operation. The team responsible for the creation of this book included:

Author	John S Mead
Sub-editor	Carole Turk
Editor & Page Make-up	Bob Jex
Workshop manager	Paul Buckland
Photo Scans	John Martin Paul Tanswell
Cover illustration & Line Art	Roger Healing

We hope the book will help you to get the maximum enjoyment from your car. By carrying out routine maintenance as described you will ensure your car's reliability and preserve its resale value.

Your Volvo 940 manual

The aim of this manual is to help you get the best value from your vehicle. It can do so in several ways. It can help you decide what work must be done (even should you choose to get it done by a garage). It will also provide information on routine maintenance and servicing, and give a logical course of action and diagnosis when random faults occur. However, it is hoped that you will use the manual by tackling the work yourself. On simpler jobs it may even be quicker than booking the car into a garage and going there twice, to leave and collect it. Perhaps most important, a lot of money can be saved by avoiding the costs a garage must charge to cover its labour and overheads.

The manual has drawings and descriptions to show the function of the various components so that their layout can be understood. Tasks are described and photographed in a clear step-by-step sequence.

References to the 'left' and 'right' of the vehicle are in the sense of a person in the driver's seat facing forward.

Acknowledgements

Thanks are due to Loders of Yeovil who provided several of the project vehicles used in the origination of this manual. Thanks are also due to Draper Tools Limited, who provided some of the workshop tools, and to all those people at Sparkford who helped in the production of this manual.

We take great pride in the accuracy of information given in this manual, but vehicle manufacturers make alterations and design changes during the production run of a particular vehicle of which they do not inform us. No liability can be accepted by the author or publisher for loss, damage or injury caused by any errors in, or omissions from, the information given.

Safety first! 0•5

Working on your car can be dangerous. This page shows just some of the potential risks and hazards, with the aim of creating a safety-conscious attitude.

General hazards

Scalding
• Don't remove the radiator or expansion tank cap while the engine is hot.
• Engine oil, automatic transmission fluid or power steering fluid may also be dangerously hot if the engine has recently been running.

Burning
• Beware of burns from the exhaust system and from any part of the engine. Brake discs and drums can also be extremely hot immediately after use.

Crushing
• When working under or near a raised vehicle, always supplement the jack with axle stands, or use drive-on ramps. *Never venture under a car which is only supported by a jack.*
• Take care if loosening or tightening high-torque nuts when the vehicle is on stands. Initial loosening and final tightening should be done with the wheels on the ground.

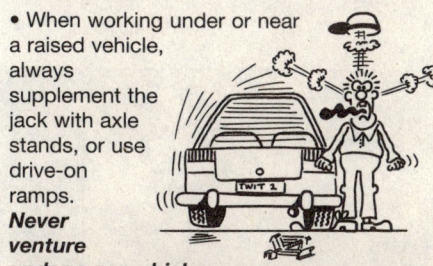

Fire
• Fuel is highly flammable; fuel vapour is explosive.
• Don't let fuel spill onto a hot engine.
• Do not smoke or allow naked lights (including pilot lights) anywhere near a vehicle being worked on. Also beware of creating sparks (electrically or by use of tools).
• Fuel vapour is heavier than air, so don't work on the fuel system with the vehicle over an inspection pit.
• Another cause of fire is an electrical overload or short-circuit. Take care when repairing or modifying the vehicle wiring.
• Keep a fire extinguisher handy, of a type suitable for use on fuel and electrical fires.

Electric shock
• Ignition HT voltage can be dangerous, especially to people with heart problems or a pacemaker. Don't work on or near the ignition system with the engine running or the ignition switched on.
• Mains voltage is also dangerous. Make sure that any mains-operated equipment is correctly earthed. Mains power points should be protected by a residual current device (RCD) circuit breaker.

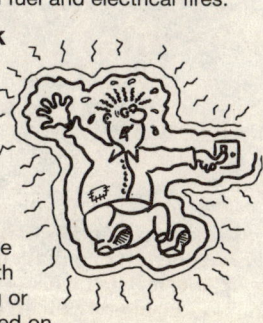

Fume or gas intoxication
• Exhaust fumes are poisonous; they often contain carbon monoxide, which is rapidly fatal if inhaled. Never run the engine in a confined space such as a garage with the doors shut.
• Fuel vapour is also poisonous, as are the vapours from some cleaning solvents and paint thinners.

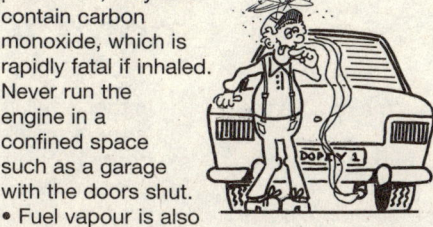

Poisonous or irritant substances
• Avoid skin contact with battery acid and with any fuel, fluid or lubricant, especially antifreeze, brake hydraulic fluid and Diesel fuel. Don't syphon them by mouth. If such a substance is swallowed or gets into the eyes, seek medical advice.
• Prolonged contact with used engine oil can cause skin cancer. Wear gloves or use a barrier cream if necessary. Change out of oil-soaked clothes and do not keep oily rags in your pocket.
• Air conditioning refrigerant forms a poisonous gas if exposed to a naked flame (including a cigarette). It can also cause skin burns on contact.

Asbestos
• Asbestos dust can cause cancer if inhaled or swallowed. Asbestos may be found in gaskets and in brake and clutch linings. When dealing with such components it is safest to assume that they contain asbestos.

Special hazards

Hydrofluoric acid
• This extremely corrosive acid is formed when certain types of synthetic rubber, found in some O-rings, oil seals, fuel hoses etc, are exposed to temperatures above 400°C. The rubber changes into a charred or sticky substance containing the acid. *Once formed, the acid remains dangerous for years. If it gets onto the skin, it may be necessary to amputate the limb concerned.*
• When dealing with a vehicle which has suffered a fire, or with components salvaged from such a vehicle, wear protective gloves and discard them after use.

The battery
• Batteries contain sulphuric acid, which attacks clothing, eyes and skin. Take care when topping-up or carrying the battery.
• The hydrogen gas given off by the battery is highly explosive. Never cause a spark or allow a naked light nearby. Be careful when connecting and disconnecting battery chargers or jump leads.

Air bags
• Air bags can cause injury if they go off accidentally. Take care when removing the steering wheel and/or facia. Special storage instructions may apply.

Diesel injection equipment
• Diesel injection pumps supply fuel at very high pressure. Take care when working on the fuel injectors and fuel pipes.

⚠ *Warning: Never expose the hands, face or any other part of the body to injector spray; the fuel can penetrate the skin with potentially fatal results.*

Remember...

DO
• Do use eye protection when using power tools, and when working under the vehicle.
• Do wear gloves or use barrier cream to protect your hands when necessary.
• Do get someone to check periodically that all is well when working alone on the vehicle.
• Do keep loose clothing and long hair well out of the way of moving mechanical parts.
• Do remove rings, wristwatch etc, before working on the vehicle – especially the electrical system.
• Do ensure that any lifting or jacking equipment has a safe working load rating adequate for the job.

DON'T
• Don't attempt to lift a heavy component which may be beyond your capability – get assistance.
• Don't rush to finish a job, or take unverified short cuts.
• Don't use ill-fitting tools which may slip and cause injury.
• Don't leave tools or parts lying around where someone can trip over them. Mop up oil and fuel spills at once.
• Don't allow children or pets to play in or near a vehicle being worked on.

0•6 Roadside repairs

The following pages are intended to help in dealing with common roadside emergencies and breakdowns. You will find more detailed fault finding information at the back of the manual, and repair information in the main chapters.

If your car won't start and the starter motor doesn't turn

- ☐ If it's a model with automatic transmission, make sure the selector is in 'P' or 'N'.
- ☐ Open the bonnet and make sure that the battery terminals are clean and tight.
- ☐ Switch on the headlights and try to start the engine. If the headlights go very dim when you're trying to start, the battery is probably flat. Get out of trouble by jump starting (see next page) using a friend's car.

If your car won't start even though the starter motor turns as normal

- ☐ Is there fuel in the tank?
- ☐ Is there moisture on electrical components under the bonnet? Switch off the ignition, then wipe off any obvious dampness with a dry cloth. Spray a water-repellent aerosol product (WD-40 or equivalent) on ignition and fuel system electrical connectors like those shown in the photos. Pay special attention to the ignition coil, ignition coil wiring connector, and HT leads.

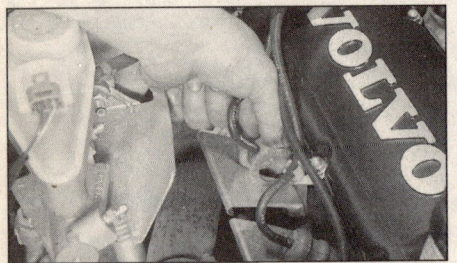

A Check that the spark plug HT leads (where applicable) are securely connected by pushing them home.

B The throttle potentiometer wiring plug may cause problems if not connected securely.

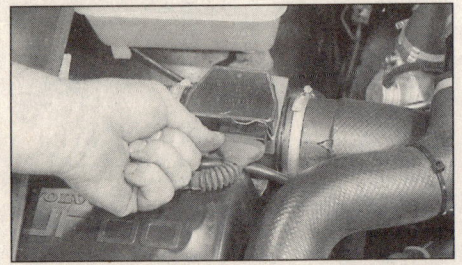

C Check the electronic control unit multi-plug for security (where applicable) with the ignition switched off.

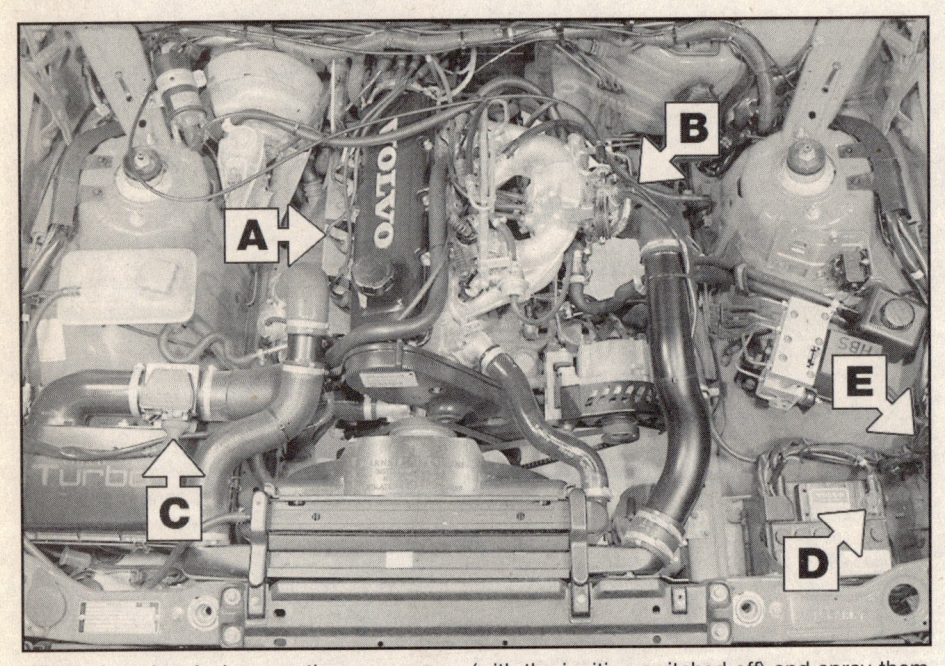

Check that electrical connections are secure (with the ignition switched off) and spray them with a water dispersant spray like WD40 if you suspect a problem due to damp

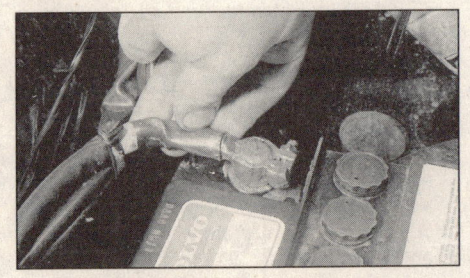

D Check the security and condition of the battery connections.

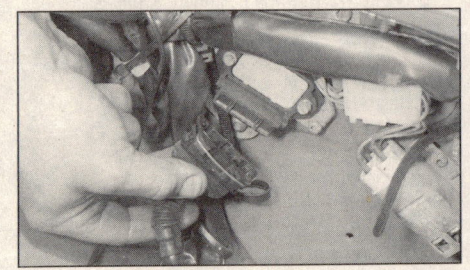

E Check that the ignition coil wiring plug is secure, and spray with water-dispersant if necessary.

Roadside repairs 0•7

Jump starting

HAYNES HiNT
Jump starting will get you out of trouble, but you must correct whatever made the battery go flat in the first place. There are three possibilities:

1 *The battery has been drained by repeated attempts to start, or by leaving the lights on.*

2 *The charging system is not working properly (alternator drivebelt slack or broken, alternator wiring fault or alternator itself faulty).*

3 *The battery itself is at fault (electrolyte low, or battery worn out).*

When jump-starting a car using a booster battery, observe the following precautions:

✔ Before connecting the booster battery, make sure that the ignition is switched off.

✔ Ensure that all electrical equipment (lights, heater, wipers, etc) is switched off.

✔ Take note of any special precautions printed on the battery case.

✔ Make sure that the booster battery is the same voltage as the discharged one in the vehicle.

✔ If the battery is being jump-started from the battery in another vehicle, the two vehicles MUST NOT TOUCH each other.

✔ Make sure that the transmission is in neutral (or PARK, in the case of automatic transmission).

1 Connect one end of the red jump lead to the positive (+) terminal of the flat battery

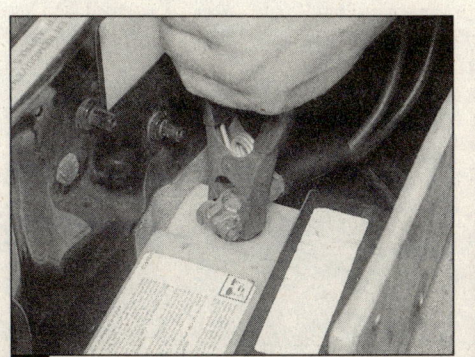

2 Connect the other end of the red lead to the positive (+) terminal of the booster battery.

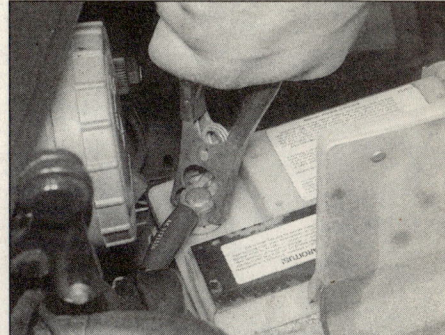

3 Connect one end of the black jump lead to the negative (-) terminal of the booster battery

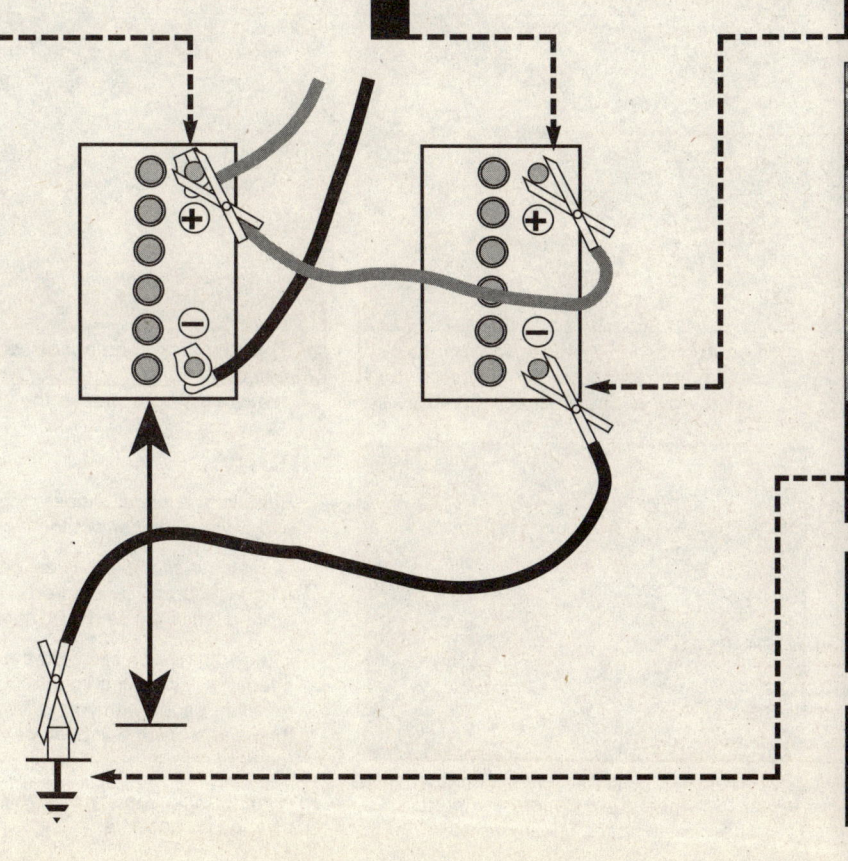

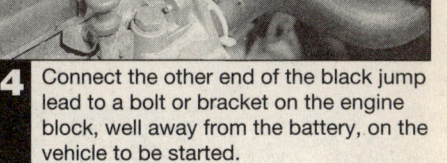

4 Connect the other end of the black jump lead to a bolt or bracket on the engine block, well away from the battery, on the vehicle to be started.

5 Make sure that the jump leads will not come into contact with the fan, drivebelts or other moving parts of the engine.

6 Start the engine using the booster battery and run it at idle speed. Switch on the lights, rear window demister and heater blower motor, then disconnect the jump leads in the reverse order of connection. Turn off the lights etc.

0•8 Roadside repairs

Wheel changing

Some of the details shown here will vary according to model. For instance, the location of the spare wheel and jack is not the same on all cars. However, the basic principles apply to all vehicles.

⚠️ *Warning: Do not change a wheel in a situation where you risk being hit by other traffic. On busy roads, try to stop in a lay-by or a gateway. Be wary of passing traffic while changing the wheel – it is easy to become distracted by the job in hand.*

Preparation

- [ ] When a puncture occurs, stop as soon as it is safe to do so.
- [ ] Park on firm level ground, if possible, and well out of the way of other traffic.
- [ ] Use hazard warning lights if necessary.
- [ ] If you have one, use a warning triangle to alert other drivers of your presence.
- [ ] Apply the handbrake and engage first or reverse gear (or Park on models with automatic transmission).
- [ ] Chock the wheel diagonally opposite the one being removed – a couple of large stones will do for this.
- [ ] If the ground is soft, use a flat piece of wood to spread the load under the jack.

Changing the wheel

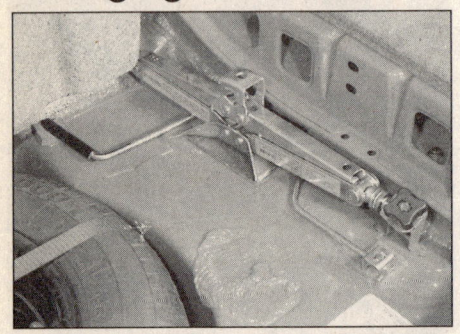

1 From inside the boot area, use the wheelbrace to lower the spare wheel cradle.

2 Slide the spare wheel out from the underside of the car.

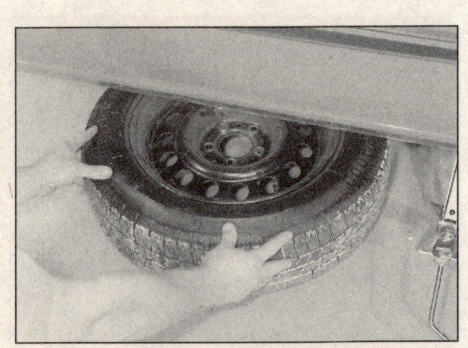

3 For safety in the event of the jack slipping, position the spare wheel under the sill, close to the jacking point.

4 Remove the wheel trim (where fitted) then slacken each wheel bolt by a half turn.

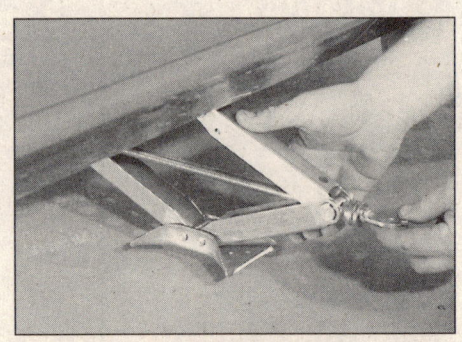

5 Locate the jack below the reinforced jacking point and on firm ground (don't jack the car at any other point on the sill).

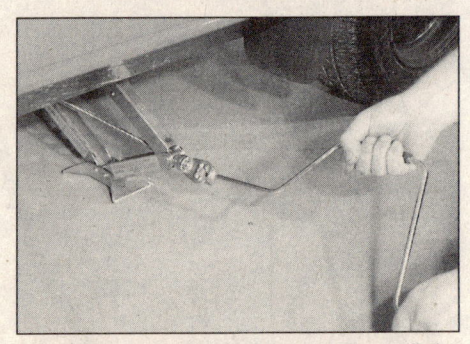

6 Turn the jack handle clockwise until the wheel is raised clear of the ground, remove the bolts and lift the wheel clear.

7 Position the spare wheel and fit the bolts. Tighten moderately with the wheel-brace, then lower the car to the ground.

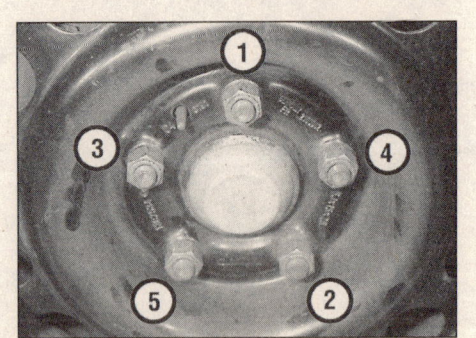

8 Tighten the wheel bolts in sequence, and fit the wheel trim. Secure the punctured wheel in the spare wheel cradle.

Finally...

- [ ] Remove the wheel chocks. Stow the jack and tools in the correct locations.
- [ ] Don't leave the spare wheel cradle empty and unsecured - it could drop onto the ground while the car is moving.
- [ ] Check the tyre pressure on the wheel just fitted. If it is low, or if you don't have a pressure gauge with you, drive slowly to the nearest garage and inflate the tyre to the right pressure.
- [ ] Have the damaged tyre or wheel repaired as soon as possible.

Roadside repairs 0•9

Identifying leaks

Puddles on the garage floor or drive, or obvious wetness under the bonnet or underneath the car, suggest a leak that needs investigating. It can sometimes be difficult to decide where the leak is coming from, especially if the engine bay is very dirty already. Leaking oil or fluid can also be blown rearwards by the passage of air under the car, giving a false impression of where the problem lies.

Warning: Most automotive oils and fluids are poisonous. Wash them off skin, and change out of contaminated clothing, without delay.

HAYNES HiNT *The smell of a fluid leaking from the car may provide a clue to what's leaking. Some fluids are distinctively coloured. It may help to clean the car carefully and to park it over some clean paper overnight as an aid to locating the source of the leak.*
Remember that some leaks may only occur while the engine is running.

Sump oil
Engine oil may leak from the drain plug...

Oil from filter
...or from the base of the oil filter.

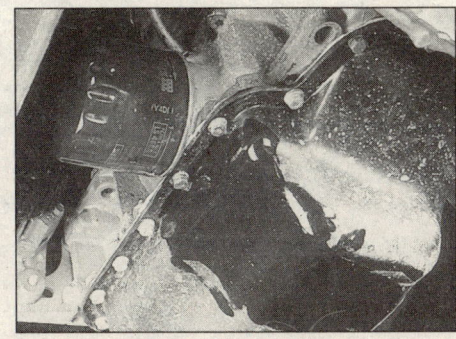

Gearbox oil
Gearbox oil can leak from the seals at the inboard ends of the driveshafts.

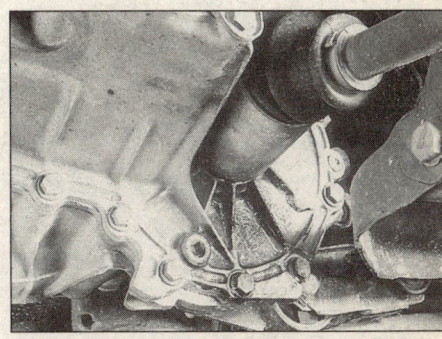

Antifreeze
Leaking antifreeze often leaves a crystalline deposit like this.

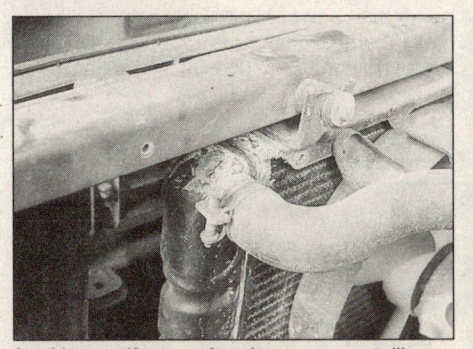

Brake fluid
A leak occurring at a wheel is almost certainly brake fluid.

Power steering fluid
Power steering fluid may leak from the pipe connectors on the steering rack.

Towing

When all else fails, you may find yourself having to get a tow home – or of course you may be helping somebody else. Long-distance recovery should only be done by a garage or breakdown service. For shorter distances, DIY towing using another car is easy enough, but observe the following points:

☐ Use a proper tow-rope – they are not expensive. The vehicle being towed must display an 'ON TOW' sign in its rear window.
☐ Always turn the ignition key to the 'on' position when the vehicle is being towed, so that the steering lock is released, and that the direction indicator and brake lights will work.
☐ Only attach the tow-rope to the towing eyes provided.
☐ Before being towed, release the handbrake and select neutral on the transmission.
☐ Note that greater-than-usual pedal pressure will be required to operate the brakes, since the vacuum servo unit is only operational with the engine running.
☐ On models with power steering, greater-than-usual steering effort will also be required.
☐ The driver of the car being towed must keep the tow-rope taut at all times to avoid snatching.
☐ Make sure that both drivers know the route before setting off.
☐ Only drive at moderate speeds and keep the distance towed to a minimum. Drive smoothly and allow plenty of time for slowing down at junctions.
☐ On models with automatic transmission, special precautions apply. If in doubt, do not tow, or transmission damage may result.

0•10 Weekly checks

Introduction

There are some very simple checks which need only take a few minutes to carry out, but which could save you a lot of inconvenience and expense.

These "Weekly checks" require no great skill or special tools, and the small amount of time they take to perform could prove to be very well spent, for example;

☐ Keeping an eye on tyre condition and pressures, will not only help to stop them wearing out prematurely, but could also save your life.

☐ Many breakdowns are caused by electrical problems. Battery-related faults are particularly common, and a quick check on a regular basis will often prevent the majority of these.

☐ If your car develops a brake fluid leak, the first time you might know about it is when your brakes don't work properly. Checking the level regularly will give advance warning of this kind of problem.

☐ If the oil or coolant levels run low, the cost of repairing any engine damage will be far greater than fixing the leak, for example.

Underbonnet check points

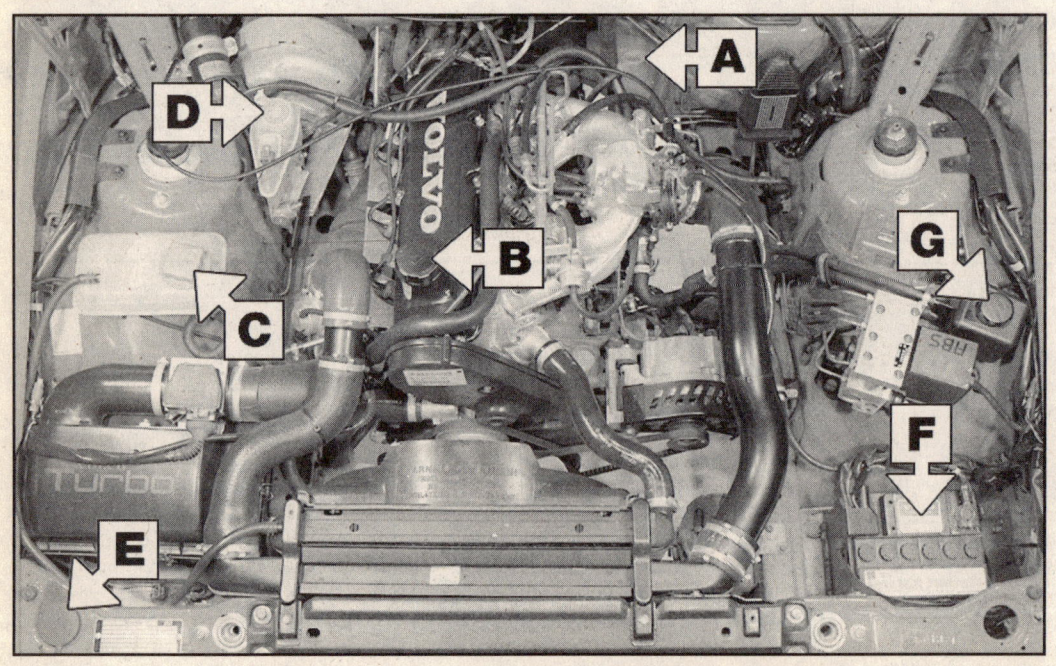

◀ **2.0 litre Turbo**

A *Engine oil level dipstick*
B *Engine oil filler cap*
C *Coolant expansion tank*
D *Brake/clutch fluid reservoir*
E *Screen washer fluid reservoir*
F *Battery*
G *Power steering fluid reservoir*

Weekly checks 0•11

Engine oil level

Before you start

✔ Make sure that your car is on level ground.
✔ Check the oil level before the car is driven, or at least 5 minutes after the engine has been switched off.

HAYNES HiNT: *If the oil is checked immediately after driving the vehicle, some of the oil will remain in the upper engine components, resulting in an inaccurate reading on the dipstick!*

The correct oil

Modern engines place great demands on their oil. It is very important that the correct oil for your car is used (See "Lubricants, fluids and tyre pressures").

Car Care

- If you have to add oil frequently, you should check whether you have any oil leaks. Place some clean paper under the car overnight, and check for stains in the morning. If there are no leaks, the engine may be burning oil.

- Always maintain the level between the upper and lower dipstick marks (see photo 3). If the level is too low severe engine damage may occur. Oil seal failure may result if the engine is overfilled by adding too much oil.

1 The dipstick top is often brightly coloured for easy identification (see "*Underbonnet check points*" on page 0•10 for exact location). Withdraw the dipstick.

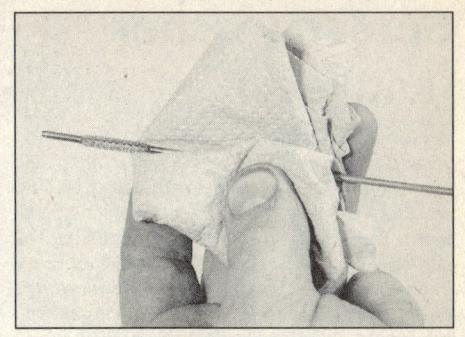

2 Using a clean rag or paper towel remove all oil from the dipstick. Insert the clean dipstick into the tube as far as it will go, then withdraw it again.

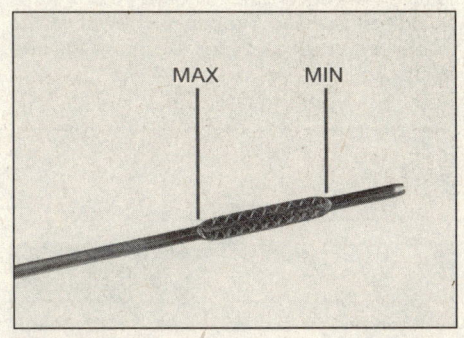

3 Note the oil level on the end of the dipstick, which should be between the upper ("MAX") mark and lower ("MIN") mark. Approximately 0.5 to 1.0 litre of oil will raise the level from the lower to the upper portion of the hatched area.

4 Oil is added through the filler cap. Unscrew the cap and top-up the level; a funnel may help to reduce spillage. Add the oil slowly, checking the level on the dipstick often. Don't overfill (see "*Car Care*" left).

Coolant level

⚠ **Warning: DO NOT attempt to remove the expansion tank pressure cap when the engine is hot, as there is a very great risk of scalding. Do not leave open containers of coolant about, as it is poisonous.**

Car Care

- With a sealed-type cooling system, adding coolant should not be necessary on a regular basis. If frequent topping-up is required, it is likely there is a leak. Check the radiator, all hoses and joint faces for signs of staining or wetness, and rectify as necessary.

- It is important that antifreeze is used in the cooling system all year round, not just during the winter months. Don't top-up with water alone, as the antifreeze will become too diluted.

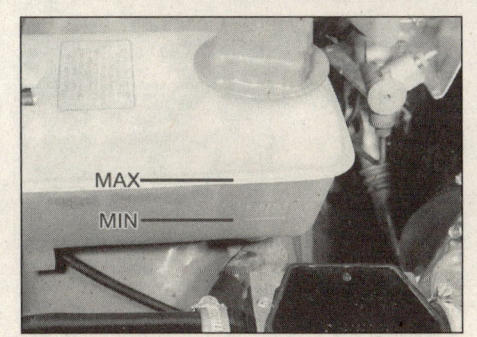

1 The coolant level varies with engine temperature. When cold, the coolant level should be up to the "MAX" mark on the side of the tank. When hot, the level may rise slightly above the "MAX" mark.

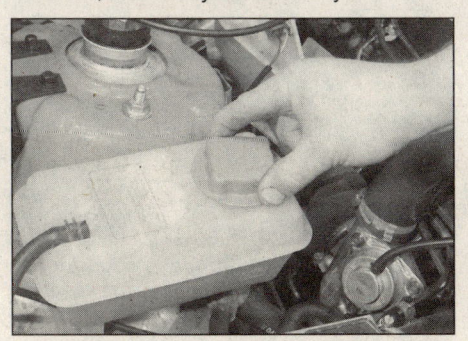

2 If topping up is necessary, **wait until the engine is cold**. Slowly unscrew the expansion tank cap, to release any pressure present in the cooling system, and remove it.

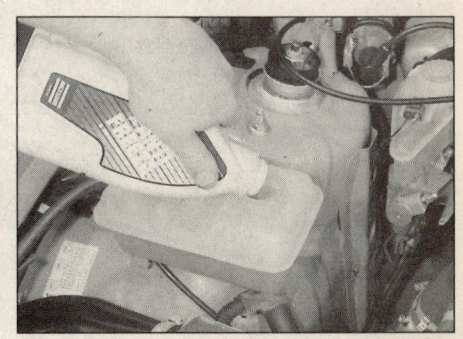

3 Add a mixture of water and antifreeze to the expansion tank until the coolant level is up to the "MAX" level mark. Refit the cap and tighten it securely.

0•12 Weekly checks

Screen washer fluid level

Screenwash additives not only keep the winscreen clean during foul weather, they also prevent the washer system freezing in cold weather - which is when you are likely to need it most. Don't top up using plain water as the screenwash will become too diluted, and will freeze during cold weather. **On no account use coolant antifreeze in the washer system - this could discolour or damage paintwork.**

1 The windscreen/tailgate/headlight washer fluid reservoir filler is located at the front right-hand corner of the engine compartment on Turbo models, or at the front left-hand corner on all other models. To check the fluid level, release the cap and observe the level in the reservoir by looking down the filler neck.

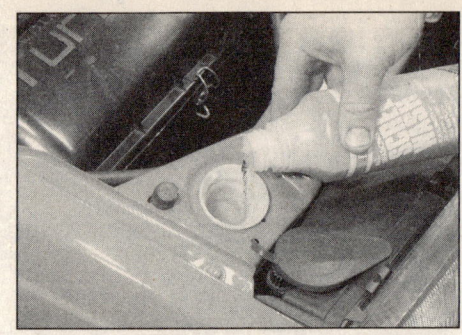

2 When topping-up the reservoir, a screenwash additive should be added in the quantities recommended on the bottle.

Brake/clutch fluid level

⚠️ **Warning:**
● Brake fluid can harm your eyes and damage painted surfaces, so use extreme caution when handling and pouring it.
● Do not use fluid that has been standing open for some time, as it absorbs moisture from the air, which can cause a dangerous loss of braking effectiveness.

HAYNES HiNT
● Make sure that your car is on level ground.
● The fluid level in the reservoir will drop slightly as the brake pads wear down, but the fluid level must never be allowed to drop below the "MIN" mark.

Safety First!
● If the reservoir requires repeated topping-up this is an indication of a fluid leak somewhere in the system, which should be investigated immediately.

● If a leak is suspected, the car should not be driven until the braking system has been checked. Never take any risks where brakes are concerned.

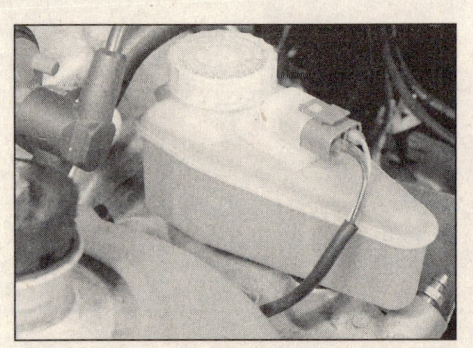

1 The MAX and MIN marks are indicated on the side of the reservoir The fluid level must be kept between the marks. On cars with an hydraulically operated clutch, the brake fluid reservoir also supplies the clutch hydraulic system.

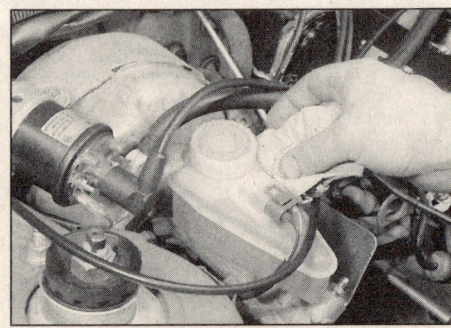

2 If topping-up is necessary, first wipe clean the area around the filler cap to prevent dirt entering the hydraulic system.

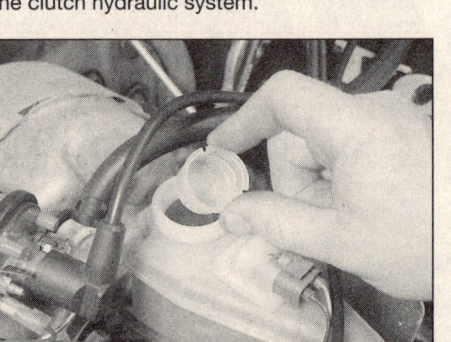

3 When adding fluid, it's a good idea to inspect the fluid filter and the reservoir itself. Wipe out the filter with a clean lint-free cloth if any particles can be seen. The system should be drained and refilled if dirt has found its way into the reservoir and can be seen in the fluid (see Chapter 9 for details).

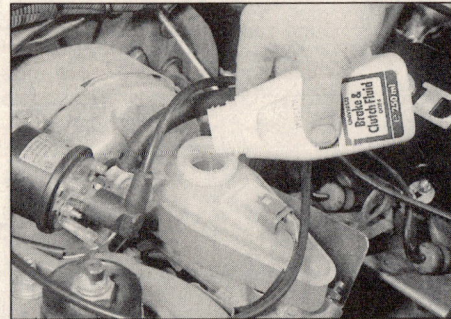

4 Carefully add fluid avoiding spilling it on surrounding paintwork. Use only the specified hydraulic fluid; mixing different types of fluid can cause damage to the system. After filling to the correct level, refit the cap securely, to prevent leaks and the entry of foreign matter. Wipe off any spilt fluid.

Weekly checks 0•13

Power steering fluid level

Before you start:
✔ Park the vehicle on level ground.
✔ Set the steering wheel straight-ahead.
✔ The engine should be turned off.

HAYNES HiNT *For the check to be accurate, the steering must not be turned once the engine has been stopped.*

Safety First!
● The need for frequent topping-up indicates a leak, which should be investigated immediately.

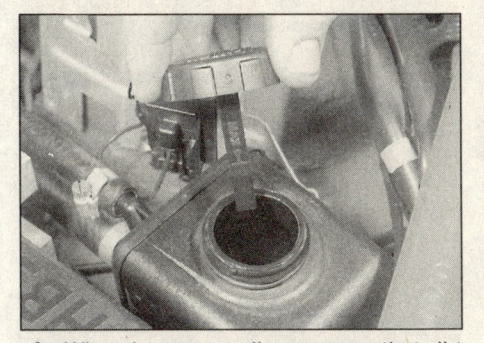

1 Wipe the surrounding area so that dirt does not enter the reservoir then unscrew the filler cap. Wipe the dipstick incorporated in the filler cap with a clean rag, then refit the cap and remove it again. The "MAX" mark is shown on one side of the dipstick.

2 On the other side of the dipstick there is a "MIN" mark. The fluid level must be maintained between the "MIN" and "MAX" marks.

3 If topping up is necessary, add a little fluid of the specified type, then recheck the level on the dipstick. Take great care not to allow any dirt into the hydraulic system and do not overfill the reservoir. When the level is correct, refit the cap.

Wiper blades

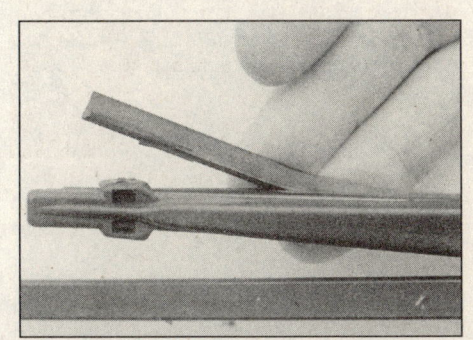

1 Check the condition of the wiper blades; if they are cracked or show any signs of deterioration, or if the glass swept area is smeared, renew them. Wiper blades should be renewed annually.

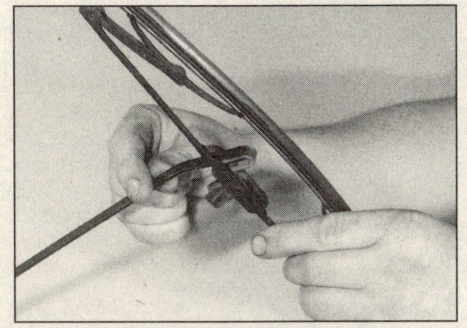

2 To remove a windscreen or tailgate wiper blade, pull the arm fully away from the glass until it locks. Swivel the blade through 90° depress the catch on the blade attachment, then withdraw the blade assembly off the arm.

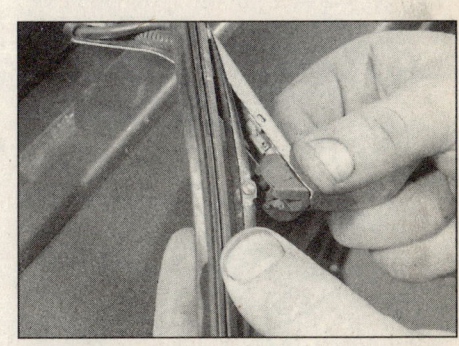

3 To remove a headlight wiper blade, simply pull the locating stud on the blade out of the socket on the arm and lift the blade away.

0•14 Weekly checks

Tyre condition and pressure

It is very important that tyres are in good condition, and at the correct pressure - having a tyre failure at any speed is highly dangerous. Tyre wear is influenced by driving style - harsh braking and acceleration, or fast cornering, will all produce more rapid tyre wear. As a general rule, the front tyres wear out faster than the rears. Interchanging the tyres from front to rear ("rotating" the tyres) may result in more even wear. However, if this is completely effective, you may have the expense of replacing all four tyres at once! Remove any nails or stones embedded in the tread before they penetrate the tyre to cause deflation. If removal of a nail does reveal that the tyre has been punctured, refit the nail so that its point of penetration is marked. Then immediately change the wheel, and have the tyre repaired by a tyre dealer.

Regularly check the tyres for damage in the form of cuts or bulges, especially in the sidewalls. Periodically remove the wheels, and clean any dirt or mud from the inside and outside surfaces. Examine the wheel rims for signs of rusting, corrosion or other damage. Light alloy wheels are easily damaged by "kerbing" whilst parking; steel wheels may also become dented or buckled. A new wheel is very often the only way to overcome severe damage.

New tyres should be balanced when they are fitted, but it may become necessary to re-balance them as they wear, or if the balance weights fitted to the wheel rim should fall off. Unbalanced tyres will wear more quickly, as will the steering and suspension components. Wheel imbalance is normally signified by vibration, particularly at a certain speed (typically around 50 mph). If this vibration is felt only through the steering, then it is likely that just the front wheels need balancing. If, however, the vibration is felt through the whole car, the rear wheels could be out of balance. Wheel balancing should be carried out by a tyre dealer or garage.

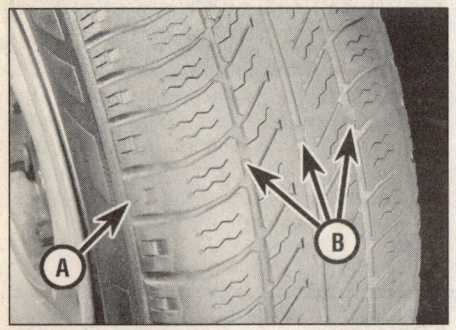

1 Tread Depth - visual check
The original tyres have tread wear safety bands (B), which will appear when the tread depth reaches approximately 1.6 mm. The band positions are indicated by a triangular mark on the tyre sidewall (A).

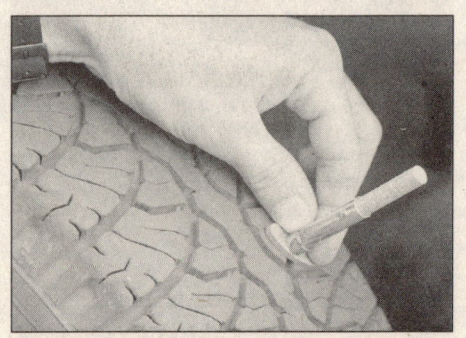

2 Tread Depth - manual check
Alternatively, tread wear can be monitored with a simple, inexpensive device known as a tread depth indicator gauge.

3 Tyre Pressure Check
Check the tyre pressures regularly with the tyres cold. Do not adjust the tyre pressures immediately after the vehicle has been used, or an inaccurate setting will result.

Tyre tread wear patterns

Shoulder Wear

Underinflation (wear on both sides)
Under-inflation will cause overheating of the tyre, because the tyre will flex too much, and the tread will not sit correctly on the road surface. This will cause a loss of grip and excessive wear, not to mention the danger of sudden tyre failure due to heat build-up.
Check and adjust pressures
Incorrect wheel camber (wear on one side)
Repair or renew suspension parts
Hard cornering
Reduce speed!

Centre Wear

Overinflation
Over-inflation will cause rapid wear of the centre part of the tyre tread, coupled with reduced grip, harsher ride, and the danger of shock damage occurring in the tyre casing.
Check and adjust pressures

If you sometimes have to inflate your car's tyres to the higher pressures specified for maximum load or sustained high speed, don't forget to reduce the pressures to normal afterwards.

Uneven Wear

Front tyres may wear unevenly as a result of wheel misalignment. Most tyre dealers and garages can check and adjust the wheel alignment (or "tracking") for a modest charge.
Incorrect camber or castor
Repair or renew suspension parts
Malfunctioning suspension
Repair or renew suspension parts
Unbalanced wheel
Balance tyres
Incorrect toe setting
Adjust front wheel alignment
Note: *The feathered edge of the tread which typifies toe wear is best checked by feel.*

Weekly checks 0•15

Bulbs and fuses

✔ Check all external lights and the horn. Refer to the appropriate Sections of Chapter 12 for details if any of the circuits are found to be inoperative.

✔ Visually check all accessible wiring connectors, harnesses and retaining clips for security, and for signs of chafing or damage.

HAYNES HiNT
If you need to check your brake lights and indicators unaided, back up to a wall or garage door and operate the lights. The reflected light should show if they are working properly.

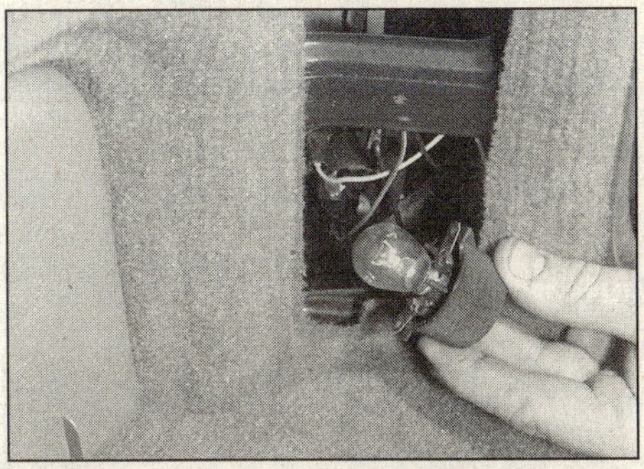

1 If an indicator light, brake light or headlight has failed, it is likely that a bulb has blown and will need to be replaced. Refer to Chapter 12 for details. If both brake lights have failed, it is possible that the brake light switch above the brake pedal needs adjusting. This simple operation is described in Chapter 12.

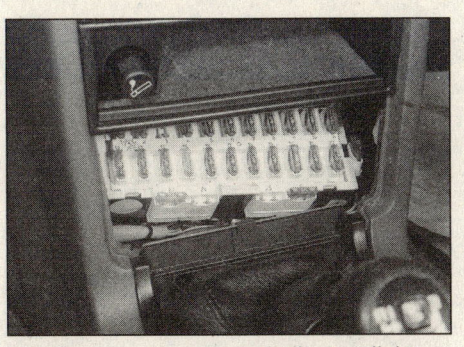

2 If more than one indicator light or headlight has failed it is likely that either a fuse has blown or that there is a fault in the circuit (see *"Electrical fault finding"* in Chapter 12). The fuses are mounted in a panel located in the centre console behind the ashtray.

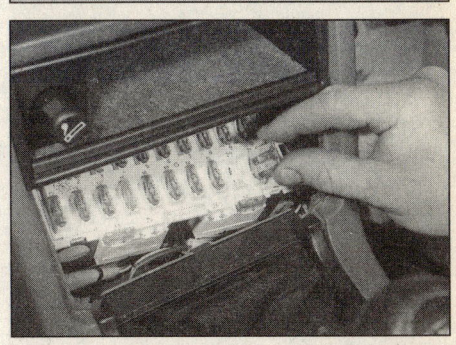

3 To replace a blown fuse, simply prise it out. Fit a new fuse of the same rating, available from car accessory shops. It is important that you find the reason that the fuse blew - a complete checking procedure is given in Chapter 12.

Battery

Caution: *Before carrying out any work on the vehicle battery, read the precautions given in "Safety first" at the start of this manual.*

✔ Make sure that the battery tray is in good condition, and that the clamp is tight. Corrosion on the tray, retaining clamp and the battery itself can be removed with a solution of water and baking soda. Thoroughly rinse all cleaned areas with water. Any metal parts damaged by corrosion should be covered with a zinc-based primer, then painted.

✔ Periodically (approximately every three months), check the charge condition of the battery as described in Chapter 5A.

✔ If the battery is flat, and you need to jump start your vehicle, see *Roadside Repairs*.

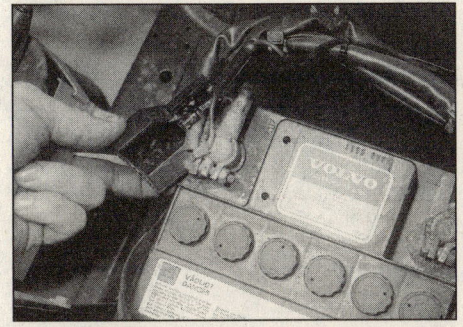

1 The battery is located at the front of the engine compartment on the left-hand, or right-hand side according to model. The exterior of the battery should be inspected periodically for damage such as a cracked case or cover.

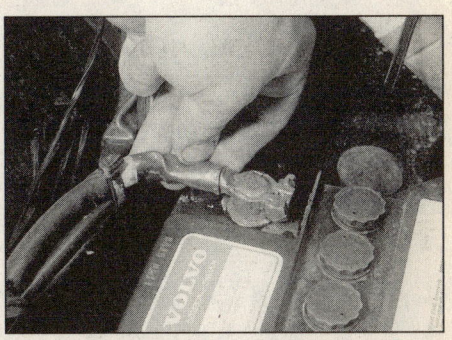

2 Check the tightness of battery clamps (A) to ensure good electrical connections. You should not be able to move them. Also check each cable (B) for cracks and frayed conductors.

HAYNES HiNT 
Battery corrosion can be kept to a minimum by applying a layer of petroleum jelly to the clamps and terminals after they are reconnected.

3 If corrosion (white, fluffy deposits) is evident, remove the cables from the battery terminals, clean them with a small wire brush, then refit them. Automotive stores sell a tool for cleaning the battery post . . .

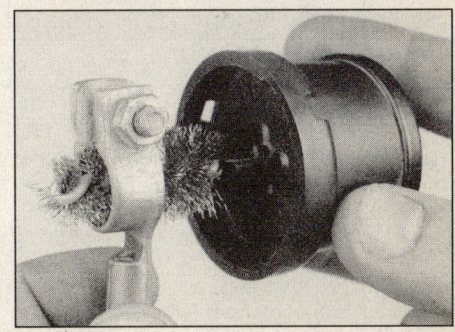

4 . . . as well as the battery cable clamps

0•16 Lubricants, fluids and tyre pressures

Lubricants and fluids

Engine oil	Multigrade engine oil, SAE 10W/30 to 15W/50, to API SG/CD
Coolant	50/50 mixture of water and ethylene glycol-based antifreeze
Brake/clutch fluid	Universal brake fluid to DOT 4
Power steering fluid	Automatic transmission fluid type Dexron IID
Manual transmission:	
M46 and M47 transmissions	Automatic transmission fluid type F or G, or Volvo thermo oil
M90 transmissions	Volvo synthetic oil
Automatic transmission	Automatic transmission fluid type Dexron IID

Choosing your engine oil

Engines need oil, not only to lubricate moving parts and minimise wear, but also to maximise power output and to improve fuel economy.

HOW ENGINE OIL WORKS

- *Beating friction*

Without oil, the moving surfaces inside your engine will rub together, heat up and melt, quickly causing the engine to seize. Engine oil creates a film which separates these moving parts, preventing wear and heat build-up.

- *Cooling hot-spots*

Temperatures inside the engine can exceed 1000° C. The engine oil circulates and acts as a coolant, transferring heat from the hot-spots to the sump.

- *Cleaning the engine internally*

Good quality engine oils clean the inside of your engine, collecting and dispersing combustion deposits and controlling them until they are trapped by the oil filter or flushed out at oil change.

OIL CARE - FOLLOW THE CODE

To handle and dispose of used engine oil safely, always:

- *Avoid skin contact with used engine oil. Repeated or prolonged contact can be harmful.*
- *Dispose of used oil and empty packs in a responsible manner in an authorised disposal site. Call 0800 663366 to find the one nearest to you. Never tip oil down drains or onto the ground.*

Tyre pressures

	Front	Rear
Saloon, up to 3 occupants	1.9 bars	1.9 bars
Saloon, fully laden	2.1 bars	2.6 bars
Estate, up to 3 occupants	1.9 bars	2.1 bars
Estate, fully laden	2.1 bars	2.8 bars
For sustained high speeds (over 113 kph) add	0.3 bars	0.3 bars
"Space saver" spare		
155/R15	3.5 bars	3.5 bars
165/14	2.8 bars	2.8 bars

Note: *Refer to the tyre pressure data sticker on the driver's door for the correct tyre pressures for your particular vehicle. Pressures apply only to original-equipment tyres, and may vary if other makes or type is fitted; check with the tyre manufacturer or supplier for correct pressures if necessary.*

Chapter 1
Routine maintenance and servicing

Contents

Accessory drivebelts check and renewal ... 20
Air cleaner element renewal ... 27
Automatic transmission fluid level check ... 19
Automatic transmission fluid renewal ... 26
Automatic transmission kickdown cable operation and selector cable adjustment ... 17
Bodywork, paint and exterior trim check ... 16
Brake fluid renewal ... 22
Brake pad wear check ... 4
Camshaft drivebelt renewal ... 28
Clutch hydraulic check/cable adjustment ... 8
Coolant renewal ... 21
Distributor, rotor arm and HT lead check ... 23
Door, boot, tailgate and bonnet check and lubrication ... 15
Emission control equipment check ... 30
Engine oil and filter renewal ... 3
Exhaust system check ... 12
Fuel filter renewal ... 29
Handbrake check and adjustment ... 6
Intensive maintenance ... 2
Introduction ... 1
Manual transmission oil level check ... 9
Propeller shaft, centre bearing and universal joint check ... 11
Rear axle oil level check ... 13
Road test ... 18
Seat belt check ... 14
Spark plug renewal ... 24
Steering and suspension check ... 7
Underbody and fuel/brake line check ... 10
Fluid leaks and hose condition checks ... 5
Valve clearance check and adjustment ... 25

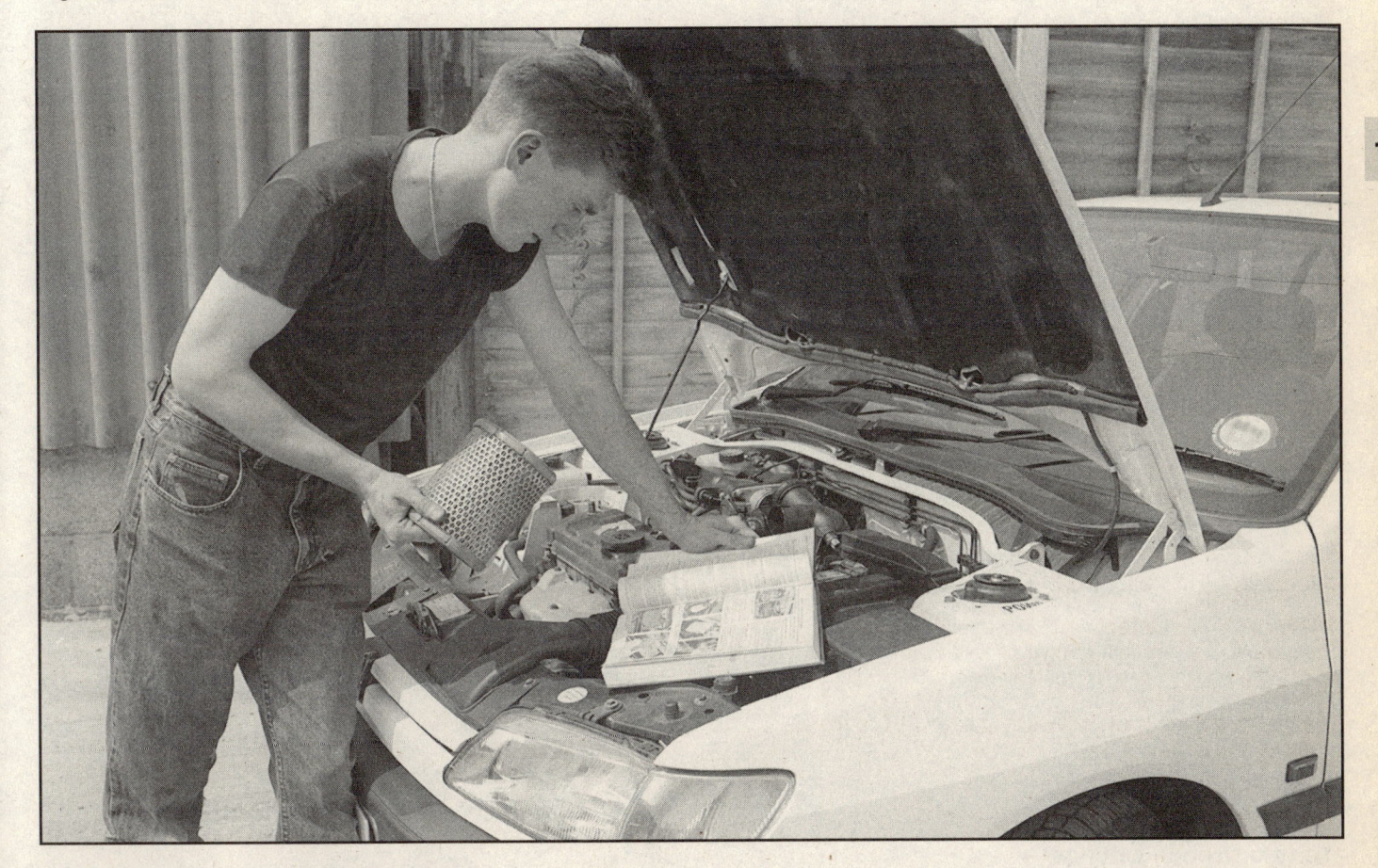

Degrees of difficulty

| **Easy,** suitable for novice with little experience | **Fairly easy,** suitable for beginner with some experience | **Fairly difficult,** suitable for competent DIY mechanic | **Difficult,** suitable for experienced DIY mechanic | **Very difficult,** suitable for expert DIY or professional |

Servicing Specifications

Lubricants and fluids
Refer to *"Weekly checks"*

Capacities

Engine oil
Drain and refill including filter change .... 3.85 litres (plus 0.6 litres for turbo oil cooler - if drained)

Cooling system .... 8.5 litres

Transmission
Manual transmission:
  M46 .... 2.3 litres
  M47 .... 1.6 litres
  M90 .... 1.75 litres
Automatic transmission:
  Drain and refill:
    AW70/71/72 .... 3.9 litres
    ZF4HP22 .... 2.0 litres
  From dry:
    AW70/71/72 .... 7.5 litres
    ZF4HP22 .... 7.7 litres

Rear axle .... 1.6 to 1.75 litres

Fuel tank .... 60 litres

Engine

Valve clearances:
  Checking value:
    Cold engine .... 0.30 to 0.40 mm
    Warm engine .... 0.35 to 0.45 mm
  Setting value:
    Cold engine .... 0.35 to 0.40 mm
    Warm engine .... 0.40 to 0.45 mm
  Adjusting shims available .... 3.30 to 4.50 mm in steps of 0.05 mm

Cooling system

Specified antifreeze mixture .... 50% antifreeze/50% water

Ignition system

Spark plugs: **Type**   **Electrode gap**

	Type	Electrode gap
B200F	Bosch WR 7 D+	0.8 mm
B200FT	Bosch WR 6 D+	0.8 mm
B230F	Bosch WR 7 D+	0.8 mm
B230FB	Bosch WR 7 D+	0.8 mm
B230FD	Bosch WR 7 D+	0.8 mm
B230FK	Bosch WR 7 D+	0.8 mm
B230FT	Bosch WR 7 D+	0.8 mm

Clutch

Cable free play at release fork .... 1.0 to 3.0 mm

Brakes

Front brake pad minimum lining thickness .... 3.0 mm
Rear brake pad minimum lining thickness .... 2.0 mm
Handbrake lever travel:
  After adjustment .... 3 to 5 clicks
  In service .... 11 clicks maximum

Tyres

Tyre pressures .... See *"Weekly checks"*

Torque wrench settings   Nm

Roadwheel nuts 85
Spark plugs (dry threads) 25

Maintenance Schedule   1•3

The maintenance intervals in this manual are provided with the assumption that you, not the dealer, will be carrying out the work. These are the minimum maintenance intervals recommended by the manufacturer for vehicles driven daily. If you wish to keep your vehicle in peak condition at all times, you may wish to perform some of these procedures more often. We encourage frequent maintenance because it enhances the efficiency, performance and resale value of your vehicle.

If the vehicle is driven in dusty areas, used to tow a trailer, driven frequently at slow speeds (idling in traffic) or on short journeys, more frequent maintenance intervals are recommended.

Every 250 miles (400 km) or weekly
☐ Refer to *"Weekly Checks"*

Every 10 000 (15 000 km) or 12 months, whichever comes first
In addition to the items listed above, carry out the following:
☐ Renew the engine oil and filter (Section 3).
☐ Check the condition of the brake pads (Section 4).
☐ Thoroughly inspect the engine for fluid leaks (Section 5).
☐ Check the handbrake adjustment (Section 6).
☐ Check the condition and security of the steering and suspension components (Section 7).
☐ Inspect the clutch hydraulic components (where applicable) (Section 8).
☐ Check the adjustment of the clutch cable (where applicable) (Section 8).
☐ Check the manual transmission oil level (Section 9).
☐ Inspect the underbody and the brake hydraulic pipes and hoses (Section 10).
☐ Check the condition of the fuel lines (Section 10)
☐ Inspect the propeller shaft, centre bearing and universal joints (Section 11).
☐ Check the condition and security of the exhaust system (Section 12).
☐ Check the rear axle oil level (Section 13).
☐ Check the condition of the seat belts (Section 14).
☐ Lubricate the locks and hinges (Section 15).
☐ Check the condition of the underseal and paintwork (Section 16).
☐ Check the automatic transmission selector adjustment (Section 17).
☐ Check the operation of the kickdown cable (automatic transmission models) (Section 17).
☐ Road test (Section 18)
☐ Check the operation of the brake servo (Section 18).
☐ Check the automatic transmission fluid level (Section 19).

Every 20 000 miles (30 000 km) or 2 years, whichever comes first
In addition to the items listed above, carry out the following:
☐ Check the condition and tension of accessory drivebelts (Section 20).
☐ Renew the coolant (Section 21).
☐ Renew the brake fluid (Section 22).

Every 30 000 miles (45 000 km) or 3 years, whichever comes first
In addition to the items listed above, carry out the following:
☐ Inspect the distributor cap, rotor arm and HT leads (Section 23).
☐ Renew the spark plugs (Section 24).
☐ Check the valve clearances (Section 25).

Every 40 000 miles (60 000 km) or 4 years, whichever comes first
In addition to the items listed above, carry out the following:
☐ Renew the automatic transmission fluid (Section 26).
☐ Renew the air cleaner element (Section 27).

Every 50 000 miles (75 000 km) or 5 years, whichever comes first
In addition to the items listed above, carry out the following:
☐ Renew the camshaft drivebelt (Section 28).
☐ Renew the fuel filter (Section 29).
☐ Check the emission control equipment (Section 30).

1•4 Maintenance & Servicing

Underbonnet view of a 2.0 litre Turbo model

1 Ignition coil
2 Brake/clutch fluid reservoir
3 Distributor cap
4 Engine oil filler cap
5 Engine oil dipstick
6 Power steering fluid reservoir
7 ABS hydraulic modulator
8 Battery
9 Alternator
10 Washer fluid reservoir filler
11 Air cleaner
12 Coolant expansion tank filler
13 Turbocharger

Front underside view of a 2.0 litre Turbo model

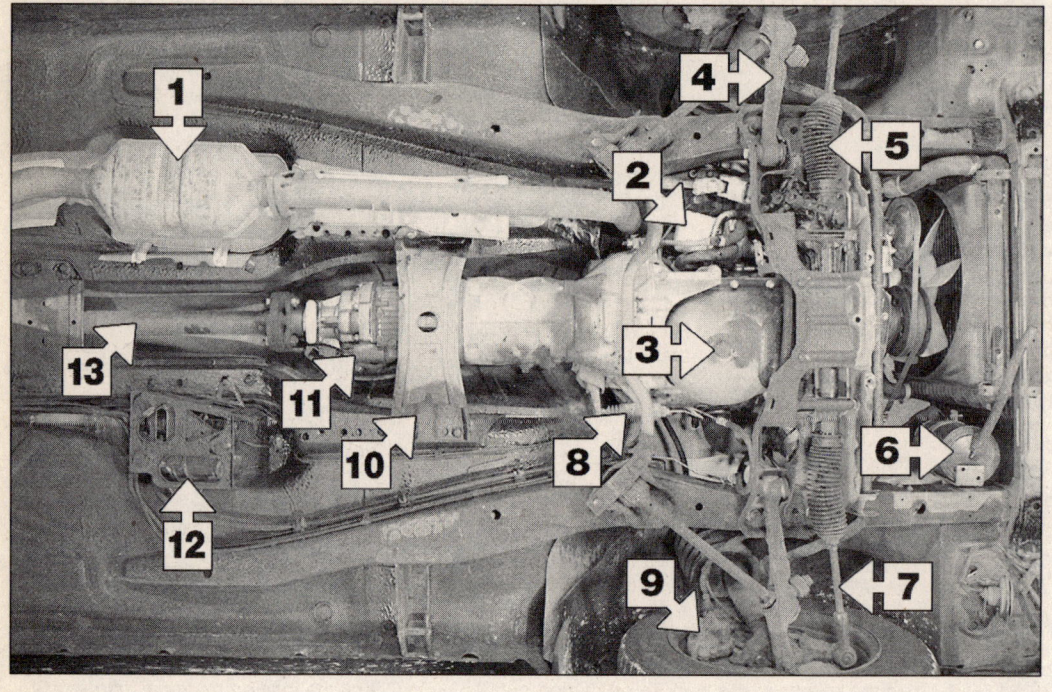

1 Catalytic converter
2 Oil filter
3 Engine oil drain plug
4 Control arm
5 Steering rack bellows
6 Carbon canister
7 Track rod
8 Clutch slave cylinder
9 Brake caliper
10 Transmission support crossmember
11 Overdrive unit
12 Fuel pump/filter cradle
13 Propeller shaft

Maintenance & Servicing 1•5

Rear underside view of a 2.0 litre Turbo model

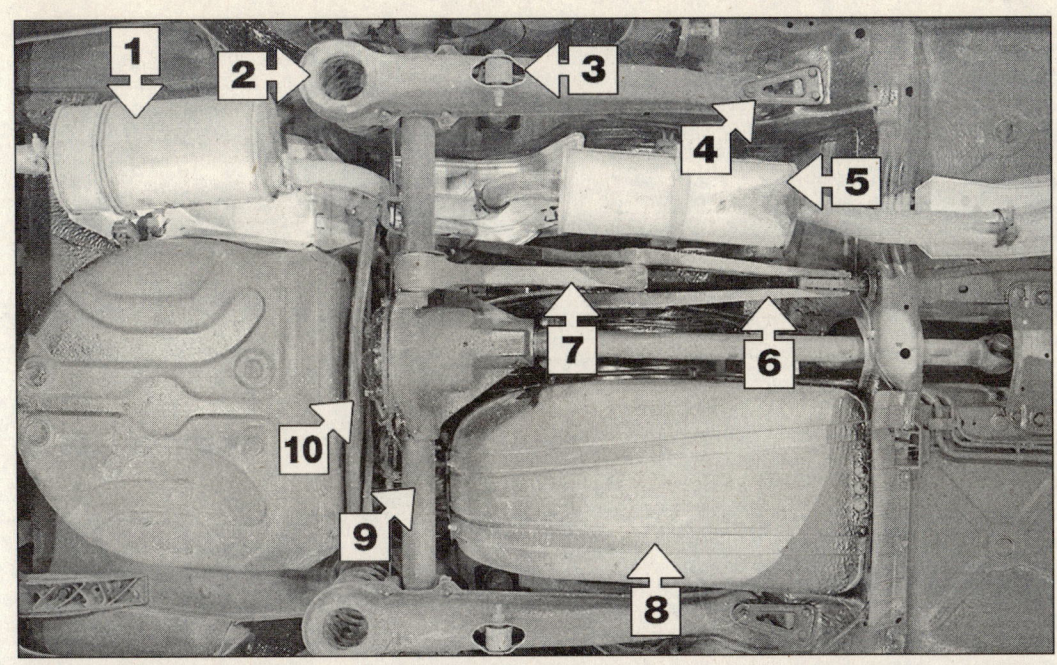

1 Rear silencer
2 Spring pan
3 Shock absorber lower mounting
4 Trailing arm bracket
5 Intermediate silencer
6 Subframe
7 Torque rod
8 Fuel tank
9 Rear axle
10 Panhard rod

Maintenance procedures

1 Introduction

This Chapter is designed to help the home mechanic maintain his/her vehicle for safety, economy, long life and peak performance.

This Chapter contains a master maintenance schedule, followed by Sections dealing specifically with each task in the schedule. Visual checks, adjustments, component renewal and other items are included. Refer to the accompanying illustrations of the engine compartment and the underside of the vehicle for the locations of the various components.

Servicing your vehicle in accordance with the distance/time maintenance schedule and the following Sections will provide a planned maintenance programme, which should result in a long and reliable service life. This is a comprehensive plan, so maintaining some items but not others at the specified service intervals will not produce the same results.

As you service your vehicle, you will discover that many of the procedures can - and should - be grouped together, because of the particular procedure being performed, or because of the close proximity of two otherwise unrelated components to one another. For example, if the vehicle is raised for any reason, the exhaust should be inspected at the same time as the suspension and steering components.

The first step of this maintenance programme is to prepare yourself before the actual work begins. Read through all the Sections relevant to the work to be carried out, then make a list and gather together all the parts and tools required. If a problem is encountered, seek advice from a parts specialist or a dealer service department.

2 Intensive maintenance

1 If, from the time the vehicle is new, the routine maintenance schedule is followed closely, and frequent checks are made of fluid levels and high-wear items, as suggested throughout this manual, the engine will be kept in relatively good running condition, and the need for additional work will be minimised.

2 It is possible that there will be times when the engine is running poorly due to the lack of regular maintenance. This is even more likely if a used vehicle, which has not received regular and frequent maintenance checks, is purchased. In such cases, additional work may need to be carried out, outside of the regular maintenance intervals.

3 If engine wear is suspected, a compression test (refer to Part A of Chapter 2) will provide valuable information regarding the overall performance of the main internal components. Such a test can be used as a basis to decide on the extent of the work to be carried out. If, for example, a compression test indicates serious internal engine wear, conventional maintenance as described in this Chapter will not greatly improve the performance of the engine, and may prove a waste of time and money, unless extensive overhaul work (Chapter 2B) is carried out first.

4 The following series of operations are those often required to improve the performance of a generally poor-running engine:

Primary operations

a) Clean, inspect and test the battery (See "Weekly checks").
b) Check all the engine-related fluids (See "Weekly checks").
c) Check the condition and tension of the accessory drivebelts (Section 20).
d) Adjust the valve clearances (Section 25).
e) Renew the spark plugs (Section 24).
f) Inspect the distributor cap, rotor arm and HT leads (Section 23).
g) Check the condition of the air cleaner filter element and renew if necessary (Section 27).
h) Renew the fuel filter (Section 29).
i) Check the condition of all hoses, and check for fluid leaks (Section 5).

5 If the above operations do not prove fully effective, carry out the following operations:

Secondary operations

All the items listed under "Primary operations", plus the following:

a) Check the charging system (Chapter 5A).
b) Check the ignition system (Chapter 5B).
c) Check the fuel system (Chapter 4).
d) Renew the distributor cap and rotor arm (Section 23).
e) Renew the ignition HT leads (Section 23).

10 000 Mile / 12 Month Service

3 Engine oil and filter renewal

1 Frequent oil changes are the best preventive maintenance the home mechanic can give the engine, because ageing oil becomes diluted and contaminated, which leads to premature engine wear.
2 Make sure that you have all the necessary tools before you begin this procedure. You should also have plenty of rags or newspapers handy, for mopping up any spills. The oil should preferably be changed just after a run when the engine is still fully warmed-up to normal operating temperature, as warm oil and sludge will flow out more easily. Take care, however, not to touch the exhaust or any other hot parts of the engine when working under the vehicle. To avoid any possibility of scalding, and to protect yourself from possible skin irritants and other harmful contaminants in used engine oils, it is advisable to wear gloves when carrying out this work. Access to the underside of the vehicle is greatly improved if the vehicle can be lifted on a hoist, driven onto ramps, or supported by axle stands. (see *"Jacking and vehicle support"*). Whichever method is chosen, make sure that the vehicle remains level, or if it is at an angle, that the drain point is at the lowest point.
3 Position the draining container under the drain plug, and unscrew the plug (see illustration). If possible, try to keep the plug pressed into the sump while unscrewing it by hand the last couple of turns.

> **HAYNES HiNT**
> As the drain plug releases from the threads, move it away sharply, so the stream of oil issuing from the sump runs into the container, not up your sleeve!

4 Allow the oil to drain into the container, and check the condition of the plug's sealing washer; renew it if worn or damaged.
5 Allow some time for the old oil to drain, noting that it may be necessary to reposition the container as the oil flow slows to a trickle. When the oil has completely drained, wipe clean the drain plug and its threads in the sump and refit the plug, tightening it securely.
6 The oil filter is located low down on the right-hand side of the cylinder block; access is not very good on Turbo models.
7 Reposition the draining container under the oil filter then, using a suitable filter removal tool if necessary, slacken the filter initially, then unscrew it by hand the rest of the way; be prepared for some oil spillage (see illustration). Empty the oil in the old filter into the container.
8 Using a clean, lint-free rag, wipe clean the cylinder block around the filter mounting. Check the old filter to make sure that the rubber sealing ring hasn't stuck to the engine; if it has, carefully remove it.
9 Apply a light coating of clean engine oil to the sealing ring on the new filter. Screw the filter into position on the engine until it seats, then tighten it firmly by hand only - **do not** use any tools.
10 Remove the old oil and all tools from under the vehicle, then lower the vehicle to the ground.
11 Remove the dipstick and the oil filler cap from the engine. Fill the engine with oil, using the correct grade and type of oil, (see Specifications). Pour in half the specified quantity of oil first, then wait a few minutes for the oil to fall to the sump. Continue adding oil a small quantity at a time, until the level is up to the lower portion of hatch marks on the dipstick. Adding approximately 0.5 to 1.0 litre will raise the level to the upper portion of hatch marks on the dipstick.
12 Start the engine. The oil pressure warning light will take a few seconds to go out while the new filter fills with oil; do not race the engine while the light is on. Run the engine for a few minutes, while checking for leaks around the oil filter seal and the drain plug.
13 Switch off the engine, and wait a few minutes for the oil to settle in the sump once more. With the new oil circulated and the filter now completely full, recheck the level on the dipstick, and add more oil as necessary.

Note: It is antisocial and illegal to dump oil down the drain. To find the location of your local oil recycling bank, call this number free.

OIL CARE — FOLLOW THE CODE
OIL BANK LINE
0800 66 33 66
www.oilbankline.org.uk

14 Dispose of the used engine oil safely and in accordance with environmental regulations (see *"General repair procedures"*).

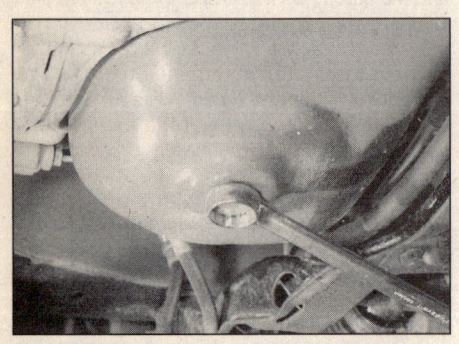

4 Brake pad wear check

1 Jack up the front or rear of the vehicle in turn, and support it on axle stands (see *"Jacking and vehicle support"*).
2 For better access to the brake calipers, remove the wheels.
3 Look through the inspection window in the caliper, and check that the thickness of the friction lining material on each of the pads is not less than the recommended minimum thickness given in the Specifications. If any one of the brake pads has worn down to, or below, the specified limit, *all four* pads at that end of the car must be renewed as a set (ie all the front pads or all the rear pads).
4 For a comprehensive check, the brake pads should be removed and cleaned. The operation of the brake calipers can then be checked, and the brake discs can be fully examined. Refer to Chapter 9 for details.

5 Fluid leaks and hose condition check

⚠ **Warning:** *Renewal of air conditioning hoses must be left to a dealer service department or air conditioning specialist who has the equipment to depressurise the system safely. Never remove air conditioning components or hoses until the system has been depressurised.*

General

1 High temperatures in the engine compartment can cause the deterioration of the rubber and plastic hoses used for engine, accessory and emission systems operation. Periodic inspection should be made for cracks, loose clamps, material hardening and leaks.
2 Carefully check the large top and bottom radiator hoses, along with the other smaller-diameter cooling system hoses and metal

3.3 Removing the sump drain plug

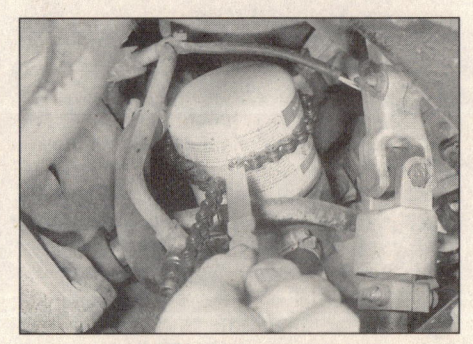

3.7 Oil filter removal

10 000 Mile / 12 Month Service

pipes; do not forget the heater hoses/pipes which run from the engine to the bulkhead. Inspect each hose along its entire length, replacing any that is cracked, swollen or shows signs of deterioration. Cracks may become more apparent if the hose is squeezed.

3 Make sure that all hose connections are tight. If the spring clamps that are used to secure the hoses in this system appear to be slackening, they should be renewed to prevent the possibility of leaks.

> **HAYNES HiNT** *A leak in the cooling system will usually show up as white or rust-coloured deposits on the areas adjoining the leak.*

4 Some other hoses are secured to their fittings with clamps. Where clamps are used, check to be sure they haven't lost their tension, allowing the hose to leak. If clamps aren't used, make sure the hose has not expanded and/or hardened where it slips over the fitting, allowing it to leak.

5 Check all fluid reservoirs, filler caps, drain plugs and fittings etc, looking for any signs of leakage of oil, transmission and/or brake hydraulic fluid, coolant and power steering fluid. If the vehicle is regularly parked in the same place, close inspection of the ground underneath it will soon show any leaks; ignore the puddle of water which will be left if the air conditioning system is in use. As soon as a leak is detected, its source must be traced and rectified. Where oil has been leaking for some time, it is usually necessary to use a steam cleaner, pressure washer or similar, to clean away the accumulated dirt, so that the exact source of the leak can be identified.

Vacuum hoses

6 It's quite common for vacuum hoses, especially those in the emissions system, to be numbered or colour-coded, or to be identified by coloured stripes moulded into them. Various systems require hoses with different wall thicknesses, collapse resistance and temperature resistance. When renewing hoses, be sure the new ones are made of the same material.

7 Often the only effective way to check a hose is to remove it completely from the vehicle. If more than one hose is removed, be sure to label the hoses and fittings to ensure correct installation.

8 When checking vacuum hoses, be sure to include any plastic T-fittings in the check. Inspect the fittings for cracks, and check the hose where it fits over the fitting for distortion, which could cause leakage.

9 A small piece of vacuum hose can be used as a stethoscope to detect vacuum leaks. Hold one end of the hose to your ear, and probe around vacuum hoses and fittings, listening for the "hissing" sound characteristic of a vacuum leak.

> **Warning: When probing with the vacuum hose stethoscope, be very careful not to come into contact with moving engine components such as the auxiliary drivebelt, radiator electric cooling fan, etc.**

Fuel hoses

> **Warning: Before carrying out the following operation, refer to the precautions given in "Safety first!" at the beginning of this manual, and follow them implicitly. Petrol is a highly dangerous and volatile liquid, and the precautions necessary when handling it cannot be overstressed.**

10 Check all fuel hoses for deterioration and chafing. Check especially for cracks in areas where the hose bends, and also just before fittings, such as where a hose attaches to the fuel filter.

11 High-quality fuel line, usually identified by the word "Fluoroelastomer" printed on the hose, should be used for fuel line renewal. Never, under any circumstances, use un-reinforced vacuum line, clear plastic tubing or water hose for fuel lines.

12 Spring-type clamps are commonly used on fuel lines. These clamps often lose their tension over a period of time, and can be "sprung" during removal. Replace all spring-type clamps with screw clamps whenever a hose is replaced.

Metal lines

13 Sections of metal piping are often used for fuel line between the fuel filter and the engine. Check carefully to be sure the piping has not been bent or crimped, and that cracks have not started in the line.

14 If a section of metal fuel line must be renewed, only seamless steel piping should be used, since copper and aluminium piping don't have the strength necessary to withstand normal engine vibration.

15 Check the metal brake lines where they enter the master cylinder and ABS hydraulic unit (if used) for cracks in the lines or loose fittings. Any sign of brake fluid leakage calls for an immediate and thorough inspection of the brake system.

6 Handbrake check and adjustment

1 The handbrake should be fully applied within the specified number of clicks of the lever ratchet. Adjustment will be necessary periodically to compensate for lining wear and cable stretch.

2 Remove the rear ashtray and the cigarette lighter/seat belt warning light panel for access to the cable adjuster **(see illustration)**.

3 Release the locking sleeve from the front of the adjuster, either by driving the sleeve forwards or by pulling the adjuster back. Turn

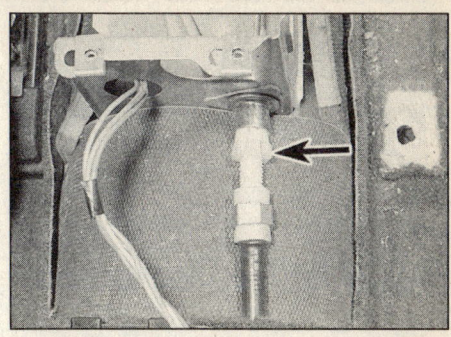

6.2 Handbrake cable adjuster (arrowed) with surrounding trim removed

the adjuster nut until handbrake operation occurs within the specified number of clicks. Check that the brake is not binding when the lever is released.

4 Re-engage the locking sleeve and refit the panel and rear ashtray.

7 Steering and suspension check

Front suspension and steering check

1 Apply the handbrake, then raise the front of the vehicle and support it on axle stands (see *"Jacking and vehicle support"*).

2 Visually inspect the balljoint dust covers and the steering gear gaiters for splits, chafing or deterioration. Any wear of these components will cause loss of lubricant, together with dirt and water entry, resulting in rapid deterioration of the balljoints or steering gear.

3 Check the power-assisted steering fluid hoses for chafing or deterioration, and the pipe and hose unions for fluid leaks. Also check for signs of fluid leakage under pressure from the steering gear rubber gaiters, which would indicate failed fluid seals within the steering gear.

4 Check for signs of fluid leakage around the shock absorber body, or from the rubber boot around the piston rod (where fitted). Should any fluid be noticed, the shock absorber is defective internally, and renewal is necessary.

5 Grasp the roadwheel at the 12 o'clock and 6 o'clock positions, and try to rock it. Very slight free play may be felt, but if the movement is appreciable, further investigation is necessary to determine the source. Continue rocking the wheel while an assistant depresses the footbrake. If the movement is now eliminated or significantly reduced, it is likely that the wheel bearings are at fault. If the free play is still evident with the footbrake depressed, then there is wear in the suspension joints or mountings.

6 Now grasp the wheel at the 9 o'clock and 3 o'clock positions, and try to rock it as before. Any movement felt may again be caused by wear in the wheel bearings or the

1•8 10 000 Mile / 12 Month Service

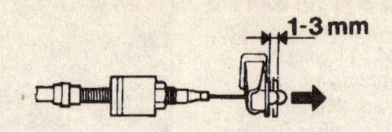

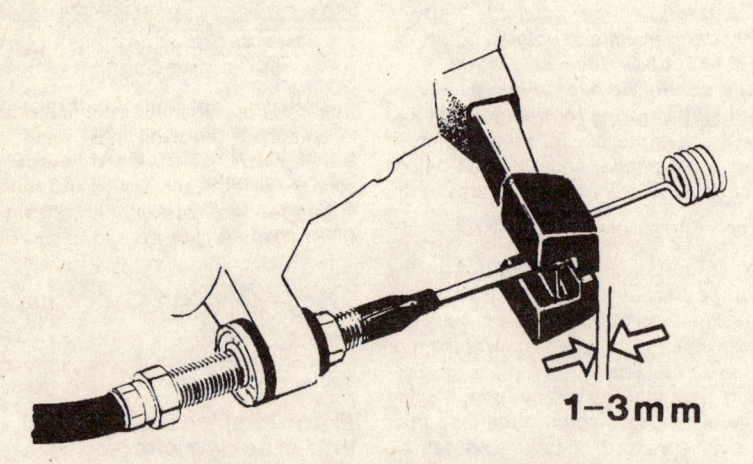

8.4 Clutch cable adjustment at the release fork - with return spring (bottom) or without (top)

steering track rod balljoints. If the outer track rod end balljoint is worn, the visual movement will be obvious. If the inner joint is suspect, it can be felt by placing a hand over the rack-and-pinion rubber gaiter, and gripping the track rod. If the wheel is now rocked, movement will be felt at the inner joint if wear has taken place.

7 Using a large screwdriver or flat bar, check for wear in the suspension mounting bushes by levering between the relevant suspension component and its attachment point. Some movement is to be expected as the mountings are made of rubber, but excessive wear should be obvious. Also check the condition of any visible rubber bushes, looking for splits, cracks or contamination of the rubber.

8 With the vehicle standing on its wheels, have an assistant turn the steering wheel back-and-forth, about an eighth of a turn each way. There should be very little, If any, lost movement between the steering wheel and roadwheels. If this is not the case, closely observe the joints and mountings previously described, but in addition, check the steering column universal joints for wear, and also check the rack-and-pinion steering gear itself.

9 The efficiency of the shock absorber may be checked by bouncing the car at each front corner. Generally speaking, the body will return to its normal position and stop after being depressed. If it rises and returns on a rebound, the shock absorber is probably suspect. Examine also the shock absorber upper and lower mountings for any signs of wear or fluid leakage.

Rear suspension check

10 Chock the front wheels, then raise the rear of the vehicle and support it on axle stands (see "*Jacking and vehicle support*").

11 Check the rear hub bearings for wear, using the method described for the front hub bearings (paragraph 4).

12 Using a large screwdriver or flat bar, check for wear in the suspension mounting bushes by levering between the relevant suspension component and its attachment point. Some movement is to be expected as the mountings are made of rubber, but excessive wear should be obvious. Check the condition of the shock absorbers as described previously.

8 Clutch hydraulic check/cable adjustment

Hydraulic check

1 On models with an hydraulically operated clutch, check that the clutch pedal moves smoothly and easily through its full travel, and that the clutch itself functions correctly, with no trace of slip or drag.

2 Remove the closing panels under the facia for access to the clutch pedal and apply light oil to the pedal pivot. Refit the panel.

3 From within the engine compartment check the condition of the fluid lines and hoses. Now have a look under the car at the clutch slave cylinder. Check for signs of fluid leaks around the rubber boot and check the security of the linkage. Apply a few drops of oil to the pushrod clevis pin and linkage.

Cable adjustment

4 On models with a cable-operated clutch, check the clutch operation generally as described in paragraphs 1 and 2, and in addition check that the clutch cable is adjusted correctly. Cable adjustment is correct when the free play at the release fork is as given in the Specifications. Adjust if necessary by means of the locknuts and threaded adjuster at the end of the cable outer **(see illustration)**.

9 Manual transmission oil level check

1 The manual transmission does not have a dipstick. To check the oil level, raise the vehicle and support it securely on axle stands, making sure that the vehicle is level (see "*Jacking and vehicle support*"). On the left-hand side of the transmission casing you will see the filler/level plug and drain plug **(see illustration)**. Wipe all around the filler/level plug (the upper one of the two) with a clean rag then unscrew and remove it. If the lubricant level is correct, the oil should be up to the lower edge of the hole.

2 If the transmission needs more lubricant (if the oil level is not up to the hole), use a syringe, or a plastic bottle and tube, to add more **(see illustration)**. Stop filling the transmission when

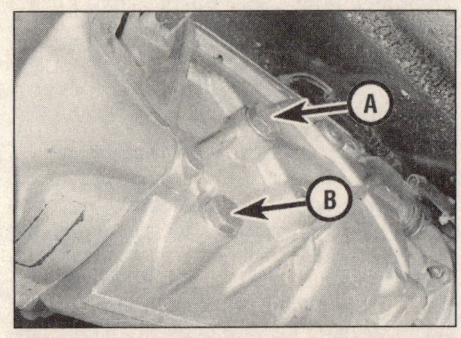

9.1 Manual transmission filler/level plug (A) and drain plug (B)

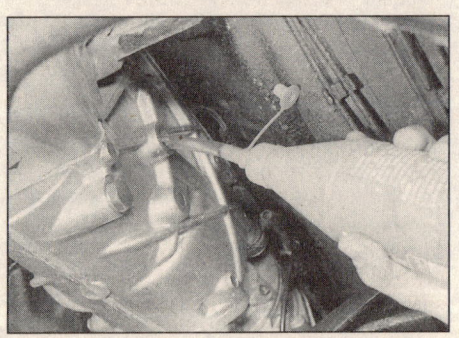

9.2 Topping-up the manual transmission oil

10 000 Mile / 12 Month Service

the lubricant begins to run out of the hole. Make sure that you use the correct type of lubricant.
3 Refit the filler/level plug, and tighten it securely. Drive the vehicle a short distance, then check for leaks.
4 A need for regular topping-up can only be due to a leak, which should be found and rectified without delay.

10 Underbody and fuel/brake line check

1 With the vehicle raised and supported on axle stands (see *"Jacking and vehicle support"*), or over an inspection pit, thoroughly inspect the underbody and wheel arches for signs of damage and corrosion. In particular, examine the bottom of the side sills, and any concealed areas where mud can collect. Where corrosion and rust is evident, press and tap firmly on the panel with a screwdriver, and check for any serious corrosion which would necessitate repairs. If the panel is not seriously corroded, clean away the rust, and apply a new coating of underseal. Refer to Chapter 11 for more details of body repairs.
2 At the same time, inspect the PVC coated lower body panels for stone damage and general condition.
3 Inspect all of the fuel and brake lines on the underbody for damage, rust, corrosion and leakage. Also make sure that they are correctly supported in their clips. Where applicable, check the PVC coating on the lines for damage.
4 Inspect the flexible brake hoses in the vicinity of the calipers, where they are subjected to most movement. Bend them between the fingers (but do not bend them double, or the casing may be damaged) and check that this does not reveal previously hidden cracks, cuts or splits.

11 Propeller shaft, centre bearing and universal joint check

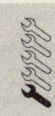

1 Ideally the vehicle should be raised at the front and rear and securely supported on axle stands with the rear wheels free to rotate (see *"Jacking and vehicle support"*).
2 Check around the rubber portion of the centre bearing for any signs of cracks, oil contamination or deformation of the rubber. If any of these conditions are apparent, the centre bearing should be renewed as described in Chapter 8.
3 At the same time, check the condition of the universal joints by holding the propeller shaft in one hand and the transmission or rear axle flange in the other. Try to twist the two components in opposite direction and look for any movement in the universal joint spiders.

Repeat this check at the centre bearing and in all other areas where the individual parts of the propeller shaft or universal joints connect. If any wear is evident, refer to Chapter 8 for repair procedures. If grating or squeaking noises have been heard from below the vehicle, or if there is any sign of rust coloured deposits around the universal joint spiders, this indicates an advanced state of wear and should be seen to immediately.
4 Also check the condition of the rubber coupling, looking for any signs of swelling, oil contamination or cracks and splits in the rubber, particularly around the bolt holes.

12 Exhaust system check

1 With the engine cold (at least three hours after the vehicle has been driven), check the complete exhaust system, from its starting point at the engine to the end of the tailpipe. Ideally, this should be done on a hoist, where unrestricted access is available; if a hoist is not available, raise and support the vehicle on axle stands (see *"Jacking and vehicle support"*).
2 Check the pipes and connections for evidence of leaks, severe corrosion, or damage. Make sure that all brackets and rubber mountings are in good condition, and tight; if any of the mountings are to be renewed, ensure that the replacements are of the correct type. Leakage at any of the joints or in other parts of the system will usually show up as a black sooty stain in the vicinity of the leak.
3 At the same time, inspect the underside of the body for holes, corrosion, open seams, etc. which may allow exhaust gases to enter the passenger compartment. Seal all body openings with silicone or body putty.
4 Rattles and other noises can often be traced to the exhaust system, especially the rubber mountings. Try to move the system, silencer(s) and catalytic converter. If any components can touch the body or suspension parts, secure the exhaust system with new mountings.

13 Rear axle oil level check

1 Ideally, the vehicle should be standing on its wheels for this check but if this is a problem (and you can't squeeze underneath) either raise it at the front and rear and support it on axle stands or use a hoist or pit (see *"Jacking and vehicle support"*).
2 Wipe all around the filler/level plug on the rear axle then unscrew the plug. The filler/level is located on the rear of the final drive casing cover. The best way to check the level is to use a "dipstick" made up from a bent piece of

13.3 Topping-up the rear axle oil

wire. Put the wire in the hole (but don't drop it in) and check the level.
3 If the axle needs more lubricant, use a syringe, or a plastic bottle and tube, to add more **(see illustration)**. Stop filling the axle when the lubricant begins to run out of the hole. Make sure that you use the correct grade of lubricant.
4 Refit the filler/level plug, and tighten it securely.
5 A need for regular topping-up can only be due to a leak, which should be found and rectified without delay.

14 Seat belt check

Check the seat belts for satisfactory operation and condition. Inspect the webbing for fraying and cuts. Check that they retract smoothly and without binding into their reels.
Check the seat belt mountings, ensuring that all the bolts are securely tightened.

15 Door, boot, tailgate and bonnet check and lubrication

Check that the doors, bonnet and tailgate/boot lid close securely. Check that the bonnet safety catch operates correctly. Check the operation of the door check straps.
Lubricate the hinges, door check straps, the striker plates and the bonnet catch sparingly with a little oil or grease.

16 Bodywork, paint and exterior trim check

1 The best time to carry out this check is after the car has been washed so that any surface blemish or scratch will be clearly evident and not hidden by a film of dirt.
2 Starting at one front corner check the paintwork all around the car, looking for minor scratches or more serious dents. Check all the trim and make sure that it is securely attached over its entire length.

10 000 Mile / 12 Month Service

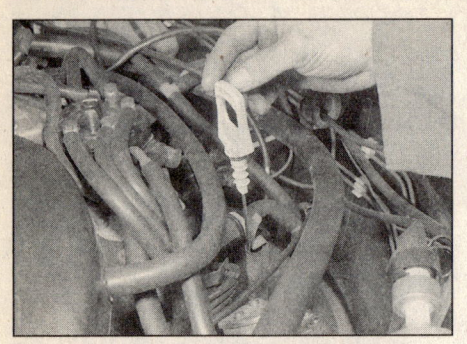

19.4 Withdrawing the automatic transmission dipstick

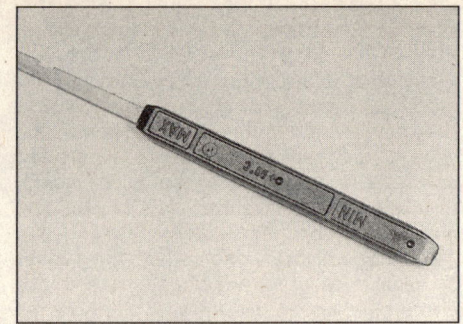

19.6a Automatic transmission dipstick markings

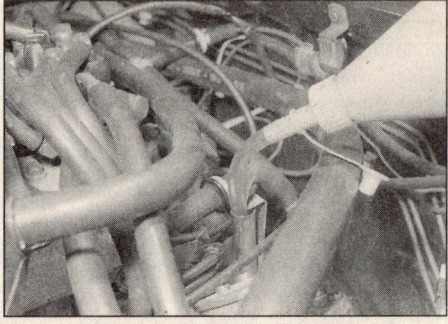

19.6b Topping-up the automatic transmission fluid

3 Check the security of all door locks, door mirrors, badges, bumpers radiator grille and wheel trim. Anything found loose, or in need of further attention should be done with reference to the relevant Chapters of this manual.
4 Rectify any problems noticed with the paintwork or body panels as described in Chapter 11.

17 Automatic transmission kickdown operation and selector cable adjustment

Refer to Chapter 7B.

18 Road test

Braking system

1 Make sure that the vehicle does not pull to one side when braking, and that the wheels do not lock prematurely when braking hard.
2 Check that there is no vibration through the steering when braking.
3 Check that the handbrake operates correctly, without excessive movement of the lever, and that it holds the vehicle stationary on a slope.
4 With the engine switched off, test the operation of the brake servo unit as follows. Depress the footbrake four or five times to exhaust the vacuum, then start the engine. As the engine starts, there should be a noticeable "give" in the brake pedal as vacuum builds up. Allow the engine to run for at least two minutes, and then switch it off. If the brake pedal is now depressed again, it should be possible to detect a hiss from the servo as the pedal is depressed. After about four or five applications, no further hissing should be heard, and the pedal should feel considerably harder.

Steering and suspension

5 Check for any abnormalities in the steering, suspension, handling or road "feel".

6 Drive the vehicle, and check that there are no unusual vibrations or noises.
7 Check that the steering feels positive, with no excessive sloppiness or roughness, and check for any suspension noises when cornering and driving over bumps.

Drivetrain

8 Check the performance of the engine, transmission and driveline.
9 Check that the engine starts correctly, both when cold and when hot.
10 Listen for any unusual noises from the engine and transmission.
11 Make sure that the engine runs smoothly when idling, and that there is no hesitation when accelerating.
12 On manual transmission models, check that all gears can be engaged smoothly without noise, and that the gear lever action is not abnormally vague or "notchy".
13 On automatic transmission models, make sure that the drive seems smooth without jerks or engine speed "flare-ups". Check that all the gear positions can be selected with the vehicle at rest. If any problems are found, they should be referred to a Volvo dealer.

Clutch

14 Check that the clutch pedal moves smoothly and easily through its full travel, and that the clutch itself functions correctly, with no trace of slip or drag. If the movement is uneven or stiff in places, check the system components with reference to Chapter 6.

Instruments and electrical equipment

15 Check the operation of all instruments and electrical equipment.
16 Make sure that all instruments read correctly, and switch on all electrical equipment in turn, to check that it functions properly.

19 Automatic transmission fluid level check

1 The level of the automatic transmission fluid should be carefully maintained. Low fluid level can lead to slipping or loss of drive, while overfilling can cause foaming, loss of fluid and transmission damage.
2 The transmission fluid level should only be checked when the transmission is hot (at its normal operating temperature). If the vehicle has just been driven over 20 km (25 km in a cold climate), and the fluid temperature is 160 to 175°F, the transmission is hot.
3 Park the vehicle on level ground, apply the handbrake, and start the engine. While the engine is idling, depress the brake pedal and move the selector lever through all gear positions then returning to the "P" position.
4 Wait two minutes then, with the engine still idling, remove the dipstick from its tube which is located at the rear of the engine **(see illustration)**. Note the condition and colour of the fluid on the dipstick.
5 Wipe the fluid from the dipstick with a clean rag, and re-insert it into the filler tube until the cap seats.
6 Pull the dipstick out again, and note the fluid level. The level should be between the "MIN" and "MAX" marks, on the side of the dipstick marked "HOT". If the level is on the "MIN" mark, stop the engine, and add the specified automatic transmission fluid through the dipstick tube, using a clean funnel if necessary **(see illustrations)**. It is important not to introduce dirt into the transmission when topping-up.
7 Add the fluid a little at a time, and keep checking the level as previously described until it is correct. The difference between the "MIN" and "MAX" marks on the dipstick is approximately 0.5 litre.
8 The need for regular topping-up of the transmission fluid indicates a leak, which should be found and rectified without delay.
9 The condition of the fluid should also be checked along with the level. If the fluid at the end of the dipstick is black or a dark reddish-brown colour, or if it has a burned smell, the fluid should be changed. If you are in doubt about the condition of the fluid, purchase some new fluid, and compare the two for colour and smell.

20 000 Mile / 2 Year Service

20 Accessory drivebelts check and renewal

1 The accessory drivebelts transmit power from the crankshaft pulley to the alternator, water pump/viscous fan, steering pump and air conditioning compressor (as applicable). A variety of belt arrangements and tensioning methods will be found, according to equipment and engine type.

Check

2 With the engine switched off, open and support the bonnet, then locate the accessory drivebelts fitted to your car (be very careful, and wear protective gloves to minimise the risk of burning your hands on hot components, if the engine has recently been running).

3 Using an inspection light or a small electric torch, and rotating the engine when necessary with a spanner applied to the crankshaft pulley bolt, check the whole length of the drivebelt for cracks, separation of the rubber, and torn or worn ribs. Also check for fraying and glazing, which gives the drivebelt a shiny appearance. Both sides of the drivebelt should be inspected, which means you will have to twist the drivebelt to check the underside. Use your fingers to feel the drivebelt where you can't see it. If you are in any doubt as to the condition of the drivebelt, renew it.

Renewal and adjustment

4 When removing a particular drivebelt, it will obviously be necessary to remove those in front of it first.

5 Twin belts should always be renewed in pairs, even if only one is broken.

Water pump/alternator drivebelt(s)

6 Slacken the alternator pivot and adjusting strap nuts and bolts.

7 Move the alternator towards the engine to release the belt tension. On some models a positive tensioning device is used: undo the tensioner screw to move the alternator inwards.

8 Slip the belts off the pulleys and remove them.

9 When refitting, move the alternator away from the engine until the belts can be deflected 5 to 10 mm by firm thumb pressure in the middle of the longest run. Tighten the pivot and adjusting strap nuts and bolts in this position and recheck the tension.

10 On models with a positive tensioning device, be careful not to over tension the belt. On models without such a device, it may be helpful to lever the alternator away from the engine to achieve the desired tension. Only use a wooden or plastic lever, and only lever at the pulley end.

Steering pump drivebelt

11 Proceed as for the water pump/alternator drivebelt, noting the location of the pivot and adjuster strap nuts and bolts.

Air conditioning compressor drivebelt

12 On models where the compressor mountings allow it to be pivoted, proceed as for the water pump/alternator drivebelt. Note, however, that the desired deflection of the belt is only 1 to 2 mm.

13 On models where the compressor mounting is rigid, belt tension is controlled by varying the number of shims between segments of the crankshaft pulley **(see illustration)**.

14 To remove the drivebelt, unbolt the pulley from its hub. Remove the pulley segments and the shims. The drivebelt can now be removed **(see illustration)**.

15 When refitting, experiment with the number of shims between the segments until belt tension is correct. Inserting shims decreases the tension, and *vice versa*. Fit unused shims in front of the pulley for future use.

All drivebelts

16 Recheck the tension of a new belt after a few hundred kilometres.

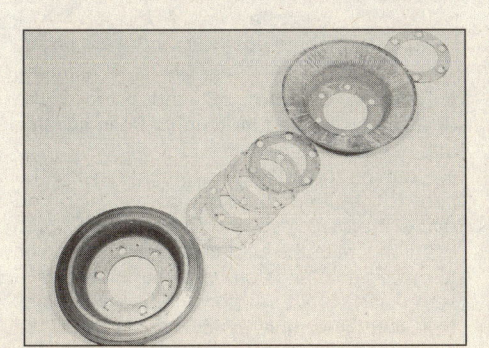

21 Coolant renewal

> **Warning: Wait until the engine is cold before starting this procedure. Do not allow antifreeze to come into contact with your skin, or with painted surfaces of the vehicle. Rinse off spills immediately with plenty of water. Never leave antifreeze lying around in an open container, or in a puddle in the driveway or on the garage floor. Children and pets are attracted by its sweet smell, but antifreeze can be fatal if ingested.**

Coolant draining

1 To drain the system, first remove the expansion tank filler cap (see *"Weekly checks"*). Move the heater temperature control to the hot position.

2 If the additional working clearance is required, raise the front of the vehicle and support it securely on axle stands (see *"Jacking and vehicle support"*).

3 Where fitted, remove the engine undertray, then place a large drain tray underneath the radiator. Slacken the radiator bottom hose clip and pull the bottom hose off the radiator stub. Direct as much of the escaping coolant as possible into the tray.

4 When the radiator has drained, move the tray to the right-hand side of the engine and unscrew the cylinder block drain tap. Allow the cylinder block to drain.

System flushing

5 With time, the cooling system may gradually lose its efficiency, as the radiator core becomes choked with rust, scale deposits from the water, and other sediment. To minimise this, as well as using only good-quality antifreeze and clean soft water, the system should be flushed as follows whenever any part of it is disturbed, and/or when the coolant is renewed.

6 With the coolant drained, refit the hose and drain plug and refill the system with fresh water. Refit the expansion tank filler cap, start the engine and warm it up to normal operating temperature, then stop it and (after allowing it to cool down completely) drain the system again. Repeat as necessary until only clean water can be seen to emerge, then refill finally with the specified coolant mixture.

7 If only clean, soft water and good-quality antifreeze has been used, and the coolant has been renewed at the specified intervals, the above procedure will be sufficient to keep the system clean for a considerable length of time. If, however, the system has been neglected, a more thorough operation will be required, as follows.

20.13 Crankshaft pulley segments and shims

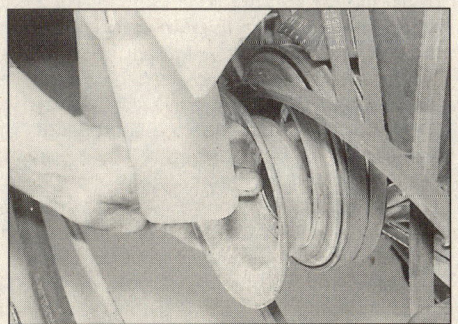

20.14 Removing the pulley front segment

20 000 Mile / 2 Year Service

8 First drain the coolant, then disconnect the radiator top and bottom hoses. Insert a garden hose into the top hose, and allow water to circulate through the radiator until it runs clean from the bottom outlet.

9 To flush the engine, insert the garden hose into the thermostat water outlet, and allow water to circulate until it runs clear from the bottom hose. If, after a reasonable period, the water still does not run clear, the radiator should be flushed with a good proprietary cleaning agent.

10 In severe cases of contamination, reverse-flushing of the radiator may be necessary. To do this, remove the radiator (Chapter 3), invert it, and insert the garden hose into the bottom outlet. Continue flushing until clear water runs from the top hose outlet. A similar procedure can be used to flush the heater matrix.

11 The use of chemical cleaners should be necessary only as a last resort. Normally, regular renewal of the coolant will prevent excessive contamination of the system.

Coolant filling

12 With the cooling system drained and flushed, ensure that all disturbed hose unions are correctly secured, and that the cylinder block drain taps are securely tightened. Refit the engine undertray if it was removed for access. If it was raised, lower the vehicle to the ground.

13 Prepare a sufficient quantity of the specified coolant mixture (see Chapter 3); allow for a surplus, so as to have a reserve supply for topping-up.

14 Slowly fill the system through the expansion tank; since the tank is the highest point in the system, all the air in the system should be displaced into the tank by the rising liquid. Slow pouring reduces the possibility of air being trapped and forming air-locks.

15 Continue filling until the coolant level reaches the expansion tank "MAX" level line, then cover the filler opening to prevent coolant splashing out.

16 Start the engine and run it at idle speed, until it has warmed-up to normal operating temperature. If the level in the expansion tank drops significantly, top-up to the "MAX" level line, to minimise the amount of air circulating in the system.

17 Stop the engine, allow it to cool down *completely* (overnight, if possible), then uncover the expansion tank filler opening and top-up the tank to the "MAX" level line. Refit the filler cap, tightening it securely, and wash off any spilt coolant from the engine compartment and bodywork.

18 After refilling, always check carefully all components of the system (but especially any unions disturbed during draining and flushing) for signs of coolant leaks. Fresh antifreeze has a searching action, which will rapidly expose any weak points in the system.

Note: *If, after draining and refilling the system, symptoms of overheating are found which did not occur previously, then the fault is almost certainly due to trapped air at some point in the system, causing an air-lock and restricting the flow of coolant; usually, the air is trapped because the system was refilled too quickly. In some cases, air-locks can be released by tapping or squeezing the various hoses. If the problem persists, stop the engine and allow it to cool down completely, before unscrewing the expansion tank filler cap or disconnecting hoses to bleed out the trapped air.*

22 Brake fluid renewal

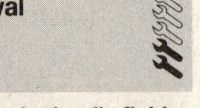

⚠️ **Warning: Brake hydraulic fluid can harm your eyes and damage painted surfaces, so use extreme caution when handling and pouring it. Do not use fluid that has been standing open for some time as it absorbs moisture from the air. Excess moisture can cause a dangerous loss of braking effectiveness.**

The procedure is similar to that for the bleeding of the hydraulic system as described in Chapter 9, except that the brake fluid reservoir should be emptied by syphoning, and allowance should be made for the old fluid to be removed from the circuit when bleeding a section of the circuit.

> **HAYNES HINT:** Old hydraulic fluid is usually much darker in colour than fresh fluid, making it easy to distinguish the two.

30 000 Mile / 3 Year Service

23 Distributor, rotor arm and HT lead check

⚠️ **Warning: Voltages produced by an electronic ignition system are considerably higher than those produced by conventional ignition systems. Extreme care must be taken when working on the system if the ignition is switched on. Persons with surgically-implanted cardiac pacemaker devices should keep well clear of the ignition circuits, components and test equipment.**

1 The spark plug (HT) leads should be inspected one at a time, to prevent mixing up the firing order, which is essential for proper engine operation. Gain access to the leads and disconnect them as described for the spark plug check and renewal.

2 Check inside the boot for corrosion, which will look like a white crusty powder. Clean this off as much as possible; if it is excessive, or if cleaning leaves the metal connector too badly corroded to be fit for further use, the lead must be renewed. Push the lead and boot back onto the end of the spark plug. The boot should fit tightly onto the end of the plug - if it doesn't, remove the lead and use pliers carefully to crimp the metal connector inside the boot until the fit is snug.

3 Using a clean rag, wipe the entire length of the lead to remove built-up dirt and grease. Once the lead is clean, check for burns, cracks and other damage. Do not bend the lead sharply, because the conductor might break.

4 Inspect the remaining spark plug (HT) leads, ensuring that each is securely fastened at the distributor cap and spark plug when the check is complete. If any sign of arcing, severe connector corrosion, burns, cracks or other damage is noticed, obtain new spark plug (HT) leads, renewing them as a set.

> **HAYNES HINT:** If new spark plug leads are to be fitted, remove the leads one at a time and fit each new lead in exactly the same position as the old one.

5 Refer to Chapter 5B and remove the distributor cap then thoroughly clean it inside and out with a dry lint-free rag.

6 Examine the HT lead segments inside the cap. If they appear badly burned or pitted renew the cap. Also check the carbon brush in the centre of the cap, ensuring that it is free to move and stands proud of its holder. Make sure that there are no signs of cracks or black "tracking" lines running down the inside of the cap, which will also mean renewal if evident.

7 Refit the cap as described in Chapter 5B on completion.

30 000 Mile / 3 Year Service 1•13

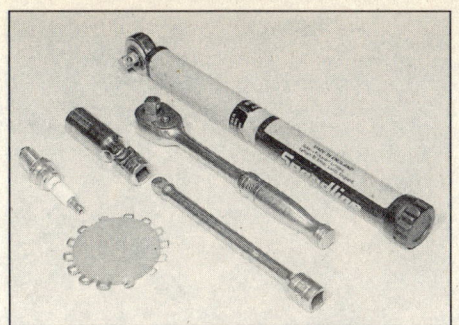

24.2 Tools required for spark plug removal, gap adjustment and refitting

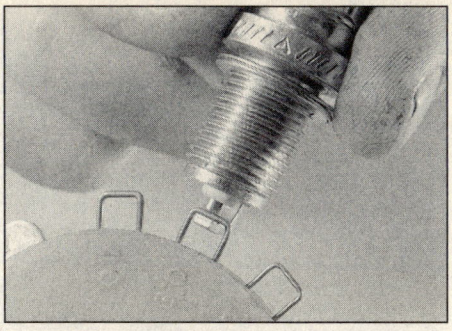

24.11a Measuring the spark plug gap with a wire gauge

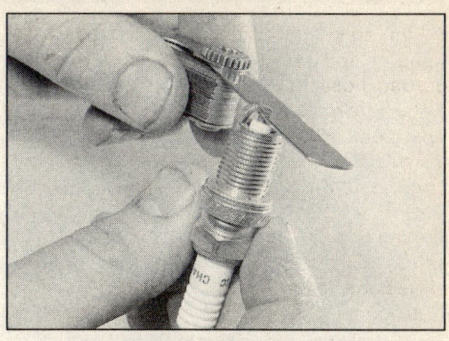

24.11b Measuring the spark plug gap with a feeler blade

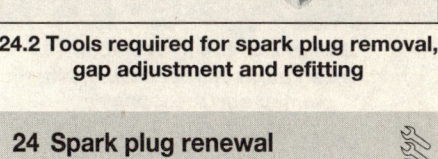

24 Spark plug renewal

1 It is vital for the correct running, full performance and proper economy of the engine that the spark plugs perform with maximum efficiency. The most important factor in ensuring this is that the plugs fitted are appropriate for the engine (see Specifications). If this type is used and the engine is in good condition, the spark plugs should not need attention between scheduled renewal intervals. Spark plug cleaning is rarely necessary, and should not be attempted unless specialised equipment is available, as damage can easily be caused to the firing ends.

2 Spark plug removal and refitting requires a spark plug socket, with an extension which can be turned by a ratchet handle or similar. This socket is lined with a rubber sleeve, to protect the porcelain insulator of the spark plug, and to hold the plug while you insert it into the spark plug hole. You will also need a wire-type feeler blade, to check and adjust the spark plug electrode gap, and a torque wrench to tighten the new plugs to the specified torque **(see illustration)**.

3 To remove the spark plugs, open the bonnet and remove any items obstructing access to the spark plugs. Note how the spark plug (HT) leads are routed and secured by clips, and on some engines, how they're positioned along the camshaft cover. To prevent the possibility of mixing up spark plug (HT) leads, it is a good idea to try to work on one spark plug at a time.

4 If the marks on the original-equipment spark plug (HT) leads cannot be seen, mark the leads 1 to 4, to correspond to the cylinder the lead serves.

5 Pull the leads from the plugs by gripping the rubber boot, not the lead, otherwise the lead connection may be fractured.

6 Unscrew the spark plugs, ensuring that the socket is kept in alignment with each plug - if the socket is forcibly moved to either side, the porcelain top of the plug may be broken off. If any undue difficulty is encountered when unscrewing any of the spark plugs, carefully check the cylinder head threads and tapered sealing surfaces for signs of wear, excessive corrosion or damage; if any of these conditions is found, seek the advice of a dealer as to the best method of repair.

7 As each plug is removed, examine it as follows - this will give a good indication of the condition of the engine. If the insulator nose of the spark plug is clean and white, with no deposits, this is indicative of a weak mixture.

8 If the tip and insulator nose are covered with hard black-looking deposits, then this is indicative that the mixture is too rich. Should the plug be black and oily, then it is likely that the engine is fairly worn, as well as the mixture being too rich.

9 If the insulator nose is covered with light tan to greyish-brown deposits, then the mixture is correct, and it is likely that the engine is in good condition.

10 The spark plug electrode gap is of considerable importance as, if it is too large or too small, the size of the spark and its efficiency will be seriously impaired. The gap should be set to the value given in the Specifications.

11 To set the electrode gap, measure the gap with a feeler blade or adjusting tool, and then bend open, or closed, the outer plug electrode until the correct gap is achieved **(see illustrations)**. The centre electrode should never be bent, as this may crack the insulation and cause plug failure, if nothing worse. If the outer electrode is not exactly over the centre electrode, bend it gently to align them.

12 Before fitting the spark plugs, check that the threaded connector sleeves at the top of the plugs are tight, and that the plug exterior surfaces and threads are clean.

13 On installing the spark plugs, first check that the cylinder head thread and sealing surface are as clean as possible; use a clean rag wrapped around a paintbrush to wipe clean the sealing surface. Apply a smear of copper-based grease or anti-seize compound to the threads of each plug, and screw them in by hand where possible. Take extra care to enter the plug threads correctly.

> **HAYNES HiNT** *It's often difficult to insert spark plugs into their holes without cross-threading them. To avoid this possibility, fit a short piece of rubber hose over the end of the spark plug. The flexible hose acts as a universal joint, to help align the plug with the plug hole. Should the plug begin to crossthread, the hose will slip on the spark plug, preventing thread damage.*

14 When each spark plug is started correctly on its threads, screw it down until it just seats lightly, then tighten it to the specified torque wrench setting.

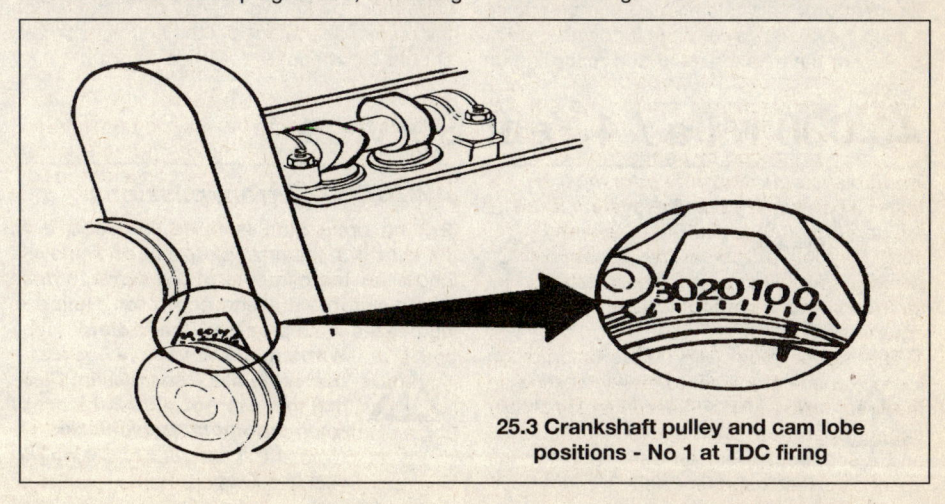

25.3 Crankshaft pulley and cam lobe positions - No 1 at TDC firing

30 000 Mile / 3 Year Service

25.4 Measuring No 1 exhaust valve clearance

25.10a Freeing a tappet shim - the tappet is being held down with a square section screwdriver

25.10b Extracting the shim. Here a C-spanner is being used to depress the tappet

15 Reconnect the spark plug (HT) leads in their correct order, using a twisting motion on the boot until it is firmly seated.

25 Valve clearance check and adjustment

1 Disconnect or remove items such as HT leads, vacuum/breather hoses, and if necessary the throttle cable, in order to gain access to the camshaft cover.
2 Remove the securing nuts and lift off the camshaft cover. Note the location of the earth strap, the HT lead clip and similar items (refer to Chapter 2A if necessary). Recover the gasket.
3 Using a spanner on the crankshaft pulley centre bolt, bring the engine to TDC, No 1 cylinder firing. (This will be easier if the spark plugs are removed.) No 1 piston is at TDC when the notch on the crankshaft pulley is in line with the figure "O" on the timing scale, and the cam lobes for No 1 cylinder (at the front) are both pointing obliquely upwards **(see illustration)**.
4 With the engine in this position, measure and record the clearance between the base of the front cam lobe and the tappet shim beneath it. Insert various thicknesses of feeler blade until a firm sliding fit is obtained **(see illustration)**. This thickness is the clearance for No 1 exhaust valve. Write it down.
5 Repeat the measurement and recording on the second cam from the front. This gives No 1 inlet valve clearance.
6 Turn the crankshaft 180° (half a turn) clockwise so that the cam lobes for No 3 cylinder are pointing obliquely upwards. Measure and record the clearances for these two valves. The exhaust valve is always nearer the front.
7 Turn the crankshaft a further 180° and deal with No 4 cylinder, then 180° again for No 2.
8 Compare the clearances recorded with those given in the Specifications. If the recorded clearances are within limits, commence reassembly (paragraph 16). Otherwise, adjust the clearances as follows.
9 Gather together a small screwdriver or scriber, a pair of long-nosed pliers and a stout C-spanner or square section screwdriver. These will substitute for the special tools normally required to change the shims with the camshaft in position. (Alternatively, the camshaft can be removed, but this involves much extra work.)
10 With the cam lobes in the same position as for checking, depress the tappet with the C-spanner or screwdriver. Only press on the edge of the tappet. Flick the shim out of the top of the tappet with the small screwdriver and remove it with the long-nosed pliers. Release the tappet **(see illustrations)**.
11 The correct thickness of shim must now be calculated. First the thickness of the old shim must be known. It may be engraved on the underside, but ideally the actual thickness should be measured with a micrometer or vernier gauge. This will take account of any wear.
12 The required shim thickness can now be calculated as shown in this example:

Specified clearance $(A) = 0.40$ mm
Measured clearance $(B) = 0.28$ mm
Original shim thickness $(C) = 3.95$ mm
Shim thickness required =
$C - A + B = 3.83$ mm

In this example the shim to be fitted would have to be 3.85 mm or 3.80 mm, giving clearances of 0.38 mm or 0.43 mm respectively.
13 Lubricate a new shim of the required thickness. Depress the tappet and insert the shim, marked side downwards. Release the tappet and check that the shim is properly located.
14 Repeat the operations on the adjacent tappet, if necessary, then proceed to the other valves, each time turning the crankshaft to position the cam lobes upwards. **Do not** turn the crankshaft whilst shims are missing from tappets, as the cam lobes may jam in them.
15 When all the required shims have been fitted, turn the crankshaft through several complete turns, then check all the clearances again.
16 Refit the camshaft cover, using a new gasket. Fit and tighten the nuts, remembering to fit the HT lead bracket and earth strap.
17 Reconnect the HT leads, vacuum hoses etc, then run the engine and check that there are no oil leaks from the camshaft cover.

40 000 Mile / 4 Year Service

26 Automatic transmission fluid renewal

1 Raise and securely support the vehicle (see "Jacking and vehicle support").

> **Warning:** This procedure may entail the engine to be running with the car raised and supported. Ensure adequate safety precautions are taken.

AW70/71/72 transmissions

2 If no drain plug is fitted, proceed from paragraph 3. If a drain plug is fitted, remove it and allow the contents of the sump to drain into a suitable draining container. Refit and tighten the drain plug **(see illustration)**.

> **Warning:** If the vehicle has just been run, the transmission fluid may be very hot. Add 2.0 litres of fresh automatic transmission fluid of the specified type via the dipstick tube.

3 Clean the oil cooler return union (the rearmost one) on the side of the transmission **(see illustration)**. Disconnect the union and attach a clear plastic hose to the line from the cooler. Lead the hose into the draining container.
4 Start the engine and allow it to idle. Fluid will flow into the draining container. When bubbles appear in the fluid, stop the engine.
5 Add 2.0 litres of fresh automatic transmission fluid of the specified type via the dipstick tube.

40 000 Mile / 4 Year Service 1•15

26.2 Automatic transmission drain plug (where fitted) - AW70/71/72 transmissions

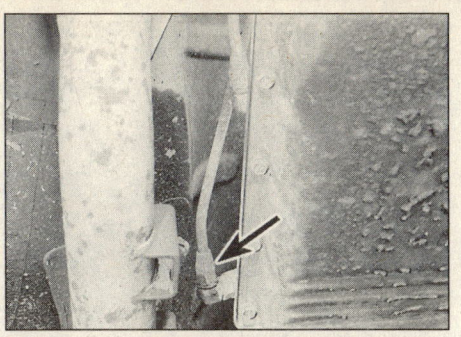

26.3 Oil cooler return union (arrowed) - AW70/71/72 transmissions

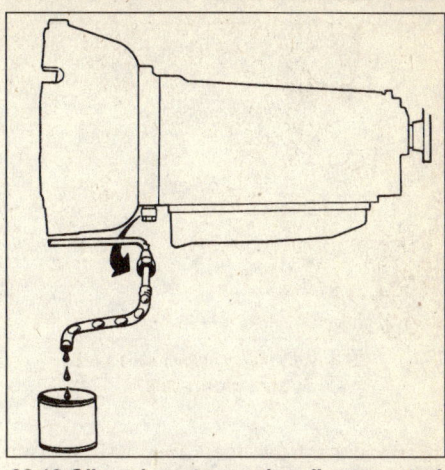

26.10 Oil cooler return union disconnected from transmission for fluid changing (ZF transmission)

6 Repeat paragraph 4, then remove the plastic hose and reconnect the oil cooler union.
7 Add a further 2.0 litres of fresh automatic transmission fluid.
8 Lower the vehicle. Check the fluid level as described in Section 19, but use the "COLD" or "+ 40°C" side of the dipstick. Top-up as necessary.
9 Dispose of the old fluid safely (see "General repair procedures").

ZFHP422 transmission

10 Proceed as described above for the AW70/71/72 transmissions, but note the following points:

a) Add fluid in increments of 2.5 litres.
b) The oil cooler return union is the lower of the two **(see illustration)**.

27 Air cleaner element renewal

1 Release the clips which secure the air cleaner lid.
2 On Turbo models, disconnect the mass air flow sensor multi-plug and the sensor-to-turbo trunking. The multi-plug is released by levering out the wire clip.
3 Lift off the lid, with mass air flow sensor when applicable, and remove the air cleaner element **(see illustration)**.
4 Wipe clean inside the housing and lid with a cloth. Be careful not to sweep debris into the air inlet.
5 Fit the new element, making sure it is the right way up. Press the seal on the rim of the element into the groove on the housing.
6 Refit the lid and secure it with the clips.
7 When applicable, reconnect the mass air flow sensor.

50 000 Mile / 5 Year Service

28 Camshaft drivebelt renewal

Refer to Chapter 2A.

29 Fuel filter renewal

⚠ **Warning:** Before carrying out the following operation, refer to the precautions given in "Safety first!" at the beginning of this manual, and follow them implicitly. Petrol is a highly dangerous and volatile liquid, and the precautions necessary when handling it cannot be overstressed.

1 Disconnect the battery negative lead.
2 Raise the vehicle on ramps or drive it over a pit (see "Jacking and vehicle support").
3 Unbolt the fuel pump cradle from the underside of the vehicle **(see illustration)**. Pull the cradle off the grommets.
4 Disconnect the fuel supply and outlet pipes from the filter. Be prepared for fuel spillage.
5 Unbolt the filter clamp and lift out the filter.

6 Fit the new filter, making sure it is the same way round as the old one. Observe the arrow on the new filter showing the direction of fuel flow. Use new copper washers on the unions (when applicable) and secure the filter in the clamp.
7 Locate the cradle on the grommets and secure in position. Lower the vehicle to the ground.
8 Reconnect the battery. Run the engine and check that there are no leaks.
9 Dispose of the old filter safely.

30 Emission control equipment check

Of the emission control systems that may be fitted, only the crankcase ventilation system and the fuel evaporative emission control systems requires regular checking, and even then, the components of this system require no attention other than to check that the hoses are clear and undamaged. Details of these checks will be found in Chapter 4B.

Should it be felt that the other systems are not functioning correctly, the advice of a dealer should be sought.

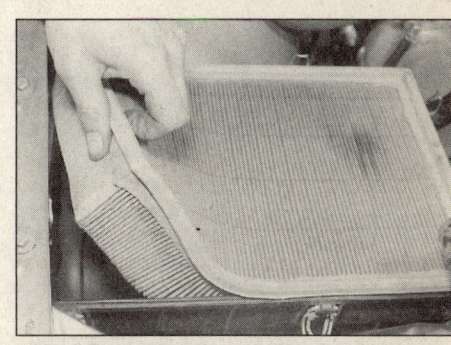

27.3 Removing the air cleaner element

29.3 The fuel filter is located in a cradle on the underside of the vehicle

Chapter 2 Part A:
In-car engine repair procedures

Contents

Camshaft and tappets - removal, inspection and refitting 6	Engine oil level check .... See "Weekly checks"
Camshaft/auxiliary shaft oil seals - renewal 5	Engine mountings - removal and refitting 12
Camshaft drivebelt - removal, refitting and tensioning 4	Flywheel/driveplate - removal and refitting 11
Camshaft cover - removal and refitting 3	General information 1
Compression test - description and interpretation 2	Oil pump - removal, inspection and refitting 9
Crankshaft oil seals - renewal 10	Sump - removal and refitting 8
Cylinder head - removal and refitting 7	Valve clearance check and adjustment .... See Chapter 1
Engine oil and filter renewal .... See Chapter 1	

Degrees of difficulty

Easy, suitable for novice with little experience	Fairly easy, suitable for beginner with some experience	Fairly difficult, suitable for competent DIY mechanic	Difficult, suitable for experienced DIY mechanic	Very difficult, suitable for expert DIY or professional

Specifications

General
Identification:
- B200F .... 2.0 litre, normally-aspirated
- B200FT .... 2.0 litre, turbocharged
- B230F/FB/FD .... 2.3 litre, normally-aspirated
- B230FT/FK .... 2.3 litre, turbocharged

Bore:
- B200 engines .... 88.9 mm (nominal)
- B230 engines .... 96 mm (nominal)

Stroke .... 80 mm

Cubic capacity:
- B200 engines .... 1986 cc
- B230 engines .... 2316 cc

Compression ratio:
- B200F 10.0:1
- B200FT 8.5:1
- B230F 9.8:1
- B230FB 9.3:1
- B230FD 9.8:1
- B230FK 8.7:1
- B230FT 8.7:1

Compression pressure:
- Overall value .... 9 to 11 bar
- Variation between cylinders .... 2 bar maximum

Firing order .... 1-3-4-2 (No 1 at front of engine)
Direction of crankshaft rotation .... Clockwise (viewed from front of engine)
Valve clearances .... See Chapter 1 Specifications

Camshaft
Identification letter (stamped on end):
- B200F .... M
- B200FT .... T
- B230F .... M
- B230FB VX3
- B230FD .... M
- B230FK .... T
- B230FT .... T

Maximum lift:
- M .... 9.50 mm (inlet), 10.50 mm (exhaust)
- T .... 9.93 mm (inlet and exhaust)
- VX3 .... 11.37 mm (inlet), 10.65 mm (exhaust)

2A•2 Engine in-car repair procedures

Camshaft (continued)
Bearing journal diameter	29.950 to 29.970 mm
Bearing running clearance:	
New	0.030 to 0.071 mm
Wear limit	0.15 mm
Endfloat	0.1 to 0.4 mm

Tappets (cam followers)
Diameter	36.975 to 36.995 mm
Height	30.000 to 31.000 mm
Shim clearance in tappet	0.009 to 0.064 mm
Tappet clearance in cylinder head	0.030 to 0.075 mm

Flywheel
Run-out	0.02 mm per 100 mm diameter

Lubrication system
Oil pressure (warm engine @ 2000 rpm)	2.5 to 6.0 bar
Oil pump type	Gear, driven from intermediate shaft
Oil pump clearances:	
Endfloat	0.02 to 0.12 mm
Gear side clearance	0.02 to 0.09 mm
Backlash	0.15 to 0.35 mm
Driving gear bearing clearance	0.032 to 0.070 mm
Idler gear bearing clearance	0.014 to 0.043 mm
Relief valve spring free length	39.20 mm

Torque wrench settings*
	Nm
Cylinder head bolts:	
Stage 1	20
Stage 2	60
Stage 3	Angle tighten 90° further
Main bearing caps	110
Connecting rod bearing caps†:	
Stage 1	20
Stage 2	Angle tighten 90° further
Flywheel/driveplate (use new bolts)	70
Camshaft sprocket	50
Intermediate shaft sprocket	50
Camshaft bearing caps	20
Crankshaft pulley/sprocket bolt:	
Stage 1	60
Stage 2	Angle tighten 60° further
Sump bolts	11

*Oiled threads unless otherwise stated
†Renew bolts if length exceeds 55.5 mm

1 General information

How to use this Chapter

This Part of Chapter 2 describes those repair procedures that can reasonably be carried out on the engine while it remains in the car. If the engine has been removed from the car and is being dismantled as described in Part B, any preliminary dismantling procedures can be ignored.

Note that, while it may be possible physically to overhaul items such as the piston/connecting rod assemblies while the engine is in the car, such tasks are not normally carried out as separate operations. Usually, several additional procedures (not to mention the cleaning of components and of oilways) have to be carried out. For this reason, all such tasks are classed as major overhaul procedures, and are described in Part B of this Chapter.

Part B describes the removal of the engine/transmission from the vehicle, and the full overhaul procedures that can then be carried out.

Engine description

The four-cylinder engine is of the overhead camshaft type. The cylinders are in line and the engine is mounted vertically and is in a "north-south" attitude in the engine bay. Cooling is by water.

The B200 series engines are all of 2.0 litre capacity while the B230 series are 2.3 litre units. The different capacity being achieved by the use of a larger cylinder bore diameter on the B230 series engines.

Drive to the camshaft is by toothed belt and sprockets. The camshaft drivebelt also drives an auxiliary shaft, which in turn drives the oil pump. Other accessories are driven from the crankshaft pulley by V-belts.

The cylinder block is of cast iron and the cylinder head of aluminium alloy, with pressed-in valve guides and valve seats. The cylinder head is of the crossflow type, the inlet ports being on the left-hand side and the exhaust ports on the right.

The crankshaft runs in five shell type main bearings; the connecting rod big-end bearings are also of the shell type. Crankshaft endfloat is taken by separate thrustwashers on No 3 main bearing. The camshaft runs in plain bearings machined directly in the cylinder head.

Valve actuation is direct, the camshaft being located above the valves. The cam lobes depress bucket type tappets; valve clearance is determined by the thickness of the shim in the recess in the top of each tappet.

The lubrication system is of the full-flow, pressure-feed type. Oil is drawn from the sump by a gear type pump, driven from the auxiliary shaft. Oil under pressure passes through a full-flow filter before being fed to the various shaft bearings and to the valve gear. On some models an external oil cooler is fitted, mounted next to the radiator. Turbo models also have an oil feed and return for the turbocharger bearings.

Repair operations possible with the engine in the car

The following work can be carried out with the engine in the car:
a) *Compression pressure - testing.*
b) *Camshaft cover - removal and refitting.*
c) *Camshaft drivebelt - removal, refitting and tensioning.*
d) *Camshaft/auxiliary shaft oil seals - renewal.*
e) *Camshaft and tappets - removal, inspection and refitting.*
f) *Cylinder head - removal and refitting.*
g) *Cylinder head and pistons - decarbonising.*
h) *Sump - removal and refitting**
i) *Oil pump - removal, inspection and refitting**
j) *Crankshaft oil seals - renewal.*
k) *Flywheel/driveplate - removal, inspection and refitting.*
l) *Engine mountings - removal and refitting.*

*It is possible to remove the sump with the engine installed, but the amount of preparatory work is formidable - see Section 8. With the sump removed, the oil pump may be dealt with.

2 Compression test - description and interpretation

1 When engine performance is down, or if misfiring occurs which cannot be attributed to the ignition or fuel systems, a compression test can provide diagnostic clues as to the engine's condition. If the test is performed regularly, it can give warning of trouble before any other symptoms become apparent.
2 The engine must be fully warmed-up to normal operating temperature, the battery must be fully charged, and all the spark plugs must be removed (Chapter 1). The aid of an assistant will also be required.
3 Disable the ignition system by disconnecting the ignition coil LT feed. Also disconnect the wiring connectors to each fuel injector to prevent fuel from contaminating the engine oil.
4 Fit a compression tester to the No 1 cylinder spark plug hole - the type of tester which screws into the plug thread is to be preferred.

5 Have the assistant hold the throttle wide open, and crank the engine on the starter motor; after one or two revolutions, the compression pressure should build up to a maximum figure, and then stabilise. Record the highest reading obtained.
6 Repeat the test on the remaining cylinders, recording the pressure in each.
7 All cylinders should produce very similar pressures; a difference of more than 2 bars between any two cylinders indicates a fault. Note that the compression should build up quickly in a healthy engine; low compression on the first stroke, followed by gradually-increasing pressure on successive strokes, indicates worn piston rings. A low compression reading on the first stroke, which does not build up during successive strokes, indicates leaking valves or a blown head gasket (a cracked head could also be the cause). Deposits on the undersides of the valve heads can also cause low compression.
8 If the pressure in any cylinder is low, carry out the following test to isolate the cause. Introduce a teaspoonful of clean oil into that cylinder through its spark plug hole, and repeat the test.
9 If the addition of oil temporarily improves the compression pressure, this indicates that bore or piston wear is responsible for the pressure loss. No improvement suggests that leaking or burnt valves, or a blown head gasket, may be to blame.
10 A low reading from two adjacent cylinders is almost certainly due to the head gasket having blown between them; the presence of coolant in the engine oil will confirm this.
11 If one cylinder is about 20 percent lower than the others and the engine has a slightly rough idle, a worn camshaft lobe could be the cause.
12 If the compression reading is unusually high, the combustion chambers are probably coated with carbon deposits. If this is the case, the cylinder head should be removed and decarbonised.
13 On completion of the test, refit the spark plugs and reconnect the ignition system and fuel injectors.

3 Camshaft cover - removal and refitting

Removal

1 Disconnect the battery negative lead.
2 Check that the spark plug HT leads are numbered to aid refitting, then detach them from the spark plugs. If no numbers can be seen, label them accordingly. Also detach the HT lead support clip where this is attached to the camshaft cover.
3 Remove the securing nuts and lift off the camshaft cover. Note the location of the earth strap, support clips and similar items. Recover the gasket. Examine the gasket for signs of damage and deterioration, and if necessary, renew it.

Refitting

4 Carefully clean the cylinder head and cover mating surfaces, and remove all traces of oil.
5 Apply silicone sealant to the camshaft front and rear bearing caps, then fit the gasket to the cylinder head, ensuring that it is correctly seated along its entire length.
6 Locate the cover over the cylinder head then fit and tighten the nuts, remembering to fit the HT lead bracket and earth strap.
7 Reconnect the HT leads, any other components removed for access. Reconnect the battery then run the engine and check that there are no oil leaks from the camshaft cover joint.

4 Camshaft drivebelt - removal, refitting and tensioning

Removal

1 Disconnect the battery negative lead.
2 Remove the accessory drivebelts (see Chapter 1).
3 Refer to Chapter 3 and remove the viscous coupled fan, the fan shroud, and the water pump pulley.
4 Unbolt and remove the top half of the camshaft drivebelt cover.

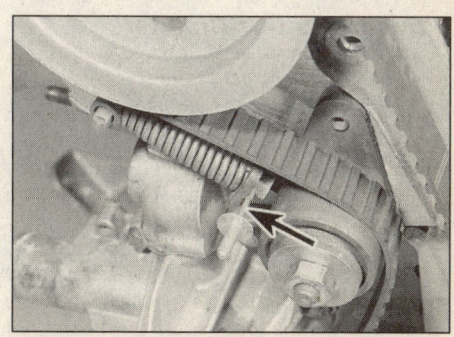

4.7a Slacken the tensioner nut . . .

4.7b . . . and insert a nail or rivet (arrowed) to restrain the spring

2A•4 Engine in-car repair procedures

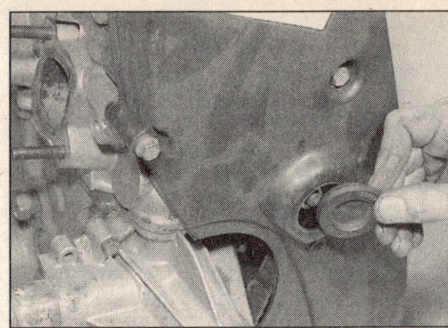

4.11 Sprocket alignment marks (arrowed) - No 1 at TDC firing. Auxiliary shaft sprocket marks are not critical

4.16 The tensioner nut access plug

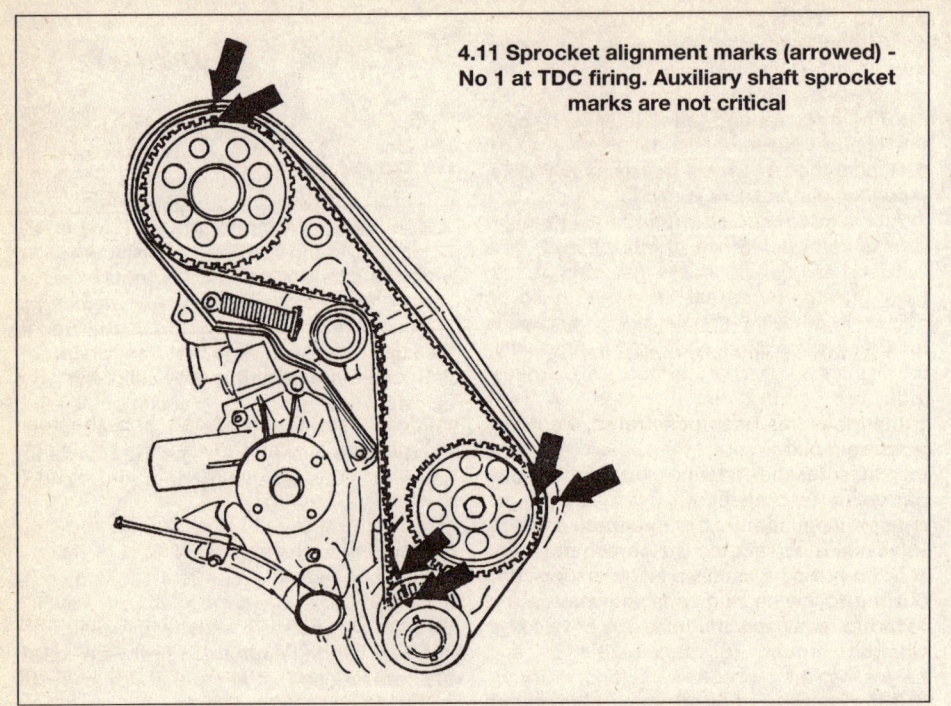

5 Using a spanner on the crankshaft pulley centre bolt, bring the engine to TDC with No 1 piston on the firing stroke. This is indicated when the mark on the camshaft sprocket is in line with the mark on the camshaft cover or the drivebelt backplate. At the same time the marks on the crankshaft pulley should align with the "0" mark on the drivebelt lower cover.
6 Remove the starter motor (see Chapter 5), or the flywheel bottom cover plate. Have an assistant lock the ring gear teeth, then slacken the crankshaft pulley bolt without disturbing the set position of the crankshaft. Remove the bolt and the pulley, then remove the lower half of the camshaft drivebelt cover.
7 Slacken the belt tensioner nut. Pull on the belt to compress the tensioner spring. Lock the tensioner in this position, either by tightening the nut again or by inserting a nail or similar into the hole in the tensioner shaft **(see illustrations)**.
8 Mark the running direction of the belt if it is to be re-used, then slip it off the sprockets and tensioner roller and remove it. Do not rotate the crankshaft, camshaft or auxiliary shaft with the belt removed.
9 Spin the tensioner roller and check for roughness or shake; renew if necessary.
10 Check the drivebelt carefully for any signs of uneven wear, splitting, or oil contamination. Pay particular attention to the roots of the teeth. Renew the belt if there is the slightest doubt about its condition. If the engine is undergoing an overhaul, and has covered more than 36 000 miles (60 000 km) with the existing belt fitted, renew the belt as a matter of course, regardless of its apparent condition. The cost of a new belt is nothing when compared to the cost of repairs, should the belt break in service. If signs of oil contamination are found, trace the source of the oil leak, and rectify it. Wash down engine drivebelt area and all related components, to remove all traces of oil.

Refitting and tensioning

11 Before refitting, make sure that the sprockets are in the correct positions (paragraph 5). The crankshaft position can be checked by ensuring that the mark on the drivebelt sprocket aligns with a corresponding mark on the oil seal housing **(see illustration)**. Slip the belt over the sprockets and round the roller, observing the correct running direction if the old belt is being re-used.
12 Recheck the alignment of the sprocket marks, then release the belt tensioner by slackening the nut or pulling out the nail. Tighten the tensioner nut.
13 Refit the drivebelt lower cover and the crankshaft pulley. Make sure that the dowel (guide pin) on the sprocket engages with the hole in the pulley. Lock the ring gear teeth and tighten the pulley bolt to the specified torque. Refit the starter motor or flywheel cover.
14 Rotate the crankshaft two full turns clockwise. Stop at TDC, No 1 piston on the firing stroke, and check that the various timing marks still align. Slacken and retighten the tensioner nut.
15 Refit the drivebelt cover top half, then refit the accessory drivebelts, pulleys, fan etc, referring to the relevant Chapters of this manual as necessary. Reconnect the battery negative lead.
16 Run the engine to operating temperature, then switch it off. Once again, bring the engine to TDC, No 1 piston on the firing stroke. Remove the access plug from the front of the drivebelt cover, slacken the tensioner nut once more and then retighten it. Refit the access plug **(see illustration)**.
17 If a new belt has been fitted, repeat paragraph 16 after approximately 600 miles (1000 km).

5 Camshaft/auxiliary shaft oil seals - renewal

1 Remove the camshaft drivebelt (see Section 4).
2 Unbolt and remove the appropriate sprockets for access to the failed seal. Restrain the sprockets with a suitable tool through the holes in their faces, or by clamping an old drivebelt around them **(see illustration)**. If removing the camshaft sprocket, **do not** allow the camshaft to move, or piston/valve contact may occur. Note the position of any front plates, backplates and/or washers when removing the sprockets. If necessary, also remove the drivebelt tensioner and backplate.
3 Carefully extract the seal by prising it out with a small screwdriver or hooked tool. Do not damage the shaft sealing face.
4 Clean the seal seat. Examine the shaft sealing face for wear or damage which could cause premature failure of the new seal.
5 Lubricate the new oil seal. Fit the seal over the shaft, lips inwards, and tap it home with a piece of tube.
6 Refit the other disturbed components, then refit and tension the camshaft drivebelt (Section 4). Fit a new drivebelt if the old one was oil-soaked.

5.2 Unbolting the auxiliary shaft sprocket

Engine in-car repair procedures 2A•5

6.3a Removing the bolt, washer and front plate . . .

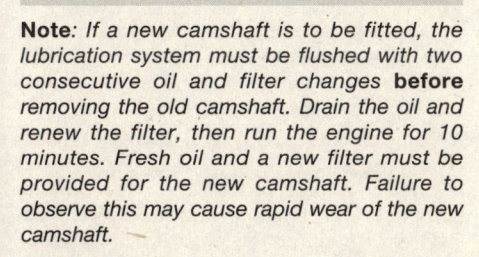

6.3b the camshaft sprocket itself . . .

6.3c . . . and the sprocket backplate. Other engines may differ slightly

6 Camshaft and tappets - removal, inspection and refitting

Note: *If a new camshaft is to be fitted, the lubrication system must be flushed with two consecutive oil and filter changes **before** removing the old camshaft. Drain the oil and renew the filter, then run the engine for 10 minutes. Fresh oil and a new filter must be provided for the new camshaft. Failure to observe this may cause rapid wear of the new camshaft.*

Removal

1 Remove the camshaft drivebelt (see Section 4). The belt can stay on the lower sprockets if wished.
2 Restrain the camshaft sprocket with a suitable tool through the holes in its face, or by clamping an old drivebelt around it. Slacken the camshaft sprocket bolt. **Do not** allow the camshaft to move, or piston/valve contact may occur.
3 Remove the sprocket bolt and the sprocket itself. Note the position of any front plates, backplates and washers **(see illustrations)**.
4 Refer to Chapter 5B and remove the distributor.
5 Remove the camshaft cover (refer to Section 3).
6 Make identification marks if necessary, then progressively slacken the camshaft bearing cap nuts **(see illustration)**. The camshaft will rise up under the pressure of the valve springs - be careful that it does not stick and then suddenly jump up. Remove the bearing caps.
7 Lift out the camshaft complete with front oil seal. Be careful of the lobes, which may have sharp edges.
8 Have ready a box divided into eight segments, or some other means of keeping matched components together.
9 Lift out the tappets and shims, keeping them identified for position by placing them in the segmented box **(see illustration)**.

Inspection

10 Inspect the cam lobes and the camshaft bearing journals for scoring or other visible evidence of wear. Once the surface hardening of the lobes has been penetrated, wear will progress rapidly.
11 Measure the bearing journals with a micrometer and check for ovality and taper. The bearing running clearances can be established by refitting the camshaft to the head and using Plastigage (see Part B of this Chapter). If the bearing caps and seats in the head are damaged, the head will have to be renewed.
12 Inspect the tappets for scuffing, cracking or other damage; measure their diameter in several places with a micrometer. Tappet clearance in the bore can be established by measuring bore diameter and subtracting tappet diameter from it. Renew the tappets if they are damaged or worn.
13 Inspect the tappet shims for visible damage; renew them if they are obviously worn. A selection of new shims should be available in any case for setting the valve clearances.
14 If it is wished to measure the camshaft endfloat, refit the camshaft and the rear bearing cap; measure the endfloat between the cap and the camshaft flange **(see illustration)**. Excessive endfloat, if not due to wear of the camshaft itself, can be corrected by renewing the rear bearing cap.

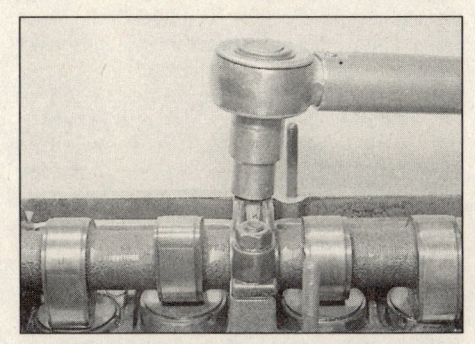

Refitting

15 Liberally oil the tappets, shims, camshaft bearings and caps, and the cam lobes. Use clean engine oil, or special camshaft lubricant if supplied with a new shaft.
16 Insert the tappets into their original bores unless they have been renewed. Measure and record the thickness of each tappet shim for reference later, then place each shim on its original tappet.
17 Fit the camshaft in approximately the correct position for No 1 piston on the firing stroke (No 1 lobes both pointing obliquely upwards). Apply sealant to the head mating surfaces of the front and rear bearing caps **(see illustration)**. Fit all the bearing caps in

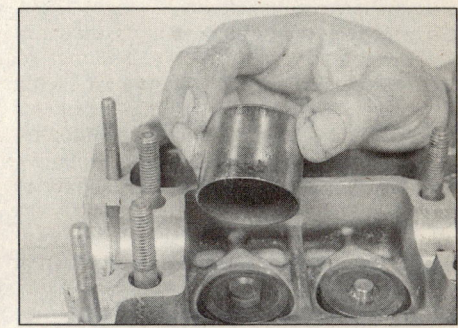

6.6 Slackening a camshaft bearing cap nut

6.9 Removing a tappet

6.14 Measuring camshaft endfloat

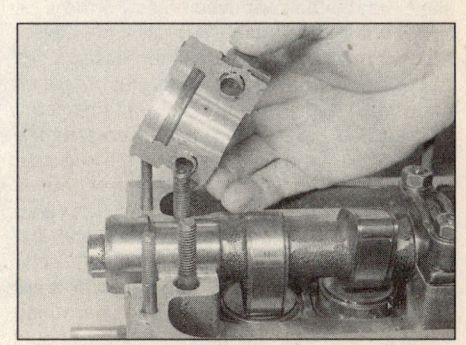

6.17 Fitting the camshaft front bearing cap

2A•6 Engine in-car repair procedures

their correct positions and pull them down by tightening the nuts a little at a time. When all the caps are seated, tighten the nuts to the specified torque.
18 Lubricate a new oil seal and fit it to the front of the camshaft, lips inwards. Tap it home with a piece of tube.
19 Refit the camshaft sprocket and associated components. Restrain the sprocket and tighten the bolt to the specified torque.
20 Refit the distributor if it was removed (Chapter 5B).
21 Refit and tension the camshaft drivebelt (Section 4).
22 Check and adjust the valve clearances as described in Chapter 1.
23 Refit the camshaft cover (Section 3)
24 If a new camshaft has been fitted, run it in at moderate engine speeds for a few minutes (neither idling nor racing), or as directed by the manufacturer.

7 Cylinder head - removal and refitting

Removal

1 Disconnect the battery negative lead.
2 Drain the cooling system (see Chapter 1).
3 Remove the camshaft cover (refer to Section 3).
4 Disconnect the radiator top hose from the thermostat housing.
5 Remove the fan and fan shroud.
6 Remove all accessory drivebelts and the water pump pulley (see Chapter 1).
7 Remove the distributor cap.
8 Remove the camshaft drivebelt cover upper section.
9 Bring the engine to TDC, No 1 piston on the firing stroke, then remove the camshaft drivebelt and tensioner (see Section 4). The drivebelt can stay on the lower sprockets if wished. **Do not** rotate the crankshaft or camshaft from now on.
10 Unbolt and remove the camshaft sprocket and the spacer washer. Also remove the camshaft drivebelt tensioner stud.
11 Remove the bolts which secure the drivebelt backplate to the cylinder head.
12 Remove the nuts which secure the inlet and exhaust manifolds to the cylinder head. Pull the manifolds off their studs to the sides of the engine bay, supporting them if necessary. Recover the gaskets.
13 Remove the camshaft cover. Recover the gasket.
14 Slacken the cylinder head bolts, half a turn at a time to begin with, in the reverse order to that shown in illustration 7.24. Remove the bolts.
15 Lift off the cylinder head noting that it will be necessary to bend the drivebelt backplate forwards a little for clearance.
16 Set the head down on a couple of wooden blocks to avoid damage to protruding valves. Recover the old head gasket.
17 If the cylinder head is to be dismantled for overhaul, remove the camshaft as described in Section 6, then refer to Part B of this Chapter.

Preparation for refitting

18 The mating faces of the cylinder head and cylinder block must be perfectly clean before refitting the head. Use a hard plastic or wood scraper to remove all traces of gasket and carbon; also clean the piston crowns. Take particular care during the cleaning operations, as aluminium alloy is easily damaged. Also, make sure that the carbon is not allowed to enter the oil and water passages - this is particularly important for the lubrication system, as carbon could block the oil supply to the engine's components. Using adhesive tape and paper, seal the water, oil and bolt holes in the cylinder block/crankcase. To prevent carbon entering the gap between the pistons and bores, smear a little grease in the gap. After cleaning each piston, use a small brush to remove all traces of grease and carbon from the gap, then wipe away the remainder with a clean rag. Clean all the pistons in the same way.
19 Check the mating surfaces of the cylinder block and the cylinder head for nicks, deep scratches and other damage. If slight, they may be removed carefully with a file, but if excessive, machining may be the only alternative to renewal.
20 If warpage of the cylinder head gasket surface is suspected, use a straight-edge to check it for distortion. Refer to Part B of this Chapter if necessary.
21 Check the condition of the cylinder head bolts, and particularly their threads, whenever they are removed. Wash the bolts in suitable solvent, and wipe them dry. Check each for any sign of visible wear or damage, renewing any bolt if necessary. Measure the length of each bolt, to check for stretching (although this is not a conclusive test, in the event that all ten bolts have stretched by the same amount. It is strongly recommended that the bolts should be renewed as a complete set whenever they are disturbed.

Refitting

22 Commence refitting by placing a new head gasket on the cylinder block. Make sure it is the right way up - all the bolt holes, oilways etc must line up.
23 Make sure that the camshaft to set to the No 1 piston on the firing stroke position, both cam lobes for No 1 cylinder pointing obliquely upwards. Lower the head into position.
24 Oil the threads of the cylinder head bolts. Fit the bolts and tighten them, in the sequence shown, to the specified Stage 1 torque **(see illustration)**.
25 In the same sequence tighten the bolts to the Stage 2 torque, then go round again and tighten the bolts through the angle specified

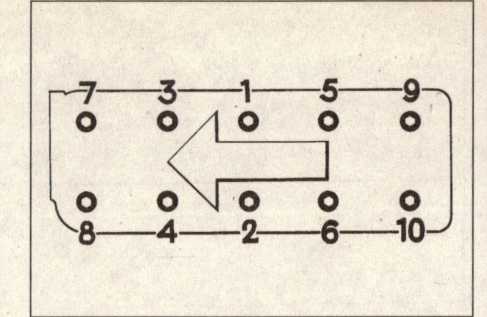

7.24 Cylinder head bolt tightening sequence

for Stage 3. (If the engine is on the bench, it may be preferable to leave Stage 3 tightening until after engine refitting.) No further tightening is required.
26 The remainder of refitting is a reversal of the removal procedure. Use new gaskets etc where necessary.
27 Check the valve clearances (Chapter 1) before starting the engine.

8 Sump - removal and refitting

Note: *Although it is possible to remove the sump with the engine in the car, it is a complicated operation. Read through this procedure first to see what is involved. Depending on facilities and experience, it may be preferable to remove the engine.*

Removal

1 Raise and securely support the front of the vehicle, or drive it over a pit.
2 Disconnect the battery negative lead.
3 Drain the engine oil (see Chapter 1).
4 Remove the splash guard from below the engine.
5 Disconnect the exhaust downpipe from the silencer.
6 Remove the nuts which secure the engine mountings to the crossmember.
7 Release the clamp bolts and disconnect the shaft from the steering gear.
8 Support the engine from above, either with a hoist or with an adjustable support resting on the inner wings or suspension turrets. Satisfy yourself as to the security of the support arrangements before proceeding.
9 Release the fan shroud and remove the engine oil dipstick, then raise the engine slightly to take the weight off the mountings. Be careful not to crush the distributor against the bulkhead.
10 Remove the engine mounting on the left-hand side. Cut the cable-tie which secures the power steering hose nearby.
11 Remove the bolts which secure the front crossmember to the body.
12 Remove the flywheel/driveplate bottom cover plate.

Engine in-car repair procedures 2A•7

9.5 Separating the pick-up pipe and cover from the pump body

9.9 Measuring oil pump gear endfloat

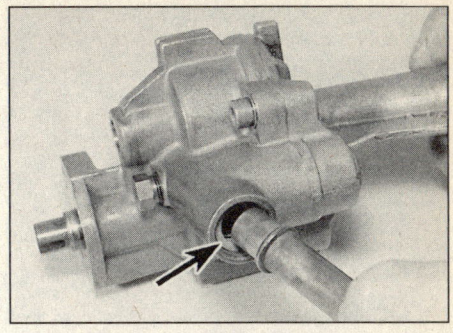

9.12 Fitting the delivery pipe to the oil pump. New seal (arrowed) is in the pump

13 Pull the front crossmember downwards to give adequate clearance below the sump. Disconnect or move aside power steering hoses as necessary.
14 Remove the sump securing bolts. Separate the sump from the block - if it is stuck, tap it with a soft-faced hammer. Do not lever between the mating faces.
15 Lower the sump, twist it to free it from the oil pump pick-up and remove it.

Refitting

16 Clean the sump internally. Remove all traces of gasket from the sump and block faces.
17 Commence refitting by sticking a new gasket to the sump with grease.
18 Offer the sump to the block, being careful not to displace the gasket. Secure the sump with two bolts in opposite corners.
19 Fit all the sump bolts and tighten them progressively to the specified torque.
20 The remainder of refitting is a reversal of the removal procedure. Check that the drain plug is tight, then refill the engine with oil on completion (Chapter 1).

9 Oil pump - removal, inspection and refitting

Removal

1 Remove the sump (see Section 8).
2 Remove the two bolts which secure the oil pump. Note that one of these bolts also secures the oil trap drain hose guide. Remove the pump and the guide.
3 Separate the oil pump delivery pipe from the pump. Recover the seals from each end of the pipe.

Inspection

4 Remove the Allen screws which hold the two halves of the pump together.
5 Remove the pick-up pipe and gear cover from the gear housing. Be prepared for the ejection of the relief valve spring **(see illustration)**.
6 Remove the relief valve spring and plunger (or ball on early models) and the pump gears.
7 Clean all components, paying particular attention to the pick-up screen, which is partly obscured by its housing. Inspect the gears, housing and gear cover for signs of wear or damage.
8 Measure the relief valve spring, and if possible compare its characteristics with those in the Specifications. Renew it if it is weak or distorted. Also inspect the plunger or ball for scoring or other damage.
9 Refit the gears to the casing. Using a straight-edge and feeler blades, check the gear side clearance and endfloat **(see illustration)**. Also check the backlash between the teeth. If the clearances are outside the specified limits, renew the pump.
10 If the clearances are satisfactory, liberally lubricate the gears. Lubricate and fit the relief valve plunger (or ball) and spring.
11 Refit the pick-up pipe and gear cover. Fit and tighten the Allen screws.

Refitting

12 Commence refitting by fitting the delivery pipe, with new seals, to the pump **(see illustration)**.
13 Fit the pump to the block, engaging the pump drivegear and the delivery pipe at the same time **(see illustration)**.
14 Fit the two bolts and the drain hose guide. Tighten the bolts.
15 Make sure that the oil drain hose is correctly positioned, then refit the sump **(see illustration)**.

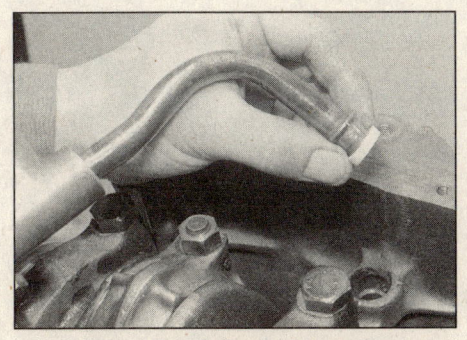

10 Crankshaft oil seals - renewal

Front oil seal

1 The front oil seal renewal procedure is essentially the same as that for the camshaft/auxiliary shaft oil seals. Refer to Section 5 for details.

Rear oil seal

2 Remove the flywheel or driveplate (see Section 11).
3 Note whether the old seal is flush with the end of its carrier, or recessed into it.
4 Carefully prise out the old oil seal. Do not damage the carrier or the surface of the crankshaft **(see illustration)**. Alternatively, punch or drill two small holes opposite each other in the oil seal. Screw a self-tapping screw into each, and pull on the screws with pliers to extract the seal.
5 Clean the oil seal carrier and the crankshaft. Inspect the crankshaft for a wear groove or ridge left by the old seal.
6 Lubricate the carrier, the crankshaft and the new seal. Fit the seal, lips inwards, and use a piece of tube (or the old seal, inverted) to tap it home. If there is any wear on the crankshaft sealing surface, fit the new seal more deeply recessed than the old one. The seal may be recessed up to 6 mm within the carrier.
7 Refit the flywheel or driveplate (Section 11).

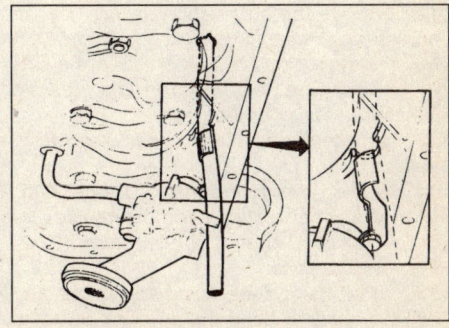

9.13 Fitting the delivery pipe and a new seal to the block

9.15 Correct positioning of oil drain hose

2A•8 Engine in-car repair procedures

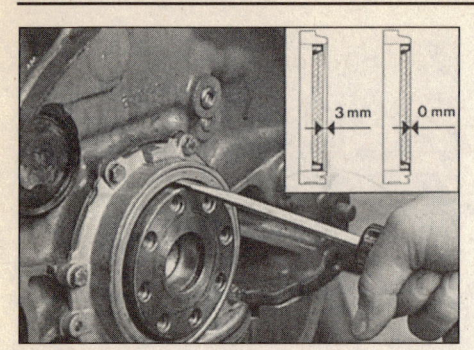

10.4 Levering out the rear oil seal. Note recessed depth (inset)

11 Flywheel/driveplate - removal and refitting

Note: New flywheel/driveplate retaining bolts will be required for refitting.

Removal

Flywheel (models with manual transmission)

1 Remove the transmission (see Chapter 7, Part A).
2 Remove the clutch pressure plate and driven plate (see Chapter 6).
3 Make alignment marks so that the flywheel can be refitted in the same position relative to the crankshaft.
4 Unbolt the flywheel and remove it. Do not drop it, it is heavy. Obtain new bolts for reassembly.

Driveplate (models with automatic transmission)

5 Remove the automatic transmission (see Chapter 7B).
6 Make alignment marks so that the driveplate can be refitted in the same position relative to the crankshaft.
7 Unbolt the driveplate and remove it, Noting the location and orientation of the large washers on each side. Obtain new bolts for reassembly.

Inspection

8 On manual transmission models, If the flywheel's clutch mating surface is deeply scored, cracked or otherwise damaged, the flywheel must be renewed. However, it may be possible to have it surface ground; seek the advice of a Volvo dealer or engine reconditioning specialist.
9 If the ring gear is badly worn or has missing teeth, it must be renewed. This job is best left to a Volvo dealer or engine reconditioning specialist. The temperature to which the new ring gear must be heated for installation is critical and, if not done accurately, the hardness of the teeth will be destroyed.
10 On models equipped with automatic transmission, check the torque converter driveplate carefully for signs of distortion. Look for any hairline cracks around the bolt holes or radiating outwards from the centre, and inspect the ring gear teeth for signs of wear or chipping. If any signs of wear or damage are found, the driveplate must be renewed.

Refitting

Flywheel (models with manual transmission)

11 Clean the mating surfaces of the flywheel and crankshaft. Remove any remaining locking compound from the threads of the crankshaft holes, using the correct-size tap, if available **(see Haynes Hint)**.
12 Continue refitting by reversing the removal operations. Apply thread locking

> **HAYNES HINT** *If a suitable tap is not available, cut two slots into the threads of one of the old flywheel bolts and use the bolt to remove the locking compound from the threads.*

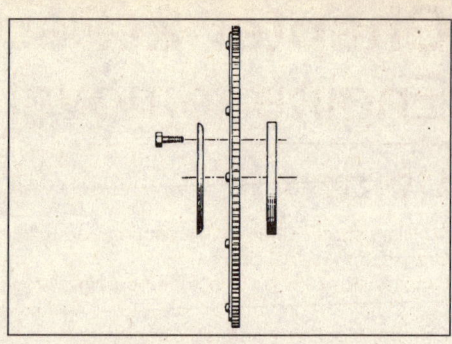

11.14 Driveplate and washers

compound to the new flywheel retaining bolts (if not already pre-coated) and tighten them to the specified torque.
13 Refit the clutch as described in Chapter 6.

Driveplate (models with automatic transmission)

14 Proceed as described above for manual transmission models but ignoring any references to clutch. Note the location and orientation of the large washers on each side of the driveplate **(see illustration)**.

12 Engine mountings - removal and refitting

Removal

1 Disconnect the battery negative lead.
2 Remove the nuts from the mounting to be removed.
3 Fit lifting tackle to the engine, or support it in some other way. Do not jack up directly onto the sump, as damage may result.
4 Take the weight off the mounting and remove it. It may be necessary to move aside power steering hoses, and to remove the inlet manifold bracing strut.

Refitting

5 Refit by reversing the removal operations.

Chapter 2 Part B:
Engine removal and overhaul procedures

Contents

Auxiliary shaft - removal, inspection and refitting	10
Crankshaft - inspection	15
Crankshaft - refitting and main bearing running clearance check	19
Crankshaft - removal	12
Cylinder block/crankcase - cleaning and inspection	13
Cylinder head - dismantling	7
Cylinder head - reassembly	9
Cylinder head and valves - cleaning and inspection	8
Engine - initial start-up after overhaul	21
Engine overhaul - dismantling sequence	6
Engine overhaul - general information	2
Engine overhaul - reassembly sequence	17
Engine/transmission removal - methods and precautions	3
General information	1
Engine (with transmission) - removal, separation and refitting	5
Engine (without transmission) - removal and refitting	4
Main and big-end bearings - inspection	16
Piston/connecting rod assemblies - inspection	14
Piston/connecting rod assemblies - refitting and big-end bearing running clearance check	20
Piston/connecting rod assemblies - removal	11
Piston rings - refitting	18

Degrees of difficulty

Easy, suitable for novice with little experience   **Fairly easy,** suitable for beginner with some experience   **Fairly difficult,** suitable for competent DIY mechanic   **Difficult,** suitable for experienced DIY mechanic   **Very difficult,** suitable for expert DIY or professional

Specifications

Cylinder head
Warp limit - acceptable for use:
- Lengthways .... 0.50 mm
- Across .... 0.25 mm

Warp limit - acceptable for refinishing:
- Lengthways .... 1.00 mm
- Across .... 0.50 mm

Height:
- New .... 146.1 mm
- Minimum after refinishing .... 145.6 mm

Inlet valves
Head diameter .... 44 mm

Stem diameter:
- New .... 7.955 to 7.970 mm
- Wear limit .... 7.935 mm

Valve head angle .... 44° 30'

Exhaust valves
Head diameter .... 35 mm

Stem diameter:
- New .... 7.945 to 7.960 mm
- Wear limit .... 7.925 mm

Valve seat inserts
Diameter (standard):
- Inlet .... 46.00 mm
- Exhaust .... 38.00 mm

Oversizes available .... + 0.25 and 0.50 mm
Fit in cylinder head .... Interference
Valve seat angle .... 45° 00'

Valve guides
Length .... 52 mm
Internal diameter .... 8.000 to 8.022 mm

Height above cylinder head:
- Inlet .... 15.4 to 15.6 mm
- Exhaust .... 17.9 to 18.1 mm

2B•2 Engine removal and overhaul procedures

Valve guides (continued)
Stem-to-guide clearance:
   New (inlet) .... 0.030 to 0.060 mm
   New (exhaust) .... 0.060 to 0.090 mm
   Wear limit (inlet and exhaust) .... 0.15 mm
Fit in head .... Interference
External oversizes available .... 3 (marked by grooves)

Valve springs
Diameter .... 25.9 mm
Free length .... 45.5 mm
Length under load of:
   280 to 320 N .... 38.0 mm
   702 to 782 N .... 27.5 mm

Cylinder bores
Standard sizes (B200):
   C .... 88.90 to 88.91 mm
   D .... 88.91 to 88.92 mm
   E .... 88.92 to 88.93 mm
   G .... 88.94 to 88.95 mm
First oversize .... 89.29 mm
Second oversize .... 89.67 mm
Wear limit .... 0.1 mm
Standard sizes (B230):
   C .... 96.00 to 96.01 mm
   D .... 96.01 to 96.02 mm
   E .... 96.02 to 96.03 mm
   G .... 96.04 to 96.05 mm
First oversize .... 96.30 mm
Second oversize .... 96.60 mm
Wear limit .... 0.1 mm

Pistons
Height .... 64.7 mm
Weight variation in same engine .... 16 g max
Running clearance in bore .... 0.01 to 0.03 mm

Piston rings
Clearance in groove (B200):
   Top compression .... 0.060 to 0.092 mm
   Second compression .... 0.030 to 0.062 mm
   Oil control .... 0.020 to 0.055 mm
Clearance in groove (B230):
   Top compression .... 0.060 to 0.092 mm
   Second compression .... 0.040 to 0.072 mm
   Oil control .... 0.030 to 0.065 mm
End gap (B200):
   Compression rings .... 0.30 to 0.50 mm
   Oil control .... 0.25 to 0.50 mm
End gap (B230):
   Compression rings .... 0.30 to 0.55 mm
   Oil control .... 0.30 to 0.60 mm

Gudgeon pins
Diameter, standard .... 23.00 mm
Oversize available .... + 0.05 mm
Fit in connecting rod .... Light thumb pressure
Fit in piston .... Firm thumb pressure

Auxiliary shaft
Bearing journal diameter:
   Front .... 46.975 to 47.000 mm
   Centre .... 43.025 to 43.050 mm
   Rear .... 42.925 to 42.950 mm
Bearing running clearance .... 0.020 to 0.075 mm
Endfloat .... 0.20 to 0.46 mm

Engine removal and overhaul procedures 2B•3

Crankshaft
Run-out	0.04 mm max
Endfloat	0.080 to 0.270 mm
Main bearing journal diameter:	
Standard	63.00 mm
First undersize	62.75 mm
Second undersize	62.50 mm
Main bearing running clearance	0.024 to 0.072 mm
Main bearing out-of-round	0.006 mm max
Main bearing taper	0.006 mm max
Connecting rod bearing journal diameter:	
Standard	49.00 mm
First undersize	48.75 mm
Second undersize	48.50 mm
Connecting rod bearing running clearance	0.023 to 0.067 mm
Connecting rod bearing out-of-round	0.1 mm max
Connecting rod bearing taper	0.01 mm max

Connecting rods
Length between centres	152 mm
Endfloat on crankshaft	0.25 to 0.45 mm
Weight variation in same engine	20 g max

Torque wrench settings
Refer to Chapter 2A Specifications

1 General information

Included in this Part of Chapter 2 are details of removing the engine/transmission from the car and general overhaul procedures for the cylinder head, cylinder block and all other engine internal components.

The information ranges from advice concerning preparation for an overhaul and the purchase of replacement parts, to detailed step-by-step procedures covering removal, inspection, renovation and refitting of engine internal components.

After Section 6, all instructions are based on the assumption that the engine has been removed from the car. For information concerning in-car engine repair, as well as removal and installation of those external components necessary for full overhaul, refer to Part A of this Chapter and to Section 6. Ignore any preliminary dismantling operations described in Part A that are no longer relevant once the engine has been removed from the car.

Apart from torque wrench settings, which are given at the beginning of Part A, all specifications relating to engine overhaul are at the beginning of this Part of Chapter 2.

2 Engine overhaul - general information

1 It's not always easy to determine when, or if, an engine should be completely overhauled, as a number of factors must be considered.

2 High mileage is not necessarily an indication that an overhaul is needed, while low mileage doesn't preclude the need for an overhaul. Frequency of servicing is probably the most important consideration. An engine that's had regular and frequent oil and filter changes, as well as other required maintenance, will most likely give many thousands of miles of reliable service. Conversely, a neglected engine may require an overhaul very early in its life.

3 Excessive oil consumption is an indication that piston rings, valve seals and/or valve guides are in need of attention. Make sure that oil leaks aren't responsible before deciding that the rings and/or guides are worn. Perform a compression test as described in Part A of this Chapter, to determine the likely cause of the problem.

4 Check the oil pressure with a gauge fitted in place of the oil pressure switch, and compare it with that specified. If it is extremely low, the main and big-end bearings, and/or the oil pump, are probably worn-out.

5 Loss of power, rough running, knocking or metallic engine noises, excessive valve gear noise and high fuel consumption may also point to the need for an overhaul, especially if they are all present at the same time. If a complete service does not remedy the situation, major mechanical work is the only solution.

6 An engine overhaul involves restoring all internal parts to the specification of a new engine.

7 During an overhaul, the pistons and the piston rings are renewed. New main and big-end bearings are generally fitted and, if necessary, the crankshaft may be reground (or renewed) to restore the journals. The valves are also serviced as well, since they are usually in less-than-perfect condition at this point. The end result should be an as-new engine that will give many trouble-free miles.

Note: Critical cooling system components such as the hoses, drivebelt, thermostat and water pump should be renewed when an engine is overhauled. The radiator should be checked carefully, to ensure that it isn't clogged or leaking. Also, it is a good idea to renew the oil pump when an engine is overhauled.

8 Before beginning the engine overhaul, read through the entire procedure to familiarise yourself with the scope and requirements of the job. Overhauling an engine is not difficult if you follow carefully all of the instructions, have the necessary tools and equipment, and pay close attention to all specifications. It can, however, be time-consuming. Plan on the vehicle being off the road for a minimum of two weeks, especially if parts must be taken to an engineering works for repair or reconditioning. Check on availability of parts, and make sure that any necessary special tools and equipment are obtained in advance. Most work can be done with typical hand tools, although a number of precision measuring tools are required, for inspecting parts to determine if they must be renewed. Often, the engineering works will handle the inspection of parts, and will offer advice concerning reconditioning and renewal.

Note: Always wait until the engine has been completely dismantled, and until all components, (especially the cylinder block/crankcase and the crankshaft) have been inspected, before deciding what service and repair operations must be performed by an engineering works. The condition of these components will be the major factor to consider when determining whether to

2B•4 Engine removal and overhaul procedures

overhaul the original engine or buy a reconditioned unit. Do not, therefore, purchase parts or have overhaul work done on other components until they have been thoroughly inspected. As a general rule, time is the primary cost of an overhaul, so it doesn't pay to fit worn or sub-standard parts.
9 As a final note, to ensure maximum life and minimum trouble from a reconditioned engine, everything must be assembled with care, in a spotlessly-clean environment.

3 Engine/transmission removal - methods and precautions

1 If you have decided that an engine must be removed for overhaul or major repair work, several preliminary steps should be taken.
2 Locating a suitable place to work is extremely important. Adequate work space, along with storage space for the car, will be needed. If a workshop or garage is not available, at the very least, a flat, level, clean work surface is required.
3 Cleaning the engine compartment and engine/transmission before beginning the removal procedure will help keep tools clean and organised.
4 An engine hoist or A-frame will also be necessary. Make sure the equipment is rated in excess of the combined weight of the engine and transmission. Safety is of primary importance, considering the potential hazards involved in lifting the engine/transmission from the car.
5 If this is the first time you have removed an engine, an assistant should ideally be available. Advice and aid from someone more experienced would also be helpful. There are many instances when one person cannot simultaneously perform all of the operations required when lifting the engine/transmission out of the vehicle.
6 Plan the operation ahead of time. Before starting work, arrange for the hire of or obtain, all of the tools and equipment you will need. Some of the equipment necessary to perform engine/transmission removal and installation safely and with relative ease (in addition to an engine hoist) is as follows: a heavy-duty trolley jack, complete sets of spanners and sockets as described elsewhere in this manual, wooden blocks, and plenty of rags and cleaning solvent for mopping up spilled oil, coolant and solvent. If the hoist must be hired, make sure that you arrange for it in advance, and perform all of the operations possible without it beforehand. This will save you money and time.
7 Plan for the vehicle to be out of use for quite a while. An engineering works will be required to perform some of the work which the do-it-yourselfer cannot accomplish without special equipment. These places often have a busy schedule, so it would be a good idea to consult them before removing the engine, to accurately estimate the amount of time required to rebuild or repair components that may need work.
8 Always be extremely careful when removing and installing the engine/transmission. Serious injury can result from careless actions. Plan ahead and take your time, and a job of this nature can be accomplished successfully.

4 Engine (without transmission) - removal and refitting

Removal

Note: *The engine can be removed from the car either on its own, or as a complete unit with the transmission. Removal of the engine on its own is described in this Section; removal of the unit with the transmission attached is described in Section 5.*

1 Disconnect the battery negative lead.
2 Either remove the bonnet (see Chapter 11), or open it to its widest setting.
3 Remove the radiator (see Chapter 3).
4 On Turbo models, remove the intercooler and associated hoses (see Chapter 4). Also remove the mass air flow sensor and its associated hoses.
5 Remove the air cleaner hot air trunking on all other models.
6 Remove the distributor cap and HT leads.
7 Disconnect the throttle cable.
8 Disconnect the brake servo vacuum hose.
9 Disconnect the fuel supply and return pipes. Be prepared for fuel spillage.
10 Disconnect the various crankcase ventilation, vacuum and pressure sensing hoses. Make notes or identifying marks if there is any possibility of confusion later.
11 Disconnect the engine wiring harness multi-plug(s), again making notes if necessary.
12 Disconnect the starter motor feed lead, then remove the battery completely.
13 Disconnect the engine earth strap(s).
14 Disconnect the air conditioning compressor clutch lead.
15 Remove the power steering pump without disconnecting the hoses and wire it up out of the way. See Chapter 10 if necessary.
16 Disconnect the heater hoses at the rear of the engine.
17 Remove the starter motor (see Chapter 5).
18 Disconnect the exhaust downpipe from the manifold or turbo exit.
19 If an oil cooler is fitted, unbolt its mounting bracket.
20 Raise and support the vehicle. Remove the engine undertray, if not already done.
21 Drain the engine oil and remove the oil filter (see Chapter 1).
22 If an oil cooler is fitted, disconnect the flexible hoses at their unions with the rigid pipes. The contents of the oil cooler will drain out of the open unions. Remove the oil cooler.
23 Remove those engine-to-transmission nuts and bolts which are accessible from below. Also remove the flywheel/driveplate bottom cover.
24 On automatic transmission models, unbolt the torque converter from the driveplate. Turn the crankshaft as necessary to gain access. Make alignment marks for reference when refitting.
25 Remove the air conditioning compressor drivebelt (see Chapter 1).
26 Remove the nuts which secure the air conditioning compressor bracket to the engine. Move the compressor aside without disconnecting the refrigerant hoses. It will rest in the space vacated by the battery.
27 Support the transmission from below, using a trolley jack for preference. Pad the jack head with rags or wood.
28 Attach the lifting tackle to the engine using the lifting eyes provided. Take the weight of the engine.
29 Remove the nuts which secure the engine bearers to the engine mountings.
30 Remove the remaining engine-to-transmission nuts and bolts.
31 Check that no wires, hoses etc have been overlooked. Raise the engine and draw it forwards off the transmission, at the same time raising the jack under the transmission. Do not allow the weight of the transmission to hang on the input shaft.
32 Once the engine is clear of the transmission, carefully lift it out of the engine bay and take it to the bench.

Refitting

33 Make sure that the clutch is properly centred, or that the torque converter is fully engaged in the transmission. Put a smear of grease or anti-seize compound on the transmission input shaft or the torque converter locating spigot.
34 Lower the engine into position; have an assistant watch to see that no pipes, wires etc, are trapped.
35 On manual transmission models, rock the engine from side to side, or rotate the crankshaft slightly, to encourage the input shaft to enter the clutch driven plate. Do not allow the engine to hang on the input shaft.
36 When the bellhousing is engaged on the engine dowels, insert a couple of engine-to-bellhousing nuts and bolts and nip them up.
37 The remainder of refitting is now a reversal of removal noting the following points:
a) *Refill the engine with oil and coolant (Chapter 1).*
b) *Refer to Section 21 before starting the engine.*

5 Engine (with transmission) - removal, separation and refitting

Note: *The engine can be removed from the car either on its own, or as a complete unit*

Engine removal and overhaul procedures 2B•5

with the transmission. Removal of the engine on its own is described in Section 4; removal of the unit with the transmission attached is described in this Section.

Removal

1 Proceed as in Section 4, paragraphs 1 to 16, 18 to 22, 25 and 26.
2 Disconnect the leads from the starter motor solenoid.
3 Remove the exhaust downpipe completely.

Manual transmission models

4 Remove the clutch slave cylinder (without disconnecting the hydraulic hose) or disconnect the clutch cable, as applicable (see Chapter 6).
5 Disconnect the gear lever (see Chapter 7A).

Automatic transmission models

6 Disconnect the kickdown and control linkages (see Chapter 7B).

All models

7 Disconnect electrical services from the transmission.
8 Unbolt the propeller shaft from the rear of the transmission.
9 Support the transmission. Unbolt the crossmember from the transmission and from the side rails and remove it.
10 Unbolt the bracing strut from below the bellhousing (when fitted).
11 Attach suitable lifting tackle to the engine using the eyes provided. Take the weight of the engine.
12 Remove the nuts which secure the engine bearers to the engine mountings.
13 Check that no attachments have been overlooked. Raise the engine, at the same time lowering the support under the transmission, until the whole assembly can be lifted from the engine bay.

Separation

14 With the engine/transmission assembly removed, support the assembly on suitable blocks of wood, on a workbench (or failing that, on a clean area of the workshop floor).
15 Remove the starter motor.
16 Remove the bellhousing-to-engine nuts and bolts. Also remove the flywheel/driveplate bottom cover plate (if applicable).

Manual transmission models

17 With the aid of an assistant, draw the transmission off the engine. Once it is clear of the dowels, do not allow it to hang on the input shaft.

Automatic transmission models

18 Unbolt the torque converter from the driveplate, turning the crankshaft to gain access from below or through the starter motor hole. Make alignment marks for reference when refitting.
19 With the aid of an assistant, draw the transmission off the engine. Make sure that the torque converter stays in the bellhousing.

Refitting

Manual transmission models

20 Make sure that the clutch is correctly centred and that the clutch release components are fitted to the bellhousing. Put a smear of grease or anti-seize compound on the input shaft splines.
21 Offer the transmission to the engine. Rotate the crankshaft or the input shaft if necessary to align the input shaft and clutch driven plate splines. Do not allow the weight of the transmission to hang on the input shaft.
22 Engage the transmission on the engine dowels. Fit a couple of bellhousing-to-engine nuts and bolts.

Automatic transmission models

23 Make sure that the torque converter is fully engaged in the transmission. Put a smear of grease or anti-seize compound on the torque converter locating spigot.
24 Offer the transmission to the engine, engaging the locating dowels. Fit a couple of bellhousing-to-engine nuts and bolts.
25 Insert the torque converter-to-driveplate bolts, turning the crankshaft to gain access. Just nip the bolts up at first, then tighten them in cross sequence to the specified torque (see Chapter 7B Specifications).

All models

26 Fit the remaining bellhousing nuts and bolts, and (when applicable) the flywheel/driveplate bottom cover plate. Tighten the nuts and bolts progressively.
27 Refit the starter motor.
28 The remainder of refitting is essentially a reversal of removal, noting the following points.
 a) On automatic transmission models, adjust the gear selector mechanism (Chapter 7B).
 b) Refill the engine with oil and coolant (Chapter 1).
 c) Refill the transmission with lubricant if necessary (Chapter 1).
 d) Refer to Section 21 before starting the engine.

6 Engine overhaul - dismantling sequence

1 It is much easier to dismantle and work on the engine if it is mounted on a portable engine stand. These stands can be hired from a tool hire shop. Before the engine is mounted on a stand, the flywheel/driveplate should be removed so that the stand bolts can be tightened into the end of the cylinder block/crankcase.
2 If a stand is not available, it is possible to dismantle the engine with it suitably supported on a sturdy workbench or on the floor. Be careful not to tip or drop the engine when working without a stand.
3 If you are going to obtain a reconditioned engine, all the external components must be removed first to be transferred to the replacement engine (just as they will if you are doing a complete engine overhaul yourself). These components include the following, according to engine type.
 a) *Engine mountings (Chapter 2A).*
 b) *Alternator and brackets (Chapter 5A).*
 c) *Exhaust manifold, with turbocharger if fitted (Chapter 4A).*
 d) *Fan and water pump (Chapter 3).*
 e) *Distributor (Chapter 5B).*
 f) *Inlet manifold with fuel injection components (Chapter 4A).*
 g) *Spark plugs (Chapter 1).*
 h) *Clutch pressure and driven plates (Chapter 6).*
 i) *Ignition sensors and brackets (Chapter 5B).*
 j) *Flywheel/driveplate (Chapter 2A).*
 k) *Oil filter (Chapter 1).*
 l) *Oil cooler and pipework (Chapter 3)*
 m) *Water pump with hoses and distribution pipe (Chapter 3).*
 n) *Dipstick, tube and bracket.*

Note: *When removing the external components from the engine, pay close attention to details that may be helpful or important during refitting. Note the fitting positions of gaskets, seals, washers, bolts and other small items.*

4 If you are obtaining a "short" engine (cylinder block/crankcase, crankshaft, pistons and connecting rods all assembled), then the cylinder head, sump, oil pump and camshaft drivebelt will have to be removed also.
5 If a complete overhaul is planned, the engine can be dismantled and the internal components removed in the following order.
 a) *Camshaft drivebelt, tensioner and sprockets.*
 b) *Cylinder head.*
 c) *Flywheel/driveplate.*
 d) *Auxiliary shaft.*
 e) *Sump.*
 f) *Oil pump.*
 g) *Pistons/connecting rods.*
 h) *Crankshaft.*

6 Before beginning the dismantling and overhaul procedures, make sure that you have all of the correct tools necessary. Refer to *"Tools and working facilities"* for further information.

7 Cylinder head - dismantling

1 Remove the cylinder head as described in Part A of this Chapter.
2 Remove the camshaft, tappets and shims as described in Part A of this Chapter.
3 According to components still in place, remove the inlet and exhaust manifolds (Chapter 4A), the thermostat housing (Chapter 3), the spark plugs (Chapter 1) and any other unions, pipes, sensors or brackets as necessary.
4 Recover the rubber rings from the valve stem tips **(see illustration)**.

2B•6 Engine removal and overhaul procedures

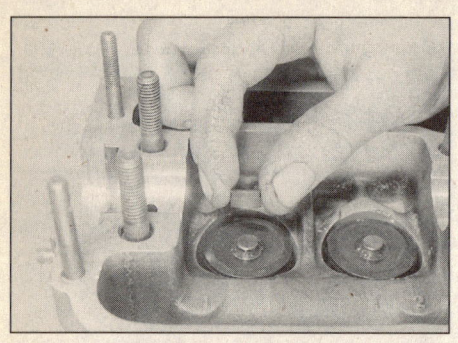

7.4 Recover the rubber ring from the valve stem tips

7.6 Extracting a collet with a magnet

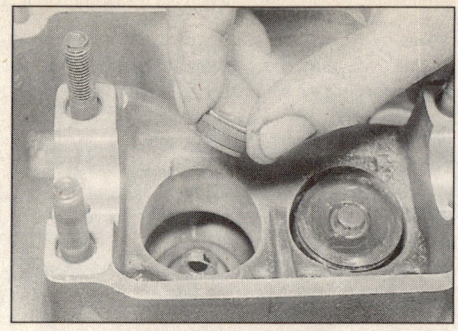

7.7 Removing a valve

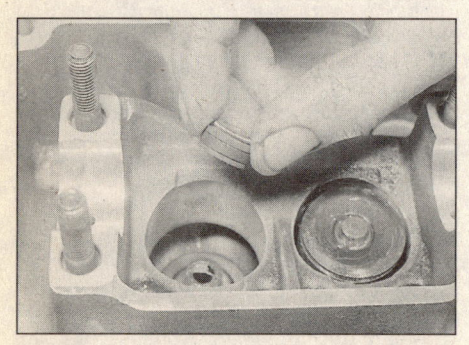

7.8 Removing the inlet valve stem oil seal

7.10 Place each valve and its associated components in a labelled polythene bag

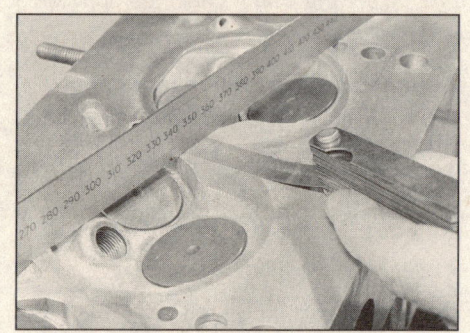

8.6 Checking the cylinder head gasket surface for distortion

5 Tap each valve stem smartly, using a light hammer and drift, to free the spring and associated items.

6 Fit a valve spring compressor to each valve in turn and compress each spring until the collets are exposed. Lift out the collets using a small screwdriver, a magnet or a pair of tweezers may be useful **(see illustration)**. Carefully release the spring compressor and remove it.

7 Remove the valve spring upper seat and the valve spring. Pull the valve out of its guide **(see illustration)**.

8 Pull off the valve stem oil seal with a pair of long-nosed pliers. Recover the seal **(see illustration)**. Note that valve stem oil seals are only fitted to the inlet valves.

9 Recover the valve spring lower seat. If there is much carbon build-up round the outside of the valve guide, this will have to be scraped off before the seat can be removed.

10 It is essential that each valve is stored together with its collets, spring and seats. The valves should also be kept in their correct sequence, unless they are so badly worn or burnt that they are to be renewed. If they are going to be kept and used again, place each valve assembly in a labelled polythene bag or similar container **(see illustration)**.

8 Cylinder head and valves - cleaning and inspection

1 Thorough cleaning of the cylinder head and valve components, followed by a detailed inspection, will enable you to decide how much valve service work must be carried out during the engine overhaul. **Note:** *If the engine has been severely overheated, it is best to assume that the cylinder head is warped, and to check carefully for signs of this.*

Cleaning

2 Scrape away all traces of old gasket material from the cylinder head.

3 Scrape away the carbon from the combustion chambers and ports, then wash the cylinder head thoroughly with paraffin or a suitable solvent.

4 Scrape off any heavy carbon deposits that may have formed on the valves, then use a power-operated wire brush to remove deposits from the valve heads and stems.

Inspection

Note: *Be sure to perform all the following inspection procedures before concluding that the services of an engineering works are required. Make a list of all items that require attention.*

Cylinder head

5 Inspect the head very carefully for cracks, evidence of coolant leakage, and other damage. If cracks are found, a new cylinder head should be obtained.

6 Use a straight edge and feeler blade to check that the cylinder head gasket surface is not distorted. If it is, it may be possible to re-surface it **(see illustration)**.

7 Examine the valve seats in each of the combustion chambers. If they are severely pitted, cracked or burned, then they will need to be renewed or re-cut by an engine overhaul specialist. If they are only slightly pitted, this can be removed by grinding-in the valve heads and seats with fine valve-grinding compound, as described below.

8 If the valve guides are worn, indicated by a side-to-side motion of the valve, new guides must be fitted. Measure the diameter of the existing valve stems (see below) and the bore of the guides, then calculate the clearance, and compare the result with the specified value; if the clearance is excessive, renew the valves or guides as necessary.

9 The renewal of valve guides is best carried out by an engine overhaul specialist.

10 If the valve seats are to be re-cut, this must be done *only after* the guides have been renewed.

Valves

11 Examine the head of each valve for pitting, burning, cracks and general wear, and check the valve stem for scoring and wear ridges. Rotate the valve, and check for any obvious indication that it is bent. Look for pits and excessive wear on the tip of each valve stem. Renew any valve that shows any such signs of wear or damage.

Caution: Exhaust valves on Turbo engines contain sodium and must not be mixed with other scrap metal. Consult a Volvo dealer for safe disposal of these valves.

12 If the valve appears satisfactory at this stage, measure the valve stem diameter at several points, using a micrometer **(see illustration)**. Any significant difference in the

Engine removal and overhaul procedures 2B•7

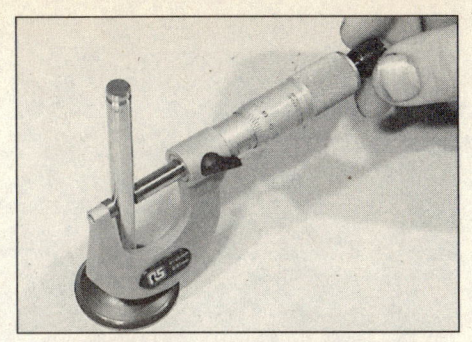

8.12 Measuring a valve stem diameter

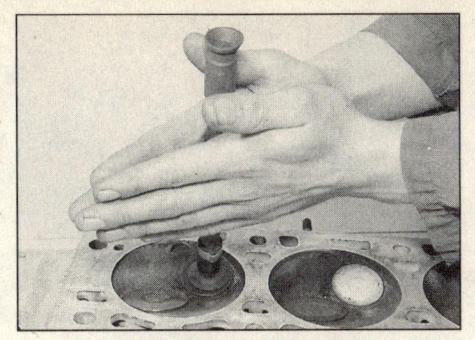

8.15 Grinding in a valve

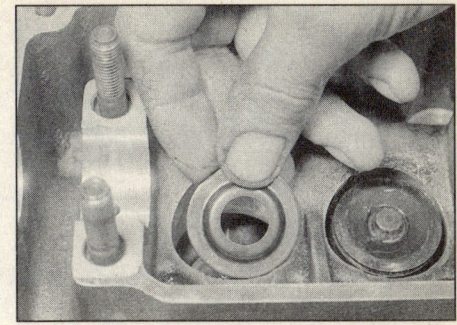

9.1 Fitting a valve spring lower seat

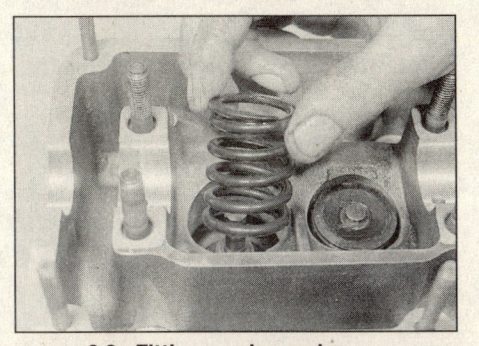

9.3a Fitting a valve spring . . .

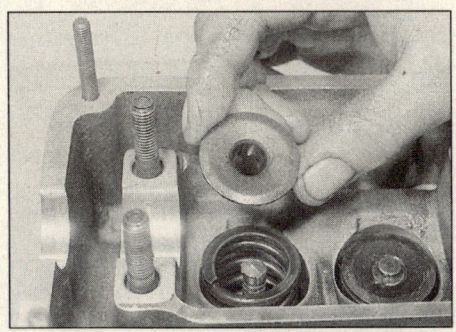

9.3b . . . and the spring upper seat

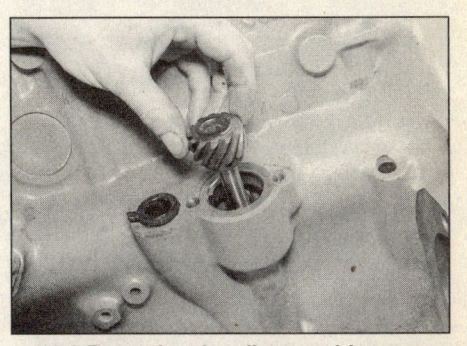

10.2 Removing the oil pump drivegear

readings obtained indicates wear of the valve stem. Should any of these conditions be apparent, the valve(s) must be renewed.
13 If the valves are in satisfactory condition, they should be ground (lapped) into their respective seats, to ensure a smooth gas-tight seal. If the seat is only lightly pitted, or if it has been re-cut, fine grinding compound *only* should be used to produce the required finish. Coarse valve-grinding compound should *not* be used unless a seat is badly burned or deeply pitted; if this is the case, the cylinder head and valves should be inspected by an expert, to decide whether seat re-cutting, or even the renewal of the valve or seat insert, is required.
14 Valve grinding is carried out as follows. Place the cylinder head upside-down on a bench, with a block of wood at each end to give clearance for the valve stems.
15 Smear a trace of (the appropriate grade of) valve-grinding compound on the seat face, and press a suction grinding tool onto the valve head. With a semi-rotary action, grind the valve head to its seat, lifting the valve occasionally to redistribute the grinding compound **(see illustration)**. A light spring placed under the valve head will greatly ease this operation.
16 If coarse grinding compound is being used, work only until a dull, matt even surface is produced on both the valve seat and the valve, then wipe off the used compound, and repeat the process with fine compound. When a smooth unbroken ring of light grey matt finish is produced on both the valve and seat, the grinding operation is complete. Do *not*

grind in the valves any further than absolutely necessary, or the seat will be prematurely sunk into the cylinder head.
17 When all the valves have been ground-in, carefully wash off *all* traces of grinding compound, using paraffin or a suitable solvent, before reassembly of the cylinder head.

Valve components
18 Examine the valve springs for signs of damage and discoloration, and also measure their free length by comparing each of the existing springs with a new component.
19 Stand each spring on a flat surface, and check it for squareness. If any of the springs are damaged, distorted, or have lost their tension, obtain a complete set of new springs. It is normal to fit new springs as a matter of course if a major overhaul is being carried out.
20 Renew the valve stem oil seals regardless of their apparent condition.

9 Cylinder head - reassembly

1 Oil the stem of one valve and insert it into its guide. Fit the spring lower seat, dished side up **(see illustration)**.
2 On the inlet valves, fit the valve stem oil seal, pushing it onto the valve guide with a piece of tube. Be careful not to damage the seal lips on the valve stem: if a protective sleeve is supplied with the seals, cover the collet grooves with it when fitting the seal.
3 Fit the valve spring and upper seat **(see

illustrations). Compress the spring and fit the two collets in the recesses in the valve stem. Carefully release the compressor.

> **HAYNES HiNT** *Use a little dab of grease to hold the collets in position on the valve stem while the spring compressor is released.*

4 Cover the valve stem with a cloth and tap it smartly with a light hammer to verify that the collets are properly seated.
5 Repeat these procedures on all the other valves.
6 Fit new rubber rings to the valve stem tips.
7 Refit the camshaft, tappets and shims as described in Part A of this Chapter.
8 Refit the remainder of the disturbed components then refit the cylinder head also as described in Part A of this Chapter.

10 Auxiliary shaft - removal, inspection and refitting

Removal
1 Remove the camshaft drivebelt, sprockets, tensioner and backplate, the sump, the oil pump and any additional external components necessary for access.
2 Unbolt the crankcase ventilation system oil trap and pull out the long drain hose. Working through that hole, lift up the oil pump drivegear/shaft and remove it **(see illustration)**.

2B•8 Engine removal and overhaul procedures

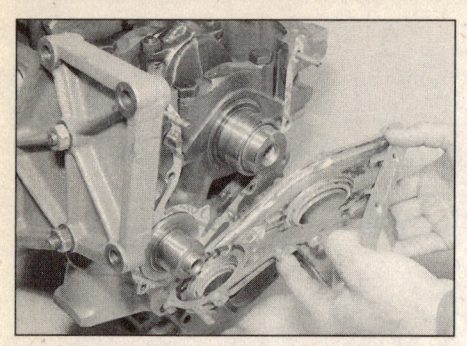

10.3 Removing the front oil seal housing

10.4 Removing the auxiliary shaft

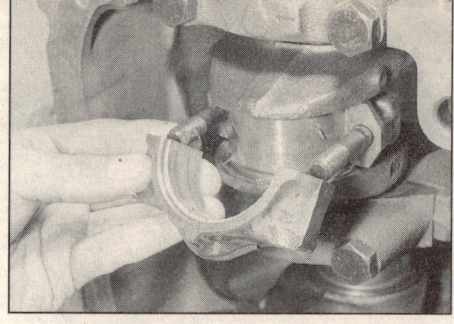

11.4 Removing a connecting rod cap

3 Unbolt and remove the front oil seal housing **(see illustration)**. Note the cable clips attached to the bottom studs. Recover the gasket.
4 Withdraw the auxiliary shaft, being careful not to damage the bearings in the block **(see illustration)**.

Inspection

5 Inspect the shaft bearing journals and gears for wear or damage. Measure the journals with a micrometer. Renew the shaft if it is worn or damaged.
6 If the auxiliary shaft bearings in the block are damaged, have them renewed by a Volvo dealer or other specialist.

Refitting

7 Lubricate the auxiliary shaft bearing surfaces and feed the shaft into the block, being careful not to damage the bearings.
8 Fit the front oil seal housing, using a new gasket. Trim the ends of the gasket level with the sump mating face. Some of the housing bolts cannot be fitted yet because they also secure the camshaft drivebelt backplate.
9 Fit new oil seals in the front oil seal housing, lips inwards and lubricated. Use a piece of tube to seat the seals.
10 Refit the oil pump drivegear/shaft, making sure it engages with the auxiliary shaft.
11 Refit the oil trap drain hose, making sure that it is inserted fully into its hole and secured towards its lower end by the guide.
12 Fit a new O-ring to the crankcase ventilation system oil trap, refit and secure the trap.
13 Refit the previously removed components with reference to the relevant Chapters of this manual.

11 Piston/connecting rod assemblies - removal

1 Remove the cylinder head, sump and oil pump as described in Part A of this Chapter
2 Feel inside the tops of the bores for a pronounced wear ridge. Some authorities recommend that such a ridge be removed (with a scraper or ridge reamer) before attempting to remove the pistons. However, a ridge big enough to damage the pistons will almost certainly mean that a rebore and new pistons are needed anyway.
3 Turn the crankshaft to bring a pair of connecting rod caps into an accessible position. Check that there are identification numbers or marks on each connecting rod and cap; paint or punch suitable marks if necessary, so that each rod can be refitted in the same position and the same way round.
4 Remove two connecting rod bolts. Tap the cap with a soft-faced hammer to free it. Remove the cap and bearing shell **(see illustration)**.
5 Push the connecting rod and piston up and out of the bore. Recover the other half bearing shell if it is loose.
6 Refit the cap to the connecting rod so that they do not get mixed up. Keep the bearing shells in their original positions if there is any chance that they will be re-used.
7 Repeat the operations on the remaining connecting rods and pistons, turning the crankshaft as necessary to gain access to the connecting rod caps.

12 Crankshaft - removal

1 Remove the pistons and connecting rods, and the front and rear oil seal housings (if not already done).
2 Before the crankshaft is removed, check the endfloat. Mount a DTI (Dial Test Indicator, or dial gauge) with the stem in line with the

12.6 Removing the rear main bearing cap

crankshaft and just touching the crankshaft.
3 Push the crankshaft fully away from the gauge, and zero it. Next, lever the crankshaft towards the gauge as far as possible, and check the reading obtained. The distance that the crankshaft moved is its endfloat; if it is greater than specified, check the crankshaft thrust surfaces for wear. If no wear is evident, new thrustwashers should correct the endfloat.
4 If no dial gauge is available, feeler blades can be used. Gently lever or push the crankshaft all the way towards the right-hand end of the engine. Slip feeler blades between the crankshaft and the main bearing incorporating the thrustwashers to determine the clearance.
5 Inspect the main bearing caps for identifying numbers or marks. Paint or punch marks if necessary.
6 Remove the main bearing cap bolts, then lift off the main bearing caps, tapping them with a soft-faced hammer if necessary to free them. Keep the bearing shells with their caps if they may be re-used **(see illustration)**.
7 Lift out the crankshaft. Do not drop it, it is heavy.
8 Recover the two half thrustwashers from each side of the centre main bearing.
9 Remove the upper half main bearing shells from their seats in the crankcase by pressing the end of the shell furthest from the locating tab. Again, keep the shells in order if they are to be re-used.

13 Cylinder block/crankcase - cleaning and inspection

Cleaning

1 Prior to cleaning, remove all external components and senders, and any gallery plugs or caps that may be fitted.
2 If any of the castings are extremely dirty, all should be steam-cleaned.
3 After the castings are returned from steam-cleaning, clean all oil holes and oil galleries one more time. Flush all internal passages with warm water until the water runs clear, then dry thoroughly and apply a light film of oil

Engine removal and overhaul procedures 2B•9

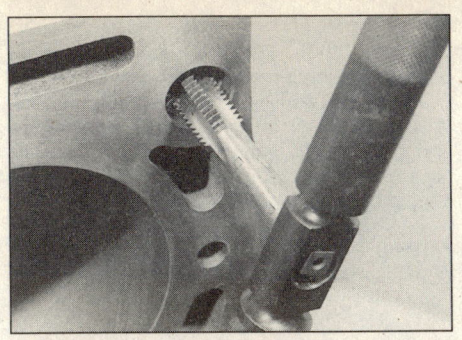

13.5 Cleaning a cylinder block threaded hole using a suitable tap

to all machined surfaces, to prevent rusting. If you have access to compressed air, use it to speed the drying process, and to blow out all the oil holes and galleries.

⚠️ **Warning: Wear appropriate eye protection when using compressed air!**

4 If the castings are not very dirty, you can do an adequate cleaning job with hot soapy water (as hot as you can stand!) and a stiff brush. Take plenty of time, and do a thorough job. Regardless of the cleaning method used, be sure to clean all oil holes and galleries very thoroughly, and to dry all components completely; protect the machined surfaces as described above, to prevent rusting.

5 All threaded holes must be clean and dry, to ensure accurate torque readings during reassembly. To clean the threads, run the correct-size tap into each of the holes to remove rust, corrosion, thread sealant or sludge, and to restore damaged threads **(see illustration)**. If possible, use compressed air to clear the holes of debris caused by this operation.

HAYNES HiNT *A good alternative is to inject aerosol-applied water dispersant lubricant into each hole, using the long spout usually supplied. Make sure each hole is dried thoroughly afterwards.*

⚠️ **Warning: Wear eye protection when cleaning out these holes in this way!**

6 If the engine is not going to be reassembled right away, cover it with a large plastic bag to keep it clean; protect the machined surfaces as described above, to prevent rusting.

Inspection

7 Visually check the castings for cracks and corrosion. Look for stripped threads in the threaded holes. If there has been any history of internal coolant leakage, it may be worthwhile having an engine overhaul specialist check the cylinder block/crankcase for cracks with special equipment. If defects are found, have them repaired, if possible, or renew the assembly.

8 Check each cylinder bore for scuffing and scoring. Check for signs of a wear ridge at the top of the cylinder, indicating that the bore is excessively worn.

9 If the necessary measuring equipment is available, measure the diameter of each cylinder at the top (just under the ridge area), centre and bottom of the cylinder bore, parallel to the crankshaft axis. Next, measure the bore diameter at the same three locations across the crankshaft axis. Note the measurements obtained.

10 Measure the piston diameter at right-angles to the gudgeon pin axis, just above the bottom of the skirt; again, note the results.

11 If it is wished to obtain the piston-to-bore clearance, measure the bore and piston skirt as described above, and subtract the skirt diameter from the bore measurement. If the precision measuring tools shown are not available, the condition of the pistons and bores can be assessed, though not quite as accurately, by using feeler blades as follows. Select a feeler blade of thickness equal to the specified piston-to-bore clearance, and slip it into the cylinder along with the matching piston. The piston must be positioned exactly as it normally would be. The feeler blade must be between the piston and cylinder on one of the thrust faces (at right-angles to the gudgeon pin bore). The piston should slip through the cylinder (with the feeler blade in place) with moderate pressure; if it falls through or slides through easily, the clearance is excessive, and a new piston will be required. If the piston binds at the lower end of the cylinder, and is loose toward the top, the cylinder is tapered. If tight spots are encountered as the piston/feeler blade is rotated in the cylinder, the cylinder is out-of-round (oval).

12 Repeat these procedures for the remaining pistons and cylinder bores.

13 Compare the results with the Specifications at the beginning of this Chapter; if any measurement is beyond the dimensions specified for that class, or if any bore measurement is significantly different from the others (indicating that the bore is tapered or oval), the piston or bore is excessively-worn.

14 If the cylinder bores are badly scuffed or scored, or if they are excessively-worn, out-of-round or tapered, the usual course of action would be to have the cylinder block/crankcase rebored, and to fit new, oversized, pistons on reassembly. Consult a dealer or engine reconditioning specialist for advice.

15 If the bores are in reasonably good condition and not excessively-worn, then it may only be necessary to renew the piston rings.

16 If this is the case, the bores should be honed, to allow the new rings to bed in correctly and provide the best possible seal. Honing is an operation that will be carried out for you by an engine reconditioning specialist.

17 After all machining operations are completed, the entire block/crankcase must be washed very thoroughly with warm soapy water to remove all traces of abrasive grit produced during the machining operations. When the cylinder block/crankcase is completely clean, rinse it thoroughly and dry it, then lightly oil all exposed machined surfaces, to prevent rusting.

18 The cylinder block/crankcase should now be completely clean and dry, with all components checked for wear or damage, and repaired or overhauled as necessary. Refit as many ancillary components as possible, for safekeeping. If reassembly is not to start immediately, cover the block with a large plastic bag to keep it clean, and protect the machined surfaces as described above to prevent rusting.

14 Piston/connecting rod assemblies - inspection

1 Before the inspection process can be carried out, the piston/connecting rod assemblies must be cleaned, and the original piston rings removed from the pistons

2 Carefully expand the old rings over the top of the pistons. The use of two or three old feeler blades will be helpful in preventing the rings dropping into empty grooves. Be careful not to scratch the pistons with the ends of the ring. The rings are brittle and will snap if they are spread too far. They are also very sharp - protect your hands and fingers. Note that the third ring incorporates an expander. Always remove the rings from the top of the piston. Keep each set of rings with its piston if the old rings are to be re-used, and mark or label each ring so that its original top surface can be identified on reassembly, and so that it can be returned to its original groove.

3 Scrape all traces of carbon from the top of the piston. A hand-held wire brush (or a piece of fine emery cloth) can be used, once the majority of the deposits have been scraped away.

4 Remove the carbon from the ring grooves in the piston, using an old ring. Break the ring in half to do this (be careful not to cut your fingers - piston rings are sharp). Be careful to remove only the carbon deposits - do not remove any metal, and do not nick or scratch the sided of the ring grooves **(see illustration)**.

5 Once the deposits have been removed, clean the piston/rod assemblies with paraffin or a suitable solvent, and dry thoroughly. Make sure the oil return holes in the ring grooves, are clear.

14.4 Cleaning a piston ring groove

2B•10 Engine removal and overhaul procedures

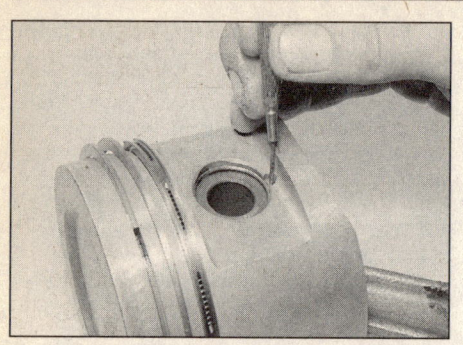

14.13a Removing a piston circlip

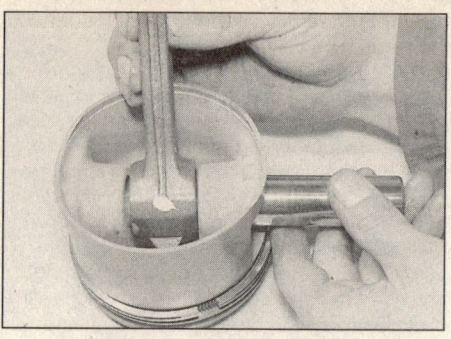

14.13b Pulling out the gudgeon pin

6 If the pistons and cylinder bores are not damaged or worn excessively, and if the cylinder block does not need to be rebored (where applicable), the original pistons can be refitted. Normal piston wear appears as even vertical wear on the piston thrust surfaces, and slight looseness of the top ring in its groove. New piston rings should always be used when the engine is reassembled.

7 Carefully inspect each piston for cracks around the skirt, around the gudgeon pin holes, and at the ring "lands" (between the ring grooves).

8 Look for scoring and scuffing on the piston skirt, holes in the piston crown, and burned areas at the edge of the crown. If the skirt is scored or scuffed, the engine may have been suffering from overheating and/or abnormal combustion, which caused excessively-high operating temperatures. The cooling and lubrication systems should be checked thoroughly. Scorch marks on the sides of the piston show that blow-by has occurred. A hole in the piston crown or burned areas at the edge of the piston crown, indicates that abnormal combustion (pre-ignition, knocking, or detonation) has been occurring. If any of the above problems exist, the causes must be investigated and corrected, or the damage will occur again. The causes may include inlet air leaks, incorrect fuel/air mixture or incorrect ignition timing.

9 Corrosion of the piston, in the form of pitting, indicates that coolant has been leaking into the combustion chamber and/or the crankcase. Again, the cause must be corrected, or the problem may persist in the rebuilt engine.

10 Examine each connecting rod carefully for signs of damage, such as cracks around the big-end and small end bearings. Check that the rod is not bent or distorted. Damage is highly unlikely, unless the engine has been seized or badly overheated. Detailed checking of the connecting rod assembly can only be carried out by an engine overhaul specialist with the necessary equipment.

11 The gudgeon pins are of the floating type, secured in position by two circlips. Where necessary, the pistons and connecting rods can be separated as follows.

12 Check that each piston and connecting rod carry identification and orientation marks, for correct reassembly. If in doubt, examine the connecting rod and piston and note any markings which can be used as a guide to fitting the new pistons.

13 Remove one of the circlips which secure the gudgeon pin. Push the gudgeon pin out of the piston and connecting rod **(see illustrations)**.

14 If new pistons of standard size are required, note that four grades are available - see Specifications. The grade letter is stamped on the piston crown and adjacent to each bore.

15 Check the fit of the gudgeon pin in the connecting rod bush and in the piston. If there is perceptible play, a new bush or an oversize gudgeon pin must be fitted. Consult a Volvo dealer or engine reconditioning specialist.

16 Examine all components and obtain any new parts required. If new pistons are purchased, they will be supplied complete with gudgeon pins and circlips. Circlips can also be purchased separately.

17 Oil the gudgeon pin. Reassemble the connecting rod and piston, making sure the rod is the right way round, and secure the gudgeon pin with the circlip.

15 Crankshaft - inspection

1 Clean the crankshaft using paraffin or a suitable solvent, and dry it, preferably with compressed air if available. Be sure to clean the oil holes with a pipe cleaner or similar probe to ensure that they are not obstructed.

⚠️ *Warning: Wear appropriate eye protection when using compressed air!*

2 Check the main and big-end bearing journals for uneven wear, scoring, pitting and cracking.

3 Big-end bearing wear is accompanied by distinct metallic knocking when the engine is running (particularly noticeable when the engine is pulling from low speed) and some loss of oil pressure.

4 Main bearing wear is accompanied by severe engine vibration and rumble - getting progressively worse as engine speed increases - and again by loss of oil pressure.

5 Check the bearing journal for roughness by running a finger lightly over the bearing surface. Any roughness (which will be accompanied by obvious bearing wear) indicates that the crankshaft requires regrinding (where possible) or renewal.

6 If the crankshaft has been reground, check for burrs around the crankshaft oil holes (the holes are usually chamfered so burrs should not be a problem unless regrinding has been carried out carelessly). Remove any burrs with a fine file or scraper.

7 Using a micrometer, measure the diameter of the main and big-end journals, and compare the results with the Specifications. By measuring the diameter at a number of points around each journal's circumference, you will be able to determine whether or not the journal is out-of-round. Take the measurement at each end of the journal, near the webs, to determine if the journal is tapered. Compare the results obtained with those given in the Specifications.

8 Check the oil seal contact surfaces at each end of the crankshaft for wear and damage. If either seal has worn a deep groove in the surface of the crankshaft, consult an engine overhaul specialist; repair may be possible, otherwise a new crankshaft will be required.

16 Main and big-end bearings - inspection

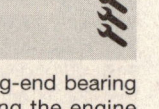

1 Even though the main and big-end bearing shells should be renewed during the engine overhaul, the old shells should be retained for close examination, as they may reveal valuable information about the condition of the engine.

2 Bearing failure occurs because of lack of lubrication, the presence of dirt or other foreign particles, overloading the engine, and corrosion **(see illustration)**. Regardless of the cause of bearing failure, the cause must be corrected (where applicable) before the engine is reassembled, to prevent it from happening again.

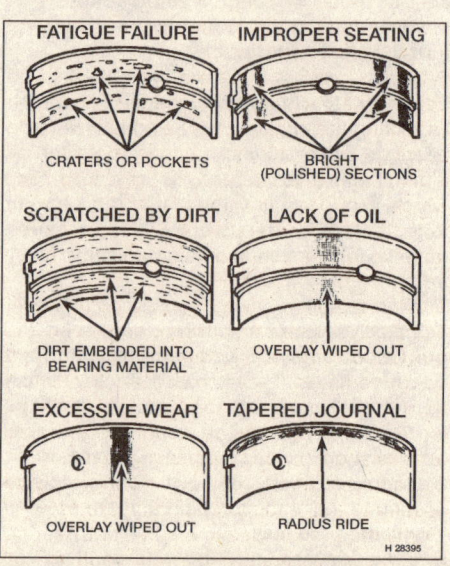

FATIGUE FAILURE	IMPROPER SEATING
CRATERS OR POCKETS	BRIGHT (POLISHED) SECTIONS
SCRATCHED BY DIRT	LACK OF OIL
DIRT EMBEDDED INTO BEARING MATERIAL	OVERLAY WIPED OUT
EXCESSIVE WEAR	TAPERED JOURNAL
OVERLAY WIPED OUT	RADIUS RIDE

16.2 Typical bearing failure

3 When examining the bearing shells, remove them from the cylinder block/crankcase and main bearing caps, and from the connecting rods and the big-end bearing caps, then lay them out on a clean surface in the same general position as their location in the engine. This will enable you to match any bearing problems with the corresponding crankshaft journal. *Do not* touch any shell's bearing surface with your fingers while checking it, or the delicate surface may be scratched.

4 Dirt or other foreign matter gets into the engine in a variety of ways. It may be left in the engine during assembly, or it may pass through filters or the crankcase ventilation system. It may get into the oil, and from there into the bearings. Metal chips from machining operations and normal engine wear are often present. Abrasives are sometimes left in engine components after reconditioning, especially when parts are not thoroughly cleaned using the proper cleaning methods. Whatever the source, these foreign objects often end up embedded in the soft bearing material, and are easily recognised. Large particles will not embed in the material, and will score or gouge the shell and journal. The best prevention for this cause of bearing failure is to clean all parts thoroughly, and to keep everything spotlessly-clean during engine assembly. Frequent and regular engine oil and filter changes are also recommended.

5 Lack of lubrication (or lubrication breakdown) has a number of inter-related causes. Excessive heat (which thins the oil), overloading (which squeezes the oil from the bearing face) and oil leakage (from excessive bearing clearances, worn oil pump or high engine speeds) all contribute to lubrication breakdown. Blocked oil passages, which usually are the result of misaligned oil holes in a bearing shell, will also starve a bearing of oil, and destroy it. When lack of lubrication is the cause of bearing failure, the bearing material is wiped or extruded from the shell's steel backing. Temperatures may increase to the point where the steel backing turns blue from overheating.

6 Driving habits can have a definite effect on bearing life. Full-throttle, low-speed operation (labouring the engine) puts very high loads on bearings, which tends to squeeze out the oil film. These loads cause the shells to flex, which produces fine cracks in the bearing face (fatigue failure). Eventually, the bearing material will loosen in pieces, and tear away from the steel backing.

7 Short-distance driving leads to corrosion of bearings, because insufficient engine heat is produced to drive off condensed water and corrosive gases. These products collect in the engine oil, forming acid and sludge. As the oil is carried to the engine bearings, the acid attacks and corrodes the bearing material.

8 Incorrect shell refitting during engine assembly will lead to bearing failure as well. Tight-fitting shells leave insufficient bearing running clearance, and will result in oil starvation. Dirt or foreign particles trapped behind a bearing shell result in high spots on the bearing, which lead to failure.

9 *Do not* touch any shell's bearing surface with your fingers during reassembly; there is a risk of scratching the delicate surface, or of depositing particles of dirt on it.

17 Engine overhaul - reassembly sequence

1 Before reassembly begins ensure that all new parts have been obtained and that all necessary tools are available. Read through the entire procedure to familiarise yourself with the work involved, and to ensure that all items necessary for reassembly of the engine are at hand. In addition to all normal tools and materials, jointing and thread locking compound will be needed in some areas during engine reassembly. In all other cases, provided the relevant mating surfaces are clean and flat, new gaskets will be sufficient to ensure joints are oil-tight.

2 In order to save time and avoid problems, engine reassembly can be carried out in the following order (as applicable).
 a) Crankshaft (see Section 19).
 b) Pistons/connecting rods (see Section 20).
 c) Oil pump (see Part A).
 d) Auxiliary shaft (see Section 10).
 e) Sump (see Part A).
 f) Flywheel/driveplate (see Part A).
 g) Cylinder head (see Part A).
 h) Camshaft drivebelt, tensioner and sprockets (see Part A).
 i) Engine external components.

3 At this stage, all engine components should be absolutely clean and dry, with all faults repaired. The components should be laid out (or in individual containers) on a completely clean work surface.

18 Piston rings - refitting

1 Before installing new piston rings, the ring end gaps must be checked as follows.
2 Lay out the piston/connecting rod assemblies and the new piston ring sets, so the ring sets will be matched with the same piston and cylinder during the end gap measurement and subsequent engine reassembly.
3 Insert the top ring into the first cylinder, and push it down the bore using the top of the piston. This will ensure that the ring remains square with the cylinder walls. Position the ring near the bottom of the cylinder bore, at the lower limit of ring travel. Note that the top and second compression rings are different. The second ring is easily identified by the step on its lower surface or by the fact that its outer face is tapered.
4 Measure the ring gap using feeler blades.
5 Repeat the procedure with the ring at the

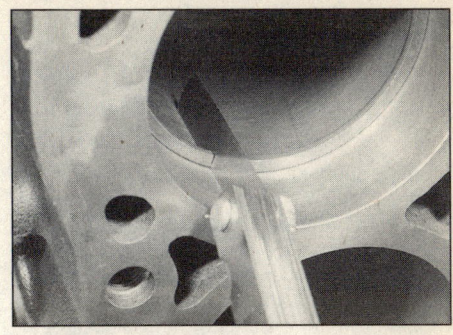

18.5 Measuring a piston ring end gap

top of the cylinder bore, at the upper limit of its travel and compare the measurements with the specified figures **(see illustration)**.
6 If the gap is still too small, it must be enlarged or the ring ends may contact each other during engine operation, causing serious damage. Ideally, new piston rings providing the correct end gap should be fitted. As a last resort the end gaps can be increased by filing the ring ends very carefully with a fine file. Mount the ring in a vice equipped with soft jaws, slip the ring over the file with the ends contacting the file face, and slowly move the ring to remove material from the ends. Take care as piston rings are sharp and are easily broken.
7 With new piston rings, it is unlikely that the end gap will be too large. If the gaps are too large, check that you have the correct rings for your engine and for the cylinder bore size.
8 Repeat the checking procedure for each ring in the first cylinder, and then for the rings in the remaining cylinders. Remember to keep rings, pistons and cylinders matched up.
9 Once the ring end gaps have been checked and if necessary corrected, the rings can be fitted to the pistons.
10 Fit the piston rings using the same technique as for removal. Fit the bottom (oil control) ring first, and work up. Observe the "TOP" marking on the second compression ring. The other rings can be fitted either way up, unless the top ring is stepped, in which case the step must be uppermost **(see illustration)**. Do not expand the compression rings too far or they will break. **Note:** *Always follow any instructions supplied with the new piston ring sets - different manufacturers may specify different procedures. Do not mix up the top and second compression rings, as they have different cross-sections.*

18.10 Piston ring profiles

19 Crankshaft - refitting and main bearing running clearance check

1 It is assumed at this point that the cylinder block/crankcase and crankshaft have been cleaned, inspected and repaired or reconditioned as necessary. Position the engine upside-down.
2 Remove the main bearing cap nuts or bolts, and lift out the caps. Lay the caps out in the proper order, to ensure correct installation.
3 If they're still in place, remove the old bearing shells from the block and the main bearing caps. Wipe the bearing recesses of the block and caps with a clean, lint-free cloth. They must be kept spotlessly-clean!

Main bearing running clearance check

4 Wipe clean the main bearing shell seats in the crankcase and clean the backs of the bearing shells. Insert the respective upper shells (dry) into position in the crankcase and the lower shells into their respective caps. Fit the bearing shells to the same locations as previously occupied if they are being re-used. Press the shells home so that the tangs engage in the recesses provided.
5 The most accurate method of checking the main bearing running clearance is to use an American product known as "Plastigage". This consists of a fine thread of perfectly-round plastic, which is compressed between the bearing shell and the journal. When the shell is removed, the plastic is deformed, and can be measured with a special card gauge supplied with the kit. The running clearance is determined from this gauge. Plastigage should be available from your Volvo dealer, otherwise enquiries at one of the larger specialist motor factors should produce the name of a stockist in your area. The procedures for using Plastigage are as follows.
6 Clean the bearing surfaces of the shells in the block, and the crankshaft main bearing journals with a clean, lint-free cloth. Check or clean the oil holes in the crankshaft, as any dirt here can go only one way - straight through the new bearings.
7 Once you are certain the crankshaft is clean, carefully lay it in position in the main bearings. Trim several pieces of the appropriate-size Plastigage (they must be slightly shorter than the width of the main bearings), and place one piece on each crankshaft main bearing journal, parallel with the crankshaft centre-line **(see illustration)**.
8 Clean the bearing surfaces of the cap shells, and install the caps in their respective positions. Take care not to disturb the Plastigage, and *do not* rotate the crankshaft at any time during this operation..
9 Working on one cap at a time, from the centre main bearing outwards (and ensuring that each cap is tightened down squarely and evenly onto the block), tighten the main bearing cap bolts to the specified torque wrench setting.
10 Remove the bolts, and carefully lift off the main bearing caps, keeping them in order. Again, take care not to disturb the Plastigage or rotate the crankshaft.
11 Compare the width of the crushed Plastigage on each journal with the scale printed on the Plastigage envelope to obtain the main bearing running clearance **(see illustration)**. Check the Specifications to make sure that the clearance is correct.
12 If the clearance is significantly different from that expected, the bearing shells may be the wrong size (or excessively worn, if the original shells are being re-used). Before deciding that different-size shells are required, make sure that no dirt or oil was trapped between the bearing shells and the caps or block when the clearance was measured. If the Plastigage is noticeably wider at one end than the other, the journal may be tapered.
13 Carefully scrape all traces of the Plastigage material off the main bearing journals and the bearing surfaces. Be very careful not to scratch the bearing - use your fingernail or a wooden or plastic scraper which is unlikely to score the bearing surfaces.

Final crankshaft refitting

14 Carefully lift the crankshaft out of the engine, then clean the bearing surfaces of the shells in the block.
15 Smear some grease on the smooth sides of the half thrustwashers. Place the washers in position on each side of the centre bearing in the crankcase. The slotted sides of the washers face outwards.
16 Liberally lubricate the bearing shells in the crankcase with clean engine oil.
17 Wipe clean the crankshaft journals, then lower the crankshaft into position. Make sure that the shells (and thrustwashers, when applicable) are not displaced.
18 Inject oil into the crankshaft oilways. Oil the shells in the main bearing caps and fit the caps, each to its correct position and the right way round.
19 Fit the main bearing cap bolts and tighten them progressively to the specified torque.
20 Rotate the crankshaft. Some stiffness is to be expected with new components, but there must be no tight spots or binding.
21 It is a good idea at this stage, to once again check the crankshaft endfloat as described in Section 12.
22 Fit the rear oil seal carrier, using a new gasket. Trim the protruding ends of the gasket level with the sump mating face.
23 Fit a new rear oil seal to the carrier as described in Part A.
24 Refit the piston/connecting rod assemblies to the crankshaft as described in Section 20.

20 Pistons/connecting rods - refitting and big-end bearing running clearance check

1 Before refitting the piston/connecting rod assemblies, the cylinder bores must be perfectly clean, the top edge of each cylinder must be chamfered, and the crankshaft must be in place.
2 Remove the big-end bearing cap from No 1 cylinder connecting rod (refer to the marks noted or made on removal). Remove the original bearing shells, and wipe the bearing recesses of the connecting rod and cap with a clean, lint-free cloth. They must be kept spotlessly-clean!

Big-end bearing running clearance check

3 Note that the following procedure assumes that the crankshaft and main bearing caps are in place.
4 Clean the back of the new upper bearing shell, fit it to No 1 connecting rod, then fit the other shell of the bearing set to the big-end bearing cap. Make sure the tab on each shell fits into the notch in the rod or cap recess.
5 It is critically important that all mating surfaces of the bearing components are perfectly clean and oil-free when they're assembled.
6 Position the piston ring gaps evenly around the piston, lubricate the piston and rings with clean engine oil, and attach a piston ring compressor to the piston. Leave the skirt protruding slightly, to guide the piston into the

19.7 Plastigage in place on a main bearing journal

19.11 Measuring the width of the deformed Plastigage using the scale on the card

20.10 Fitting a piston to the bore

cylinder bore. The rings must be compressed until they're flush with the piston.

7 Rotate the crankshaft until No 1 big-end journal is at BDC (Bottom Dead Centre), and apply a coat of engine oil to the cylinder walls.

8 Arrange the No 1 piston/connecting rod assembly so that the arrow on the piston crown points to the camshaft drivebelt end of the engine. Gently insert the assembly into the No 1 cylinder bore, and rest the bottom edge of the ring compressor on the engine block.

9 Tap the top edge of the ring compressor to make sure it's contacting the block around its entire circumference.

10 Gently tap on the top of the piston with the end of a wooden hammer handle **(see illustration)**, while guiding the connecting rod big-end onto the crankpin. The piston rings may try to pop out of the ring compressor just before entering the cylinder bore, so keep some pressure on the ring compressor. Work slowly, and if any resistance is felt as the piston enters the cylinder, stop immediately. Find out what is binding, and fix it before proceeding. *Do not*, for any reason, force the piston into the cylinder - you might break a ring and/or the piston.

11 The most accurate method of checking the big-end bearing running clearance is to use Plastigage (see Section 19).

12 Cut a piece of the appropriate-size Plastigage slightly shorter than the width of the connecting rod bearing, and lay it in place on the No 1 big-end journal, parallel with the crankshaft centre-line.

13 Clean the connecting rod-to-cap mating surfaces, and refit the big-end bearing cap. Tighten the cap bolts to the specified torque. Do not rotate the crankshaft at any time during this operation!

14 Unscrew the bolts and detach the cap, being very careful not to disturb the Plastigage.

15 Compare the width of the crushed Plastigage to the scale printed on the Plastigage envelope, to obtain the running clearance. Compare it to the Specifications, to make sure the clearance is correct.

16 If the clearance is significantly different from that expected, the bearing shells may be the wrong size (or excessively worn, if the original shells are being re-used). Before deciding that different-size shells are required, make sure that no dirt or oil was trapped between the bearing shells and the cap or rod when the clearance was measured. If the Plastigage is noticeably wider at one end than the other, the journal may be tapered.

17 Carefully scrape all traces of the Plastigage material off the big-end bearing journal and the bearing surface. Be very careful not to scratch the bearing - use your fingernail or a wooden or plastic scraper which is unlikely to score the bearing surfaces.

Final piston/connecting rod refitting

18 Make sure the bearing surfaces are perfectly clean, then apply a uniform layer of clean engine oil, to both of them. You will have to push the piston into the cylinder to expose the bearing surface of the shell in the connecting rod.

19 Slide the connecting rod back into place on the big-end journal, refit the big-end bearing cap, and then tighten the nuts as described above.

20 Repeat the entire procedure for the remaining piston/connecting rod assemblies.

21 The important points to remember are:
a) *Keep the backs of the bearing shells and the recesses of the connecting rods and caps perfectly clean when assembling them.*
b) *Make sure you have the correct piston/rod assembly for each cylinder.*
c) *The arrow on the piston crown must face the camshaft drivebelt end of the engine.*
d) *Lubricate the cylinder bores with clean engine oil.*
e) *Lubricate the bearing surfaces when refitting the big-end bearing caps after the running clearance has been checked.*

22 After all the piston/connecting rod assemblies have been properly installed, rotate the crankshaft a number of times by hand, to check for any obvious binding.

23 Continue with engine reassembly in the sequence given in Section 17.

21 Engine - initial start-up after overhaul

1 With the engine refitted in the vehicle, double-check the engine oil and coolant levels. Make a final check that everything has been reconnected, and that there are no tools or rags left in the engine compartment.

2 Refit the spark plugs, and connect all the spark plug (HT) leads (Chapter 1).

3 Start the engine, noting that this also may take a little longer than usual, due to the fuel system components being empty.

4 While the engine is idling, check for fuel, coolant and oil leaks. Don't be alarmed if there are some odd smells and smoke from parts getting hot and burning off oil deposits

5 Keep the engine idling until hot water is felt circulating through the top hose, check that it idles reasonably smoothly and at the usual speed, then switch it off.

6 After a few minutes, recheck the oil and coolant levels, and top-up as necessary (Chapter 1).

7 If new components such as pistons, rings or crankshaft bearings have been fitted, the engine must be run-in for the first 500 miles (800 km). Do not operate the engine at full-throttle, or allow it to labour in any gear during this period. It is recommended that the oil and filter be changed at the end of this period.

Notes

Chapter 3
Cooling, heating and air conditioning systems

Contents

Accessory drivebelts check and renewal .... See Chapter 1	Cooling system hoses - disconnection and renewal 2
Air conditioning system - general information and precautions 13	Electric fan - removal and refitting 6
Air conditioning system components - testing, removal and refitting .. 14	General information and precautions 1
Antifreeze - general information 3	Heating and ventilation system - general information 11
Coolant level check .... See "Weekly checks"	Heater/ventilation system components - removal and refitting 12
Cooling system - draining .... See Chapter 1	Oil coolers - removal and refitting 10
Cooling system electrical switches and sensors -	Radiator - removal and refitting 4
testing, removal and refitting 7	Thermostat - removal, testing and refitting 9
Cooling system - filling .... See Chapter 1	Viscous coupled fan - removal and refitting 5
Cooling system - flushing .... See Chapter 1	Water pump - removal and refitting 8

Degrees of difficulty

Easy, suitable for novice with little experience | **Fairly easy,** suitable for beginner with some experience | **Fairly difficult,** suitable for competent DIY mechanic | **Difficult,** suitable for experienced DIY mechanic | **Very difficult,** suitable for expert DIY or professional

Specifications

Thermostat
Opening commences:
- Type 1 thermostat .... 87°C
- Type 2 thermostat .... 92°C

Fully open at:
- Type 1 thermostat .... 97°C
- Type 2 thermostat .... 102°C

1 General information and precautions

General information

The cooling system is conventional in operation. Water-based coolant is circulated around the cylinder block and head by a belt-driven pump. A thermostat restricts circulation to the engine and heater matrix until operating temperature is achieved. When the thermostat opens, coolant circulates through the radiator at the front of the engine bay.

Cooling airflow through the radiator is provided by the forward motion of the vehicle, and by a viscous coupled fan on the water pump pulley. The design of the viscous coupling is such that fan speed remains low at low air temperatures, increasing as the temperature of the air coming through the radiator rises. In this way overcooling, unnecessary power loss and noise are minimised. On some models, an electric cooling fan is placed in front of the air conditioning condenser, itself in front of the radiator, to supplement the airflow.

The cooling system is pressurised, which increases the efficiency of the system by raising the boiling point of the coolant. An expansion tank accommodates variations in coolant volume with temperature.

Because the system is sealed, evaporative losses are minimal.

Heat from the coolant is used in the heating system. The heating and air conditioning systems are described in Sections 11 and 13.

Precautions

Warning: Do not attempt to remove the expansion tank filler cap, or to disturb any part of the cooling system, while it or the engine is hot, as there is a very great risk of scalding. If the expansion tank filler cap must be removed before the engine and radiator have fully cooled down (even though this is not recommended) the pressure in the cooling system must first be released. Cover the cap with a thick layer of cloth, to avoid scalding, and slowly unscrew the filler cap until a hissing sound can be heard. When the hissing has stopped, showing that pressure is released, slowly unscrew the filler cap further until it can be removed; if more hissing sounds are heard, wait until they have stopped before unscrewing the cap completely. At all times, keep well away from the filler opening.

Warning: Do not allow antifreeze to come in contact with your skin, or with the painted surfaces of the vehicle. Rinse off spills immediately with plenty of water. Never leave antifreeze lying around in an open container, or in a puddle in the driveway or on the garage floor. Children and pets are attracted by its sweet smell, but antifreeze is fatal if ingested.

Warning: Refer to Section 13 for precautions to be observed when working on vehicles equipped with air conditioning.

2 Cooling system hoses - disconnection and renewal

Note: *Refer to the warnings given in Section 1 of this Chapter before proceeding. Hoses should only be disconnected once the engine has cooled sufficiently to avoid scalding.*

1 If the checks described in Chapter 1 reveal a faulty hose, it must be renewed as follows.
2 First drain the cooling system (Chapter 1); if the antifreeze is not due for renewal, the drained coolant may be re-used, if it is collected in a clean container.

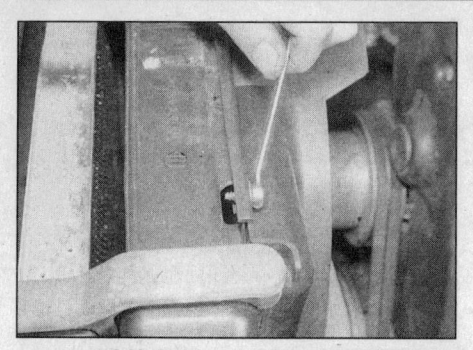

3•2 Cooling, heating and air conditioning systems

4.6 Unbolting the fan shroud

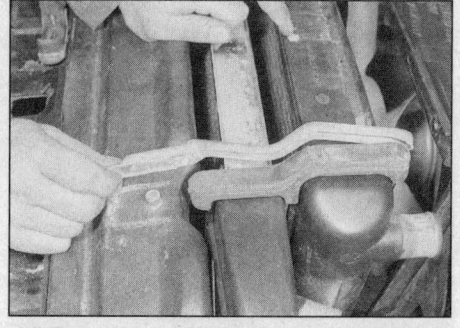

4.7 Removing a radiator mounting bracket

5.3 Removing the fan and viscous coupling

3 To disconnect any hose, use a pair of pliers to release the spring clamps (or a screwdriver to slacken screw-type clamps), then move them along the hose clear of the union. Carefully work the hose off its stubs. The hoses can be removed with relative ease when new - on an older vehicle, they may have stuck.

4 If a hose proves stubborn, try to release it by rotating it on its unions before attempting to work it off. Gently prise the end of the hose with a blunt instrument (such as a flat-bladed screwdriver), but do not apply too much force, and take care not to damage the pipe stubs or hoses. Note in particular that the radiator hose unions are fragile; do not use excessive force when attempting to remove the hoses. If all else fails, cut the hose with a sharp knife, then slit it so that it can be peeled off in two pieces. While expensive, this is preferable to buying a new radiator. Check first, however, that a new hose is readily available.

5 When refitting a hose, first slide the clamps onto the hose, then engage the hose with its unions. Work the hose into position, then check that the hose is settled correctly and is properly routed. Slide each clip along the hose until it is behind the union flared end, before tightening it securely.

> **HAYNES HiNT** *If the hose is stiff, use a little soapy water as a lubricant, or soften the hose by soaking it in hot water. Do not use oil or grease, which may attack the rubber.*

6 Refill the system with coolant (Chapter 1).
7 Check carefully for leaks as soon as possible after disturbing any part of the cooling system.

3 Antifreeze - general information

Note: *Refer to the warnings given in Section 1 of this Chapter before proceeding.*

The cooling system should be filled with a water/ethylene glycol-based antifreeze solution, of a strength which will prevent freezing down to at least -20°C, or lower if the local climate requires it. Antifreeze also provides protection against corrosion, and increases the coolant boiling point.

The cooling system should be maintained according to the schedule described in Chapter 1. If antifreeze is used that is not to Volvo's specification, old or contaminated coolant mixtures are likely to cause damage, and encourage the formation of corrosion and scale in the system. Use distilled water with the antifreeze, if available - if not, be sure to use only soft water. Clean rainwater is suitable.

Before adding antifreeze, check all hoses and hose connections, because antifreeze tends to leak through very small openings. Engines don't normally consume coolant, so if the level goes down, find the cause and correct it.

The specified mixture is 50% antifreeze and 50% clean soft water (by volume). Mix the required quantity in a clean container and then fill the system as described in Chapter 1, and *"Weekly checks"*. Save any surplus mixture for topping-up.

4 Radiator - removal and refitting

Note: *Refer to the warnings given in Section 1 of this Chapter before proceeding. If leakage is the reason for removing the radiator, bear in mind that minor leaks can often be cured using a radiator sealant with the radiator in situ.*

Removal

1 Drain the cooling system (see Chapter 1).
2 Disconnect the top hose, expansion tank hose and vent hose from the radiator.
3 On automatic transmission models, disconnect the fluid cooler lines from the radiator. Be prepared for fluid spillage. Plug or cap the lines to keep dirt out.
4 Disconnect the leads from any thermal switches, sensors etc, in the radiator.
5 Unbolt the power steering fluid reservoir (when located on the radiator) and move it aside.
6 Unbolt the fan shroud and move it rearwards **(see illustration)**.
7 Unbolt the radiator top mounting brackets **(see illustration)**.
8 Lift out the radiator. Recover the bottom mountings if they are loose.

Refitting

9 Refit by reversing the removal operations. Refill the cooling system on completion. On automatic transmission models check, and if necessary top-up, the transmission fluid level. Both these operations are described in Chapter 1.

5 Viscous coupled fan - removal and refitting

Removal

1 Remove the retaining bolts and lift away the fan shroud.
2 Remove the nuts which secure the viscous coupling to the water pump pulley studs.
3 Pull the fan and coupling off the studs and remove it **(see illustration)**.
4 The fan and viscous coupling may now be separated if required.

Refitting

5 Refit by reversing the removal operations.

6 Electric fan - removal and refitting

Removal

1 Remove the front grille panel, with reference to Chapter 11.
2 Remove the four screws which secure the fan mounting bars. Disconnect the wiring multi-plug.
3 Remove the fan complete with mounting bars. The motor can be unbolted from the bars if wished.

Refitting

4 Refit by reversing the removal operations.

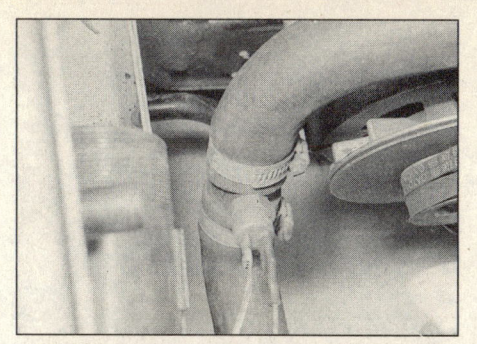

Cooling, heating and air conditioning systems 3•3

7.1 Fan thermoswitch in a hose adapter. It may also be in the radiator side tank

8.5 Removing the water pump pulley

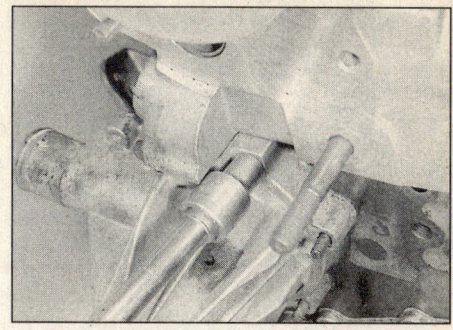

8.7 Unbolting the water pump

7 Cooling system electrical switches and sensors - testing, removal and refitting

Electric fan thermoswitch

Removal

1 Partially drain the cooling system (see Chapter 1) to below the level of the thermoswitch. The switch is located in the radiator side tank or in a hose adapter adjacent to the radiator **(see illustration)**.
2 Disconnect the thermoswitch leads, unscrew it and remove it.

Testing

3 To test the switch, connect a battery and test light to its terminals. Heat the switch in hot water. The switch should close (test light comes on) at approximately the temperature stamped on it, and open again (test light goes off) as it cools down. If not, renew it.

Refitting

4 Refit the thermoswitch, using sealant on the threads, and reconnect its leads.
5 Refill the cooling system (Chapter 1).

Coolant temperature sensor

Testing

6 If the temperature gauge indicates Hot at any time, consult the *"Fault finding"* section at the rear of this manual, to assist in tracing possible cooling system faults. If both the fuel gauge and the temperature gauge are inaccurate, the fault is probably in the instrument voltage stabiliser on the instrument panel printed circuit (see Chapter 12). If, however inaccurate gauge readings are accompanied by poor engine performance, it is highly likely that the sensor unit is at fault. The sensor performs a dual function and is also used by the fuel and ignition systems to supply information on engine temperature. To test the unit accurately, Volvo test equipment is required.

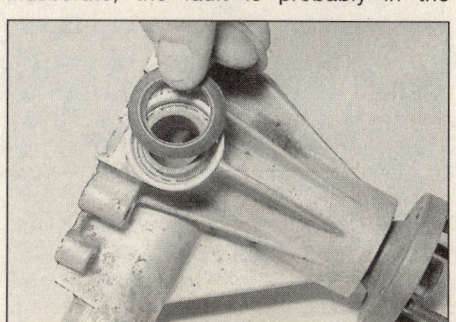

Removal

7 Partially drain the cooling system (Chapter 1) to below the level of the sensor unit.
8 Disconnect the lead from the sensor unit and unscrew it from its location in the cylinder head, below the inlet manifold.

Refitting

9 Screw in the new sensor unit, using a smear of sealant on the threads. Reconnect the lead.
10 Top-up the coolant level (Chapter 1).

8 Water pump - removal and refitting

Note: *Refer to the warnings given in Section 1 of this Chapter before proceeding.*

Removal

1 Disconnect the battery negative lead.
2 Remove the accessory drivebelts, as necessary, for access to the water pump pulley (see Chapter 1).
3 Drain the cooling system (see Chapter 1).
4 Remove the radiator and the fan shroud (see Section 4).
5 Remove the fan from the water pump (see Section 5), then remove the water pump pulley **(see illustration)**.
6 Disconnect the radiator bottom hose and the heater pipe from the pump.
7 Unbolt the water pump, slide it downwards and remove it **(see illustration)**.
8 Clean away all traces of sealant and old gasket from the mating faces.

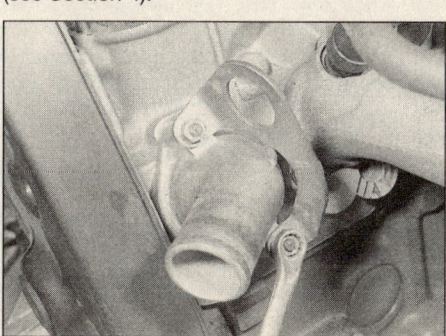

Refitting

9 Renew the pump top sealing ring and body gasket **(see illustration)**. When refitting, keep the pump pressed upwards against the cylinder head whilst tightening the nuts and bolts. Use a new seal on the heater pipe.
10 The remainder of refitting is a reversal of the removal procedure. Refit and tension the accessory drivebelt(s) and refill the cooling system (Chapter 1) to complete.

9 Thermostat - removal, testing and refitting

Note: *Refer to the warnings given in Section 1 of this Chapter before proceeding.*

Removal

1 Drain the cooling system (see Chapter 1).
2 Release the radiator top hose from the thermostat housing then undo the two housing retaining nuts. On some models an engine lifting eye may also be attached here **(see illustration)**.
3 Lift off the housing and remove the thermostat and sealing ring **(see illustration)**.

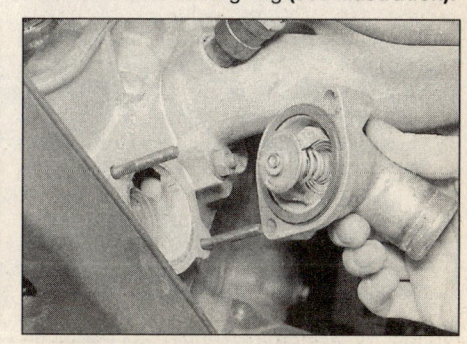

8.9 Fitting a new top sealing ring

9.2 Unbolting the thermostat housing . . .

9.3 . . . and removing the thermostat

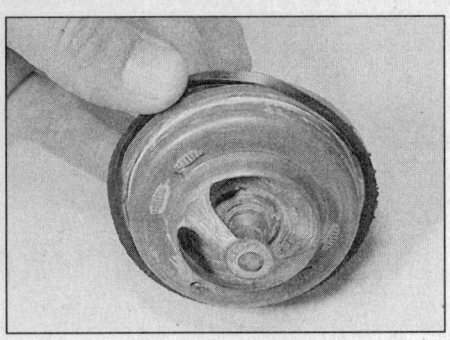

3•4 Cooling, heating and air conditioning systems

9.7 Fitting a thermostat sealing ring

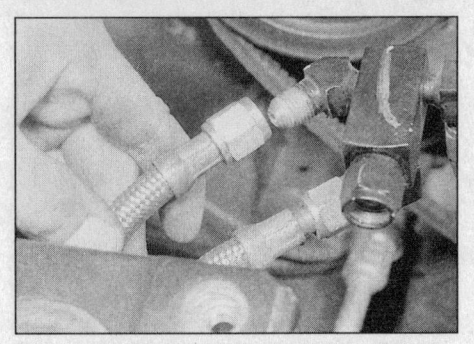

10.7 Disconnecting an ATF cooler flexible hose

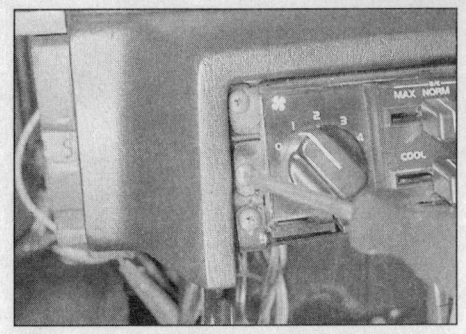

12.2 Removing a control panel securing screw

Testing

4 Suspend the (closed) thermostat on a length of string in a container of cold water, with a thermometer beside it; ensure that neither touches the side or bottom of the container.
5 Heat the water, and check the temperature at which the thermostat begins to open, or is fully open. Compare this value with the figures given in the Specifications, then remove the thermostat and allow it to cool down; check that it closes fully.
6 If the thermostat does not open and close as described, if it sticks in either position, or if it does not open at the specified temperature, it must be renewed.

Refitting

7 Fit a new sealing ring to the thermostat **(see illustration)**.
8 Refit the thermostat and housing (and the engine lifting eye, when applicable). Fit and tighten the housing nuts.
9 Reconnect the top hose then refill the cooling system (Chapter 1).

10 Oil coolers - removal and refitting

Engine oil cooler

Removal

1 When fitted, the engine oil cooler is mounted behind and to one side of the radiator.
2 Disconnect the oil cooler unions, either at the cooler itself or at the flexible hoses. Be prepared for oil spillage.
3 Unbolt the oil cooler brackets and remove it. The oil cooler can then be separated from the brackets if required.
4 If the oil cooler is to be re-used, flush it internally with solvent and then blow compressed air through it. Also clean it externally.

Refitting

5 Refit by reversing the removal operations, then run the engine and check for oil leaks.

Switch off the engine and check the oil level as described in *"Weekly checks"*.

ATF auxiliary cooler

Removal

6 When fitted, the ATF auxiliary cooler is mounted between the radiator and the air conditioning condenser.
7 Disconnect the flexible hoses from the union on the radiator **(see illustration)**. Be prepared for fluid spillage. Cap open unions to keep dirt out.
8 Remove the radiator (see Section 4).
9 Unbolt the cooler. Feed the hoses through the side panel grommets and remove the cooler and hoses together.
10 Clean the cooler fins and flush it internally with clean ATF. Renew the hoses if necessary.

Refitting

11 Refit by reversing the removal operations. Refill the cooling system (Chapter 1), then run the engine and check the transmission fluid level as described in *"Weekly checks"*.

11 Heating and ventilation system - general information

Depending on model and options selected, the heater may be fitted alone or in conjunction with an air conditioning unit. The same housings and heater components are used in all cases. The air conditioning system is described in Section 13.

The heater is of the fresh air type. Air enters through a grille in front of the windscreen. On its way to the various vents a variable proportion of the air passes through the heater matrix, where it is warmed by engine coolant flowing through the matrix.

Distribution of air to the vents, and through or around the matrix, is controlled by flaps or shutters. These are operated by vacuum motors (except for the air mix shutter on heater-only models, which is operated by cable). A vacuum tank is fitted under the vehicle on some models.

A four-speed electric blower is fitted to boost the airflow through the heater.

12 Heater/ventilation system components - removal and refitting

Heater/air conditioning control panel

Removal

1 For best access, remove the centre console side panels (see Chapter 11, Section 33).
2 Remove the trim from around the control panel, if not already done. Remove the panel securing screws **(see illustration)**.
3 Withdraw the panel and disconnect the control cables, multi-plugs and vacuum unions from it. Make notes or identifying marks if necessary for reference when refitting.

Refitting

4 Refit by reversing the removal operations. Where a mechanical temperature control cable is fitted, adjust it as described below.

Heater temperature control cable

Note: *A mechanical temperature control cable is only fitted to vehicles without air conditioning.*

Removal

5 With the temperature control in the "WARM" position, disconnect the far end of the cable from the air mix shutter lever **(see illustration)**.

12.5 Temperature control cable connections (arrowed) at shutter lever

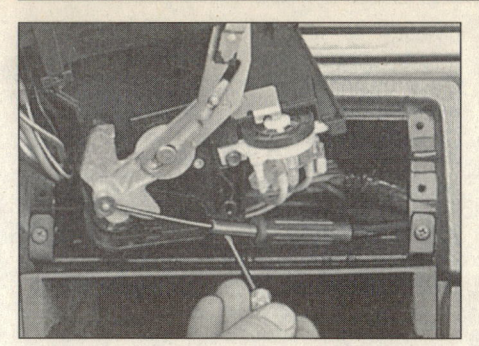

Cooling, heating and air conditioning systems 3•5

12.7 Prising out the temperature control cable sleeve

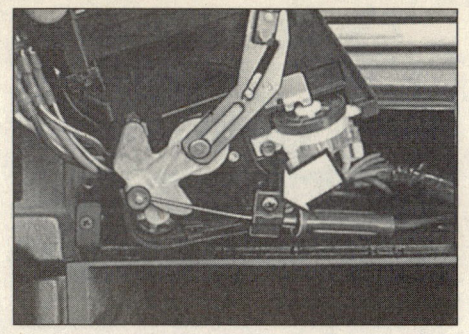

12.9 Use of a self-tapping screw (arrowed) to secure the sleeve

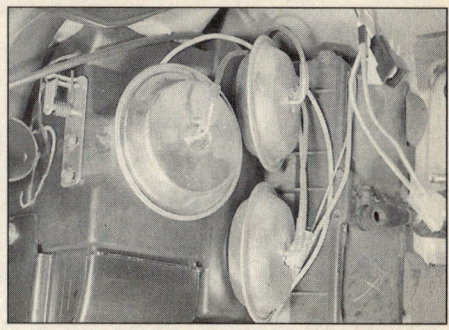

12.16 Distribution unit vacuum motors

6 Remove the trim from around the heater control panel. Remove the screws which hold the panel to the centre console.
7 Ease the heater control panel away from the centre console until the cable is accessible. Disconnect the cable from the control panel, using a screwdriver to prise free the cable sleeve **(see illustration)**.
8 The cable can now be removed.

Refitting

9 Refit by reversing the removal operations, noting the following points:
   a) If the cable sleeve was damaged during removal, use a self-tapping screw to secure it **(see illustration)**.
   b) Adjust the position of the cable sleeve so that the air mix shutter travels over its full range of movement when the temperature control is operated.

Heater matrix

Removal

Note: *Refer to the warnings given in Section 1 of this Chapter before proceeding.*
10 Disconnect the battery negative lead.
11 Depressurise the cooling system by removing the expansion tank cap. Take precautions against scalding if the coolant is hot.
12 Clamp the coolant hoses which lead to the heater matrix stubs on the bulkhead. Release the hose clips and disconnect the hoses from the stubs. Be prepared for coolant spillage.
13 Remove the glovebox, centre console and rear console (Chapter 11, Sections 32 to 34).
14 Unclip the central electrical unit and move it aside.
15 Remove the centre panel vent. Remove the screw from the distribution unit and disconnect all the air ducts from the unit. Also remove the rear vent distribution ducts.
16 Disconnect the vacuum hoses from the vacuum motors **(see illustration)**. On models with automatic climate control, also remove the hose which leads to the inner sensor (the aspirator hose).
17 Remove the distribution unit.
18 Remove the heater matrix clips. Pull the matrix out and remove it; be prepared for coolant spillage.

Refitting

19 Refit by reversing the removal operations ensuring that the vacuum hoses are connected correctly.
20 Top-up the cooling system on completion (see *"Weekly checks"*). Run the engine and check that there are no coolant leaks, then allow it to cool and recheck the coolant level.

Heater vacuum motors in distribution unit

Removal

21 Remove the distribution unit as described in the previous sub-Section, but do not disconnect the coolant pipes from the matrix.
22 Remove the appropriate panel from the distribution unit for access to the motors. Remove the motors as necessary.

Refitting

23 Refit by reversing the removal operations.

Air recirculation shutter motor

Removal

24 Remove the glovebox (see Chapter 11, Section 32). Also remove the outer panel vent and air duct.
25 Unbolt the control rod from the motor. Undo the two securing nuts, withdraw the motor and disconnect the vacuum hose **(see illustration)**.

Refitting

26 When refitting, make sure that both the shutter and the vacuum motor are in the resting position before tightening the control rod bolt.

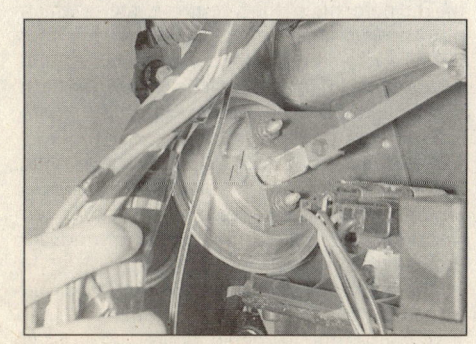

12.25 Recirculation shutter vacuum motor

27 The remainder of refitting is a reversal of the removal procedure.

Heater blower motor

Removal

28 Remove the trim panel from below the glovebox.
29 Remove the screws which secure the motor to the housing.
30 Lower the motor and disconnect the cooling hose. Disconnect the wiring and remove the motor complete with centrifugal fan **(see illustration)**.
31 Do not disturb any steel clips on the fan blades. They have been fitted for balancing purposes.

Refitting

32 When refitting, apply sealant between the motor flange and housing. Connect the wiring and secure the motor.
33 Refit the motor cooling hose this is important if premature failure is to be avoided.
34 Check for correct operation of the motor, then refit the trim panel.

Heater blower motor resistor

Removal

35 Remove the glovebox (see Chapter 11, Section 32).
36 Disconnect the multi-plug from the resistor.
37 Remove the two screws from the resistor and withdraw it **(see illustration)**. Be careful not to damage the coils of resistance wire.

Refitting

38 Refit by reversing the removal operations,

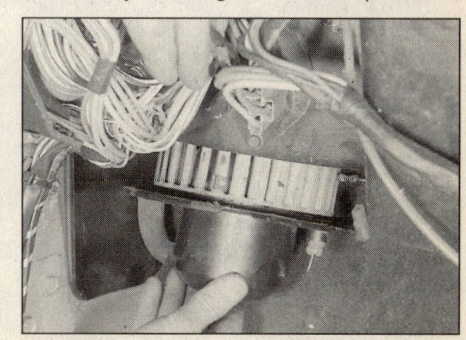

12.30 Removing the heater blower motor

3•6 Cooling, heating and air conditioning systems

12.37 Removing the motor resistor

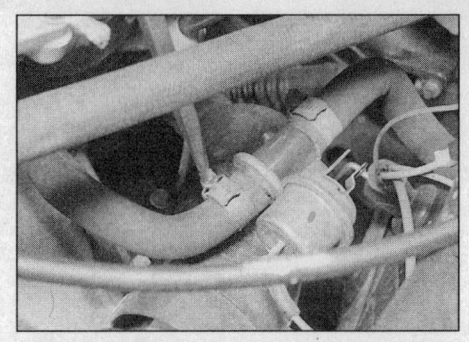

12.41 Disconnecting the heater water valve

but check the operation of the blower on all four speeds before refitting the glovebox.

Heater water valve

Removal

Note: *Refer to the warnings given in Section 1 of this Chapter before proceeding.*

39 Depressurise the cooling system by removing the expansion tank cap. Take precautions against scalding if the coolant is hot.
40 Clamp the coolant hoses on each side of the valve.
41 Disconnect the vacuum and coolant hoses from the valve and remove it **(see illustration)**.

Refitting

42 Refit by reversing the removal operations. Top-up the coolant if much was lost (see *"Weekly checks"*).

13 Air conditioning system - general information and precautions

General information

Air conditioning system

Air conditioning is fitted as standard on most models and is optionally available on others. In conjunction with the heater, the system enables any reasonable air temperature to be achieved inside the car. It also reduces the humidity of the incoming air, aiding demisting even when cooling is not required.

The refrigeration side of the air conditioning system functions in a similar way to a domestic refrigerator. A compressor, belt-driven from the crankshaft pulley, draws refrigerant in its gaseous phase from an evaporator. The compound refrigerant passes through a condenser where it loses heat and enters its liquid phase. After dehydration the refrigerant returns to the evaporator where it absorbs heat from air passing over the evaporator fins. The refrigerant becomes a gas again and the cycle is repeated.

Various subsidiary controls and sensors protect the system against excessive temperature and pressures. Additionally, engine idle speed is increased when the system is in use to compensate for the additional load imposed by the compressor.

Automatic Climate Control system

On models with Automatic Climate Control (ACC), the temperature of the incoming air is automatically regulated to maintain the cabin temperature at the level selected by the operator. An electromechanical programmer controls heater, air conditioner and blower functions to achieve this.

The four sensors peculiar to the ACC are the control panel sensor, the coolant thermal switch, the inner sensor and the outer sensor.

The control panel sensor operates in conjunction with the coolant thermal switch. If cabin temperature is below 18°C and coolant temperature is below 35°C, the blower is prevented from operating (unless "defrost" is selected). This prevents the ACC from blowing cold air into the cabin whilst the coolant warms up.

The inner sensor is located above the glovebox. It reads cabin air temperature.

The outer sensor is located in the blower housing and reads the temperature of the incoming air.

Acting on information received from the inner and outer sensors, the programmer applies the appropriate heating/cooling and blower speed settings to achieve the selected temperature.

Electronic Climate Control system

The Electronic Climate Control (ECC), optionally available on models for certain markets, is a development of the Automatic Climate Control (ACC) described earlier. The main difference is in the control system, which now incorporates a microprocessor, solenoid valves and a servo motor. Less use is made of vacuum than in the ACC system, with a consequent increase in reliability.

From the driver's point of view the two systems are very similar. When the automatic function is engaged, the selected temperature is maintained in the cabin by mixing of hot and cold air, using the heating and air conditioning systems as necessary.

The microprocessor control unit, mounted on the back of the control panel, incorporates a built-in fault diagnosis facility. A fault is signalled to the driver by the flashing of the air conditioner control button. If the fault is serious, the button will flash continuously while the engine is running. If the fault is less serious, the button will flash for about 20 seconds after the engine is started. The four sensors peculiar to the ECC are the solar sensor, the water temperature sensor, the interior air temperature sensor and the exterior air temperature sensor.

The solar system is mounted on top of the dashboard, in the left-hand loudspeaker grille. Its function is to reduce cabin air temperature by up to 3°C in bright sunlight.

The interior air temperature sensor is located inside the interior light. It measures cabin air temperature. A hose running from the sensor to the inlet manifold maintains a flow of air through the sensor when the engine is running.

The water temperature sensor is located next to the heater matrix. This sensor in fact measures air temperature adjacent to the matrix. When the automatic function is selected, this sensor prevents the fan running at maximum speed before the matrix has heated up.

The exterior air temperature sensor is mounted on the blower motor casing. It measures the temperature of the air passing through the blower; when the recirculation function is selected, this air comes from inside the car, but otherwise it comes from outside.

Precautions

When an air conditioning system is fitted, it is necessary to observe special precautions whenever dealing with any part of the system, or its associated components. If for any reason the system must be discharged, entrust this task to your Volvo dealer or a refrigeration engineer.

⚠ **Warning:** *The refrigeration circuit may contain a liquid refrigerant (Freon), and it is therefore dangerous to disconnect any part of the system without specialised knowledge and equipment.*

The refrigerant is potentially dangerous, and should only be handled by qualified persons. If it is splashed onto the skin, it can cause frostbite. It is not itself poisonous, but in the presence of a naked flame (including a cigarette) it forms a poisonous gas. Uncontrolled discharging of the refrigerant is dangerous, and potentially damaging to the environment.

In view of the above points, removal and refitting of any air conditioning system components, except for the sensors and other peripheral items covered in this Chapter, must be left to a specialist.

14 Air conditioning system components - testing, removal and refitting

1 The contents of this Section is limited to those operations which can be carried out

Cooling, heating and air conditioning systems

without discharging the refrigerant. Renewal of the compressor drivebelt is described in Chapter 1, but all other operations must be entrusted to a Volvo dealer or air conditioning specialist. If necessary, the compressor can be unbolted and moved aside, without disconnecting the refrigerant unions, after removing the compressor drivebelt.

ACC control panel sensor

Removal

2 Remove the trim from around the control panel. Remove the control panel securing screws and pull the panel out.
3 Disconnect the sensor multi-plug. Use an ohmmeter to check the sensor for continuity. Continuity should be displayed above 18°C, and no continuity (open-circuit) at lower temperatures. Cool the sensor with some ice cubes, or warm it in the hands, to check that it behaves as described.
4 To remove the sensor, insert a thin screwdriver or a stiff wire into the multi-plug and prise out the sensor terminals.

Refitting

5 Fit the new sensor by pressing its terminals into the multi-plug. Refit the control panel and trim.

ACC Coolant thermal switch

Removal

6 The coolant thermal switch is located under the bonnet. It is screwed into a T-piece inserted in the heater supply hose.
7 Unplug the electrical connector and unscrew the thermal switch from the T-piece.
8 Test the thermal switch using an ohmmeter, or a battery and test lamp, immersing the switch in a heated water bath. The switch should show continuity at temperatures of 30 to 40°C. As the water cools, continuity should be broken before the temperature reaches 10°C.

9 Note that if the lead to the thermal switch is accidentally disconnected, the heater blower will not work at cabin temperatures below 18°C, regardless of coolant temperature.

Refitting

10 Refit by reversing the removal operations.

ACC Inner sensor

Removal

11 Remove the glovebox (see Chapter 11, Section 32).
12 Pull the air hose off the sensor, unclip the sensor and remove it.
13 The only test specified for this sensor is that it should display continuity. No resistance values are given.

Refitting

14 Refit by reversing the removal operations.

ACC Outer sensor

General

15 Access to the sensor for testing can be gained by removing the windscreen wiper arms, the scuttle panel and the air inlet cover.
16 Measure the resistance of the sensor. At 20 to 23°C, the resistance should be 30 to 40 ohms. The higher the temperature, the lower the resistance.
17 For removal and refitting of the sensor, proceed by removing the air recirculation shutter motor (see Section 12). The sensor can then be removed and a new one fitted.
18 On later models, the sensor is mounted lower down in the fan housing. Access for testing and removal should therefore be possible without much dismantling.

ACC programmer

Removal

19 Remove the glovebox (see Chapter 11, Section 32). Also remove the outer panel vent and duct.

20 Disconnect the air mix shutter control rod, the electrical multi-plug and the vacuum pipe cluster from the programmer.
21 Remove the three screws which secure the programmer and remove it.

Refitting

22 When refitting, secure the programmer with the three screws, then connect the vacuum cluster and the multi-plug. The vacuum pipe connections must not be pushed right home, or an apparent loss of vacuum can result. The connection is correct when the spigot on the programmer enters the connector only as far as the entry of the vacuum line on the side of the connector.
23 Adjust the shutter control rod as follows. Run the engine to provide vacuum. Select maximum heat on the temperature control dial. Pull the control rod until it reaches its stop and secure it to the programmer arm.
24 Refit the duct, vent and glovebox.

ECC control pump and control unit

Removal

25 Disconnect the battery negative lead.
26 Remove the switch panel and ECC panel surround.
27 Remove the four screws now exposed and draw the ECC panel and control unit into the car. (This will give sufficient access for bulb renewal if this is the reason for removal.)
28 Disconnect the multi-plugs from the rear of the unit and remove it.
29 Do not attempt to dismantle the control unit, unless out of curiosity. There are no serviceable parts inside.

Refitting

30 Refit by reversing the removal operations.

Chapter 4 Part A:
Fuel and exhaust systems

Contents

Air cleaner assembly - removal and refitting 2	Fuel tank pump - removal and refitting 4
Air cleaner element renewal ....See Chapter 1	Fuel tank sender unit - removal and refitting 6
Cruise control - general information 12	General information and precautions 1
Exhaust manifold - removal and refitting 14	Inlet manifold - removal and refitting 13
Exhaust system - general information, removal and refitting 18	Intercooler - removal and refitting 17
Exhaust system check ....See Chapter 1	Main fuel pump - removal and refitting 5
Fuel filter check and renewal ....See Chapter 1	Throttle cable - removal, refitting and adjustment 7
Fuel injection system - testing 10	Throttle pedal - removal and refitting 8
Fuel injection system components - removal and refitting 11	Turbocharger - general information and precautions 15
Fuel injection systems - general information 9	Turbocharger - removal and refitting 16
Fuel tank - removal and refitting 3	Underbody and fuel/brake line check ....See Chapter 1

Degrees of difficulty

Easy, suitable for novice with little experience	Fairly easy, suitable for beginner with some experience	Fairly difficult, suitable for competent DIY mechanic	Difficult, suitable for experienced DIY mechanic	Very difficult, suitable for expert DIY or professional

Specifications

System type
All engines except B230F .... Bosch LH2.4-Jetronic fuel injection, normally-aspirated or turbocharged depending on model
B230F engines .... Bosch LH2.4-Jetronic or Bendix Regina fuel injection, normally-aspirated

Fuel system data
Idle speed*:
   All engines except B230FT and B230FK .... 775 rpm
   B230FT and B230FK engines .... 750 rpm
Basic idle speed (see text - Section 11) .... 480 to 520 rpm
Idle mixture CO content* .... 0.4 to 0.8%
*Non-adjustable - controlled by fuel system electronic control module

Recommended fuel .... 91-95 RON unleaded

---

1 General information and precautions

The fuel system consists of a rear-mounted fuel tank, one or two electric fuel pumps, and a fully electronic normally-aspirated or turbocharged fuel injection system. Further details of the fuel injection system will be found in Section 9. Depending on engine type, models for some market territories are also equipped with an exhaust gas recirculation (EGR) system, as part of an emissions control package. Further details of this system will be found in Part B of this Chapter.

The exhaust system consists of multiple sections, the number varying according to model, suspended from under the car on rubber mountings. A catalytic converter is fitted to the exhaust system of all models.

⚠️ **Warning: Many of the procedures in this Chapter require the removal of fuel lines and connections, which may result in some fuel spillage. Before carrying out any operation on the fuel system, refer to the precautions given in "Safety first!" at the beginning of this manual, and follow them implicitly. Petrol is a highly dangerous and volatile liquid, and the precautions necessary when handling it cannot be overstressed.**

2 Air cleaner assembly - removal and refitting

Removal
1 Remove the air cleaner element (see Chapter 1).
2 Disconnect the hot air inlet trunking from the housing. Also disconnect the crankcase ventilation hose.
3 To remove the complete air cleaner housing, release the securing bolt or clip. Lift out the housing, disengaging the cold air inlet from the grommet in the inner wing.

Refitting
4 Refit by reversing the removal operations.

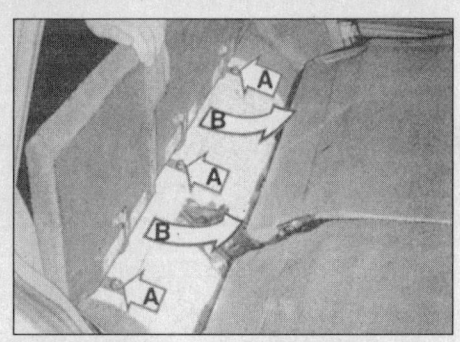

4A•2 Fuel and exhaust systems

4.2a Access to the fuel tank hatch on Estate models: remove screws (A) and pull floor forward and upwards (B)

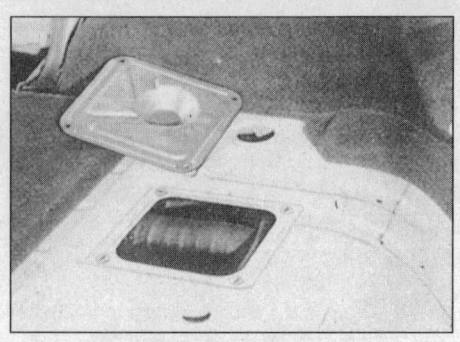

4.2b Fuel tank hatch removed on Estate models

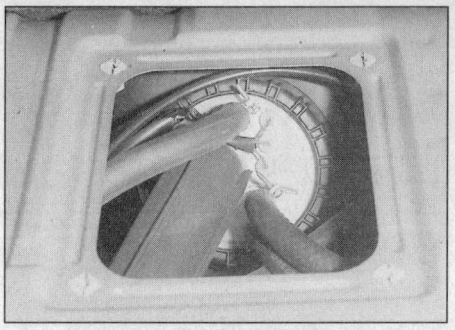

4.6 Later type fuel tank pump unit secured by a plastic ring nut

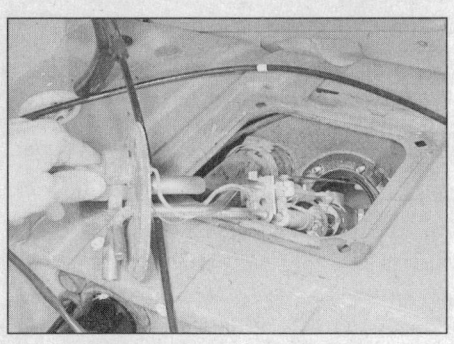

4.7 Removing the tank pump

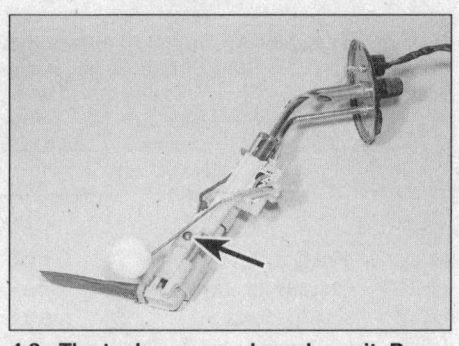

4.8a The tank pump and sender unit. Pump clamp screw arrowed

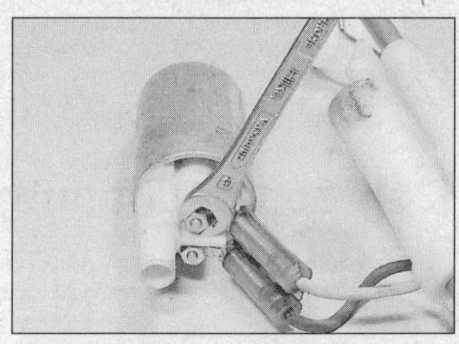

4.8b Disconnect a lead from the pump

3 Fuel tank - removal and refitting

Note: Refer to the warning note in Section 1 before proceeding.

Removal

1 Run the fuel level as low as possible prior to removing the tank.
2 Disconnect the battery negative lead.
3 Remove the fuel filler cap then syphon or pump out the remaining fuel from the fuel tank (there is no drain plug). The fuel must be emptied into a suitable container for storage.
4 Remove the access hatch from the luggage area floor.
5 Disconnect the fuel hoses, filler and breather hoses (when applicable) and the tank pump connector. See Section 4.
6 Raise and support the rear of the vehicle. Support the fuel tank, remove the securing nuts, bolts, straps and reinforcing plates then carefully lower the tank.
7 Repair of a leaking tank must only be undertaken by professionals. Even when the tank is empty, it may still contain explosive vapours. "Cold" repair compounds are available and these are suitable for DIY use.

Refitting

8 Refit by reversing the removal operations, using new hoses and clips as necessary.

4 Fuel tank pump - removal and refitting

Note: Refer to the warning note in Section 1.

Removal

1 Disconnect the battery earth lead.
2 Gain access to the top of the fuel tank by removing the access hatch from the luggage area floor **(see illustrations)**.
3 Clean around the tank pump/sender unit cover plate.
4 Disconnect and plug the fuel supply and return hoses. Also disconnect the breather hose (when applicable).
5 Follow the electrical lead back to the nearest multi-plug and disconnect it. If the

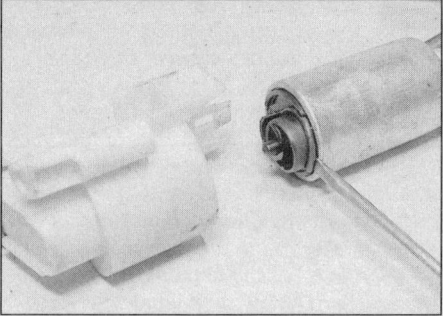

4.10 The screwdriver shows the pump O-ring

plug will not pass through the holes in the bodywork *en route* to the tank, prise the connectors out of the plug. Unbolt the earth tag and pull the lead into the same compartment as the tank.
6 Remove the nuts which secure the cover plate to the tank. On some models the pump/sender unit is secured by a large plastic ring nut; unscrew the nut using a "soft" tool such as a strap wrench **(see illustration)**.
7 The tank pump/sender unit can now be removed from the tank. Considerable manipulation will be needed. Do not force the unit out, it is delicate **(see illustration)**.
8 Unclip the pick-up screen and tube from the pump. Remove the clamp screw, disconnect the electrical leads and remove the pump **(see illustrations)**.
9 If the pump is defective it must be renewed.

Refitting

10 Fit the pump to the sender unit and secure the pick-up components. Make sure that the O-ring is in good condition and that the pick-up screen is clean **(see illustration)**. Connect the electrical leads and tighten the clamp screw.
11 The pump is spring-loaded against the cover plate to ensure that the pick-up screen sits at the very bottom of its well. Temporarily defeat the spring by pressing the pump towards the plate and wedging it in this position with a length of matchstick on a piece of string. Feed the string out through the breather hole **(see illustration)**.

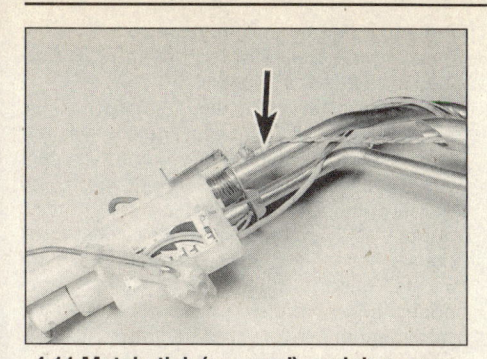

Fuel and exhaust systems 4A•3

4.11 Matchstick (arrowed) wedging pump in raised position. String goes through breather tube

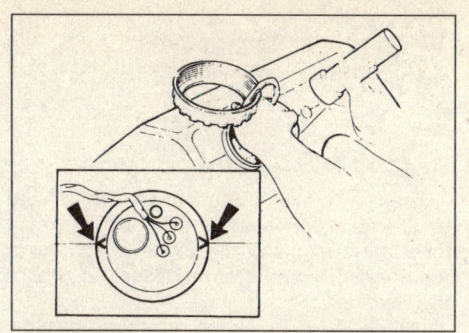

4.13 Arrows on fuel tank pump (arrowed) must align with seam on tank

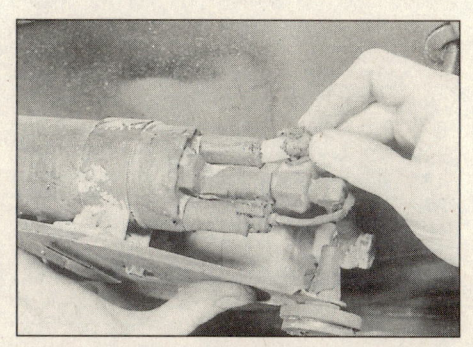

5.3 Unbolting the main fuel pump cradle

5.4 Disconnecting the electrical leads from the main fuel pump

12 Check the condition of the sealing ring on the tank and renew it if necessary.
13 Offer the pump/sender unit to the tank and work it into position. Fit and tighten the securing nuts. Where applicable, align the arrows on each side of the unit with seams of the fuel tank, then fit and tighten the ring nut **(see illustration)**.
14 Pull the piece of string to release the matchstick. The spring will force the pick-up screen to the bottom of the tank. Withdraw the string and matchstick through the breather hole. (No harm will result if the matchstick is lost.)
15 Reconnect the electrical lead, not forgetting the earth tag.
16 Reconnect the fuel hoses and (when applicable) the breather hose.
17 Refit the access hatch.
18 Reconnect the battery.

5 Main fuel pump - removal and refitting

Note: *Refer to the warning note in Section 1 before proceeding.*

Removal

1 Raise the vehicle on ramps, or drive it over an inspection pit.
2 Disconnect the battery negative lead.
3 Unbolt the fuel pump cradle from the underside of the vehicle **(see illustration)**. Pull the cradle off the grommets.
4 Disconnect the electrical leads from the pump, noting the colours of the wires and the corresponding terminals **(see illustration)**.
5 Disconnect the fuel supply and outlet pipes from the pump. Be prepared for fuel spillage. Plug or cap the open pipe unions.
6 Unbolt the pump brackets and remove the pump.

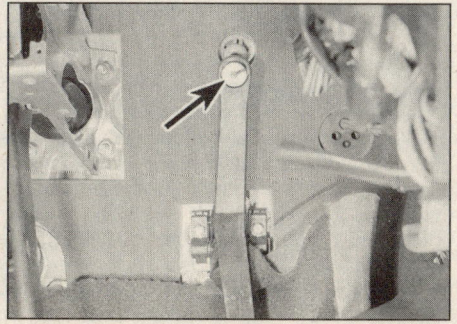

Refitting

7 Refit by reversing the removal operations, using new sealing washers as necessary.
8 Run the engine and check for leakage.

6 Fuel tank sender unit - removal and refitting

The removal and refitting procedure is as given in Section 4 for the fuel tank pump.

7 Throttle cable - removal, refitting and adjustment

Removal

1 Release the outer cable retaining clip and unhook the inner cable from the drum **(see illustration)**.
2 Inside the vehicle, remove the trim from below the steering column. Pull the cable inner through the end of the pedal and slide the split bush off the end of the cable **(see illustration)**.
3 Release the cable grommet from the bulkhead and pull the cable into the engine bay. Note the routing of the cable, release it from any clips or ties and remove it.

Refitting and adjustment

4 Refit by reversing the removal operations, then adjust the cable as follows.
5 Disconnect the link rod which joins the cable down to the throttle valve by levering off a balljoint **(see illustration)**.
6 With the throttle pedal released, the cable inner should be just taut, and the cable drum must be resting against the idle stop. With the pedal fully depressed the drum must contact the full throttle stop. Adjust if necessary by means of the threaded sleeve.
7 On automatic transmission models, first check the adjustment of the kickdown cable (see Chapter 7B).
8 Reconnect the link rod and place a 2.5 mm feeler blade between the cable drum and the

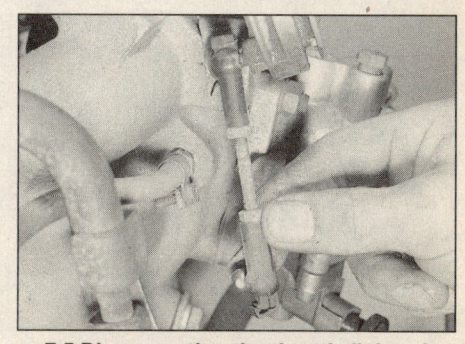

7.1 Release outer cable retaining clip (arrowed) and unhook inner from the drum

7.2 Split bush (arrowed) secures cable at pedal end

7.5 Disconnecting the throttle link rod

4A

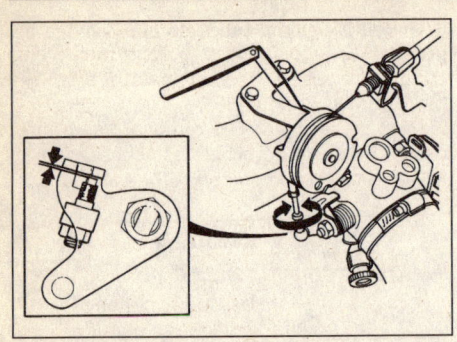

7.8 Throttle cable adjustment. Insert feeler blade as shown and adjust link rod to give specified clearance between throttle lever and adjustment screw (inset)

idle stop. In this position the clearance between the throttle lever and the adjustment screw must be between 0.1 and 0.45 mm. Adjust the link rod (**not** the adjustment screw) if necessary to achieve this **(see illustration)**.

9 Once the link rod is correctly adjusted, check the adjustment of the throttle position switch as described in Section 11.

8 Throttle pedal - removal and refitting

Removal

1 Remove the trim from below the steering column.
2 Depress the pedal fully. Grip the cable inner with pliers and release the pedal. Separate the cable inner from the split bush **(see illustration)**.
3 Remove the pedal bracket bolts and remove the pedal and bracket.

Refitting

4 Refit by reversing the removal operations. Check the throttle cable adjustment on completion (see Section 7).

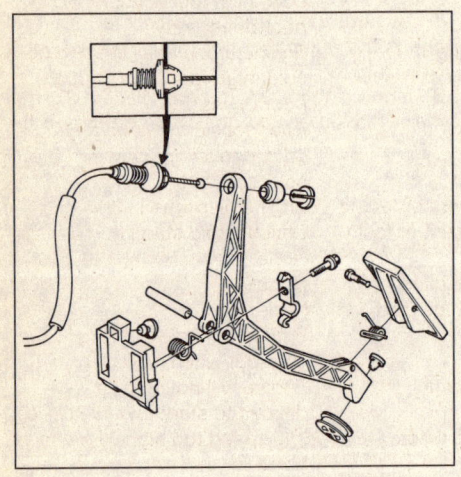

8.2 Throttle pedal and associated components

9 Fuel injection systems - general information

Bosch LH2.4-Jetronic system

The Bosch LH2.4-Jetronic system is fitted to all engines covered by this manual except for some versions of the B230F which utilise the Bendix Regina system described later in this Section.

LH2.4-Jetronic is a microprocessor-controlled fuel management system, designed to meet stringent emission control legislation whilst still providing excellent engine performance and fuel economy. This is achieved by continuously monitoring the engine using various sensors, whose data is input to the system's electronic control module. Based on this information, the control module program and memory then determine the exact amount of fuel necessary, which is then injected directly into the inlet manifold, for all actual and anticipated driving conditions.

The LH2.4 Jetronic control module interacts with the ignition system control module to provide a total engine management package. In addition, it also controls various aspects of the emissions control systems described in Part B of this Chapter.

The main components of the system and their individual operation is as follows.

Control module: The fuel control module is a microprocessor, which controls the entire operation of the fuel system. Contained in the module memory is a program which controls the fuel supply to the injectors, and their opening duration. The program enters sub-routines to alter these parameters, according to inputs from the other components of the system. In addition to this, the engine idle speed is also controlled by the control module, which uses an idle air control valve to open or close an air passage as required. The control module also incorporates a self-diagnostic facility in which the entire fuel system is continuously monitored for correct operation. Any detected faults are logged as fault codes which can be displayed by activating the on-board diagnostic unit. In the event of a fault in the system due to loss of a signal from one of the sensors, the control module reverts to an emergency ("limp-home") program. This will allow the car to be driven, although engine operation and performance will be limited.

Fuel injectors: Each fuel injector consists of a solenoid-operated needle valve, which opens under commands from the control module. Fuel from the fuel rail is then delivered through the injector nozzle into the inlet manifold.

Cold start injector: The cold start injector is used to supply additional fuel for starting, in cold conditions. The injector is located further away from the engine than the main injectors and supplies fuel in a more vaporised form. The cold start injector is only fitted to pre-1992 model year engines.

Coolant temperature sensor: This resistive device is screwed into the cylinder head, where its element is in direct contact with the engine coolant. Changes in coolant temperature are detected by the control module as a change in sensor resistance. Signals from the coolant temperature sensor are also used by the ignition system control module and by the temperature gauge in the instrument panel.

Mass air flow sensor: The MAF sensor measures the mass of air drawn into the engine. The sensor contains a wire which is heated to 150°C higher than the temperature of the inlet air passing over it. The greater the mass of air entering the engine the higher the current needed to keep the wire at the correct temperature. This current flow across the wire is used by the control module as a measure of inlet air mass. When the engine is stopped, the wire is heated to 1000°C for approximately one second to burn off any deposits that may have collected.

Throttle position switch: The throttle position switch is attached to the throttle shaft in the throttle housing. The unit sends signals to both the fuel and ignition system control modules that the throttle is either closed or fully open.

Idle air control valve: The idle air control valve contains a small electric motor that open or shuts a bypass air passage inside the valve. The valve only operates when the throttle position switch is closed, and in response to signals from the control module, maintains the engine idle speed at a constant value irrespective of any additional load from the various accessories. In addition, the valve supplies air to the engine under engine braking conditions to maintain the partial vacuum in the inlet manifold at an acceptable level.

Fuel pumps: Two electric fuel pumps are used in the LH2.4 Jetronic system; an impeller pump, located in the fuel tank, and totally submerged in the fuel, supplies fuel to the main fuel pump located under the car. This roller type pump then supplies fuel to the fuel rail on the inlet manifold via an in-line fuel filter.

Fuel pressure regulator: The regulator is a vacuum-operated mechanical device, which ensures that the pressure differential between fuel in the fuel rail and fuel in the inlet manifold is maintained at a constant value. As manifold depression increases, the regulated fuel pressure is reduced in direct proportion. When fuel pressure in the fuel rail exceeds the regulator setting, the regulator opens to allow fuel to return via the return line to the tank.

Fuses and relays: The main system relay is energised by the fuel system control module and provides power for the fuel pumps, fuel injectors, idle air control valve, the MAF sensor, the heated oxygen sensor and some

Fuel and exhaust systems 4A•5

of the control module functions. A 25 amp fuse protects the main system relay while 15 amp fuses are used to protect the fuel pumps and heated oxygen sensor.

Bendix Regina system

The Bendix Regina system is used on the B230F engine for certain market territories. The components and system operation are virtually the same as the LH2.4-Jetronic system apart from the method of calculating the volume of air entering the engine and other minor differences which are described below.

Pressure sensor: Instead of the mass air flow sensor used in the Jetronic system, the Regina system utilises a pressure sensor and inlet air temperature sensor to calculate the volume of air being drawn into the engine. The pressure sensor is connected to the inlet manifold via a hose and uses a piezo-electrical crystal to convert manifold pressure to an electrical signal to be transmitted to the fuel system control module.

Inlet air temperature sensor: This resistive device is located in the air inlet ducting, where its element is in direct contact with the air entering the engine. Changes in air temperature are detected by the control module as a change in sensor resistance. From the signals received from the inlet air temperature sensor and pressure sensor, the control module can calculate the volume of air inducted into the engine.

Fuel pump: On the Regina system only one fuel pump is used, located in the fuel tank.

Cold start injector: The cold start injector is used on all engines equipped with the Regina fuel injection system.

10 Fuel injection system - testing

General information

1 If a fault appears in the fuel injection system, first ensure that all the system wiring connectors are securely connected and free of corrosion. Ensure that the fault is not due to poor maintenance; ie, check that the air cleaner filter element is clean, the spark plugs are in good condition and correctly gapped, the valve clearances are correctly adjusted, the cylinder compression pressures are correct, and that the engine breather hoses are clear and undamaged, referring to Chapters 1, 2 and 4B for further information.

2 If these checks fail to reveal the cause of the problem the on-board diagnostic facility can be used to isolate the nature of the fault and to determine what course of action to be taken. As the fuel and ignition systems must ideally be treated as one integrated engine management package, testing and fault diagnosis of the fuel system must be done in conjunction with similar tests on the ignition system.

3 A full description of the on-board diagnostic system and the fault diagnosis procedures associated with it is given in Chapter 5B, Section 3. Listed below are the possible fuel system fault codes and, where applicable, the symptoms associated with each fault which should be used in conjunction with the procedure in Chapter 5B.

Fault code read-out

Bosch LH2.4-Jetronic system

Code	Meaning	Symptoms
1-1-1	No fault detected	None
1-1-2	Control module fault	None
1-1-3	Fuel supply too weak/rich	High fuel consumption
1-2-1	MAF sensor signal absent or faulty	Poor driveability, high fuel consumption
1-2-3	Coolant temperature sensor signal absent or faulty	Difficult starting when cold
1-3-1	Engine speed signal from ignition system absent or faulty	Engine will not start
1-3-2	Battery voltage too low or too high	None
1-3-3	Throttle position switch signal faulty at idling	Excessively high idling speed
2-1-2	Heated oxygen sensor signal absent or faulty	Poor driveability, high fuel consumption
2-1-3	Throttle position switch signal faulty at full load	None
2-2-1	Fuel supply too weak in part-load stage	Engine stops after starting from cold, high fuel consumption, poor driveability
2-2-3	Idle air control valve signal absent or faulty	Engine will not start or is difficult to start, excessively low idling speed
2-3-1	Fuel supply too weak or too rich in part-load stage	Engine stops after starting from cold, high fuel consumption, poor driveability
2-3-2	Fuel supply too weak or too rich at idling	Engine stops after starting from cold, high fuel consumption, poor driveability
3-1-1	Speedometer signal absent	Erratic idling
3-1-2	Knock sensor signal from ignition system absent	None
3-2-2	MAF sensor burn-off signal absent or faulty	Poor driveability

Bendix Regina system

Code	Meaning	Symptoms
1-1-1	No fault detected	None
1-1-2	Control module fault	None
1-1-3	Fuel injector fault	Engine will not start, engine stops or hesitates
2-2-1	Heated oxygen sensor signal absent or faulty	High fuel consumption
2-3-1	Fuel supply too weak or too rich in part-load stage	Engine stops after starting from cold, high fuel consumption, poor driveability
2-3-2	Fuel supply too weak or too rich at idling	Engine stops after starting from cold, high fuel consumption, poor driveability
1-2-1	Pressure sensor signal absent or faulty	Poor acceleration, engine cuts out when idling, difficult cold/hot starting
1-2-2	Inlet air temperature sensor signal absent or faulty	Engine dies when idling
1-2-3	Coolant temperature sensor signal absent or faulty	Difficult cold starting
1-3-2	Battery voltage too low or too high	None
1-3-3	Throttle position switch signal faulty at idling	None
2-1-3	Throttle position switch signal faulty at full load	None
2-2-2	System relay signal absent or faulty	Engine will not start, engine cuts-out when running
2-2-3	Idle air control valve signal absent or faulty	Engine will not start or is difficult to start, low idle speed
2-3-3	Adaptive idling control out of operating limits	Idle speed too high or too low
3-1-1	Speedometer signal absent	None
3-2-1	Signal to cold start valve short-circuited to earth or missing	Difficult cold starting

4A

4A•6 Fuel and exhaust systems

11.2 Disconnect the multi-plug at the mass air flow sensor

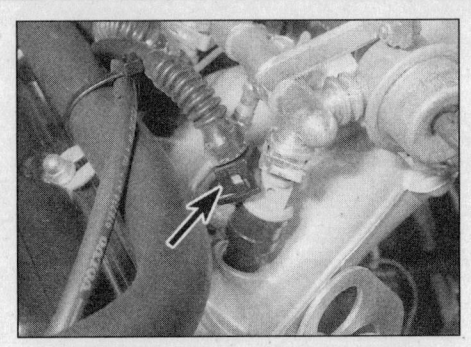

11.8 Disconnect the wiring multi-plug (arrowed) from the fuel injectors

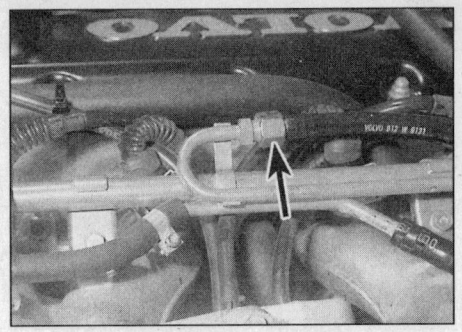

11.9 Fuel supply union nut (arrowed) at the fuel rail

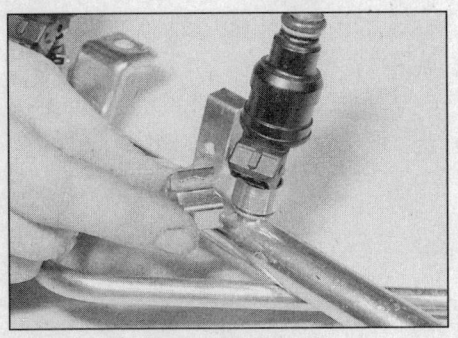

11.12a Remove the clip...

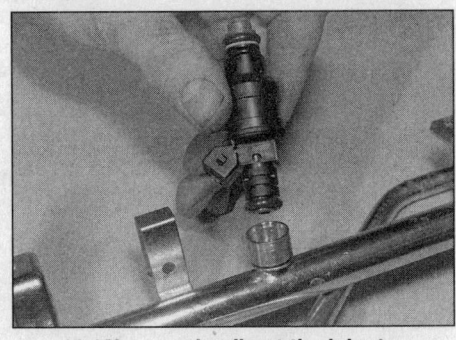

11.12b ...and pull out the injector

11.17 Fuel pressure regulator attachments at the fuel rail

11 Fuel injection system components - removal and refitting

Note: *The following procedures are applicable to both the LH2.4-Jetronic and the Regina fuel injection systems unless otherwise stated.*

1 Disconnect the battery negative lead.

Mass air flow sensor (LH2.4-Jetronic)

2 Disconnect the multi-plug from the mass air flow sensor **(see illustration)**.
3 Release the clips which secure the air mass meter to the air cleaner, and the hose clip which secures it to the trunking. Remove the air mass meter.
4 Refit by reversing the removal operations.

Pressure sensor (Regina)

5 Disconnect the air hose and the wiring multi-plug from the sensor located on the engine compartment bulkhead.
6 Undo the retaining screws and remove the unit from its location.
7 Refit by reversing the removal operations.

Injectors

Note: *Refer to the warning note in Section 1 before proceeding.*

8 Disconnect the wiring plug from each injector **(see illustration)**. Free the wiring harness from the fuel rails, cutting cable-ties where necessary.
9 Uncouple the fuel supply and return pipes from the fuel rail, counterholding the unions when slackening them. Be prepared for fuel spillage **(see illustration)**.
10 Disconnect the vacuum hose from the fuel pressure regulator.
11 Remove the bolts which secure the fuel rail to the inlet manifold, noting the location of the earth lead. Pull the rail upwards to release the injectors from the manifold and remove the rail complete with injectors and fuel pressure regulator.
12 Individual injectors may now be removed from the rail by removing the securing clips and pulling them out **(see illustrations)**.
13 Refit by reversing the removal operations. Check that the injector O-rings are in good condition and renew them if necessary; smear them with petroleum jelly or silicone grease as an assembly lubricant.

Cold start injector

Note: *Refer to the warning note in Section 1 before proceeding.*

14 Disconnect the wiring multi-plug from the cold start injector.
15 Unscrew the fuel supply banjo union and recover the copper washers. Be prepared for fuel spillage.
16 Undo the two retaining bolts and remove the injector from the manifold.
Refit by reversing the removal operations using new copper washers on the fuel supply banjo union.

Fuel pressure regulator

Note: *Refer to the warning note in Section 1 before proceeding.*

17 Disconnect the vacuum and fuel hoses from the regulator. Be prepared for fuel spillage **(see illustration)**.
18 Remove the regulator from its bracket, being prepared for further spillage.
19 Refit by reversing the removal operations.

Idle air control valve

20 Disconnect the multi-plug from the valve.
21 Slacken the hose clips and carefully pull the air hoses off the valve stubs **(see illustration)**.
22 Undo the mounting bracket retaining bolt and withdraw the valve from below the inlet manifold.
23 Refit by reversing the removal operations, using new hoses and clips if necessary.

Throttle housing

24 Disconnect the throttle position switch multi-plug.

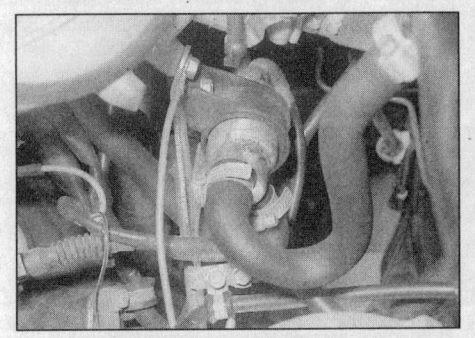

11.21 Air hose connections at the idle air control valve

Fuel and exhaust systems 4A•7

11.26 Disconnect the throttle linkage balljoint at the operating lever

25 Disconnect the air control valve hose, the vacuum hose and the air inlet trunking from the housing.
26 Prise out the spring clip and disconnect the throttle linkage balljoint from the throttle spindle operating lever **(see illustration)**.
27 Make alignment marks between the housing and the inlet manifold. Remove the nuts which secure the housing and withdraw it. Recover the gasket.
28 When refitting, observe the alignment marks if refitting the old components. Use a new gasket.
29 With the housing refitted, the basic idle speed should be checked and, if necessary adjusted, as follows.
30 Connect a tachometer to the engine in accordance with the maker's instructions. Start the engine and allow it to reach normal operating temperature.
31 Where fitted, ensure that the air conditioning is turned off. On automatic transmission models move the selector lever to the P position.
32 With the engine idling, clamp the hose that runs from the throttle housing air inlet to the idle air control valve using a suitable pair of grips **(see illustration)**. The idle speed should now fall to below 500 rpm, or the engine may even stop completely. If so, the basic idle speed is satisfactory. If the idle speed does not fall to below 500 rpm, adjust as follows.
33 Slacken the throttle spindle adjustment screw locknut. Turn the adjustment screw as

11.38 Throttle position switch adjustment
A turn clockwise   B Turn anticlockwise
Arrow indicates location of feeler blade during adjustment

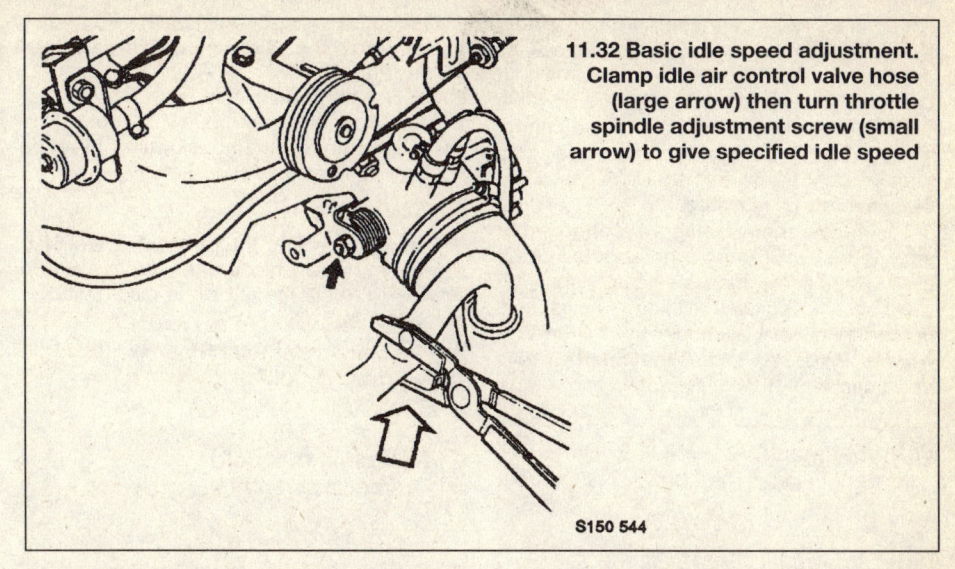

11.32 Basic idle speed adjustment. Clamp idle air control valve hose (large arrow) then turn throttle spindle adjustment screw (small arrow) to give specified idle speed

necessary until the idle speed is between 480 and 520 rpm. Hold the screw in this position and tighten the locknut.
34 Switch off the engine, disconnect the tachometer and remove the clamp from the air hose. Check the operation of the throttle position switch as described in the next sub-Section.

Throttle position switch

35 Disconnect the multi-plug from the switch.
36 Remove the two Allen screws which secure the switch and withdraw the switch from the throttle housing.
37 Refit by reversing the removal operations but before tightening the securing screws, adjust the switch position as follows.
38 Slacken the switch screws (if not already done). Turn the switch clockwise (viewed from behind) within its limits of travel. Place a 0.15 mm feeler blade between the throttle spindle operating lever and the throttle spindle adjustment screw. Turn the switch slowly anti-clockwise until a click is heard. Hold the switch in this position and tighten the screws **(see illustration)**.
39 Check the adjustment by opening the throttle slightly and insert feeler blades between the throttle spindle operating lever and the throttle spindle adjustment screw as follows. With a 0.45 mm feeler blade inserted, there should be no click from the switch as the throttle is closed. With a 0.15 mm feeler blade inserted there should be a click from the switch as the throttle is closed. If this is not the case repeat the adjustment.

Coolant temperature sensor

40 Refer to Chapter 3, Section 7.

Inlet air temperature sensor (Regina)

41 Disconnect the wiring multi-plug at the temperature sensor.
42 Slacken the retaining clips and remove

the air duct centre section from the air cleaner and inlet manifold ducting. At the time of writing it is unclear whether the sensor can be removed separately from the duct for renewal.
43 Refit by reversing the removal operations.

Electronic control module

44 Remove the lower trim panel under the facia on the right-hand side.
45 Release the forward end of the sill/seat belt reel trim by removing the screws securing it. These screws are concealed by covers.
46 Unclip the right-hand footwell trim panel and remove it.
47 Make sure the ignition is switched off, then disconnect the multi-plug from the control unit.
48 Remove the securing screws and slide the unit out of its bracket.
49 Refit by reversing the removal operations.

12 Cruise control -
general information

When fitted, the cruise control allows the vehicle to maintain a steady speed selected by the driver, regardless of gradients or prevailing winds.
The main components of the system are a control unit, a control switch, a vacuum servo and a vacuum pump. Brake and (when applicable) clutch pedal switches protect the engine against excessive speeds or loads should a pedal be depressed whilst the system is in use.
In operation, the driver accelerates to the desired speed and then brings the system into use by means of the switch. The control unit then monitors vehicle speed (from the speedometer pulses) and opens or closes the throttle by means of the servo to maintain the set speed. If the switch is moved to "OFF", or the brake or clutch pedal is depressed, the servo immediately closes the throttle. The set

4A•8 Fuel and exhaust systems

speed is stored in the control unit memory and the system can be reactivated by moving the switch to "RESUME", provided that vehicle speed has not dropped below 25 mph.

The driver can override the cruise control for overtaking simply by depressing the throttle pedal. When the pedal is released, the set speed will be resumed.

The cruise control cannot be engaged at speeds below 25 mph, and should not be used in slippery or congested conditions.

No specific removal, refitting or adjustment procedures were available at the time of writing. Problems should be referred to a Volvo dealer or other specialist.

13 Inlet manifold - removal and refitting

Note: *Refer to the warning note in Section 1 before proceeding.*

Removal

1 Disconnect the battery negative lead.
2 Disconnect the air inlet trunking from the throttle housing.
3 Disconnect the control cable(s) from the throttle drum.
4 Disconnect the injector multi-plugs and any other electrical services obstructing removal.
5 Disconnect vacuum, pressure, and breather hoses from the manifold, making identifying marks if necessary.
6 Disconnect the fuel feed and return pipes from the fuel rail or pressure regulator. Be prepared for fuel spillage.
7 Disconnect or move aside the cold start injector and the idle air control valve (as applicable).
8 Check that nothing has been overlooked, then unbolt and remove the manifold complete with throttle housing and injection equipment. Recover the gasket.

Refitting

9 Refit by reversing the removal operations, using new gaskets or O-rings. It may be necessary to cut the gasket to clear adjacent components.
10 Adjust the throttle cable (Section 7) and automatic transmission kickdown cable (Chapter 7B).

14 Exhaust manifold - removal and refitting

Non-turbocharged engines

Removal

1 Remove the hot air trunking (when so equipped).
2 Disconnect the exhaust downpipe from the manifold.
3 Unbolt the manifold from the cylinder head and remove it. Recover the gaskets.

Refitting

4 When refitting, use new gaskets. The marking "UT" must face away from the cylinder head.
5 Apply anti-seize compound to the threads. Fit the manifold to the head and tighten the nuts evenly.
6 Reconnect the exhaust downpipe and the hot air trunking.
7 Run the engine and check for leaks.

Turbocharged engines

8 On these engines, either remove the turbocharger first as described in Section 16, or disconnect the services and connections at the turbocharger then remove the exhaust manifold and turbocharger as a unit.

15 Turbocharger - general information and precautions

General information

1 Two types of water-cooled turbocharger are used on 940 models covered by this manual **(see illustration)**. The turbocharger increases the efficiency of the engine by raising the pressure in the inlet manifold above atmospheric pressure. Instead of the air/fuel mixture being simply sucked into the cylinders it is actively forced in.
2 Energy for the operation of the turbocharger comes from the exhaust gas. The gas flows through a specially-shaped housing (the turbine housing) and in so doing spins the turbine wheel. The turbine wheel is attached to a shaft, at the other end of which is another vaned wheel known as the compressor wheel. The compressor wheel spins in its own housing and compresses the inducted air on the way to the inlet manifold.
3 After leaving the turbocharger, the compressed air passes through an intercooler,

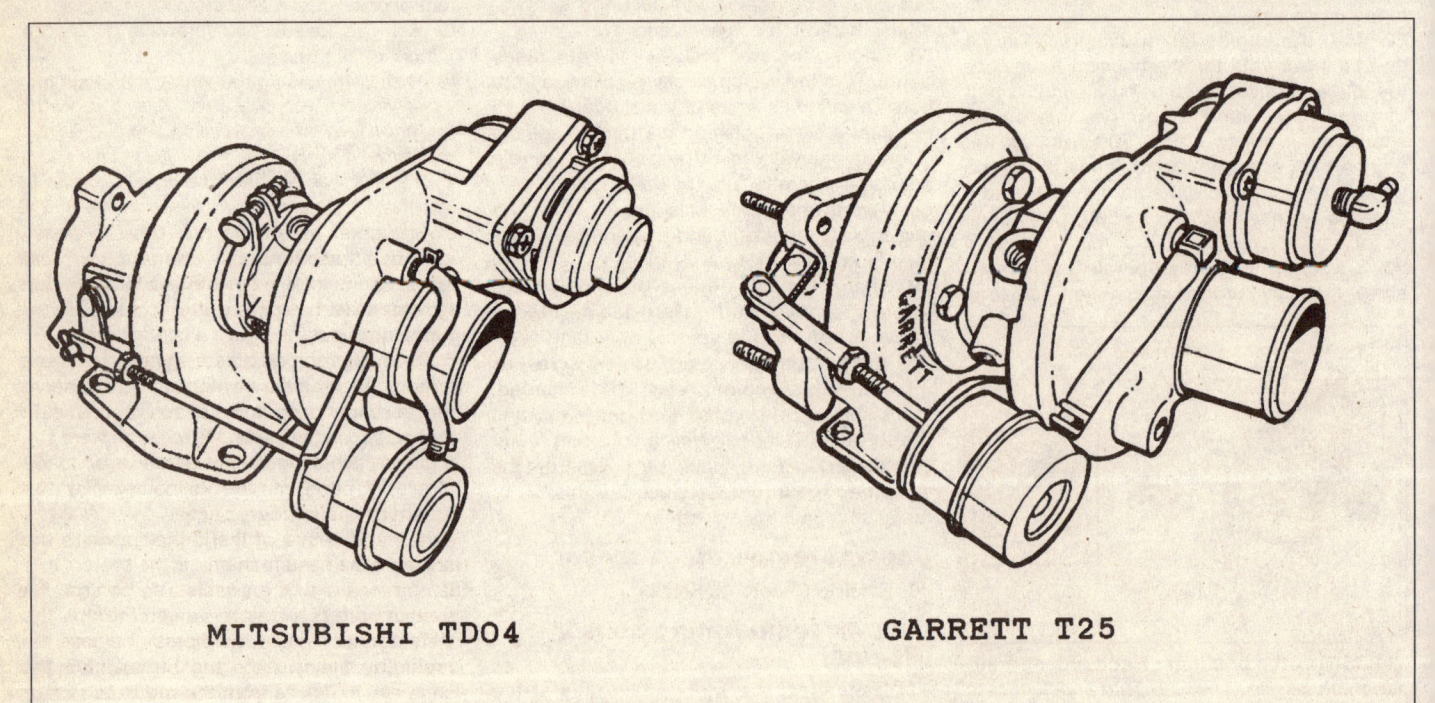

MITSUBISHI TD04   **GARRETT T25**

15.1 General view of the two turbocharger types

Fuel and exhaust systems 4A•9

which is an air-to-air heat exchanger mounted in front of the radiator. Here the air gives up heat which it acquired when being compressed. This temperature reduction improves engine efficiency and reduces the risk of detonation.

4 Boost pressure (the pressure in the inlet manifold) is limited by a wastegate, which diverts the exhaust gas away from the turbine wheel in response to a pressure-sensitive actuator. As a further precaution, a pressure-sensitive switch cuts out the fuel pump if boost pressure becomes excessive. On some models, boost pressure is displayed to the driver by a gauge on the instrument panel.

5 The turbo shaft is pressure-lubricated by means of a feed pipe from the engine's main oil gallery. The shaft "floats" on a cushion of oil. A drain pipe returns the oil to the sump.

6 Water cooling keeps the operating temperature of the turbo bearings lower than previously. Water continues to circulate by convection after the engine has stopped, so cooling the turbocharger if it is hot after a long run.

Precautions

7 The turbocharger operates at extremely high speeds and temperatures. Certain precautions must be observed to avoid premature failure of the turbo or injury to the operator.
 a) Do not operate the turbo with any parts exposed. Foreign objects falling onto the rotating vanes could cause extensive damage and (if ejected) personal injury.
 b) Do not race the engine immediately after start-up, especially if it is cold. Give the oil a few seconds to circulate.
 c) Always allow the engine to return to idle speed before switching it off - do not blip the throttle and switch off, as this will leave the turbo spinning without lubrication.
 d) Allow the engine to idle for several minutes before switching off after a high-speed run.
 e) Observe the recommended intervals for oil and filter changing, and use a reputable oil of the specified quality. Neglect of oil changing, or use of inferior oil, can cause carbon formation on the turbo shaft and subsequent failure.

16.3 Turbocharger vacuum and water hose connections

16 Turbocharger - removal and refitting

Removal

1 Disconnect the battery negative lead.
2 Drain the cooling system (Chapter 1).
3 Slacken the hose clips and disconnect the water, vacuum and air inlet hoses from the turbocharger (see illustration). Cover the air inlet openings with rags to prevent dirt entry.
4 Jack up the front of the car and securely support it on stands.
5 Undo the nuts and separate the exhaust system flanged joint forward of the catalytic converter. Remove the flywheel housing bracket then disconnect the exhaust pipe from the turbocharger. Cover the turbocharger opening with rags to prevent dirt entry.
6 Disconnect the oil feed pipe at the turbocharger and cover the opening and disconnected union. Where applicable, also release the bracket at the front of the compressor housing.
7 Undo the turbocharger to exhaust manifold securing nuts and carefully withdraw the unit, complete with return oil line. Remove the return oil line rubber seal and cover the openings. If the turbocharger is to be renewed, transfer the return oil line to the new unit, using a new gasket on the joint flange.
8 Prior to refitting, thoroughly clean all mating faces and obtain new locknuts for all fastenings.

Refitting

9 Locate a new rubber seal on the oil return line.
10 Position the turbocharger on the manifold studs and guide the return oil line into position.
11 Fit the turbocharger-to-manifold retaining nuts using thread locking compound on their threads. Tighten the nuts securely, in a diagonal sequence.
12 Fill the turbocharger oil feed hole with oil then refit the feed pipe using new washers on the union. Where applicable, re-attach the bracket at the front of the compressor housing.
13 Reconnect the exhaust system then lower the car to the ground.
14 Reconnect the water, vacuum and air inlet hoses to the turbocharger.
15 Fill the cooling system as described in Chapter 1, then reconnect the battery.

17 Intercooler - removal and refitting

Removal

1 Remove the radiator top mountings and carefully move the radiator rearwards.
2 Disconnect the hoses from the intercooler and lift it out.
3 If turbocharger failure has occurred, the intercooler may contain a substantial quantity of oil. A drain plug is provided.

Refitting

4 Refit by reversing the removal operations.

18 Exhaust system - general information, removal and refitting

General information

1 The exhaust system consists of front, intermediate and rear sections, the number varying according to model. The system is suspended from the underbody on rubber mountings, and bolted to a cast iron manifold at the front. Flanged joints incorporating gasket seals or U-type pipe clamps are used to secure the sections. On all models a catalytic converter is fitted - refer to Part B of this Chapter for further information.
2 The exhaust system should be examined for leaks, damage and security at regular intervals (see Chapter 1). To do this, apply the handbrake, and allow the engine to idle in a well-ventilated area. Lie down on each side of the car in turn, and check the full length of the system for leaks, while an assistant temporarily places a wad of cloth over the end of the tailpipe. If a leak is evident, stop the engine and use a proprietary repair kit to seal it. If the leak is excessive, or damage is evident, renew the section. Check the rubber mountings for deterioration, and renew them if necessary.

Removal

3 Details of exhaust system routing and mounting will vary with model and year, but the principles of removal and refitting remain the same.
4 In many cases it will be found easier to remove the complete system from the downpipe(s) rearwards and then to renew individual sections on the bench. One exception is where the system passes over the rear axle; here it is better to separate the joints, or to cut the pipe if it is rusty anyway.
5 To remove the complete system, raise and support the vehicle at a convenient working height. Apply penetrating oil to the nuts, bolts and clamps which will have to be undone.
6 Unbolt the flanged joint at the union of the exhaust system with the downpipe(s).
7 Where the system passes over the rear axle, remove one of the U-pipe clamps and separate the system there.
8 With the aid of an assistant, unhook the system from its mountings and remove it.
9 To remove the downpipe(s), release the mounting clamp from the bellhousing and separate the joints from the manifold(s). Also disconnect the hot air trunking; and if necessary unbolt the hot air shroud.

4A

Refitting

10 Commence refitting with the downpipe(s), using new gaskets. Apply anti-seize compound to the threads. Fit the bellhousing mounting clamp bolt but do not tighten it yet.
11 Sling the rest of the system on its mountings and couple it up, using a new sealing ring at the flanged joint. Apply exhaust jointing compound to the sliding joints and anti-seize compound to all threads.
12 Tighten all the joints from the front rearwards, but leave the bellhousing clamp loose until everything else has been tightened. Twist the sliding joints slightly if necessary so that the system hangs easily and without touching the body.
13 Run the engine for a few minutes and check the system for leaks. Allow it to cool and retighten the joints.
14 Lower the vehicle.

Chapter 4 Part B:
Emission control systems

Contents

Catalytic converter - general information and precautions 3
Emission control systems - checking and component renewal 2
Exhaust system check ....See Chapter 1
General information 1
Underbonnet hose check ....See Chapter 1

Degrees of difficulty

| **Easy,** suitable for novice with little experience | **Fairly easy,** suitable for beginner with some experience | **Fairly difficult,** suitable for competent DIY mechanic | **Difficult,** suitable for experienced DIY mechanic | **Very difficult,** suitable for expert DIY or professional |

Specifications

Torque wrench setting   Nm
Heated oxygen sensor 45

1 General information

All models covered by this manual have various features built into the fuel system to help minimise harmful emissions. These features fall broadly into three categories; crankcase emission control, fuel evaporative emission control and exhaust emission control. The main features of these systems are as follows.

Crankcase emission control

To reduce the emissions of unburned hydrocarbons from the crankcase into the atmosphere, a Positive Crankcase Ventilation (PCV) system is used whereby the engine is sealed and the blow-by gasses and oil vapour are drawn from inside the crankcase, through an oil separator, into the inlet tract to be burned by the engine during normal combustion **(see illustration)**.

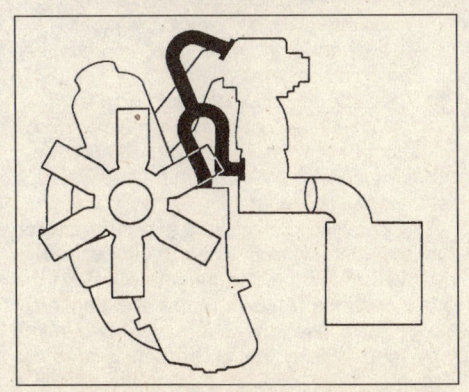

Under conditions of high manifold depression (idling, deceleration) the gasses will be sucked positively out of the crankcase. Under conditions of low manifold depression (acceleration, full-throttle running) the gasses are forced out of the crankcase by the (relatively) higher crankcase pressure; if the engine is worn, the raised crankcase pressure (due to increased blow-by) will cause some of the flow to return under all manifold conditions.

Fuel evaporative emission control

The evaporative emission control (EVAP) system is used to minimise the escape of unburned hydrocarbons into the atmosphere. To do this, the fuel tank filler cap is sealed, and a carbon canister is used to collect and store petrol vapours generated in the tank. When the engine is running, the vapours are cleared from the canister via a vacuum operated valve into the inlet tract, to be burned by the engine during normal combustion.

To ensure that the engine runs correctly when idling, the vacuum valve only opens when the engine is running under load; the valve then opens to allow the stored vapour to pass into the inlet tract.

As a safety measure, and to further reduce hydrocarbon emissions, a roll-over valve is incorporated into the tank which closes when the car tilts sideways by more than 45°. This prevents fuel leakage from the tank in the event of an accident **(see illustration)**.

Exhaust emission control

To minimise the amount of pollutants which escape into the atmosphere, all models are fitted with a catalytic converter in the exhaust system. The system is of the closed-loop type, in which a heated oxygen sensor in the exhaust system provides the fuel injection system control module with constant feedback on the oxygen content of the exhaust gasses. This enables the control module to adjust the mixture by altering injector opening time, thus provide the best possible conditions for the converter to operate. The system operates in the following way.

The oxygen sensor has a built-in heating element, activated by the control module to quickly bring the sensor's tip to an efficient operating temperature. The sensor's tip is sensitive to oxygen, and sends the control module a varying voltage depending on the amount of oxygen in the exhaust gasses; if the inlet air/fuel mixture is too rich, the exhaust gasses are low in oxygen, so the sensor sends a voltage signal proportional to the oxygen detected, the voltage altering as the mixture weakens and the amount of oxygen in the exhaust gasses rises. Peak conversion efficiency of all major pollutants occurs if the inlet air/fuel mixture is maintained at the chemically-correct ratio for complete

1.2 Crankcase ventilation hose layout

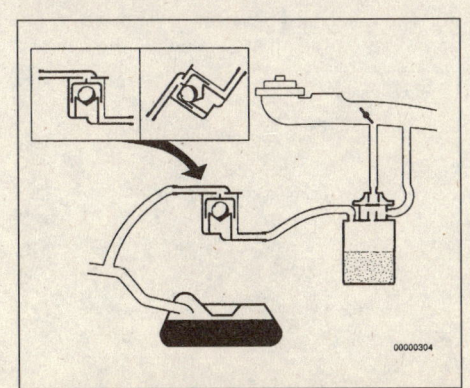

1.6 General arrangement of the evaporative emission control system

4B•2 Emission control systems

combustion of petrol - 14.7 parts (by weight) of air to 1 part of fuel (the "stoichiometric" ratio). The sensor output voltage alters in a large step at this point, the control module using the signal change as a reference point, and correcting the inlet air/fuel mixture accordingly, by altering the fuel injector opening time.

In addition to the catalytic converter, certain models are fitted with an exhaust gas recirculation (EGR) system. This system is designed to recirculate small quantities of exhaust gas into the inlet tract, and therefore into the combustion process. This reduces the level of oxides of nitrogen present in the final exhaust gas which is released into the atmosphere.

The volume of exhaust gas recirculated is controlled by vacuum (supplied from the inlet manifold) via an EGR valve mounted on the inlet manifold. Before reaching the EGR valve, the vacuum from the manifold passes to an EGR vacuum controller. The purpose of which is to modify the vacuum supplied to the EGR valve according to engine operating conditions.

The EGR system is controlled by the ignition system electronic control module, which receives information on engine operating parameters from its various sensors.

2 Emission control systems - checking and component renewal

Crankcase emission control

1 The components of this system require no attention other than to check that the hoses are clear and undamaged at regular intervals.

Fuel evaporative emission control

Checking

2 Poor idle, stalling and poor driveability can be caused by an inoperative canister vacuum valve, a damaged canister, split or cracked hoses, or hoses connected to the wrong fittings. Check the fuel filler cap for a damaged or deformed gasket.
3 Fuel loss or fuel odour can be caused by liquid fuel leaking from fuel lines, a cracked or damaged canister, an inoperative canister vacuum valve, and disconnected, mis-routed, kinked or damaged vapour or control hoses.
4 Inspect each hose attached to the canister for kinks, leaks and cracks along its entire length. Repair or renew as necessary.
5 Inspect the canister. If it is cracked or damaged, renew it. Look for fuel leaking from the bottom of the canister. If fuel is leaking, renew the canister, and check the hoses and hose routing.

Carbon canister renewal

6 The canister is located in the front of the engine compartment on the right-hand or left-hand side according to model.
7 Note the location of the vacuum and fuel vent hose connections at the canister and carefully disconnect them (see illustration).
8 Release the canister retaining strap and remove the unit from the engine compartment.
9 Refitting is a reversal of removal.

Exhaust emission control

Checking

10 Checking of the system as a whole entails a close visual inspection of all hoses, pipes and connections for condition and security. Apart from this, any known or suspected faults should be attended to by a Volvo dealer. At the time of writing, no information was available on the exhaust gas recirculation system. Detailed checks in the event of a fault in the system, or component renewal should also be entrusted to a dealer.

Heated oxygen sensor - renewal

Note: *The sensor is delicate. It will not work if dropped or knocked, if its power supply is disrupted, or if any cleaning materials are used on it.*
11 Jack up the front of the car and support it on axle stands (see "*Jacking and vehicle support*").
12 Disconnect the electrical connector from the sensor which will be located either in the catalytic converter, or in the exhaust pipe just in front of the converter (see illustration).
13 Unscrew the sensor and collect the sealing washer (where fitted).
14 On refitting, clean the sealing washer (where fitted) and renew it if it is damaged or worn. Apply a smear of anti-seize compound to the sensor's threads, then refit the sensor, tightening it to the specified torque. Reconnect the wiring and refit the connector plug.

Catalytic converter - renewal

15 The catalytic converter is renewed in the same way as the other sections of the exhaust system. Refer to the next Section for general information and to Chapter 4A, Section 18 for details of removal and refitting.

3 Catalytic converter - general information and precautions

The catalytic converter is a reliable and simple device, which needs no maintenance in itself, but there are some facts of which an owner should be aware if the converter is to function properly for its full service life.

a) DO NOT use leaded petrol in a vehicle equipped with a catalytic converter - the lead will coat the precious metals, reducing their converting efficiency, and will eventually destroy the converter.
b) Always keep the ignition and fuel systems well-maintained in accordance with the manufacturer's schedule (see Chapter 1).
c) If the engine develops a misfire, do not drive the vehicle at all (or at least as little as possible) until the fault is cured.
d) DO NOT push - or tow-start the vehicle - this will soak the catalytic converter in unburned fuel, causing it to overheat when the engine does start.
e) DO NOT switch off the ignition at high engine speeds, ie do not "blip" the throttle immediately before switching off.
f) DO NOT use fuel or engine oil additives - these may contain substances harmful to the catalytic converter.
g) DO NOT continue to use the vehicle if the engine burns oil to the extent of leaving a visible trail of blue smoke.
h) Remember that the catalytic converter operates at very high temperatures. DO NOT, therefore, park the vehicle in dry undergrowth, over long grass or piles of dead leaves, after a long run.
i) Remember that the catalytic converter is FRAGILE. Do not strike it with tools during servicing work.
j) In some cases, a sulphurous smell (like that of rotten eggs) may be noticed from the exhaust. This is common to many catalytic converter-equipped vehicles. Once the vehicle has covered a few thousand miles, the problem should disappear - in the meantime, try changing the brand of petrol used.
k) The catalytic converter used on a well-maintained and well-driven vehicle should last for between 80 000 and 160 000 km. If the converter is no longer effective, it must be renewed.

The catalytic converter is located between the exhaust system front sections and is removed and refitted in the same way as the other sections. Always renew the converter flange seals when the unit is disturbed in any way, and ensure that all retaining nuts are securely tightened. Refer to the relevant earlier Parts of this Chapter, for details of exhaust system removal and refitting.

2.7 Vacuum, fuel and vent hose connections at the carbon canister

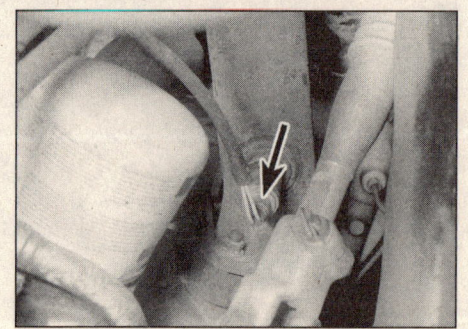

2.12 Heated oxygen sensor location in the exhaust front pipe

Chapter 5 Part A:
Starting and charging systems

Contents

Accessory drivebelts check and renewal ....See Chapter 1
Alternator drivebelt - removal, refitting and tensioning 6
Alternator - removal and refitting 7
Alternator - testing and overhaul 8
Battery check ....See "Weekly checks"
Battery - removal and refitting 4
Battery - testing and charging 3
Charging system - testing 5
Electrical fault finding - general information 2
Electrical system check ....See "Weekly checks"
General information and precautions 1
Oil pressure warning light switch - removal and refitting 12
Starter motor - removal and refitting 10
Starter motor - testing and overhaul 11
Starting system - testing 9

Degrees of difficulty

Easy, suitable for novice with little experience	Fairly easy, suitable for beginner with some experience	Fairly difficult, suitable for competent DIY mechanic	Difficult, suitable for experienced DIY mechanic	Very difficult, suitable for expert DIY or professional

Specifications

System type .... 12 volt, negative earth

Battery
Type .... Lead acid
Charge condition:
  Poor .... 12.5 volts
  Normal .... 12.6 volts
  Good .... 12.7 volts

Alternator
Type .... Bosch K1, N1, NC, or Nippon-Denso

Starter motor
Type .... Bosch GF, DW, or EW

1 General information and precautions

General information

The engine electrical system consists mainly of the charging and starting systems. Because of their engine-related functions, these components are covered separately from the body electrical devices such as the lights, instruments, etc (which are covered in Chapter 12). Information on the ignition system will be found in Part B of this Chapter.

The electrical system id of the 12-volt negative earth type.

The battery is charged by the alternator which is belt driven from the crankshaft pulley.

The starter motor is of the pre-engaged type incorporating an integral solenoid. On starting, the solenoid moves the drive pinion into engagement with the flywheel/driveplate ring gear teeth before the starter motor is energised. Once the engine is started, a one-way clutch prevents the motor armature being turned by the engine until the pinion disengages from the ring gear.

Precautions

Further details of the various systems are given in the relevant Sections of this Chapter. While some repair procedures are given, the usual course of action is to renew the component concerned. The owner whose interest extends beyond mere component renewal should obtain a copy of the *"Automobile Electrical & Electronic Systems Manual"* from the publishers of this manual.

It is necessary to take extra care when working on the electrical system to avoid damage to semi-conductor devices (diodes and transistors), and to avoid the risk of personal injury. In addition to the precautions given in *"Safety First!"* at the beginning of this manual, observe the following when working on the electrical system:

Always remove rings, watches, etc before working on the electrical system. Even with the battery disconnected, capacitive discharge could occur if a component's live terminal is earthed through a metal object. This could cause a shock or nasty burn.

Do not reverse the battery connections. Components such as the alternator, or any other components having semi-conductor circuitry could be irreparably damaged.

If the engine is being started using jump leads and a slave battery, connect the batteries positive-to-positive and negative-to-negative (see "Booster battery (jump) starting"). This also applies when connecting a battery charger.

Never disconnect the battery terminals, the alternator, or any electrical wiring or any test instruments when the engine is running.

Do not let the engine to turn the alternator when the alternator is not connected.

Never "test" for alternator output by "flashing" the output lead to earth.

Never use an ohmmeter of the type incorporating a hand-cranked generator for circuit or continuity testing.

5A•2 Starting and charging systems

Always ensure that the battery negative lead is disconnected when working on the electrical system.

Before using electric-arc welding equipment on the vehicle, disconnect the battery and alternator to protect them from the risk of damage.

Certain later radio/cassette units fitted as standard equipment by Volvo are equipped with built-in security codes to deter thieves. If the power source to the unit is interrupted, the anti-theft system will activate. Even if the power source is immediately reconnected, the radio/cassette unit will not function until the correct security code has been entered. Therefore, if you do not know the correct security code for the radio/cassette unit, do not disconnect the negative terminal of the battery or remove the radio/cassette unit from the vehicle. Refer to "Radio/cassette unit anti-theft system precaution" Section for further information.

2 Electrical fault finding - general information

Refer to Chapter 12.

3 Battery - testing and charging

Standard and low maintenance battery - testing

1 If the vehicle covers a small annual mileage, it is worthwhile checking the specific gravity of the electrolyte every three months to determine the state of charge of the battery. Use a hydrometer to make the check and compare the results with the following table **(see illustration)**. The temperatures in the table are ambient (air) temperatures. Note that the specific gravity readings assume an electrolyte temperature of 15°C; for every 10°C below 15°C subtract 0.007. For every 10°C above 15°C add 0.007.

	Above 25°C	Below 25°C
Fully charged	1.210 to 1.230	1.270 to 1.290
70% charged	1.170 to 1.190	1.230 to 1.250
Discharged	1.050 to 1.070	1.110 to 1.130

2 If the battery condition is suspect, first check the specific gravity of electrolyte in each cell. A variation of 0.040 or more between any cells indicates loss of electrolyte or deterioration of the internal plates.
3 If the specific gravity variation is 0.040 or more, the battery should be renewed. If the cell variation is satisfactory but the battery is discharged, it should be charged as described later in this Section.

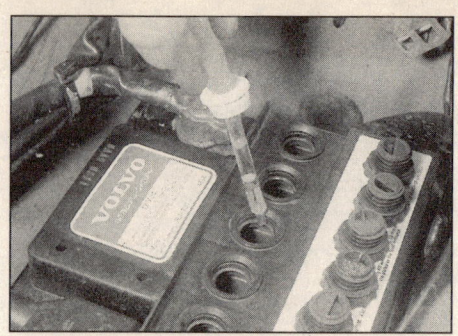

3.1 Checking battery specific gravity using a hydrometer

Maintenance-free battery - testing

4 In cases where a "sealed for life" maintenance-free battery is fitted, topping-up and testing of the electrolyte in each cell is not possible. The condition of the battery can therefore only be tested using a battery condition indicator or a voltmeter.
5 If testing the battery using a voltmeter, connect the voltmeter across the battery and compare the results with those given in the Specifications under "charge condition" The test is only accurate if the battery has not been subjected to any kind of charge for the previous six hours. If this is not the case, switch on the headlights for 30 seconds, then wait four to five minutes before testing the battery after switching off the headlights. All other electrical circuits must be switched off, so check that the doors, boot and/or tailgate are fully shut when making the test.
6 If the voltage reading is less than 12.2 volts, then the battery is discharged, whilst a reading of 12.2 to 12.4 volts indicates a partially discharged condition.
7 If the battery is to be charged, remove it from the vehicle (Section 4) and charge it as described later in this Section.

Standard and low-maintenance battery - charging

Note: *The following is intended as a guide only. Always refer to the manufacturer's recommendations (often printed on a label attached to the battery) before charging a battery.*
8 Charge the battery at a rate of 3.5 to 4 amps and continue to charge the battery at this rate until no further rise in specific gravity is noted over a four hour period.
9 Alternatively a trickle charger charging at the rate of 1.5 amps can safely be used overnight.
10 Specially rapid "boost" charges which are claimed to restore the power of the battery in 1 to 2 hours are not recommended, as they can cause serious damage to the battery plates through overheating.
11 While charging the battery, note that the temperature of the electrolyte should never exceed 37.8°C.

Maintenance-free battery - charging

Note: *The following is intended as a guide only. Always refer to the manufacturer's recommendations (often printed on a label attached to the battery) before charging a battery.*
12 This battery type takes considerably longer to fully recharge than the standard type, the time taken being dependent on the extent of discharge, but it can take anything up to three days.
13 A constant voltage type charger is required, to be set, when connected, to 13.9 to 14.9 volts with a charger current below 25 amps. Using this method, the battery should be usable within three hours, giving a voltage reading of 12.5 volts, but this is for a partially discharged battery and, as mentioned, full charging can take considerably longer.
14 If the battery is to be charged from a fully discharged state (condition reading less than 12.2 volts), have it recharged by your Volvo dealer or local automotive electrician, as the charge rate is higher and constant supervision during charging is necessary.

4 Battery - removal and refitting

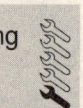

Note: *If a radio/cassette unit with built-in security code is fitted, refer to "Radio/cassette unit anti-theft system precaution".*

Removal

1 Disconnect the battery negative (earth) lead **(see illustration)**.
2 Disconnect the battery positive leads. These may be protected by a plastic cover. Do not allow the spanner to bridge the positive and negative terminals.
3 Release the battery hold-down clamps. Lift out the battery. Keep it upright and be careful not to drop it - it is heavy.

Refitting

4 Commence refitting by placing the battery in its tray, making sure it is the right way round. Secure it with the hold-down clamp.
5 Clean the battery terminals if necessary, then reconnect them. Connect the positive lead first, and the negative lead last.

4.1 Battery, showing position (+) and negative (-) terminals

5 Charging system - testing

Note: *Refer to the warnings given in "Safety First!" and in Section 1 of this Chapter before starting work.*

1 If the ignition warning light fails to illuminate when the ignition is switched on, first check the alternator wiring connections for security. If satisfactory, check that the warning light bulb has not blown and that the bulbholder is secure in its location in the instrument panel. If the light still fails to illuminate, check the continuity of the warning light feed wire from the alternator to the bulbholder. If all is satisfactory, the alternator is at fault and should be renewed or taken to an auto-electrician for testing and repair.

2 If the ignition warning light illuminates when the engine is running, stop the engine and check that the drivebelt is correctly tensioned (see Chapter 1) and that the alternator connections are secure. If all is so far satisfactory, have the alternator checked by an auto- electrician.

3 If the alternator output is suspect even though the warning light functions correctly, the regulated voltage may be checked as follows.

4 Connect a voltmeter across the battery terminals and start the engine.

5 Increase the engine speed until the voltmeter reading remains steady; the reading should be approximately 12 to 13 volts, and no more than 14 volts.

6 Switch on as many electrical accessories (eg, the headlights, heated rear window, heater blower) as possible and check that the alternator maintains the regulated voltage at around 13 to 14 volts.

7 If the regulated voltage is not as stated, the fault may be due to worn brushes, weak brush springs, a faulty voltage regulator, a faulty diode, a severed phase winding or worn or damaged slip rings. The alternator should be renewed or taken to an auto-electrician for testing and repair.

6 Alternator drivebelt - removal, refitting and tensioning

Refer to the procedure given for the auxiliary drivebelts in Chapter 1.

7 Alternator - removal and refitting

Removal

1 Disconnect the battery negative lead.
2 Slacken the alternator drivebelt(s) and slip them off the pulley (Refer to Chapter 1).
3 Disconnect the electrical wiring from the rear of the alternator - this may be a multi-plug or separate screw terminals. Make notes for reconnection if necessary **(see illustration)**.
4 Support the alternator. Remove the pivot and adjusting strap nuts, bolts and washers, noting the fitted positions of the washers. Note also that on some installations a drivebelt guard is fitted over the top of the alternator **(see illustration)**. Lift out the alternator. Do not drop it, it is fragile.

Refitting

5 Refit by reversing the removal operations. Tension the drivebelt(s) (Chapter 1) before reconnecting the battery.

8 Alternator - testing and overhaul

If the alternator is thought to be suspect, it should be removed from the vehicle and taken to an auto-electrician for testing. Most auto-electricians will be able to supply and fit brushes at a reasonable cost. However, check on the cost of repairs before proceeding as it may prove more economical to obtain a new or exchange alternator.

9 Starting system - testing

Note: *Refer to the warnings given in "Safety First!" and in Section 1 of this Chapter before starting work.*

1 If the starter motor fails to operate when the ignition key is turned to the appropriate position, the following possible causes may be to blame:
 a) The battery is faulty.
 b) The electrical connections between the switch, solenoid, battery and starter motor are somewhere failing to pass the necessary current from the battery through the starter to earth.
 c) The solenoid is faulty.
 d) The starter motor is mechanically or electrically defective.

2 To check the battery, switch on the headlights. If they dim after a few seconds, this indicates that the battery is discharged - recharge (see Section 3) or renew the battery. If the headlights glow brightly, operate the ignition switch and observe the lights. If they dim, then this indicates that current is reaching the starter motor, therefore the fault must lie in the starter motor. If the lights continue to glow brightly (and no clicking sound can be heard from the starter motor solenoid), this indicates that there is a fault in the circuit or solenoid - see following paragraphs. If the starter motor turns slowly when operated, but the battery is in good condition, then this shows that either the starter motor is faulty, or there is considerable resistance in the circuit.

3 If a fault in the circuit is suspected, disconnect the battery leads (including the earth connection to the body), the starter/solenoid wiring and the engine/transmission earth strap. Thoroughly clean the connections, and reconnect the leads and wiring, then use a voltmeter or test lamp to check that full battery voltage is available at the battery positive lead connection to the solenoid, and that the earth is sound. Smear petroleum jelly around the battery terminals to prevent corrosion - corroded connections are amongst the most frequent causes of electrical system faults.

4 If the battery and all connections are in good condition, check the circuit by disconnecting the wire from the solenoid blade terminal. Connect a voltmeter or test lamp between the wire and a good earth (such as the battery negative terminal), and check that the wire is live when the ignition switch is turned to the "start" position. If it is, then the circuit is sound - if not, the circuit wiring can be checked as described in Chapter 12.

5 The solenoid contacts can be checked by connecting a voltmeter or test lamp between the battery positive feed connection on the starter side of the solenoid, and earth. When the ignition switch is turned to the "start"

7.3 Electrical connections at the rear of the alternator

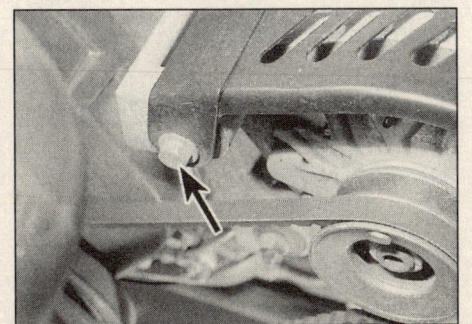

7.4 Alternator pivot and belt guard retaining bolt (arrowed)

5A•4 Starting and charging systems

10.3 Starter solenoid connections

10.4 Starter motor securing bolts

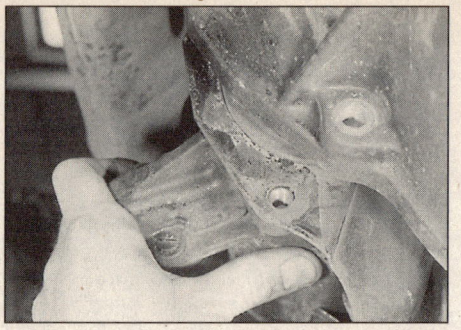

10.5 Removing a starter motor and adapter plate

position, there should be a reading or lighted bulb, as applicable. If there is no reading or lighted bulb, the solenoid is faulty and should be renewed.
6 If the circuit and solenoid are proved sound, the fault must lie in the starter motor. In this event, it may be possible to have the starter motor overhauled by a specialist, but check on the cost of spares before proceeding, as it may prove more economical to obtain a new or exchange motor.

10 Starter motor - removal and refitting

Removal

1 On some models, access to the starter motor is easier from below. Raise the front of the vehicle on ramps if necessary, and remove the undertray.
2 Disconnect the battery negative lead.
3 Disconnect the wires from the starter motor solenoid. Make notes or identifying marks if necessary **(see illustration)**.
4 Support the starter motor and remove its securing bolts. If a tail bracket is fitted, unbolt it first **(see illustration)**.
5 Remove the starter motor. When fitted, recover the adapter plate **(see illustration)**.

Refitting

6 Refit by reversing the removal operations.

11 Starter motor - testing and overhaul

If the starter motor is thought to be suspect, it should be removed from the vehicle and taken to an auto-electrician for testing. Most auto-electricians will be able to supply and fit brushes at a reasonable cost. However, check on the cost of repairs before proceeding as it may prove more economical to obtain a new or exchange motor.

12 Oil pressure warning light switch - removal and refitting

Removal

1 The oil pressure switch is located on the right-hand side of the cylinder block. Depending on model and equipment, access may be easier from below.
2 Disconnect the electrical lead from the switch. Wipe clean around the switch, unscrew it from the block and remove it. Recover the sealing washer (if fitted).

Refitting

3 Refit by reversing the removal operations. Put a smear of sealant on the switch threads and renew the sealing washer if necessary.
4 Run the engine and check for correct operation of the oil pressure warning light. Inspect the switch to see that there are no leaks.

Chapter 5 Part B:
Ignition system

Contents

Distributor - removal and refitting 5
Distributor, rotor arm and HT lead check .... See Chapter 1
Ignition HT coil - removal and refitting 4
Ignition system - general information 1
Ignition system - testing 2
Ignition system electronic control module - removal and refitting 8
Ignition system power stage - removal and refitting 7
Ignition system sensors - removal and refitting 6
Ignition timing - checking 9
On-board diagnostic system - general information and operation ... 3
Spark plug renewal .... See Chapter 1

Degrees of difficulty

Easy, suitable for novice with little experience	Fairly easy, suitable for beginner with some experience	Fairly difficult, suitable for competent DIY mechanic	Difficult, suitable for experienced DIY mechanic	Very difficult, suitable for expert DIY or professional

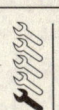

Specifications

General
Application:
  All engines except B230F .... Bosch EZ 116 K
  B230F engines .... Bosch EZ 116 K or Bendix REX-I
Firing order .... 1-3-4-2 (No. 1 cylinder at front of engine)

Spark plugs
Type .... See Chapter 1 Specifications

Ignition timing*
B200F .... 12° BTDC @ 775 ± 50 rpm
B200FT .... 12° BTDC @ 775 ± 50 rpm
B230F:
  With EZ 116 K system .... 12° BTDC @ 775 ± 50 rpm
  With REX-I system .... 10° BTDC @ 775 ± 50 rpm
B230FB .... 12° BTDC @ 775 ± 50 rpm
B230FD .... 12° BTDC @ 775 ± 50 rpm
B230FT .... 12° BTDC @ 750 ± 50 rpm
B230FK .... 12° BTDC @ 750 ± 50 rpm

*Values given are for checking purposes only, no adjustment is possible

Ignition coil
EZ 116 K system:
  Primary resistance .... 0.6 to 0.8 Ω
  Secondary resistance .... 6900 to 8500 Ω
REX-I system:
  Primary resistance .... 0.35 to 0.65 Ω
  Secondary resistance .... 4000 to 6000 Ω

1 Ignition system - general information

The ignition system is responsible for igniting the compressed fuel/air charge in each cylinder in turn at precisely the right moment for the prevailing engine speed and load. This is achieved by using a programmed electronic ignition system, which utilises computer technology and electro-magnetic circuitry to simulate the main functions of a conventional ignition distributor.

Two systems may be encountered on 940 models covered by this manual. The most common is the Bosch EZ 116 K system, although the alternative Bendix REX-I system is fitted to models for certain territories. The operation of both systems is virtually identical.

A series of holes drilled in the periphery of the engine flywheel, and an RPM sensor whose inductive head runs just above the drilled flywheel periphery, replace the operation of the contact breaker points in a conventional system. As the crankshaft rotates, the land (or "teeth") between the drilled holes in the flywheel pass the RPM sensor, which transmits a pulse to the ignition control module every time a tooth passes it. On the EZ 116 K system there is one missing hole in the flywheel periphery, which allows the land (or tooth) at that point to be twice as wide as the others. The control module recognises the absence of a pulse from the RPM sensor at this point, and uses it to establish the TDC position for Nos 1 and 4 pistons. On the REX-I system there are missing teeth at two points on the flywheel, 180° apart, allowing the TDC position for both pairs of pistons to be established. The time interval between pulses and the location of the missing pulse(s) allow the control module to accurately determine crankshaft speed and position.

Information on engine load is supplied to the ignition control module from the fuel injection system control unit. The load being determined by the quantity of air being drawn into the engine through the air mass meter. From this constantly-changing data, the ignition control module selects a particular ignition advance setting from a map of ignition characteristics stored in its memory. The basic setting can be further advanced or retarded, according to information sent to the control module from the coolant temperature sensor, knock sensor and the throttle position switch.

With the firing point established, the control module sends a signal to the power stage, which is an electronic switch controlling the current to the ignition coil primary windings (an electronic version of the contact breaker points in a conventional system). On receipt of the signal from the control module, the power stage interrupts the primary current to the ignition coil which induces a high-tension voltage in the coil secondary windings. This HT voltage is passed to the distributor and then on to the spark plugs via the distributor rotor arm and HT leads in the conventional manner. The cycle is then repeated many times a second for each cylinder in turn.

In the event of a fault in the system due to loss of a signal from one of the sensors, the ignition control module reverts to an emergency ("limp-home") program. This will allow the car to be driven, although engine operation and performance will be limited.

To facilitate fault diagnosis, both the EZ 116 K and REX-I systems are provided with an on-board diagnostic facility which displays detected faults in the system as a series of three-digit fault codes on a flashing LED.

In addition to the above operations, many of the ignition system components have a second function in the control and operation of the fuel injection system. Further details will be found in Part A of Chapter 4.

2 Ignition system - testing

Warning: Voltages produced by an electronic ignition system are considerably higher than those produced by conventional ignition systems. Extreme care must be taken when working on the system if the ignition is switched on. Persons with surgically-implanted cardiac pacemaker devices should keep well clear of the ignition circuits, components and test equipment.

General

1 The components of the electronic ignition system are normally very reliable; most faults are far more likely to be due to loose or dirty connections, or to "tracking" of HT voltage due to dirt, dampness or damaged insulation, than to the failure of any of the system's components. **Always** check all wiring thoroughly before condemning an electrical component, and work methodically to eliminate all other possibilities before deciding that a particular component is faulty.

2 The old practice of checking for a spark by holding the live end of an HT lead a short distance away from the engine is **not** recommended; not only is there a high risk of a powerful electric shock, but the HT coil, control module or power stage may be damaged. Similarly, **never** try to "diagnose" misfires by pulling off one HT lead at a time.

3 The following tests should be carried out when an obvious fault such as non-starting or a clearly detectable misfire exists. Some faults, however, are more obscure and are often disguised by the fact that the fuel and ignition system control modules will adopt an emergency program ("limp-home") mode to maintain as much driveability as possible. Faults of this nature usually appear in the form of excessive fuel consumption, poor idling characteristics, lack of performance, knocking or "pinking" noises from the engine under certain conditions, or a combination of these conditions. Where problems such as this are experienced, the on-board diagnostic facility described in Section 3 should be used to isolate the problem.

Engine will not start

4 If the engine either will not turn over at all, or only turns very slowly, check the battery and starter motor. Connect a voltmeter across the battery terminals (meter positive probe to battery positive terminal) then note the voltage reading obtained while turning the engine over on the starter for (no more than) ten seconds. If the reading obtained is less than approximately 9.5 volts, first check the battery, starter motor and charging system as described in Part A of this Chapter.

5 If the engine turns over at normal speed but will not start, check the HT circuit by connecting a timing light (following its manufacturer's instructions) and turning the engine over on the starter motor; if the light flashes, voltage is reaching the spark plugs, so these should be checked first. If the light does not flash, check the HT leads themselves, followed by the distributor cap, carbon brush and rotor arm, using the information given in Chapter 1.

6 If there is a spark, check the fuel system for faults, referring to the relevant part of Chapter 4 for further information.

7 If there is still no spark, check the voltage at the ignition coil "+" terminal; it should be the same as battery voltage (ie, at least 11.7 volts). If the voltage at the coil is more than 1 volt less than that at the battery, check the condition of all the circuit wiring, referring to the wiring diagrams at the end of this manual.

8 If the feed to the coil is sound, check the condition of the coil, if possible, by substitution with a known good unit. If the fault persists the problem lies elsewhere; if the fault is now cleared, a new coil is the obvious cure. However, check carefully the condition of the LT connections themselves before doing so, to ensure that the fault is not due to dirty or poorly-fastened connectors.

9 If the coil is in good condition, the fault is probably within the power stage, one of the system sensors, or the control module and its related components (as applicable). In this case a fault code should be logged in the diagnostic unit which should help to isolate the component concerned (see Section 3).

Engine misfires

10 An irregular misfire suggests either a loose connection or intermittent fault on the primary circuit, or an HT fault on the coil side of the rotor arm.

11 With the ignition switched off, check carefully through the system, ensuring that all connections are clean and securely fastened. If the equipment is available, check the LT circuit as described above.

12 Check that the ignition coil, the distributor cap and the HT leads are clean and dry. Check the leads themselves and the spark plugs (by substitution if necessary), then check the distributor cap, carbon brush and rotor arm as described in Chapter 1.

13 Regular misfiring is almost certainly due to a fault in the distributor cap, HT leads or spark plugs. Use a timing light (paragraph 5 above) to check whether HT voltage is present at all leads.

14 If HT voltage is not present on any particular lead, the fault will be in that lead, or in the distributor cap. If HT is present on all leads, the fault will be in the spark plugs; check and renew them if there is any doubt about their condition.

15 If no HT is present, check the ignition coil; its secondary windings may be breaking down under load.

16 Any further checking of the system components should be carried out by a Volvo dealer.

3 On-board diagnostic system - general information and operation

Note: *Both the ignition and fuel systems must ideally be treated as one inter-related engine management system. Although the contents of this section is mainly concerned with the ignition side of the system, many of the components perform dual functions and some of the following procedures of necessity relate to the fuel system.*

Ignition system

General information

1 The fuel and ignition systems on all engines covered by this manual incorporate an on-board diagnostic system to facilitate fault finding and system testing. The diagnostic system works in conjunction with the fuel and ignition system control modules to continually monitor the system components when the car is being driven. Should a fault occur, the relevant control module sends a series of signals (or fault codes) to the diagnostic unit located in the engine compartment. The diagnostic unit then stores the fault codes for subsequent read-out. In addition, the diagnostic unit can be used to check the integrity of the signals received from the various fuel/ignition system sensors, and to manually operate many of the fuel system related components under test conditions.

2 If driveability problems have been experienced and engine performance is suspect, the on-board diagnostic system can be used to pinpoint any problem areas without the use of special test equipment. Once this has been done, further tests may often be necessary to determine the exact nature of the fault; ie, whether a component itself has failed, or whether it is a wiring or other inter-related problem. Apart from checking visually the wiring and connections, these additional tests will require the use of Volvo test equipment and should be entrusted to a dealer.

Preliminary checks

Note: *When carrying out these checks to trace a fault, remember that if the fault has appeared only a short time after any part of the vehicle has been serviced or overhauled, the first place to check is where that work was carried out, however unrelated it may appear, to ensure that no carelessly-refitted components are causing the problem.*

If you are tracing the cause of a "partial" engine fault, such as lack of performance, in addition to the checks outlined below, check the valve clearances and compression pressures. Check also that the fuel filter and air cleaner element have been renewed at the recommended intervals. Refer to Chapters 1, 2 or 4 for details of these procedures.

3 Open the bonnet and check the condition of the battery connections - remake the connections or renew the leads if a fault is found (see Section 1 in Part A of this Chapter before disconnecting the battery). Use the same techniques to ensure that all earth points in the engine compartment provide good electrical contact through clean, metal-to-metal joints, and that all are securely fastened.

4 Next work methodically around the engine compartment, checking all visible wiring, and the connections between sections of the wiring loom. What you are looking for at this stage is wiring that is obviously damaged by chafing against sharp edges, or against moving suspension/transmission components and/or the accessory drivebelt(s), by being trapped or crushed between carelessly-refitted components, or melted by being forced into contact with hot engine castings, coolant pipes, etc. In almost all cases, damage of this sort is caused in the first instance by incorrect routing on reassembly after previous work has been carried out (see the note at the beginning of this sub-Section).

5 Obviously wires can break or short together inside the insulation so that no visible evidence betrays the fault, but this usually only occurs where the wiring loom has been incorrectly routed so that it is stretched taut or kinked sharply; either of these conditions should be obvious on even a casual inspection. If this is thought to have happened and the fault proves elusive, the suspect section of wiring should be checked very carefully during the more detailed checks which follow.

6 Depending on the extent of the problem, damaged wiring may be repaired by rejoining the break or splicing-in a new length of wire, using solder to ensure a good connection, and remaking the insulation with adhesive insulating tape or heat-shrink tubing, as desired. If the damage is extensive, given the implications for the vehicle's future reliability, the best long-term answer may well be to renew that entire section of the loom, however expensive this may appear.

7 When the actual damage has been repaired, ensure that the wiring loom is re-routed correctly, so that it is clear of other components, is not stretched or kinked, and is secured out of harm's way using the plastic clips, guides and ties provided.

8 Check all electrical connectors, ensuring that they are clean, securely fastened, and that each is locked by its plastic tabs or wire clip, as appropriate. If any connector shows external signs of corrosion (accumulations of white or green deposits, or streaks of "rust"), or if any is thought to be dirty, it must be unplugged and cleaned using electrical contact cleaner. If the connector pins are severely corroded, the connector must be renewed; note that this may mean the renewal of that entire section of the loom.

9 If the cleaner completely removes the corrosion to leave the connector in a satisfactory condition, it would be wise to pack the connector with a suitable material which will exclude dirt and moisture, and prevent the corrosion from occurring again; a Volvo dealer may be able to recommend a suitable product.

10 Working methodically around the engine compartment, check carefully that all vacuum hoses and pipes are securely fastened and correctly routed, with no signs of cracks, splits or deterioration to cause air leaks, or of hoses that are trapped, kinked, or bent sharply enough to restrict air flow. Check with particular care at all connections and sharp bends, and renew any damaged or deformed lengths of hose.

11 Working from the fuel tank, via the filter, to the fuel rail (and including the feed and return), check the fuel lines, and renew any that are found to be leaking, trapped or kinked.

12 Check that the accelerator cable is correctly secured and adjusted; renew the cable if there is any doubt about its condition, or if it appears to be stiff or jerky in operation. Refer to Chapter 4 for further information, if required.

13 Unclip the air cleaner cover, and check that the air filter is not clogged or soaked. (A clogged air filter will obstruct the inlet air flow, causing a noticeable effect on engine performance. Renew the filter if necessary; refer to the relevant Sections of Chapter 1 for further information, if required.

14 Start the engine and allow it to idle.

⚠ **Warning:** *Working in the engine compartment while the engine is running requires great care if the risk of personal injury is to be avoided; among the dangers are burns from contact with hot components, or contact with moving components such as the radiator cooling fan or the auxiliary drivebelt. Refer to "Safety first!" at the front of this manual before starting, and ensure your hands, and long hair or loose clothing, are kept clear of hot or moving components at all times.*

15 Working from the air inlet, via the air cleaner assembly and the mass air flow sensor to the throttle housing and inlet manifold (and including the various vacuum hoses and pipes connected to these), check for air leaks. Usually, these will be revealed by sucking or hissing noises, but minor leaks may be traced by spraying a solution of soapy water on to the suspect joint; if a leak exists, it will be shown by the change in engine note and the accompanying air bubbles (or sucking-in of the liquid, depending on the pressure difference at that point). If a leak is found at any point, tighten the fastening clamp and/or renew the faulty components, as applicable.

16 Similarly, work from the cylinder head, via the manifold to the tailpipe, to check that the exhaust system is free from leaks. The simplest way of doing this, if the vehicle can be raised and supported safely and with complete security while the check is made, is to temporarily block the tailpipe while listening for the sound of escaping exhaust gases; any leak should be evident. If a leak is found at any point, tighten the fastening clamp bolts and/or nuts, renew the gasket, and/or renew the faulty section of the system, as necessary, to seal the leak.

17 It is possible to make a further check of the electrical connections by wiggling each electrical connector of the system in turn as the engine is idling; a faulty connector will be immediately evident from the engine's response as contact is broken and remade. A faulty connector should be renewed to ensure that the future reliability of the system; note that this may mean the renewal of that entire section of the loom.

5B•4 Ignition system

3.20 On-board diagnostic unit location in engine compartment

Ignition system fault codes

Code	Meaning	Symptoms
1-1-1	No fault detected	None
1-4-2	Control module fault	None
1-4-3	Knock sensor signal absent or faulty	Poor acceleration, high fuel consumption, lack of power
1-4-4	Load signal from fuel injection system absent	Sluggish engine
1-5-4*	EGR system flow too high	Uneven idling
2-1-4	RPM sensor signal absent intermittently	Engine will not start, runs roughly, or overheats
2-2-4	Coolant temperature sensor signal absent or faulty	None
2-3-4	Throttle position switch signal in idling position absent or faulty	None
2-4-1*	EGR system flow too low	Uneven idling
4-1-3*	EGR temperature sensor signal absent or faulty	Uneven idling

* Only applicable to later engines with electronically controlled exhaust gas recirculation system (see Chapter 4, Part B).

18 Switch off the engine. If the fault is not yet identified, the next step is to check the fault code read out at the diagnostic unit as described below.

Fault code read-out

19 As noted in the general comments at the beginning of this Section, the preliminary checks outlined above should eliminate the majority of faults from the ignition (or fuel) system. If the fault has not yet been identified, the next step is to check whether a fault code has been logged in the diagnostic unit and if so, to interpret the meaning of the code.
20 Firstly, locate the diagnostic unit which is situated in the engine compartment either just in front of, or just to the rear of, the left-hand suspension strut tower (see illustration).
21 With the ignition switched off, lift up the diagnostic unit lid and unclip the flylead from the holder on the side of the unit.
22 Note that there are six numbered sockets on the face of the unit. Only two of these are used; socket 2 for fuel system checks and socket 6 for ignition system checks.
23 Have a paper and pen ready to copy down the fault codes as they are displayed - there may be as many as three. The three-digit codes will be displayed as a series of blinks of the red LED (located on the top face of the unit next to the test button) with a slight pause between each digit.
24 Insert the flylead into position 6 of the diagnostic unit then switch on the ignition. Press the test button on top of the unit once, for about one second, then release it and wait for the LED to flash (see illustration). As the LED flashes, copy down the fault codes. If more than one code is displayed, copy them all until the first is displayed again, then switch off the ignition.
25 If code 1-1-1 is obtained, this indicates that there are no ignition fault codes stored in the diagnostic unit. In this case, move the flylead to position 2 in the unit, switch on the ignition and press the test button once again as before. Record any fault codes now displayed which will be applicable to the fuel injection side of the system. Switch off the ignition. If code 1-1-1 is once again displayed, this indicates that there are no fuel related fault codes stored either, and the system is operating correctly.

26 Given above are the possible ignition system fault codes and, where applicable, the symptoms associated with each fault. A description of the fuel system fault codes is given in Chapter 4.
27 Once all the fault codes have been recorded (for both the ignition and fuel systems, they should be deleted from the diagnostic unit. To do this, insert the flylead in position 2 of the diagnostic unit. Switch on the ignition and press the test button for approximately five seconds. When the LED lights, press the test button for a further five seconds. Check that all the fuel system fault codes have been deleted by pressing the test button for one second, code 1-1-1 should appear. If a code other than 1-1-1 appears, record the code then repeat the deleting procedure. Switch off the ignition. Now move the flylead to position 6, switch on the ignition and delete the ignition system fault codes in the same way. When all the codes have been deleted, switch off the ignition, locate the flylead in its holder and close the diagnostic unit lid.
28 Once the location of a fault has been established from the fault code read-out, investigations can be concentrated in that area. Go through the checks outlined earlier in this section in case anything was missed the first time. As mentioned previously, further detailed checking of the system components will require the use of Volvo test equipment. Therefore the only alternatives possible at this time are the substitution of a suspect component with a known good unit, or entrusting further work to a Volvo dealer. If a substitute unit can be obtained (or borrowed), removal and refitting procedures are given in the following Sections of this Chapter.

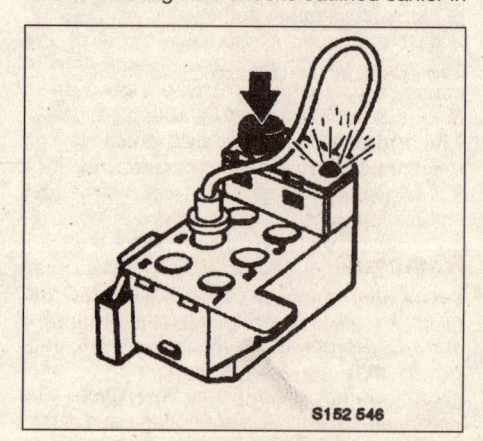

4 Ignition HT coil - removal and refitting

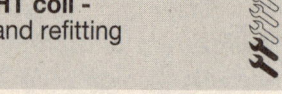

Removal

1 Disconnect the battery negative terminal.
2 Disconnect the wires from the coil, identifying their locations for refitting. Release the clamp bracket, or undo the retaining screws, according to coil type (see illustration). Slide the coil out of the bracket (where applicable) and remove it from the engine compartment.
3 Inspect the coil visually for cracks, leakage of insulating oil or other obvious damage. Renew it if such damage is evident.

Refitting

4 Refit by reversing the removal operations.

3.24 Using the diagnostic unit to display fault codes

4.2 Ignition coil location and connections on the EZ 116 K system

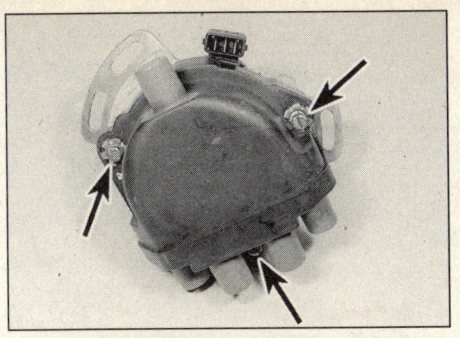

Ignition system 5B•5

5.2 Distributor cap securing screws (arrowed) - distributor removed

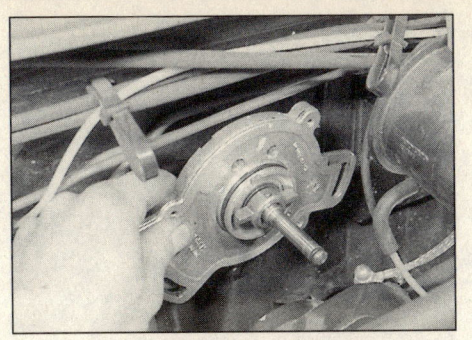

5.8 Removing the distributor

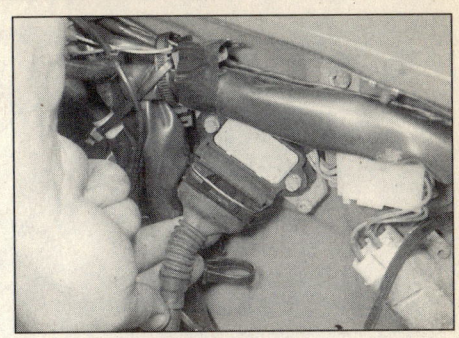

7.1 Ignition coil power stage on the EZ 116 K system

5 Distributor - removal and refitting

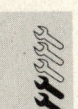

Removal

1 Identify the spark plug leads and disconnect them from the cap.
2 Undo the three screws which secure the distributor cap. Access is restricted. The screws are captive, so do not attempt to remove them from the cap **(see illustration)**.
3 Lift off the distributor cap with the coil HT lead still attached.
4 Pull off the rotor arm and, where fitted, remove the dust shield.
5 Make alignment marks between the distributor flange and the cylinder head.
6 Remove the two bolts which secure the distributor.
7 Disconnect the LT connector from the distributor (when applicable).
8 Remove the distributor from the cylinder head **(see illustration)**.
9 Renew the distributor O-rings if necessary.

Refitting

10 When refitting, offer the distributor to the head, observing the alignment marks, and turn the shaft to align the drive dogs with the slots in the camshaft. The drive is offset, so there is no possibility of incorrect fitting.
11 The remainder of refitting is a reversal of the removal procedure.

6 Ignition system sensors - removal and refitting

Flywheel (RPM) sensor

Removal

1 Disconnect the multi-plug from the RPM sensor located at the rear of the engine on the transmission bellhousing.
2 Remove the sensor retaining Allen screw.
3 Withdraw the sensor from its location and remove it.

Refitting

4 Refit by reversing the removal operations.

Knock sensor

Removal

5 Disconnect the knock sensor multi-plug.
6 Remove the sensor bolt and the sensor itself. It is located under the inlet manifold.

Refitting

7 Refit by reversing the removal operations. Apply thread locking compound to the bolt and tighten it securely.

Coolant temperature sensor

8 Refer to Chapter 3, Section 7.

7 Ignition system power stage - removal and refitting

Note: *On the EZ 116 K ignition system, the power stage is located at the front of the engine compartment on the left-hand inner wing panel. On the REX-I system the power stage is an integral part of the ignition coil and cannot be removed separately.*

Removal

Disconnect the multi-plug. Remove the two screws which secure the power stage to its heat sink and remove it **(see illustration)**.

Refitting

Refit by reversing the removal operations. Ensure that there is good contact between the power stage and the heat sink; use a thermally conductive paste if available.

8 Ignition system electronic control module - removal and refitting

Removal

1 The control module is located below the facia on the left-hand side **(see illustration)**.
2 Remove the trim from below the steering column if necessary for access.
3 Remove the two (or four) module screws and withdraw the unit from its location.
4 Disconnect the multi-plug and remove the control unit.

Refitting

5 Refit by reversing the removal operations.

9 Ignition timing - checking

Note: *The ignition timing cannot be adjusted, but it can be checked if wished.*

1 Bring the engine to operating temperature with the air conditioning switched off. With the engine stopped, connect a timing light (stroboscope) and a tachometer as instructed by the manufacturers.
2 Highlight the notch on the crankshaft pulley and the desired marks on the timing scale with white paint or typist's correction fluid. (See Specifications for the desired values).
3 Run the engine at the specified idle speed and shine the timing light on the timing scale.

⚠️ **Warning:** *Do not get electrical leads, clothing, long hair etc, caught in the drivebelts or the fan. The pulley notch will appear stationary and (if the timing is correct) in alignment with the appropriate mark on the timing scale.*

4 Stop the engine, disconnect the test gear and remake the original electrical connections.
5 If the timing is incorrect, there is likely to be a fault in the RPM sensor, the ignition system control module or associated wiring. Any faults in these areas are likely to be accompanied by a fault code which will be logged in the diagnostic unit (see Section 3).

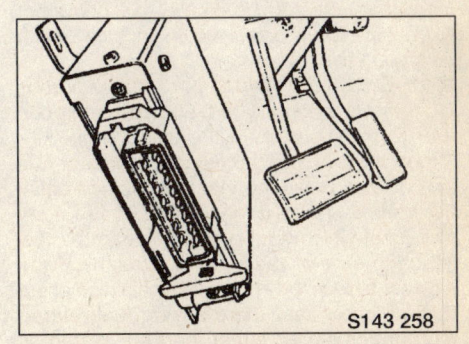

8.1 Ignition system control module location

Chapter 6
Clutch

Contents

Clutch assembly - removal, inspection and refitting 9
Clutch cable - removal and refitting 2
Clutch fluid level check . . . . .See "Weekly checks"
Clutch hydraulic check/cable adjustment . . . . .See Chapter 1
Clutch hydraulic system - bleeding 8
Clutch master cylinder - overhaul 5
Clutch master cylinder - removal and refitting 4
Clutch pedal - removal and refitting 3
Clutch release bearing - removal and refitting 10
Clutch slave cylinder - overhaul 7
Clutch slave cylinder - removal and refitting 6
General information 1

Degrees of difficulty

Easy, suitable for novice with little experience | **Fairly easy,** suitable for beginner with some experience | **Fairly difficult,** suitable for competent DIY mechanic | **Difficult,** suitable for experienced DIY mechanic | **Very difficult,** suitable for expert DIY or professional

Specifications

General
Actuation . . . . Hydraulic or cable, according to model and market

Pressure plate
Warp limit . . . . 0.2 mm

Torque wrench settings   Nm
Pressure plate retaining bolts 25

1 General information

A single dry plate diaphragm spring clutch is fitted. Operation may be hydraulic or mechanical, according to model and market.

The main components of the clutch are the pressure plate, the driven plate (sometimes called the friction plate or disc) and the release bearing. The pressure plate is bolted to the flywheel, with the driven plate sandwiched between them. The centre of the driven plate carries female splines which mate with the splines on the transmission input shaft. The release bearing is attached to the release fork and acts on the diaphragm spring fingers of the pressure plate.

When the engine is running and the clutch pedal is released, the diaphragm spring clamps the pressure plate, driven plate and flywheel firmly together. Drive is transmitted through the friction surfaces of the flywheel and pressure plate to the linings of the driven plate and thus to the transmission input shaft.

When the clutch pedal is depressed, the pedal movement is transmitted (hydraulically or by cable) to the release fork. The fork moves the bearing to press on the diaphragm spring fingers. Spring pressure on the pressure plate is relieved, and the flywheel and pressure plate spin without moving the driven plate. As the pedal is released, spring pressure is restored and the drive is gradually taken up.

The clutch hydraulic system consists of a master cylinder, a slave cylinder and the associated pipes and hoses. The fluid reservoir is shared with the brake master cylinder.

Wear in the driven plate linings is compensated for automatically by the hydraulic system components. The cable needs periodic adjustment to compensate for wear and stretch.

2 Clutch cable - removal and refitting

Removal

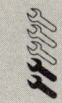

1 At the transmission end, slacken the outer cable locknut and threaded adjuster as far as possible. Disconnect the return spring (if fitted) from the release fork and unhook the cable inner. If a rubber buffer is fitted at the end of the inner, note which way round it goes **(see illustration)**.
2 Remove the trim panel below the steering column for access to the pedals. Remove the retainer which secures the cable inner to the pedal.
3 Pull the cable into the engine bay and remove it.

Refitting

4 Refit by reversing the removal operations, making sure the cable is correctly routed. Adjust the cable as described in Chapter 1 on completion.

3 Clutch pedal - removal and refitting

Removal

1 Disconnect the battery negative lead.
2 Remove the steering column (Chapter 10).
3 Disconnect the brake pedal from the servo pushrod by removing the clevis pin.
4 Similarly disconnect the clutch pedal from the master cylinder pushrod, or (when applicable) disconnect the clutch cable.
5 Remove the three bolts which secure the top of the pedal box to the scuttle.
6 Remove the six nuts which secure the pedal box to the bulkhead. (These nuts also secure the clutch master cylinder and the brake servo.)
7 Disconnect the stop-light switch. Also disconnect electrical and vacuum/pressure feeds from turbo boost and cruise control switches, or the ignition control unit (as applicable).

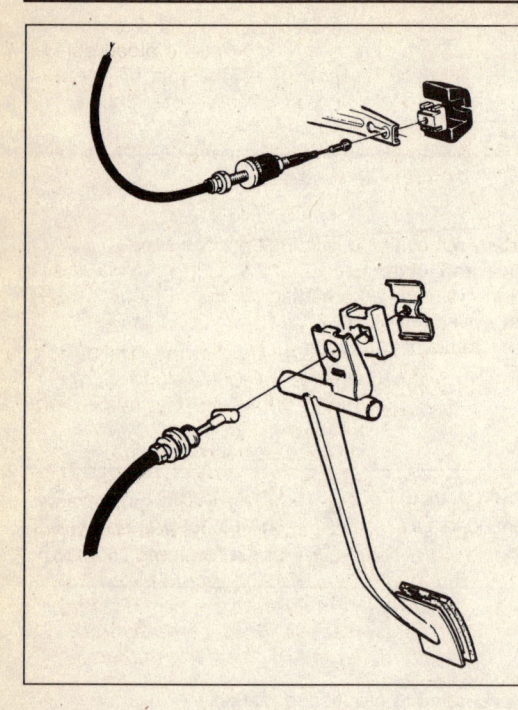

6•2 Clutch

2.1 Clutch cable attachment details

4.4 Clutch pedal clevis pin (arrowed)

8 Remove the pedal box and pedals from the vehicle. Note how the brake pedal return spring bears against the scuttle.
9 Disengage the clutch pedal return spring. Remove the pivot nut and bolt, remove the clutch pedal and recover the bushes.

Refitting
10 Refit by reversing the removal operations. Apply grease to the pedal bushes and to the pivot bolt.

4 Clutch master cylinder - removal and refitting

⚠️ **Warning: Hydraulic fluid is poisonous; wash off immediately and thoroughly in the case of skin contact, and seek immediate medical advice if any fluid is swallowed or gets into the eyes. Certain types of hydraulic fluid are inflammable, and may ignite when allowed into contact with hot components; when servicing any hydraulic system, it is safest to assume that the fluid IS inflammable, and to take precautions against the risk of fire as though it is petrol that is being handled. Hydraulic fluid is also an effective paint stripper, and will attack plastics; if any is spilt, it should be washed off immediately, using copious quantities of clean water. Finally, it is hygroscopic (it absorbs moisture from the air) - old fluid may be contaminated and unfit for further use. When topping-up or renewing the fluid, always use the recommended type, and ensure that it comes from a freshly-opened sealed container.**

Removal
1 Disconnect the fluid supply hose from the master cylinder. Have ready a container to catch the fluid which will spill.
2 Disconnect the pressure pipe union from the end of the cylinder. Be prepared for further fluid spillage. Cover the open pipe union with a piece of polythene and a rubber band to keep dirt out.
3 Remove the trim panel below the steering column.
4 Remove the clevis pin which secures the clutch pedal to the master cylinder pushrod **(see illustration)**.
5 Remove the two nuts which secure the master cylinder to the bulkhead.
6 Remove the master cylinder, being careful not to drip fluid onto the paintwork.

Refitting
7 Refit by reversing the removal operations, noting the following points:
a) With the pedal released there should be 1.0 mm clearance between the pushrod and the piston. Adjust if necessary by screwing the clevis up or down the pushrod.
b) Bleed the hydraulic system on completion (Section 8).

5 Clutch master cylinder - overhaul

Refer to Section 7. Overhaul of the master cylinder is basically the same, except that there is a washer under the piston retaining circlip, and the piston has two seals **(see illustration)**.

6 Clutch slave cylinder - removal and refitting

Note: Refer to the warning at the beginning of Section 4 before proceeding.

Removal
1 Raise the vehicle on ramps, or drive it over a pit.

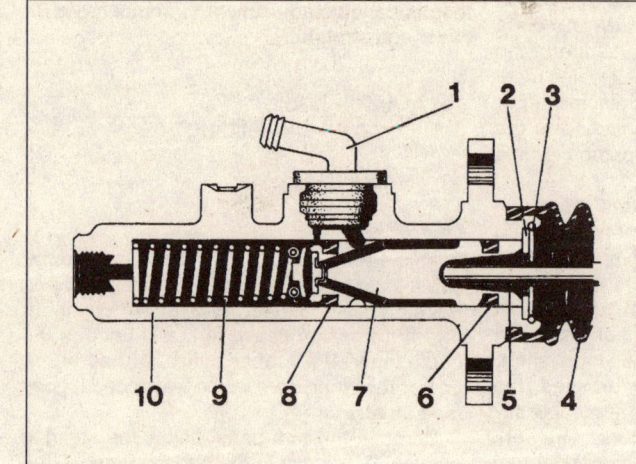

5.1 Sectional view of the clutch master cylinder
1 Fluid inlet
2 Washer
3 Circlip
4 Dust boot
5 Pushrod
6 Outer seal
7 Piston
8 Inner seal
9 Spring
10 Cylinder body

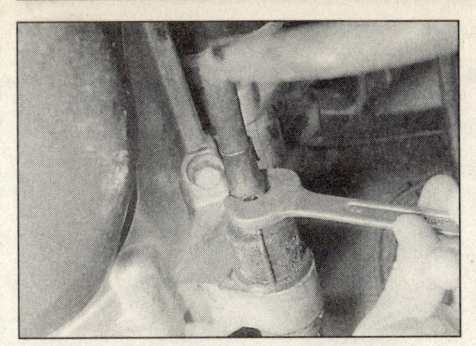

Clutch 6•3

6.2 Undoing the clutch slave cylinder hydraulic union

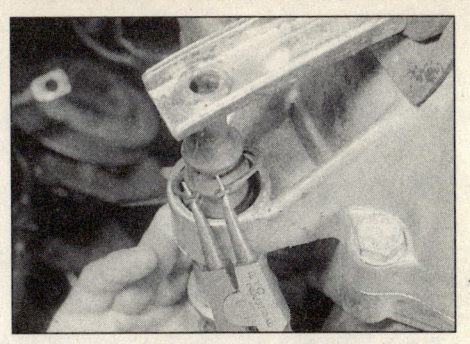

6.3 Removing the slave cylinder circlip

2 Slacken the flexible hose union on the slave cylinder **(see illustration)**.
3 Unbolt the slave cylinder or remove its securing circlip, according to type **(see illustration)**.
4 Withdraw the slave cylinder with pushrod. Unscrew the cylinder from the flexible hose. Plug or cap the open end of the hose to minimise fluid loss. Recover the sealing washer.

Refitting

5 Refit by reversing the removal operations. Check the "set" of the flexible hose after tightening; correct it if necessary by repositioning the hose-to-pipe union in the bracket.
6 Bleed the clutch hydraulic system (refer to Section 8).

7 Clutch slave cylinder - overhaul

Note: *Refer to the warning at the beginning of Section 4 before proceeding.*
1 Empty the fluid out of the cylinder and clean it externally.
2 Remove the dust boot and pushrod **(see illustration)**.
3 Remove the circlip (if fitted) from the mouth of the cylinder.
4 Shake or tap out the piston and spring. If the piston is stuck, carefully blow it out with **low** air pressure (eg from a foot pump).

5 Remove the seal from the piston.
6 Clean the piston and bore with wire wool and methylated spirit. If either is badly rusted or scored, renew the complete cylinder. Otherwise, obtain a repair kit containing a new seal and dust boot.
7 Dip the new seal in clean hydraulic fluid and fit it to the piston, using the fingers only. Make sure it is the right way round.
8 Lubricate the piston and bore with clean hydraulic fluid. Insert the spring and the piston into the bore.
9 When applicable, refit the circlip to the open end.
10 Fit the new dust boot over the pushrod. Place the pushrod in the cup of the piston and seat the dust boot on the cylinder.

8 Clutch hydraulic system - bleeding

Note: *Refer to the warning at the beginning of Section 4 before proceeding.*
1 Top-up the hydraulic fluid reservoir with fresh clean fluid of the specified type (see "Weekly checks").
2 Slacken the bleed screw on the slave cylinder. Fit a length of clear hose over the screw. Place the other end of the hose in a jar containing a small amount of hydraulic fluid.
3 Have an assistant depress the clutch pedal. Tighten the bleed screw when the pedal is depressed. Have the assistant release the pedal, then slacken the bleed screw again.

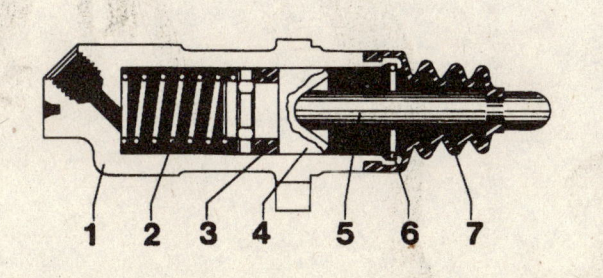

4 Repeat the process until clean fluid, free of air bubbles, emerges from the bleed screw. Tighten the screw at the end of a pedal downstroke and remove the hose and jar.
5 Top-up the hydraulic fluid reservoir.
6 Pressure bleeding equipment may be used if preferred - see Chapter 9.

9 Clutch assembly - removal, inspection and refitting

⚠️ **Warning:** *Dust created by clutch wear and deposited on the clutch components may contain asbestos which is a health hazard. DO NOT blow it out with compressed air or inhale any of it. DO NOT use petrol or petroleum-based solvents to clean off the dust. Brake system cleaner or methylated spirit should be used to flush the dust into a suitable receptacle. After the clutch components are wiped clean with rags, dispose of the contaminated rags and cleaner in a sealed, marked container.*

Removal

1 Remove the engine or transmission, as wished (see Chapter 2B or 7A as applicable):
2 Make alignment marks between the pressure plate and the flywheel.
3 Slacken the pressure plate bolts half a turn at a time until the spring pressure is released. Remove the bolts, the pressure plate and the driven plate **(see illustrations)**. Note which way round the driven plate is fitted.

9.3a Removing the clutch pressure plate . . .

9.3b . . . and the driven plate

7.2 Sectional view of the clutch slave cylinder
1 Cylinder body
2 Spring
3 Seal
4 Piston
5 Pushrod
6 Circlip
7 Dust boot

6•4 Clutch

Inspection

4 Examine the friction surfaces of the flywheel and the pressure plate for scoring or cracks. Light scoring may be ignored. Excessive scoring or cracks can sometimes be machined off the flywheel face - consult a specialist. The pressure plate must be renewed if it is badly scored or warped.

5 Inspect the pressure plate cover and the diaphragm spring for damage, or blue discoloration suggesting overheating. Pay attention to the tips of the spring fingers where the release bearing operates. Renew the pressure plate if in doubt.

6 Renew the driven plate if the friction linings are worn down to, or approaching, the rivets. If the linings are oil-soaked or have a hard black glaze, the source of oil contamination - the crankshaft rear oil seal or transmission input shaft oil seal - must be dealt with before the plate is renewed. Also inspect the driven plate springs, hub and splines.

7 Note that if the driven plate only is renewed, problems may be experienced related to the bedding-in of the driven plate and old pressure plate. It is certainly better practise to renew the driven plate and pressure plate together, if finances permit.

8 Try the fit of the driven plate (whether new or used) on the transmission input shaft splines. It must neither bind nor be slack.

9 Spin the release bearing in the clutch bellhousing and feel for roughness or shake. The bearing should be renewed without question unless it is known to be in perfect condition.

Refitting

10 Commence refitting by cleaning the friction surfaces of the flywheel and pressure plate with a non-greasy solvent, followed by a wipe with a clean cloth. Clean oil or grease off the hands before handling the clutch.

11 Offer the driven plate to the flywheel, making sure it is the right way round. It is probably marked "SCHWUNGRAD" or "FLYWHEEL SIDE".

12 Hold the driven plate in position using a proprietary centering tool and fit the pressure plate over it. Observe the alignment marks if the original plate is being refitted.

9.13 Clutch centering tool in position

13 Fit the pressure plate bolts and tighten them evenly until the driven plate is being gripped but can still be moved. Insert the centering tool, if it is not already in position, and tighten the pressure plate bolts progressively to the specified torque **(see illustration)**.

> **TOOL TIP** *An alternative centering tool can be made from a length of wooden dowel which is a snug fit in the crankshaft spigot bearing. Build up the dowel with masking tape so that it just fits through the driven plate splines.*

14 Remove the centering tool and check visually that the driven plate is central relative to the crankshaft spigot bearing. If the plate is not central, it will be impossible for the transmission input shaft to enter it.

15 Refit the engine or transmission.

10 Clutch release bearing - removal and refitting

Removal

1 Remove the engine or transmission as wished (see Chapter 2B or 7A as applicable).

2 Free the release fork dust boot from the bellhousing.

3 Disconnect the release fork from the pivot ball-stud. There may be a spring clip securing

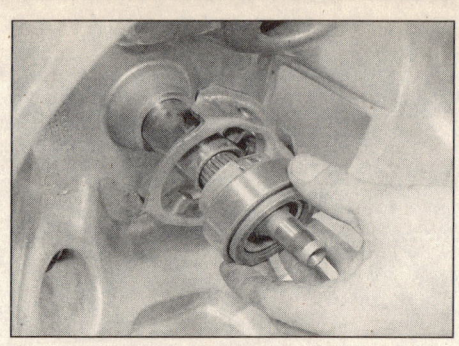

10.4 Removing the release bearing and fork

the fork to the stud, or there may be nothing.

4 Slide the bearing and fork off the guide sleeve and separate them **(see illustration)**.

5 Clean the guide sleeve and smear a little grease on it lightly around the fork pivot and tips too.

Refitting

6 Refit by reversing the removal operations. When the release fork is secured by a spring clip, note that the clip should pass below the groove in the ball-stud **(see illustration)**.

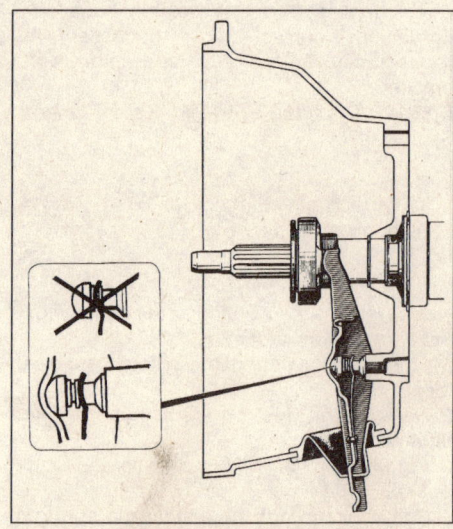

10.6 Correct fitting of release fork clip below ball-stud groove

Chapter 7 Part A:
Manual transmission and overdrive

Contents

Gear lever - removal and refitting 2	Oil seals - renewal 4
Gear lever pullrod - renewal 3	Overdrive unit - general information 8
General information 1	Overdrive unit overhaul - general information 11
Manual transmission - removal and refitting 6	Overdrive unit - removal and refitting 10
Manual transmission oil level check . . . . .See Chapter 1	Overdrive switches - removal and refitting 9
Manual transmission overhaul - general information 7	Reversing light switch - removal and refitting 5

Degrees of difficulty

Easy, suitable for novice with little experience	**Fairly easy,** suitable for beginner with some experience	**Fairly difficult,** suitable for competent DIY mechanic	**Difficult,** suitable for experienced DIY mechanic	**Very difficult,** suitable for expert DIY or professional

Specifications

General
Transmission type:
    M46 . . . . 4 forward gears, overdrive and one reverse.
                                                                                                  Synchro on all forward gears
    M47, M90 . . . . 5 forward gears and one reverse. Synchro on all forward gears
Overdrive type . . . . Laycock J, P, or J/P Hybrid

Ratios
M46 and M47 transmissions:
    1st . . . . 4.03 : 1
    2nd . . . . 2.16 : 1
    3rd . . . . 1.37 : 1
    4th . . . . 1.00 : 1
    Overdrive (M46) . . . . 0.79 : 1
    5th (M47) . . . . 0.82 : 1
    Reverse . . . . 3.68 : 1

M90 transmission:
    1st . . . . 3.54 : 1
    2nd . . . . 2.05 : 1
    3rd . . . . 1.38 : 1
    4th . . . . 1.00 : 1
    5th . . . . 0.81 : 1
    Reverse . . . . 3.45 : 1

Torque wrench settings
                                                                                                   Nm
Bellhousing nuts and bolts . . . . 35 to 50
Gear lever mounting bracket bolts . . . . 35 to 50
Drive flange nut:
    M46 175
    M47, size M16 . . . . 70 to 90
    M47, size M20 . . . . 90 to 110
Overdrive-to-intermediate case nuts 12
Overdrive solenoid 50

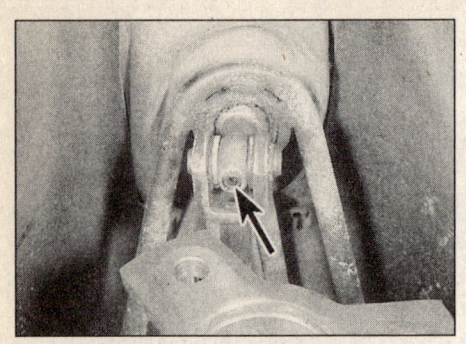

7A•2 Manual transmission and overdrive

2.2 Allen screw (arrowed) securing gear lever pin

2.3 Circlip (arrowed) at base of gear lever

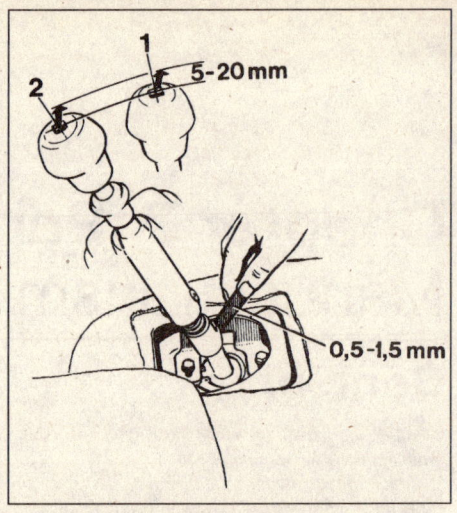

2.7 Gear lever adjustment in 1st or 2nd gear positions (1 and 2)

1 General information

Drive from the engine is transmitted to the input shaft by the clutch. The gear on the input shaft is permanently meshed with the front gear on the layshaft; the remaining layshaft gears (except reverse) are permanently meshed with their counterparts on the mainshaft. Only one mainshaft gear at a time is actually locked to the shaft, the others are freewheeling. The selection of gears is by sliding synchro units: movement of the gear lever is transmitted to selector forks, which slide the appropriate synchro unit towards the gear to be engaged and lock it to the mainshaft. In 4th gear the input shaft is locked to the mainshaft. In neutral, none of the mainshaft gears are locked.

Reverse gear is obtained by sliding an idler gear into mesh with the layshaft and mainshaft reverse gears. The introduction of the idler gear reverses the direction of rotation of the mainshaft.

A gear ratio higher than 4th is provided by the overdrive or by 5th gear. The 5th gear components are mounted at the rear of the transmission, in a housing separate from the main gearcase.

Caution: *At the time of writing, very little information applicable to the M90 transmission was available from the manufacturers. Although many of the operations contained in this chapter will still be applicable to the M90 unit, differences will be noted. The advice of a Volvo dealer should be sought before carrying out any work on models with the M90 transmission.*

2 Gear lever - removal and refitting

Removal

1 Raise and support the vehicle for access to the underside of the gear lever.
2 Remove the Allen screw which secures the pin at the end of the gear lever **(see illustration)**. Press out the pin from the gear lever and the selector rod.
3 Remove the large circlip from the base of the gear lever **(see illustration)**.
4 Inside the vehicle, remove the console section from around the gear lever.
5 Remove the outer gaiter. Undo the four screws which secure the inner gaiter clamp plate. Remove the clamp plate, noting which way round it is fitted, and peel the inner gaiter up the gear lever.
6 Pull the gear lever upwards and withdraw it. Disconnect the overdrive switch wires (when applicable). Do not disturb the reverse detent plate bolts.

Refitting

7 Refit by reversing the removal operations. Check the clearance between the reverse detent plate and finger with 1st gear engaged: it should be between 0.5 and 1.5 mm **(see illustration)**. Adjust if necessary by slackening the detent plate bolts. When adjustment is correct, side-to-side play of the gear lever knob in 1st or 2nd gear should be 5.0 to 20 mm.

3 Gear lever pullrod - renewal

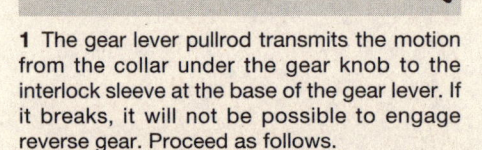

1 The gear lever pullrod transmits the motion from the collar under the gear knob to the interlock sleeve at the base of the gear lever. If it breaks, it will not be possible to engage reverse gear. Proceed as follows.
2 On models with overdrive, remove the trim panel from the right-hand side of the centre console. Separate the overdrive wiring connector there and tie a piece of string to the wire leading to the gear lever.
3 On all models, remove the gear lever boot. Drive out the roll pin which secures the lever to the stub. Lift off the gear lever, at the same time pulling the overdrive wire and string through, when applicable. Untie the string.
4 Remove the overdrive switch, where applicable. Remove the gear lever knob by gripping the lever in a soft-jawed vice and tapping the knob with a soft hammer and an open-ended spanner **(see illustration)**. The knob is glued onto splines and may not come off undamaged. Clean off the old glue.
5 Remove the old pullrod. It may be plastic or metal. The metal rod is removed by undoing the grub screw at the top of the lever, then withdrawing the pullrod, spring and interlock sleeve downwards. To remove the plastic rod, release the catch at the base and (on overdrive models) lift up the collar slightly to free the top of the rod **(see illustrations)**.
6 Soak the new pullrod in water for one hour before fitting it. Fit the new rod from below on overdrive models, being careful not to displace the rubber bushes and wiring. Make sure it engages with the collar. On models without overdrive, fit the pullrod to the collar and then insert them both from above. On all models, position the pullrod bottom lug to receive the interlock sleeve.

3.4 Removing the gear lever knob

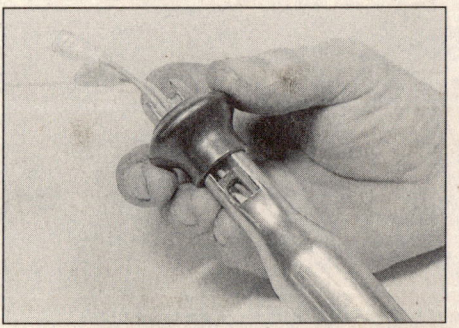

3.5a Lift up the collar . . .

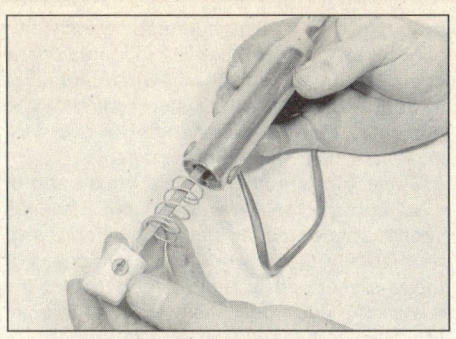

Manual transmission and overdrive 7A•3

3.5b ... and remove the pullrod with the spring and interlock sleeve

7 Fit the spring and interlock sleeve, engaging the pullrod lug in the catch on the sleeve.
8 Refit the gear lever over the splines, using a little glue if wished. Do not use powerful glue, or there will be a problem with any subsequent removal.
9 Refit the gear lever to the stub and secure it with the roll pin. On overdrive models, reattach the string to the wiring and draw the wire back to the centre console. Reconnect the wires and refit the trim panel.
10 Check the selection of all gears, including reverse. If adjustment is necessary, see Section 2, paragraph 7.
11 When adjustment is satisfactory, refit the gear lever boot, the overdrive switch and any other disturbed items.

4 Oil seals - renewal

Drive flange oil seal

1 Raise and support the vehicle.
2 Unbolt the propeller shaft from the drive flange and move it aside.
3 Counterhold the flange and undo its central nut **(see illustration)**.
4 Draw off the flange, using a puller if necessary. Do not try to hammer it off. Be prepared for oil spillage.
5 Prise out the oil seal and clean up its seat. Inspect the seal rubbing surface on the flange: clean it, or renew the flange if necessary, to avoid premature failure of the new seal.

6 Lubricate the new seal and fit it, lips inwards, using a piece of tube to tap it home. On the M47 transmission the seal should be recessed by 2.5 mm.
7 On the M46 transmission, apply locking compound to the output shaft splines. Be careful not to contaminate the seal.
8 Refit the flange and secure it with the nut, tightened to the specified torque.
9 Refit the propeller shaft.
10 Top-up the transmission oil (Chapter 1).
11 Lower the vehicle. Check for leaks after the next run.

Input shaft oil seal

12 Remove the transmission (Section 6).
13 Remove the clutch release components from the bellhousing.
14 Unbolt the bellhousing and remove it. Recover the input shaft bearing shim and clean off the old gasket.
15 Lever the old oil seal out of the bellhousing and clean out its seat **(see illustration)**.
16 Inspect the seal rubbing face of the input shaft. If it is damaged, a new shaft may be required.
17 Lubricate the new seal and fit it to the bellhousing, lips pointing to the gearcase side. Use a piece of tube to seat it **(see illustration)**.
18 Refit the bellhousing to the gearcase, using a new gasket. Remember to refit the input shaft bearing shim; use a smear of grease to hold it in position if necessary.
19 Fit the bellhousing bolts and tighten them to the specified torque.
20 Refit the clutch release components.
21 Refit the transmission.

5 Reversing light switch - removal and refitting

Removal

1 Gain access to the transmission top cover (Section 9, paragraphs 3 and 4).
2 Clean around the switch, disconnect the wires and unscrew it **(see illustration)**.

Refitting

3 Refit by reversing the removal operations.

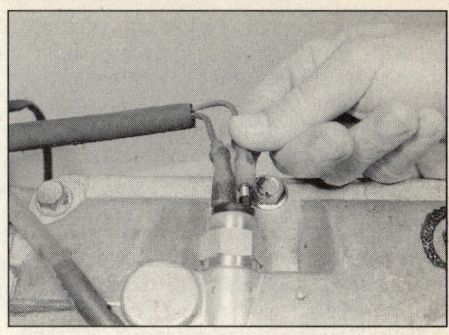

5.2 Disconnecting the reversing light switch

6 Manual transmission - removal and refitting

Note: *The transmission can be removed as a unit with the engine as described in Chapter 2B, then separated from the engine on the bench. However, if work is only necessary on the transmission or clutch unit, it is better to remove the transmission on its own from underneath the vehicle. The latter method is described in this Section. A trolley jack will be required, and the aid of an assistant during the actual removal (and refitting) procedures.*

Removal

1 On overdrive transmissions, if the overdrive is to be subsequently removed, it should first be relieved as described in Section 10, paragraph 1.
2 Disconnect the battery negative lead.
3 Arrangements must be made to support the engine from above to prevent damage to the distributor due to engine movement. The best way to support the engine is with a bar resting in the bonnet channels with an adjustable hook appropriately placed.
4 Raise and support the vehicle.
5 Unbolt the propeller shaft from the transmission output flange.
6 Remove the Allen screw which secures the gear lever to the selector rod. Push out the pin and separate the rod from the lever.
7 Slacken the exhaust downpipe-to-silencer joint so that some movement of the pipe is possible.

4.3 Transmission drive flange

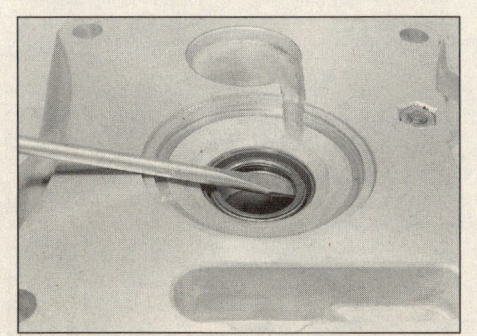

4.15 Removing the input shaft oil seal

4.17 Seating the input shaft oil seal

7A

7A•4 Manual transmission and overdrive

8 Unbolt the transmission mounting crossmember from the transmission and from the side rails. Remove the crossmember.
9 Adjust the engine support so that the distributor cap is 10 mm from the bulkhead.
10 Disconnect the transmission wiring harness multi-plugs.
11 Remove the gear lever (Section 2). Alternatively, the gear lever carrier can be unbolted now and left on the vehicle.
12 Remove the starter motor (Chapter 5).
13 Remove the clutch slave cylinder without disconnecting the hydraulic pipe, or disconnect the clutch cable, as applicable. See Chapter 6.
14 Remove all but two of the engine-to-transmission nuts and bolts. Note the position of cable clips, exhaust brackets, etc.
15 Support the transmission, preferably with a cradle and trolley jack, or with the aid of an assistant. It is too heavy for one person to remove alone.
16 Remove the rest of the engine-to-transmission fasteners. Draw the transmission off the engine. Do not allow the weight of the transmission to hang on the input shaft.
17 Remove the transmission from under the vehicle.

Refitting

18 Refit by reversing the removal operations, noting the following points:
 a) *Apply a smear of molybdenum-based grease to the input shaft splines.*
 b) *Make sure that the clutch driven plate is properly centred, and that the clutch release components have been fitted in the bellhousing (Chapter 6).*
 c) *Adjust the clutch cable (when applicable) (Chapter 1).*
 d) *Refill or top-up the transmission oil (Chapter 1).*
 e) *Check for correct operation on completion.*

7 Manual transmission overhaul - general information

Overhauling a manual transmission is a difficult job for the do-it-yourselfer. It involves the dismantling and reassembly of many small parts. Numerous clearances must be precisely measured and, if necessary, changed with selected spacers and circlips. As a result, if transmission problems arise, while the unit can be removed and refitted by a competent do-it-yourselfer, overhaul should be left to a transmission specialist. Rebuilt transmissions may be available - check with your dealer parts department, motor factors, or transmission specialists. At any rate, the time and money involved in an overhaul is almost sure to exceed the cost of a rebuilt unit.

Nevertheless, it's not impossible for an amateur mechanic to rebuild a transmission, providing the special tools are available, and the job is done in a deliberate step-by-step manner so nothing is overlooked.

The tools necessary for an overhaul include: internal and external circlip pliers, a bearing puller, a slide hammer, a set of pin punches, a dial test indicator, and possibly a hydraulic press. In addition, a large, sturdy workbench and a vice or transmission stand will be required.

During dismantling of the transmission, make careful notes of how each part comes off, where it fits in relation to other parts, and what holds it in place.

Before taking the transmission apart for repair, it will help if you have some idea what area of the transmission is malfunctioning. Certain problems can be closely tied to specific areas in the transmission, which can make component examination and replacement easier. Refer to the *"Fault finding"* section at the rear of this manual for information regarding possible sources of trouble.

8 Overdrive unit - general information

The overdrive is essentially an extra transmission, driven by the output shaft of the main transmission and producing on its own output shaft a step-up ratio of 0.797 : 1. The unit is attached to the rear of the transmission and takes the form of a hydraulically operated epicyclic gear. Overdrive operates on fourth gear to provide fast cruising at lower engine revolutions. The overdrive is engaged or disengaged by a driver operated switch which controls an electrical solenoid mounted on the overdrive unit. A further switch (inhibitor switch) is included in the electrical circuit to prevent accidental engagement of overdrive in reverse, first, second or third gears.

Satisfactory fault diagnosis, repair and/or overhaul of the overdrive unit requires specialist knowledge, factory tools and environmentally clean working conditions. For these reasons, it is recommended that the advice of a Volvo dealer is sought in the event of any unsatisfactory performance or suspected fault on the unit.

9 Overdrive switches - removal and refitting

Removal

Control switch

1 Prise off the trim plate from the top of the gear lever knob **(see illustration)**.
2 Prise out the switch and disconnect it **(see illustrations)**.

Inhibitor (transmission) switch

3 Raise and support the vehicle.
4 Support the transmission, remove the crossmember and slacken the exhaust flanged joint. Lower the rear of the transmission slightly for access to the top cover.
5 Clean around the switch, disconnect the wires and unscrew it **(see illustrations)**.

Pressure switch (Turbo only)

6 Raise and support the vehicle.
7 The switch is located in front of the overdrive solenoid. Clean around the switch, disconnect the wiring and unscrew it. Be prepared for oil spillage.
8 Refit by reversing the removal operations. Top-up the transmission oil if necessary.

Refitting

9 In all cases, refit the switches by reversing the removal operations. Top-up the transmission oil as described in Chapter 1 where necessary.

9.1 Removing the gear lever knob trim plate

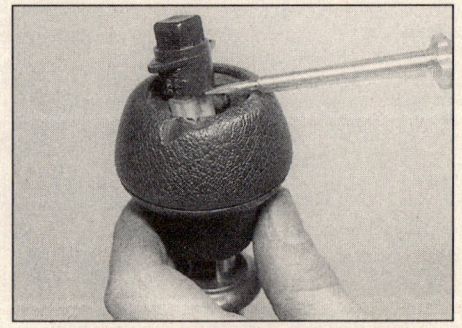

9.2a Prise out the overdrive switch . . .

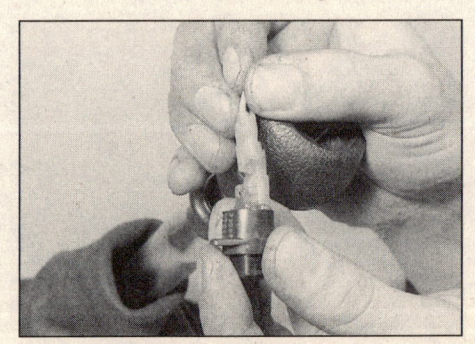

9.2b . . . and disconnect it

Manual transmission and overdrive 7A•5

9.5a Disconnect the inhibitor switch . . .

9.5b . . . and unscrew it from the cover

10 Overdrive unit - removal and refitting

Removal

1 Relieve the pressure in the overdrive by driving the vehicle with overdrive engaged, then disengaging the overdrive with the clutch pedal depressed.
2 Raise and support the vehicle.
3 Unbolt the propeller shaft from the drive flange.
4 Support the transmission and remove the crossmember. Lower the rear of the transmission, being careful not to damage the distributor.
5 Disconnect the wiring from the overdrive solenoid and (when applicable) the pressure switch **(see illustration)**.
6 Remove the eight nuts which secure the overdrive to the transmission intermediate section. Lift off the overdrive **(see illustrations)**; be prepared for oil spillage. If the overdrive will not come off, use a slide hammer on the drive flange; do not lever between the transmission and overdrive casings.

Refitting

7 Refit by reversing the removal operations, noting the following points:
 a) Use a new gasket between the transmission and the overdrive.
 b) Tighten the nuts progressively to the specified torque.
 c) Top-up the transmission oil (Chapter 1), road test the vehicle, then check the oil level again.

11 Overdrive unit overhaul - general information

In the event of a fault occurring on the overdrive unit, it is first necessary to determine whether it is of an electrical, mechanical or hydraulic nature, and to do this special test equipment is required. It is therefore essential to have the work carried out by a Volvo dealer if an overdrive fault is suspected.

Do not remove the overdrive unit from the vehicle for possible repair before professional fault diagnosis has been carried out, since most tests require the unit to be in the vehicle.

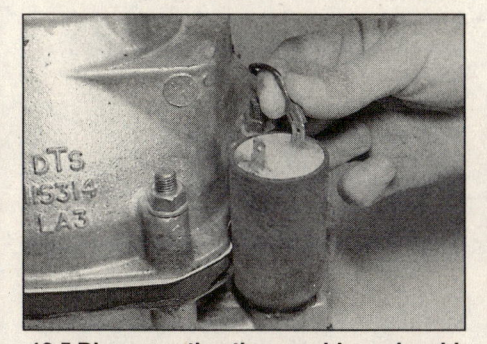

10.5 Disconnecting the overdrive solenoid

10.6a Four of the overdrive securing nuts

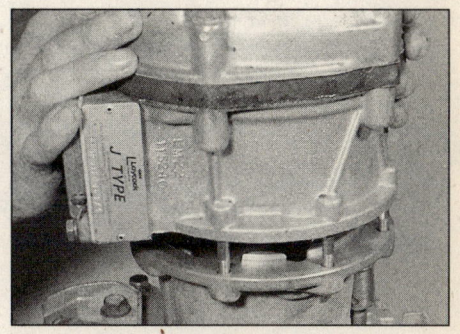

10.6b Lifting off the overdrive (gearbox on bench)

7A

Notes

Chapter 7 Part B:
Automatic transmission

Contents

Automatic transmission - removal and refitting 9
Automatic transmission fluid level check ....See Chapter 1
Automatic transmission fluid renewal ....See Chapter 1
Gear selector - checking and adjustment 2
General information 1
Kickdown cable - checking and adjustment 3
Kickdown cable - renewal 4
Kickdown marker - adjustment 5
Overdrive switch (AW70/AW71/AW72 transmission) - removal and refitting 7
Starter inhibitor/reversing light switch - removal and refitting 6
Transmission oil seals - renewal 8

Degrees of difficulty

Easy, suitable for novice with little experience	Fairly easy, suitable for beginner with some experience	Fairly difficult, suitable for competent DIY mechanic	Difficult, suitable for experienced DIY mechanic	Very difficult, suitable for expert DIY or professional

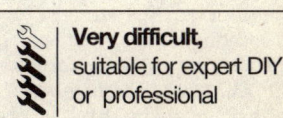

Specifications

General
Designation .... AW70, AW71, AW72, or ZF4HP22

Ratios (typical)
1st .... 2.45 : 1
2nd .... 1.45 : 1
3rd .... 1.0 : 1
4th .... 0.69 : 1
Reverse .... 2.21 : 1

Throttle cable setting
Stop-to-sleeve distance:
 Idling .... 0.25 to 1.00 mm
 Kickdown .... 51.0 ± 1.6 mm

Torque wrench settings   Nm

AW70/71/72
Converter housing to engine 48
Driveplate to torque converter 30
Centre support to gearcase (in steps of 5 Nm/4 lbf ft) ...... 24 to 28
Oil pan .... 4 to 5
Oil cooler union .... 20 to 30
Dipstick tube nut .... 65 to 70
Drive flange nut 45

ZF4HP22
Converter housing to engine:
 M10 .... 35 to 50
 M12 .... 55 to 90
Driveplate to torque converter:
 M8 .... 17 to 27
 M10 .... 41 to 50
Oil pan .... 5 to 7
Filler tube nut .... 85 to 115
Drive flange nut 100

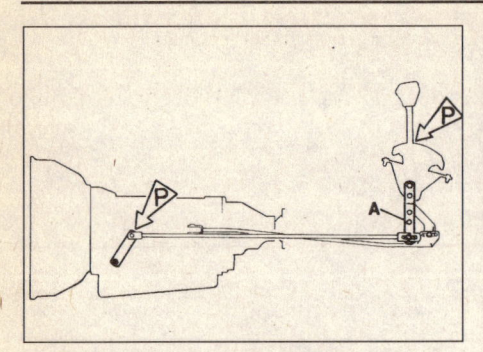

7B•2 Automatic transmission

2.1a Automatic transmission selector linkage in position P
A Actuator lever

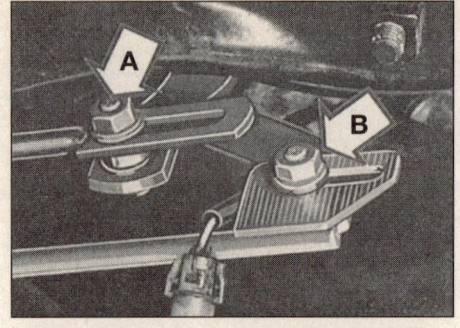

2.1b Automatic transmission selector linkage adjustment nuts
A Actuator lever   B Reaction lever

2.4 Gear selector reaction lever nut (arrowed, under cable)

1 General information

The automatic transmission has four forward speeds and one reverse. Gear changing between forward speeds is normally fully automatic, responding to speed and load, although the driver can prevent the selection of higher ratios. On the AW70/AW71/AW72 transmission the highest (4th) gear is provided by an overdrive unit fitted between the torque converter and the rest of the transmission. The ZF4HP transmission is an integrated four-speed unit.

Drive is taken from the engine to the transmission by a torque converter. This is a type of fluid coupling which under certain conditions has a torque multiplying effect. On certain models the torque converter is mechanically locked at high speeds in 3rd and 4th gear, so eliminating losses due to slip, and improving fuel economy.

The gear selector has six or seven positions: P, R, N, D, 3 (on some models), 2 and 1. The engine can only be started in positions P and N. In position P the transmission is mechanically locked: this position must only be engaged when the vehicle is stationary. In position R reverse is engaged, in N neutral. In position D gear changing is automatic throughout the range; positions 3, 2 and 1 prevent the selection of higher ratios when this is desired. These lower positions must not be selected at speeds so high as to cause engine over-revving.

When position 3 is missing from the selector, a button on the side of the selector knob serves to inhibit the engagement of 4th (overdrive) gear. A dashboard warning light reminds the driver when this has been done.

A shift lock facility is also incorporated into the gear selector mechanism. This security device prevents movement of the selector lever when the engine has been stopped, or when the ignition is switched off with the selector lever in the P position.

A "kickdown" facility causes the transmission to shift down a gear (subject to engine speed) when the throttle is fully depressed. This is useful when extra acceleration is required. Kickdown is controlled by a cable linkage from the throttle cable drum.

The transmission fluid is cooled by a heat exchanger built into one of the radiator side tanks, and (on some models) by an auxiliary cooler mounted in front of the radiator.

The automatic transmission is a complex unit, but if it is not abused it is reliable and long-lasting. Repair or overhaul operations are beyond the scope of many dealers, let alone the home mechanic; specialist advice should be sought if problems arise which cannot be solved by the procedures given in this Chapter.

2 Gear selector - checking and adjustment

Checking

1 Check that the gear lever is vertical in position P (not touching the centre console). Adjust from below if necessary by slackening the actuator lever nut **(see illustrations)**.
2 Check that the engine will only start in positions P and N, and that the reversing lights only come on in position R (ignition on).
3 Check that the free play from D to N is the same as, or less than, the play from 2 to 1 (AW70/AW71/AW72) or from 3 to 2 (ZF4HP22).

Adjustment

4 If there is insufficient play in D, slacken the reaction lever nut (beneath the vehicle) and move the lever approximately 2 mm rearwards **(see illustration)**.
5 If there is insufficient play in 3 or 2, slacken the nut and move the lever approximately 3 mm forwards.
6 Tighten the nut and recheck the adjustment.

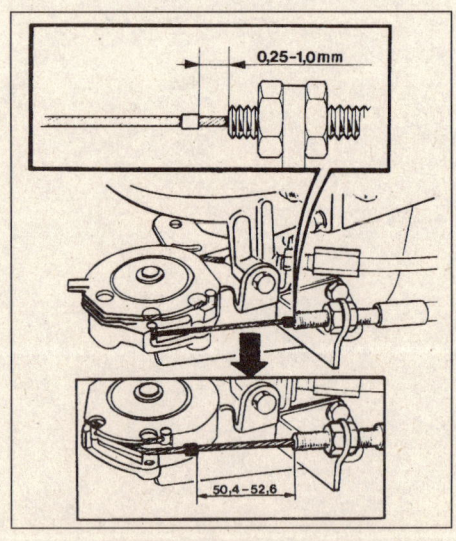

3 Kickdown cable - checking and adjustment

Checking

1 With the throttle linkage in the idle position, the distance from the crimped stop on the kickdown cable to the adjuster sleeve should be 0.25 to 1.0 mm **(see illustration)**. The cable should be taut.
2 Have an assistant depress the throttle pedal fully. Measure the distance from the stop to the adjuster again **(see illustration)**. It should be 50.4 to 52.6 mm. From this position it should be possible to pull the cable out by 2 mm.

3.1 Kickdown cable adjustment at idle (inset, top) and at full throttle (below)

3.2 Checking kickdown cable adjustment at full throttle

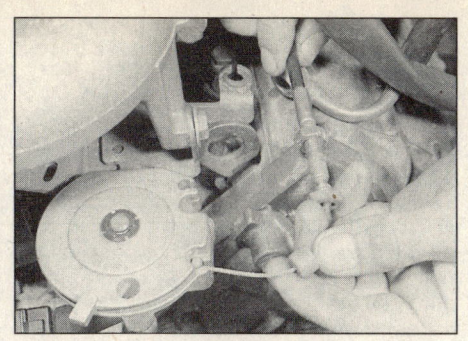

Automatic transmission 7B•3

4.1 Disconnecting the kickdown cable at the throttle end

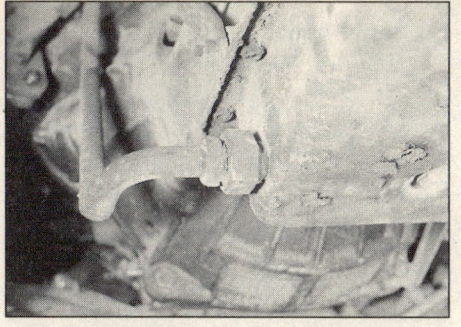

4.2 Transmission dipstick/filler tube nut

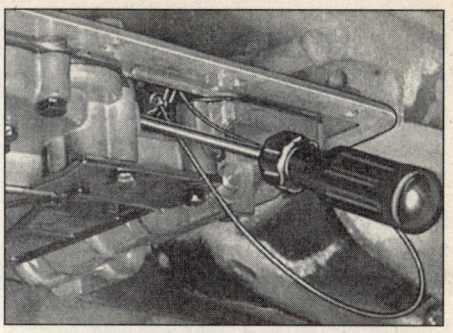

4.4a Removing the kickdown cable - AW transmission

Adjustment

3 Adjust if necessary by slackening the locknuts, turning the adjuster sleeve and tightening the locknuts.

4 If correct adjustment cannot be achieved, either the throttle linkage adjustment is incorrect (Chapter 4) or the cable crimped stop is incorrectly positioned (Section 4).

4 Kickdown cable - renewal

1 Slacken the cable adjuster at the throttle end. Disconnect the cable inner from the drum and the outer from the bracket **(see illustration)**.

2 Raise and support the vehicle (see "*Jacking and vehicle support*"). Drain the transmission oil pan by removing the drain plug (when fitted) and the dipstick/filler tube nut **(see illustration)**.

⚠️ *Warning: It is a good idea to wear gloves for this operation, as the fluid may be very hot.*

3 Clean the oil pan, then unbolt and remove it. Be prepared for fluid spillage. Recover the gasket.

4 Clean around the cable outer where it enters the transmission. Unhook the cable inner from the cam, using a screwdriver to turn the cam **(see illustrations)**. Cut the cable inner below the stop at the throttle end if there is not enough slack in the inner. Release the cable outer and remove the cable.

5 Fit the new cable to the transmission, attaching the inner to the cam and securing the outer to the transmission case. Use a new O-ring and grease the cable outer where it enters the transmission.

6 Attach the cable outer at the throttle end. Pull the cable inner until light resistance is felt, and in this position crimp the inner stop 0.25 to 1.0 mm from the adjuster.

7 Reconnect the cable inner to the throttle drum. Adjust the cable as described in Section 3.

8 Clean the inside of the oil pan, including the magnets when fitted.

9 Refit the oil pan, using a new gasket. Reconnect the dipstick/filler tube.

10 Top-up the transmission fluid (see Chapter 1).

11 Lower the vehicle. Road test the transmission, then recheck the fluid level and inspect the oil pan for leaks.

5 Kickdown marker - adjustment

Screw the marker into the pedal as far as possible.

Depress the throttle pedal by hand to the start of the kickdown position. Hold the pedal in this position and screw the marker down to meet the floor.

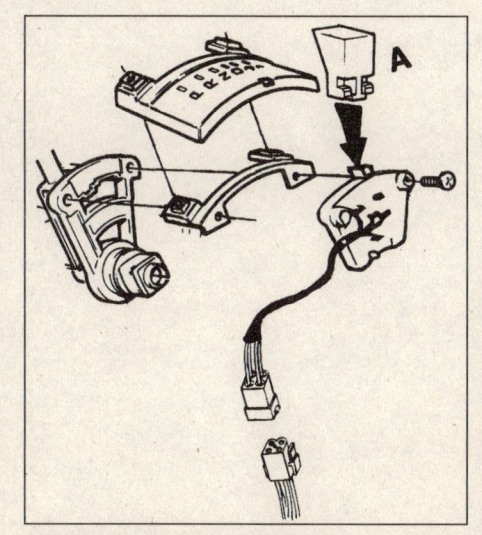

6 Starter inhibitor/reversing light switch - removal and refitting

Removal

1 Remove the ashtray and the centre console panel in front of the selector.

2 Remove the two screws which secure the left-hand half of the selector cover - one screw at each end of the brush. Lift off the half of the cover.

3 Remove the holder containing the gear position symbols from the selector housing **(see illustration)**.

4 Undo the switch securing screws, disconnect the multi-plug and remove it.

5 If a new switch is being fitted, transfer the lens to it.

Refitting

6 Refit by reversing the removal operations. Make sure that the stud on the lever enters the slot in the switch.

7 Overdrive switch (AW70/71/72 transmission) - removal and refitting

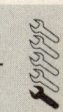

Removal

Prise the switch from the side of the selector lever and disconnect it **(see illustration)**.

Refitting

Refit by reversing the removal operations.

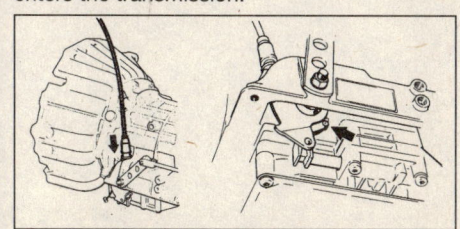

4.4b Kickdown cable attachments - ZF transmission

6.3 Starter inhibitor/reversing light switch and associated components
A Lens

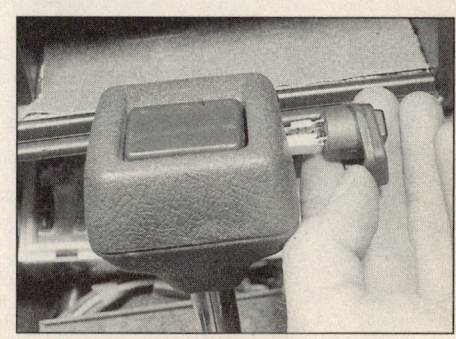

7.1 Removing the overdrive switch

7B

8 Transmission oil seals - renewal

Note: *It is important not to introduce dirt into the transmission when working on it.*

Drive flange oil seal

1 The procedure is the same as that described for the manual transmission in Part A, Section 4, except that the flange central nut may be secured by a lockwasher.

Input shaft/torque converter oil seal

2 Remove the transmission (Section 9).
3 Lift the torque converter out of its housing. Be careful, it is full of fluid.
4 Pull or lever out the old seal. Clean the seat and inspect the seal rubbing surface on the torque converter.
5 Lubricate the new seal with ATF and fit it, lips inwards. Seat it with a piece of tube.
6 Refit the torque converter and the transmission.

Selector shaft oil seal

7 Remove the selector arm nut and pull the arm off the shaft.
8 Prise the seal out with a small screwdriver. Clean the seat.
9 Grease the new seal and fit it, lips inwards. Seat the seal with a tube or socket.
10 Refit the selector arm and tighten the nut.

All seals

11 Check the transmission fluid level as described in Chapter 1 on completion.

9 Automatic transmission - removal and refitting

Note: *If the transmission is being removed for repair, check first that the repairer does not need to test it in the vehicle.*

Removal

1 Select "P" (AW70/71/72 transmissions) or "N" (ZF transmission).
2 Disconnect the battery negative lead.
3 Disconnect the kickdown cable at the throttle end.
4 Raise and support the vehicle. Drain the transmission fluid by removing the dipstick/filler tube nut.

⚠️ **Warning: It is a good idea to wear gloves for this operation, as the fluid may be very hot.**

5 Disconnect the selector linkage and (when applicable) the overdrive wiring connector from the side of the transmission.
6 Remove the starter motor (Chapter 5).
7 Remove the dipstick/filler tube.
8 Disconnect the fluid cooler unions at the transmission. Be prepared for spillage. Cap the open unions to keep dirt out.
9 Disconnect the exhaust downpipe and unbolt the exhaust support bracket from the transmission crossmember. Support the exhaust system if necessary.
10 Unbolt the propeller shaft flange.
11 When fitted, remove the cover plate from the bottom of the torque converter housing. Also remove the cooling grilles.
12 Jam the driveplate and remove the bolts which hold the torque converter to the driveplate. Turn the crankshaft to bring the bolts into view. It is possible to work through the starter motor aperture on some models.
13 Support the transmission, preferably with a properly designed cradle. Unbolt and remove the transmission crossmember.
14 Lower the transmission until it takes up a stable position. Make sure that the distributor is not crushed against the bulkhead.
15 Remove the converter housing-to-engine nuts and bolts.
16 With the aid of an assistant, draw the transmission off the engine, at the same time levering the torque converter away from the driveplate. Keep the transmission tilted rearwards and lower it from the vehicle. It is heavy.

Refitting

17 Refit by reversing the removal operations, noting the following points:
a) *Put a smear of grease on the torque converter spigot.*
b) *Tighten the torque converter-to-driveplate bolts progressively to the specified torque.*
c) *Do not fully tighten the dipstick tube nut until the tube bracket has been secured.*
d) *Adjust the selector mechanism (Section 2) and the kickdown cable (Section 3).*
e) *Refill the transmission with fluid. If a new transmission has been fitted, flush the oil cooler(s) - (see "Automatic transmission fluid renewal" in Chapter 1). Additionally, flush the auxiliary cooler (when fitted) using a hand pump. The auxiliary cooler is thermostatically controlled and will not be flushed during the fluid renewal procedure.*

Chapter 8
Propeller shaft and rear axle

Contents

Centre bearing - renewal 6	Propeller shaft, centre bearing and universal joint check . . See Chapter 1
General information 1	Rear axle - description 7
Halfshaft, bearing and seals - removal and refitting 9	Rear axle - removal and refitting 10
Pinion oil seal - renewal 8	Rear axle oil level check .... See Chapter 1
Propeller shaft - description 2	Rubber coupling - removal and refitting 3
Propeller shaft - removal and refitting 4	Universal joints - overhaul 5

Degrees of difficulty

| Easy, suitable for novice with little experience | Fairly easy, suitable for beginner with some experience | Fairly difficult, suitable for competent DIY mechanic | Difficult, suitable for experienced DIY mechanic | Very difficult, suitable for expert DIY or professional |

Specifications

Rear axle
Final drive ratio (depending on model and year) .... 3.31, 3.54, 3.73, 3.91 or 4.10:1

Torque wrench settings   Nm
Propeller shaft
Rubber coupling nuts and bolts 80
Plain flange coupling nuts and bolts:
  M8 bolts:
    Stage 1 30
    Stage 2 .... Angle tighten 60° further
  M10 bolts 50
Rear axle
Pinion flange nut (see text):
  Solid spacer .... 200 to 250
  Collapsible spacer .... 180 to 200
Speedometer sensor locknut .... 25 to 40
Halfshaft retaining plate bolts 40
Trailing arm bracket bolts 45
Trailing arm bracket nuts 85
Trailing arm to axle 45
Panhard rod 85
Shock absorber lower mountings 85
Torque rods 140

1 General information

The information in this Chapter deals with the driveline components from the transmission to the rear wheels. For the purposes of this Chapter, these components are grouped into the two categories, propeller shaft and rear axle. Separate sections within this Chapter offer general information and repair procedures for each group.

Since many of the procedures covered in this Chapter involve working under the car, make sure that it is securely supported on axle stands placed on firm level ground (see "Jacking and vehicle support").

2 Propeller shaft - description

A two-section tubular propeller shaft is fitted. Two or three universal joints are used, and on some models a rubber coupling is fitted between the transmission output flange and the propeller shaft flange. A centre bearing supports the shaft at the junction of the two sections.

The universal joints are secured with circlips instead of by staking, which makes them relatively easy to overhaul.

3 Rubber coupling - removal and refitting

Removal

1 Raise and securely support the vehicle (see "Jacking and vehicle support").
2 Make alignment marks between the shaft and the transmission output flange.
3 Remove the six nuts and bolts which hold

8•2 Propeller shaft and rear axle

3.3 Rubber coupling nuts and bolts

the flanges to the coupling **(see illustration)**. (It may not be possible actually to remove the forward-facing bolts, which will stay on the flange.)

4 Pull the shaft rearwards and lower the front section. Remove the rubber coupling, the centre sleeve and the locating plate.

Refitting

5 Refit by reversing the removal operations, observing the alignment marks and tightening the bolts to the specified torque. Apply a little anti-seize compound to the locating plate pin.

4 Propeller shaft - removal and refitting

Removal

1 Raise the vehicle on ramps or drive it over a pit.
2 Make alignment marks between the shaft flanges and the gearbox and axle flanges, and between the two sections of the shaft.
3 Remove all the flange nuts and bolts except one at each end **(see illustration)**. Leave these last ones loose.
4 Have an assistant support the shaft. Remove the bolts which secure the centre bearing carrier.
5 With the aid of the assistant, remove the remaining flange bolts. Remove the shaft and bearing from under the vehicle. Recover the rubber coupling (when fitted).

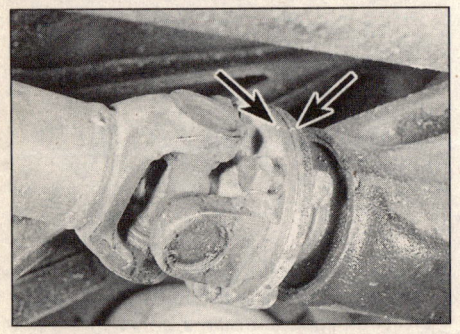

4.3 Propeller shaft rear flange - note alignment marks (arrowed)

6 In the absence of an assistant, the shaft may be removed in two sections (rear section first). The two sections simply pull apart. Release the rubber boot from the rear of the centre bearing carrier as this is done.

Refitting

7 Refit by reversing the removal operations, observing the flange alignment marks and tightening all bolts to the specified torque. Do not tighten the bearing carrier bolts until the flange bolts have been tightened; the carrier fixings are slotted to allow the bearing to take up an unstrained position.

5 Universal joints - overhaul

1 The joints may need to be overhauled because of excess play; a joint which is stiff will cause vibration and must also be overhauled.
2 Obtain an overhaul kit (spider, bearing cups and circlips) for each joint **(see illustration)**.
3 Clean the joint and apply penetrating oil or releasing fluid to the circlips.
4 Remove the circlips. If they are stuck, tap them with a punch.
5 Rest the yoke of the joint on the open jaws of a vice. Tap the flange with a plastic or copper hammer, or place a piece of tube over the bearing cup and strike that, until the cup protrudes a little way. Do not hit too hard, or clamp the shaft too firmly in the vice - if it is distorted it will be scrap.
6 Grasp the bearing cup with self-locking pliers and withdraw it. Recover any loose rollers.
7 Repeat this process until the spider can be removed from the yoke and all the bearing cups have been removed.
8 Clean the cup seats in the shaft and flange.
9 Carefully remove the cups from the new spider. Check that each cup contains its complement of rollers and that the seals are securely attached. The rollers should already be packed with grease.
10 Offer the spider to the yoke. Fit a cup to the spider, making sure that the rollers are not displaced.

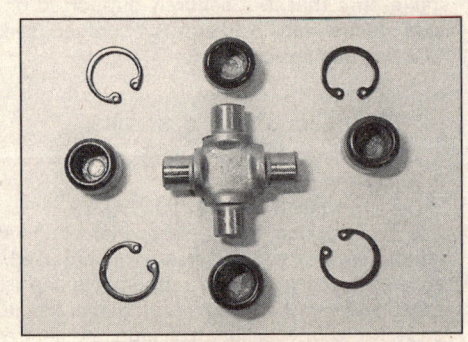

5.2 Universal joint repair kit

11 Tap the cup lightly to seat it, then press it in using the vice and a tube or socket (photo). The cup should be recessed by 3 to 4 mm.
12 Fit the circlip to secure the cup.
13 Similarly fit and secure the opposite cup, then assemble the rest of the joint in the same way.
14 Check the joint for freedom of movement. If it is stiff, tap it lightly with a plastic or copper hammer.
15 If vibration persists after overhauling the joints, it may be that the shaft needs to be balanced. This must be done by a specialist.

6 Centre bearing - renewal

Note: *Several different patterns of centre bearing and rubber boot have been fitted. If buying new components in advance, be careful to obtain the correct ones.*

1 Remove the propeller shaft (Section 4) and separate the two sections.
2 Support the front of the bearing and cage on V-blocks or with a piece of split tubing. Press or drive the shaft out of the bearing. Recover the protective rings from both sides of the bearing
3 If the bearing cage is undamaged, the old bearing can be driven out and a new one pressed in. Otherwise, renew the bearing and cage complete.
4 Fit a new front protective ring to the shaft and tap it home with a wooden or plastic mallet.
5 Fit the new bearing and cage. Seat them with a piece of tube pressing on the bearing inner race.
6 Fit the rear protective ring, keeping it square as it is tapped home.
7 Check that the bearing spins freely, then reassemble the two sections of the shaft, observing the previously made alignment marks. Use a new rubber boot and/or retaining rings if necessary.
8 Refit the shaft to the vehicle.

7 Rear axle - description

The rear axle is conventional in design. A rigid casing encloses the final drive unit and two halfshafts. The casing is located by two torque rods bolted to a central subframe, by the two trailing arms and the Panhard rod.

The final drive unit is mounted centrally in the casing. It consists of the differential unit, the crownwheel and pinion. Drive from the propeller shaft is transmitted to the crownwheel by the pinion. The differential unit is bolted to the crownwheel and transmits the drive to the halfshafts. The differential gears and pinions allow the halfshafts to turn at different speeds when necessary, for example when cornering.

Propeller shaft and rear axle 8•3

On some models the differential is of the "limited slip" type. Here the difference in speed between the two halfshafts is limited by means of friction clutches. This improves traction on slippery surfaces.

Work on the rear axle should be limited to the operations described in this Chapter. If overhaul of the final drive unit is necessary, consult a Volvo dealer or other specialist.

8 Pinion oil seal - renewal

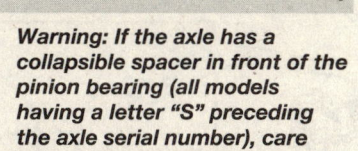

Warning: If the axle has a collapsible spacer in front of the pinion bearing (all models having a letter "S" preceding the axle serial number), care must be taken not to overtighten the pinion flange nut. If the nut is overtightened, it may be necessary to take the axle to a Volvo dealer for a new spacer to be fitted.

1 Raise and support the rear of the vehicle on ramps (see "Jacking and vehicle support"), or drive it over a pit.
2 Unbolt the propeller shaft flange from the pinion flange. Make alignment marks between the flanges.
3 Restrain the pinion flange with a bar and a couple of bolts then unscrew the flange nut.
4 Paint or scribe alignment marks between the pinion flange and the pinion shaft.
5 Pull off the pinion flange. If it is tight, strike it from behind with a copper mallet. Be prepared for oil spillage.
6 Lever out the old oil seal. Clean the seal seat and tap in the new seal, lips inwards.
7 Inspect the seal rubbing surface of the pinion flange. Clean it, or renew the flange, as necessary.
8 Oil the seal lips, then refit the flange, aligning the marks made on removal if the original flange is being refitted.
9 Refit the flange nut and tighten it to the specified torque according to axle type. On axles incorporating a collapsible spacer, take care not to exceed the maximum torque figure given, otherwise premature failure of the pinion bearings may occur.
10 Refit the propeller shaft and lower the vehicle.
11 Check the rear axle oil level as described in Chapter 1, and top-up if necessary.

9 Halfshaft, bearing and seals - removal and refitting

Removal

1 Remove the handbrake shoes (Chapter 9).
2 Remove the four bolts which secure the halfshaft retaining plate (see illustration). Recover the handbrake shoe clips.
3 Refit the brake disc the wrong way round (drum facing outwards) and secure it with the wheel nuts, flat faces inwards. Pull on the brake disc to withdraw the halfshaft. Be prepared for oil spillage.
4 With the halfshaft removed, the inner (axle oil) seal may be removed by prising it out of the axle tube. Clean the seal seat and tap the new seal into position using a mallet and a piece of tube.
5 Renewal of the outer (grease) seal and bearing should be left to a Volvo dealer or other specialist, as press tools are required.

Refitting

6 Before refitting, make sure that the bearing and seal lips are packed with grease.
7 Clean the axle tube and retaining plate mating faces and apply sealant to them.
8 Fit the halfshaft into the axle tube, being careful not to damage the inner seal. Secure it with the retaining plate and the four bolts, tightened to the specified torque. Remember to fit the handbrake shoe clips.
9 Remove the brake disc (if not already done) and refit the handbrake shoes.
10 Check the rear axle oil level as described in Chapter 1 and top-up if necessary.

10 Rear axle - removal and refitting

Removal

1 Slacken the rear wheel nuts. Raise and support the vehicle with the rear wheels free.
2 Remove the rear wheels.
3 Remove the rear brake calipers (without disconnecting them), the brake discs and the handbrake shoes. See Chapter 9 for details.
4 Disconnect the handbrake cables from the brake backplates and from the brackets on the axle.
5 Unbolt the axle torque rods from the subframe, and the lower torque rod from the axle (see illustration).
6 Support the axle with a cradle and a jack. Take the weight of the axle on the jack.
7 If the exhaust system runs below the axle, remove it.
8 Remove the Panhard rod.
9 Disconnect the speedometer sender/ABS multi-plug(s) (as applicable). The speedometer sender multi-plug may be secured by a locking wire and seal, which must be broken.
10 Unbolt the propeller shaft/axle flange joint.
11 Unbolt the upper torque rod from the axle.
12 Unbolt the rear shock absorber lower mountings.
13 Remove the trailing arm front mounting bracket nuts and bolts.

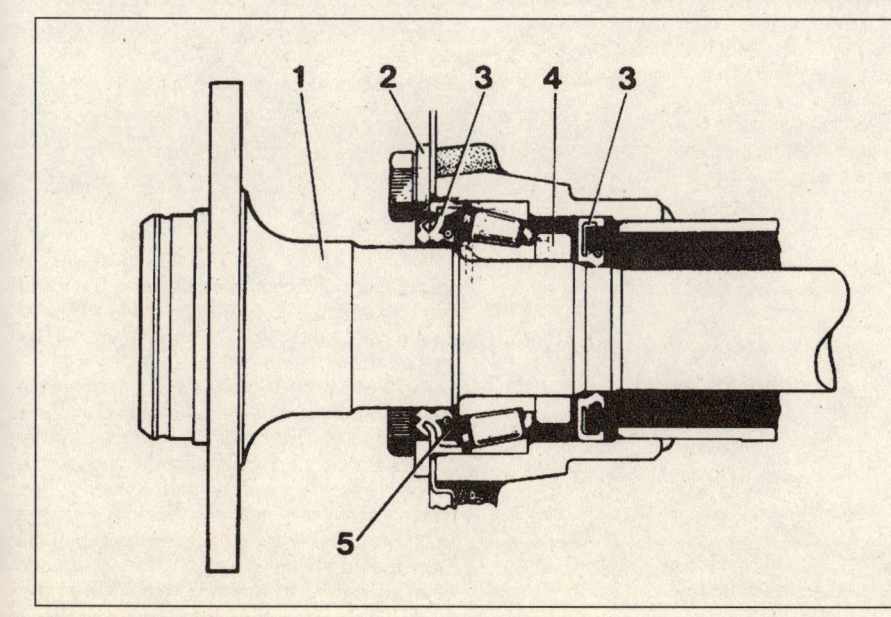

9.2 Sectional view of halfshaft, bearing and seals
1 Halfshaft
2 Lockplate
3 Seals
4 Bearing retainer
5 Grease space

8•4 Propeller shaft and rear axle

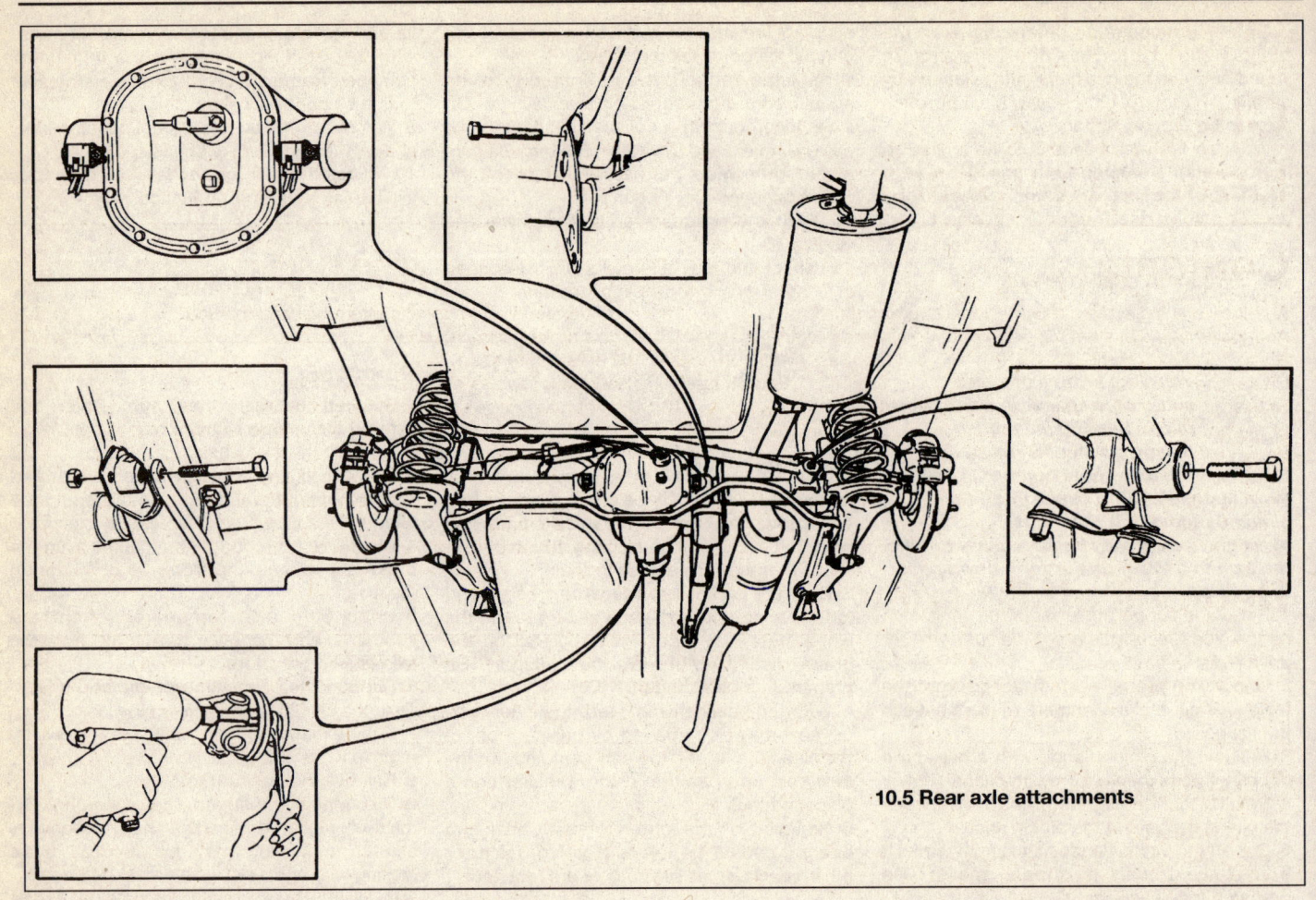

10.5 Rear axle attachments

14 Lower the axle, at the same time freeing the trailing arm front mountings, and remove it from under the vehicle.

15 The anti-roll bar (if fitted) and the trailing arms may now be removed if wished. The trailing arms are handed: do not mix them up.

Refitting

16 Refit by reversing the removal operations, noting the following points:
a) When refitting the trailing arms to the axle, tighten the nuts progressively in diagonal sequence to the specified torque.
b) Do not finally tighten the torque rods until the weight of the vehicle is back on the wheels (or jack the axle up to simulate this condition).
c) Check the rear axle oil level as described in Chapter 1 on completion.

Chapter 9
Braking system

Contents

Anti-lock braking system (ABS) - general information 15
Anti-lock braking system (ABS) components - removal and refitting .16
Brake fluid level check . . . . .See "Weekly checks"
Brake fluid renewal . . . . .See Chapter 1
Brake master cylinder - removal, overhaul and refitting 10
Brake pad wear check . . . . .See Chapter 1
Brake pedal - removal and refitting 11
Brake servo - removal and refitting 12
Braking system check (servo unit, handbrake check and
  adjustment) . . . . .See Chapter 1
Front brake caliper - removal, overhaul and refitting 8
Front brake disc - inspection, removal and refitting 6
Front brake pads - renewal 4
General information 1
Handbrake cables - removal and refitting .14
Handbrake shoes - inspection and renewal 13
Hydraulic pipes and hoses - inspection and renewal 3
Hydraulic system - bleeding 2
Rear brake caliper - removal, overhaul and refitting 9
Rear brake disc - inspection, removal and refitting 7
Rear brake pads - renewal 5
Underbody and fuel/brake line check . . . . .See Chapter 1

Degrees of difficulty

Easy, suitable for novice with little experience	**Fairly easy,** suitable for beginner with some experience	**Fairly difficult,** suitable for competent DIY mechanic	**Difficult,** suitable for experienced DIY mechanic	**Very difficult,** suitable for expert DIY or professional

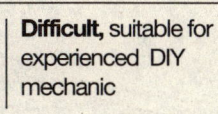

Specifications

Front brakes
Brake pad minimum lining thickness . . . . 3.0 mm
Disc thickness:
  280 mm disc:
    New . . . . 26.0 mm
    Wear limit . . . . 23.0 mm
  287 mm disc:
    New . . . . 22.0 mm
    Wear limit . . . . 20.0 mm
Maximum disc run out . . . . 0.06 mm

Rear brakes
Brake pad minimum lining thickness . . . . 2.0 mm
Disc thickness:
  New . . . . 9.6 mm
  Wear limit . . . . 8.4 mm
Maximum disc run out . . . . 0.08 mm

Handbrake
Drum diameter . . . . 160 mm
Maximum drum run-out . . . . 0.15 mm
Maximum drum out-of-round . . . . 0.20 mm

Torque wrench settings   Nm
Front caliper bracket bolts* 100
Front caliper guide pin bolts* 30
Front dust shield 24
Rear caliper mounting bolts* 58
Rear dust shield 40
Master cylinder mounting nuts 30
Servo unit mounting nuts 14
Rigid pipe unions 14
Flexible hose unions 17
*Use new bolts every time

1 General information

The brake pedal operates disc brakes on all four wheels by means of a dual circuit hydraulic system with servo assistance. The handbrake operates separate drum brakes on the rear wheels only by means of cables. An anti-lock braking system (ABS) is fitted to some models, and is described in further detail in Section 15.

The hydraulic system is split into two circuits, so that in the event of failure of one circuit, the other will still provide adequate braking power (although pedal travel and effort may increase). On pre-1992 models (except those with ABS) a triangular-split system is used, whereby each circuit serves one rear caliper and half of both front ones. On later models, and all models equipped with ABS, an axle-split system is employed in which one circuit serves the front brakes and the other circuit the rear brakes. On all models from 1992 onwards, a pressure reducing valve is incorporated into the rear brake circuit to prevent rear brake wheel lock up under severe braking conditions.

The brake servo is of the direct-acting type, being interposed between the brake pedal and the master cylinder. The servo magnifies the effort applied by the driver. It is vacuum-operated, the vacuum being derived from the inlet manifold.

Instrument panel warning lights alert the driver to low fluid level by means of a level sensor in the master cylinder reservoir. Another warning light reminds when the handbrake is applied. The stop-lights are covered by the bulb failure warning system.

Note: *When servicing any part of the system, work carefully and methodically; also observe scrupulous cleanliness when overhauling any part of the hydraulic system. Always renew components (in axle sets, where applicable) if in doubt about their condition, and use only genuine Volvo replacement parts, or at least those of known good quality. Note the warnings given in "Safety first" and at relevant points in this Chapter concerning the dangers of asbestos dust and hydraulic fluid.*

2 Hydraulic system - bleeding

Warning: *Hydraulic fluid is poisonous; wash off immediately and thoroughly in the case of skin contact, and seek immediate medical advice if any fluid is swallowed or gets into the eyes. Certain types of hydraulic fluid are inflammable, and may ignite when allowed into contact with hot components; when servicing any hydraulic system, it is safest to assume that the fluid IS inflammable, and to take precautions against the risk of fire as though it is petrol that is being handled. Hydraulic fluid is also an effective paint stripper, and will attack plastics; if any is spilt, it should be washed off immediately, using copious quantities of clean water. Finally, it is hygroscopic (it absorbs moisture from the air). The more moisture is absorbed by the fluid, the lower its boiling point becomes, leading to a dangerous loss of braking under hard use. Old fluid may be contaminated and unfit for further use. When topping-up or renewing the fluid, always use the recommended type, and ensure that it comes from a freshly-opened sealed container.*

General

1 The correct functioning of the brake hydraulic system is only possible after removing all air from the components and circuit; this is achieved by bleeding the system.
2 During the bleeding procedure, add only clean, fresh hydraulic fluid of the specified type; never re-use fluid that has already been bled from the system. Ensure that sufficient fluid is available before starting work.
3 If there is any possibility of incorrect fluid being used in the system, the brake lines and components must be completely flushed with uncontaminated fluid and new seals fitted to the components.
4 If brake fluid has been lost from the master cylinder due to a leak in the system, ensure that the cause is traced and rectified before proceeding further.
5 Park the car on level ground, switch off the ignition and select first gear (manual transmission) or Park (automatic transmission) then chock the wheels and release the handbrake.
6 Check that all pipes and hoses are secure, unions tight, and bleed screws closed. Remove the dust caps and clean any dirt from around the bleed screws.
7 Unscrew the master cylinder reservoir cap, and top-up the reservoir to the "MAX" level line. Refit the cap loosely, and remember to maintain the fluid level at least above the "MIN" level line throughout the procedure, otherwise there is a risk of further air entering the system.
8 There are a number of one-man, do-it-yourself, brake bleeding kits currently available from motor accessory shops. It is recommended that one of these kits is used wherever possible, as they greatly simplify the bleeding operation, and also reduce the risk of expelled air and fluid being drawn back into the system. If such a kit is not available, the basic (two-man) method must be used, which is described in detail below.
9 If a kit is to be used, prepare the vehicle as described previously, and follow the kit manufacturer's instructions, as the procedure may vary slightly according to the type being used; generally, they are as outlined below in the relevant sub-section.
10 Whichever method is used, the correct sequence must be followed (paragraphs 11 to 13) to ensure that the removal of all air from the system.

Bleeding sequence

11 If the hydraulic system has only been partially disconnected and suitable precautions were taken to minimise fluid loss, it should only be necessary to bleed that part of the system (ie the primary or secondary circuit).
12 If the complete system is to be bled, then it should be done in the following sequence:
a) Rear brakes (in either order).
b) Front brakes (in either order).
13 On pre-1992 non-ABS models, there are two bleed screws on each front caliper, and one on each rear caliper; all other models have a single bleed screw on each caliper. When bleeding the front brakes on calipers with two bleed screws, start with the lower bleed screw on each caliper, followed by the upper.

Bleeding - basic (two-man) method

14 Collect a clean glass jar and a suitable length of plastic or rubber tubing, which is a tight fit over the bleed screw, and a ring spanner to fit the screws. The help of an assistant will also be required.
15 If not already done, remove the dust cap from the bleed screw of the first wheel to be bled and fit the bleed tube to the screw.
16 Immerse the other end of the bleed tube in the jar, which should contain enough fluid to cover the end of the tube.
17 Ensure that the master cylinder reservoir fluid level is maintained at least above the "MIN" level line throughout the procedure.
18 Open the bleed screw approximately half a turn, and have your assistant depress the brake pedal with a smooth steady stroke down to the floor, and then hold it there. When the flow of fluid through the tube stops, tighten the bleed screw and have your assistant release the pedal slowly.
19 Repeat this operation (paragraph 18) until clean brake fluid, free from air bubbles, can be seen flowing from the end of the tube.
20 When no more air bubbles appear, tighten the bleed screw, remove the bleed tube and refit the dust cap. Repeat these procedures on the remaining calipers in sequence until all air is removed from the system and the brake pedal feels firm again.

Bleeding - using a one-way valve kit

21 As their name implies, these kits consist of a length of tubing with a one-way valve fitted, to prevent expelled air and fluid being drawn back into the system; some kits incorporate a translucent container, which can be positioned so that the air bubbles can be more easily seen flowing from the end of the tube.

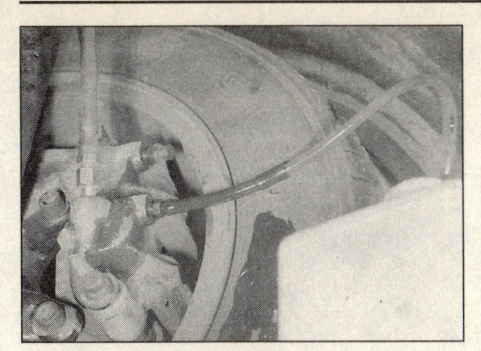

Braking system 9•3

2.22 One-way valve bleeder connected to a front bleed screw

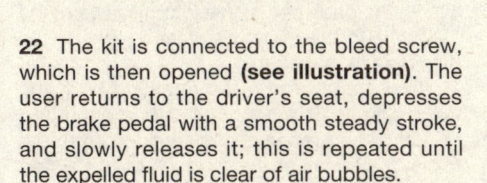

4.2 Removing a front caliper lower guide pin bolt

4.3 Pivot the caliper upwards

22 The kit is connected to the bleed screw, which is then opened **(see illustration)**. The user returns to the driver's seat, depresses the brake pedal with a smooth steady stroke, and slowly releases it; this is repeated until the expelled fluid is clear of air bubbles.
23 Note that these kits simplify work so much that it is easy to forget the master cylinder fluid level; ensure that this is maintained at least above the "MIN" level line at all times.

Bleeding - using a pressure-bleeding kit

24 These kits are usually operated by the reserve of pressurised air contained in the spare tyre. However, note that it will probably be necessary to reduce the pressure to a lower level than normal; refer to the instructions supplied with the kit.
25 By connecting a pressurised, fluid-filled container to the master cylinder reservoir, bleeding is then carried out by simply opening each bleed screw in turn (in the specified sequence) and allowing the fluid to run out, rather like turning on a tap, until no air bubbles can be seen in the expelled fluid.
26 This method has the advantage that the large reservoir of fluid provides an additional safeguard against air being drawn into the system during bleeding.
27 Pressure bleeding is particularly effective when bleeding "difficult" systems, or when bleeding the complete system at the time of routine fluid renewal. It is also the method recommended by Volvo if the hydraulic system has been drained either wholly or partially.

All methods

28 When bleeding is completed, check and top-up the fluid level in the master cylinder reservoir.
29 Check the feel of the brake pedal. If it feels at all spongy, air must still be present in the system, and further bleeding is indicated. Failure to bleed satisfactorily after a reasonable repetition of the bleeding operations may be due to worn master cylinder seals.
30 Discard brake fluid which has been bled from the system; it will not be fit for re-use.

3 Hydraulic pipes and hoses - inspection and renewal

Note: *Before starting work, refer to the warning at the beginning of Section 2 concerning the dangers of hydraulic fluid.*

Inspection

1 Raise and securely support the car at the front and rear so that the pipes and hoses under the wheel arches and on the suspension assemblies can be inspected.
2 Inspect the rigid pipes for security in their mountings. The pipes must be free from rust or impact damage.
3 Inspect the flexible hoses for cracks, splits and bulges. Bend the hoses between finger and thumb to show up small cracks. Renew any hoses whose condition is at all dubious. It is worth considering the renewal of the hoses on a precautionary basis at the time of fluid renewal.

Renewal

4 Details of pipe and hose renewal will vary according to the location of the item in question, but the basic steps are the same.
5 Where possible, minimise hydraulic fluid loss by removing the master cylinder reservoir cap, placing a piece of plastic film over the reservoir and tightening the cap over it.
6 Clean around the unions which are to be disconnected. Undo the unions - with a flexible hose, release it at the rigid pipe first, then from the caliper. Free the pipe or hose from any mounting clips and remove.
7 Before refitting, blow through the new pipe or hose with dry compressed air. Any bending needed for a rigid pipe should take place before the unions are connected. If genuine Volvo parts are used, the pipes should fit without bending.
8 When satisfied that the pipe or hose is correctly routed and will not foul adjacent components, refit and tighten the unions.
9 Bleed the hydraulic system as described in Section 2.

4 Front brake pads - renewal

⚠️ *Warning: Disc brake pads must be renewed on both front wheels at the same time - never renew the pads on only one wheel as uneven braking may result. Dust created by wear of the pads may contain asbestos, which is a health hazard. Never blow it out with compressed air and do not inhale any of it. DO NOT use petroleum-based solvents to clean brake parts. Use brake cleaner or methylated spirit only. DO NOT allow any brake fluid, oil or grease to contact the brake pads or disc. Also refer to the warning at the start of Section 2 concerning the dangers of hydraulic fluid.*

1 Slacken the front wheel nuts, raise and support the front of the car and remove the front roadwheels.
2 Remove the caliper lower guide pin bolt, if necessary counterholding the guide pin with an open-ended spanner **(see illustration)**. Obtain a new bolt for reassembly.
3 Pivot the caliper upwards and support it in this position using string or wire tied to a convenient suspension component **(see illustration)**. Do not press the brake pedal whilst the caliper is removed.
4 Recover the pads from the caliper bracket, noting their positions if they are to be re-used. Recover the anti-squeal shims (if fitted) from the backs of the pads, and the damping spring from the caliper.
5 Measure the thickness of the pad friction linings. If any one pad lining has worn down to the specified minimum, all four front pads must be renewed. Do not interchange pads in an attempt to even out wear. (Uneven pad wear may be due to the caliper sticking on the guide pins.)
6 Clean the caliper and bracket with a damp rag or an old paintbrush. Inspect the caliper piston and dust boots for signs of fluid leakage. Also inspect the rubber bellows which cover the guide pins. Repair or renew as necessary (Section 8).

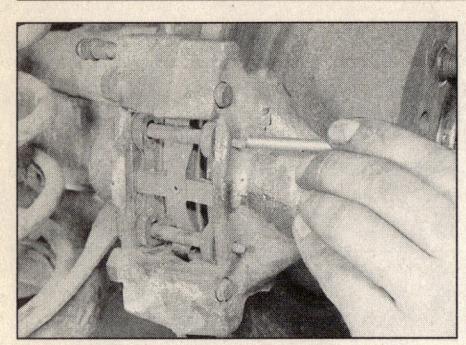

5.2 Driving out a pad retaining pin

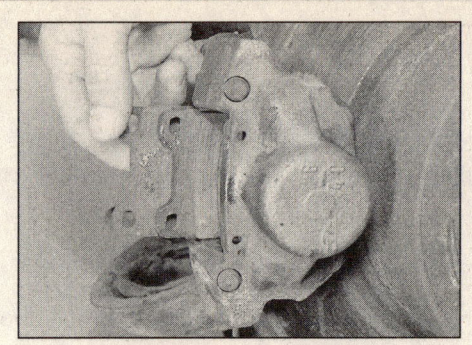

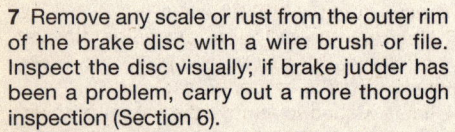

5.11 Refitting a rear pad and anti-squeal shim

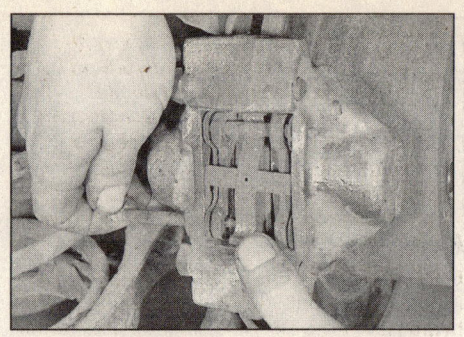

5.12 Fitting a pad retaining pin over the spring tongue

7 Remove any scale or rust from the outer rim of the brake disc with a wire brush or file. Inspect the disc visually; if brake judder has been a problem, carry out a more thorough inspection (Section 6).
8 If new pads are to be fitted, press the caliper pistons back into their bores with a pair of pliers, being careful not to damage the dust boots. Remove some fluid from the master cylinder reservoir to prevent overflowing as the pistons are pressed back.

> **HAYNES HINT**
> *Remove fluid from the master cylinder reservoir using a clean syringe or an old poultry baster.*

9 On twin-piston calipers only, apply anti-seize compound or disc brake lubricant to the backs of the brake pads (the backs of the pads are pre-coated on single-piston calipers). Do not allow lubricant to contact the disc or pad friction surfaces. Also lubricate both sides of the anti-squeal shims (when fitted) and fit them to the pads.
10 Position the pads on the caliper bracket with the friction surfaces towards the disc. Fit a new damping spring to the caliper, with the arrows pointing upwards, then swing the caliper down over the pads. Make sure that the damping spring in the caliper is sitting correctly on the pads.
11 Insert a new guide pin bolt and tighten it to the specified torque.
12 Press the brake pedal several times to bring the pads up to the disc.
13 Repeat the operations on the other front brake.
14 Refit the roadwheels, lower the vehicle and tighten the wheel nuts.
15 Check and top-up the brake fluid level.
16 If new pads have been fitted, avoid hard braking as far as possible for the first few hundred miles to allow the linings to bed in.

5 Rear brake pads - renewal

⚠ *Warning: Disc brake pads must be renewed on both rear wheels at the same time - never renew*

the pads on only one wheel, as uneven braking may result. Dust created by wear of the pads may contain asbestos, which is a health hazard. Never blow it out with compressed air and do not inhale any of it. DO NOT use petroleum-based solvents to clean brake parts. Use brake cleaner or methylated spirit only. DO NOT allow any brake fluid, oil or grease to contact the brake pads or disc. Also refer to the warning at the start of Section 2 concerning the dangers of hydraulic fluid.

1 Slacken the rear wheel nuts, raise and support the rear of the car and remove the rear wheels.
2 Drive the two retaining pins out of the caliper using a hammer and punch **(see illustration)**. Recover the anti-rattle spring. Obtain a new spring for reassembly.
3 Press each pad away from the disc, using pliers. Do not lever between the pads and the disc.
4 Pull the pads out of the caliper, along with the anti-squeal shims (if fitted). Identify their position if they are to be re-used. Do not press the brake pedal with the pads removed.
5 Measure the thickness of the pad friction linings. If any one pad lining has worn down to the specified minimum, all four rear pads must be renewed. Do not interchange pads in an attempt to even out wear.
6 Clean the caliper with a damp rag or an old paintbrush. Inspect the caliper pistons and dust boots for signs of fluid leakage. Repair or renew as necessary (Section 9).
7 Inspect the visible surface of the brake disc. If deep scoring, cracks or grooves are evident, or if brake judder or snatch has been a problem, carry out a more thorough inspection (Section 7). Remove the caliper if necessary for access to the inboard face of the disc.
8 Anti-squeal shims may be fitted if wished, even if none were fitted before.
9 If new pads are to be fitted, press the caliper pistons back into their bores. Remove some fluid from the master cylinder reservoir to prevent overflowing as the pistons are pressed back **(see Haynes Hint)**.
10 Smear the backs of the pads and both sides of the anti-squeal shims (if used) with anti-seize compound or disc brake lubricant. Keep this off the friction surfaces of the pads.

11 Fit the pads and shims into the jaws of the caliper with the friction surfaces towards the disc **(see illustration)**.
12 Insert one of the pad retaining pins and tap it home. Fit a new anti-rattle spring and the other pad retaining pin, making sure that the pins pass over the tongues of the spring **(see illustration)**.
13 Pump the brake pedal several times to bring the new pads up to the discs.
14 Repeat the operations on the other rear brake.
15 Refit the roadwheels, lower the vehicle and tighten the wheel nuts.
16 Check the brake fluid level and top-up if necessary.
17 If new pads have been fitted, avoid harsh braking as far as possible for the first few hundred miles to allow the linings to bed in.

6 Front brake disc - inspection, removal and refitting

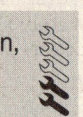

Note: *Before starting work, refer to the warning at the beginning of Section 4 concerning the dangers of asbestos dust.*

Inspection

Note: *If either disc requires renewal, BOTH should be renewed at the same time, to ensure even and consistent braking. New brake pads should also be fitted.*

1 Slacken the front wheel nuts, raise and support the front of the car and remove the front roadwheels.
2 Inspect the friction surfaces for cracks or deep scoring (light grooving is normal and may be ignored). A cracked disc must be renewed; a scored disc can be reclaimed by machining provided that the thickness is not reduced below the specified minimum.
3 Check the disc run-out using a dial test indicator with its probe positioned near the outer edge of the disc. If the run-out exceeds the figures given in the Specifications, machining may be possible, otherwise disc renewal will be necessary **(see Tool Tip)**.
4 Disc thickness variation in excess of 0.015 mm can also cause judder. Check this using a micrometer.

Braking system 9•5

TOOL TIP
If a dial test indicator is not available, check the run-out by positioning a fixed pointer near the outer edge, in contact with the disc face. Rotate the disc and measure the maximum displacement of the pointer with feeler blades.

Removal

5 Remove the brake caliper and bracket (Section 8), but do not disconnect the hydraulic hoses. Tie the caliper up so that the hoses are not strained.
6 Check whether the position of the disc in relation to the hub is marked, and if not, make your own mark as an aid to refitting. Remove the spigot pin which holds the disc to the hub and lift off the disc **(see illustrations)**.

Refitting

7 Ensure that the hub and disc mating faces are clean. Clean rustproofing compound off a new disc with methylated spirit and a rag.
8 Locate the disc on the hub with the orientation marks aligned and refit the retaining spigot pin.
9 Refit the brake caliper and bracket (Section 8).

7 Rear brake disc - inspection, removal and refitting

Note: *Before starting work, refer to the warning at the beginning of Section 5 concerning the dangers of asbestos dust.*

Inspection

1 The inspection procedures are the same as for the front brake disc, and reference should be made to Section 6, paragraphs 1 to 4 inclusive. Additionally, after removal, check the condition of the handbrake drums. Refinishing, run-out and out-of-round limits are given in the Specifications. The drums are unlikely to wear unless the handbrake is habitually used to stop the vehicle.

Removal

2 Remove the rear brake caliper without disconnecting the hydraulic hose (Section 9). Tie the caliper up out of the way.

6.6a Remove the spigot pin . . .

3 If a wheel locating spigot is fitted, unscrew it from the disc.
4 Mark the position of the disc in relation to the hub, make sure that the handbrake is released, then pull off the disc. Tap it with a soft-faced mallet if necessary to free it **(see illustration)**.

Refitting

5 Refit by reversing the removal procedure. If a new disc is being fitted, remove the traces of rustproofing compound from it.

8 Front brake caliper - removal, overhaul and refitting

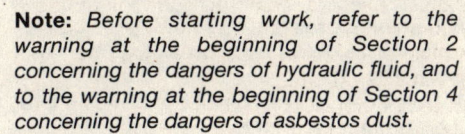

Note: *Before starting work, refer to the warning at the beginning of Section 2 concerning the dangers of hydraulic fluid, and to the warning at the beginning of Section 4 concerning the dangers of asbestos dust.*

Removal

1 Remove the brake pads as described in Section 4, then disconnect the caliper hose(s) from the hydraulic pipe(s) at the bracket on the inner wing. On twin piston calipers, identify the hoses so that they can be refitted to the same pipes; be prepared for hydraulic fluid spillage. Keep dirt out of the open unions.

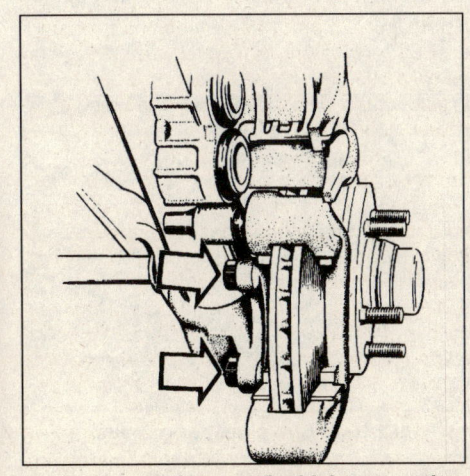

8.4 Two bolts (arrowed) which secure the front caliper bracket

6.6b . . . and lift off the brake disc

2 On ABS models, release the ABS wiring harness from the brake hose.
3 Unscrew the caliper upper guide pin bolt and remove the caliper, complete with brake hose(s) from the caliper bracket.
4 If it is wished to remove the caliper bracket, undo the two bolts which secure it to the steering knuckle **(see illustration)**. Obtain new bolts for reassembly.

Overhaul

5 With the brake caliper removed, clean it externally with methylated spirit and a soft brush.
6 Remove the hydraulic hose(s) and the bleed screws. Empty any remaining hydraulic fluid out of the caliper.
7 Remove the piston dust boot(s) and pull the piston(s) out of the bore **(see illustrations)**. If the caliper piston is reluctant to move, refit the bleed screw and apply **low** air pressure (eg from a foot pump) to the fluid inlet, but note that the piston may be ejected with some force. On twin piston calipers, refit both bleed

7.4 Removing a rear brake disc

8.7a Remove a piston dust boot . . .

8.7b . . . and the piston itself

9

9•6 Braking system

8.13 Fit a new piston seal into the groove

screws and cover the second fluid inlet with your finger. Identify the piston locations if they are to be re-used

8 Hook out the piston seal(s) from the bore using a blunt instrument.
9 Clean the pistons and bores with a lint-free rag and some clean brake fluid or methylated spirit. Slight imperfections may be polished out with steel wool. Pitting, scoring or wear ridging of bores or pistons mean that the whole caliper must be renewed.
10 Renew all rubber components (seals, dust boots and bellows) as a matter of course. Blow through the fluid inlet and bleed screw holes with compressed air.
11 Check that the guide pins slide easily in their housings. Clean or renew them as necessary, and lubricate them with a copper-based anti-seize compound.
12 Lubricate the new piston seal(s) with clean brake fluid. Insert the seal(s) into the groove in the bore, using the fingers only **(see illustration)**.
13 Fit a new dust boot to the piston(s) ensuring that it is properly seated in the piston groove. Extend the dust boot ready for fitting.
14 Lubricate the piston(s) and bore(s) with clean brake fluid, or with assembly lubricant if this is supplied with the repair kit.
15 Offer the piston and dust boot to the caliper. Engage the dust boot with the groove in the piston housing, then push the piston through the dust boot into the caliper bore. Engage the dust boot with the groove on the piston. Where applicable, repeat the above operation on the other piston and bore.
16 Refit the bleed screws, hydraulic hoses and other disturbed components.

Refitting

17 When refitting the caliper bracket, apply thread locking compound to the new retaining bolts and tighten them to the specified torque.
18 Refit the caliper to the bracket and secure with the upper guide pin bolt. Refit the brake pads as described in Section 4 and reconnect the hydraulic hoses. Check the "set" of the hoses ensuring that they aren't twisted or kinked.
19 Bleed the hydraulic system on completion (Section 2).

9 Rear brake caliper - removal, overhaul and refitting

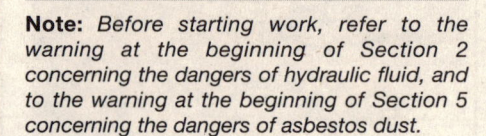

Note: *Before starting work, refer to the warning at the beginning of Section 2 concerning the dangers of hydraulic fluid, and to the warning at the beginning of Section 5 concerning the dangers of asbestos dust.*

Removal

1 Remove the rear brake pads (Section 5).
2 Clean around the hydraulic union on the caliper. Slacken the union half a turn **(see illustration)**.
3 Remove the two bolts which secure the caliper. Of the four bolts on the caliper, these are the two nearest the hub. Do not remove the other two bolts, which hold the caliper halves together. Obtain new bolts for refitting.
4 Remove the caliper from the disc and unscrew it from the hydraulic hose. Be prepared for fluid spillage. Plug or cap open unions.

Overhaul

5 This is essentially the same procedure as that described for the front caliper (Section 8).
Do not attempt to separate the caliper halves to facilitate removal of the pistons.

Refitting

6 Commence refitting by screwing the caliper onto the flexible hose. Do not tighten the union fully yet.
7 Fit the caliper over the disc and secure it to the axle bracket with two new bolts. Tighten the bolts to the specified torque.
8 Tighten the flexible hose union at the caliper. Check that the routing and "set" of the hose are such that it does not contact adjacent components. Correct if necessary by releasing the hose union at the brake pipe bracket, repositioning the hose and tightening the union.
9 Refit the brake pads (Section 5).
10 Bleed the appropriate hydraulic circuit (Section 2).

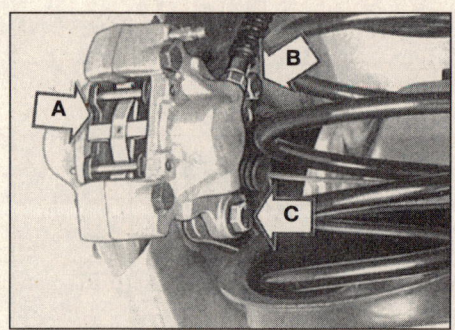

9.2 Rear brake caliper removal
A Rear pads
B Hydraulic union
C Caliper securing bolts

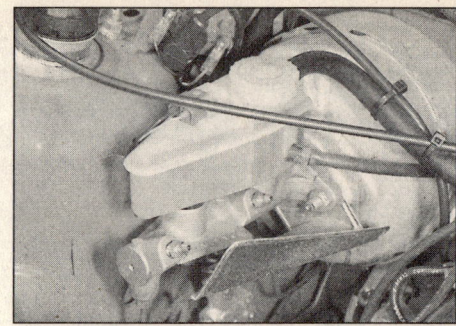

10.3 Master cylinder fitted to later models. Note heat shield at base of unit

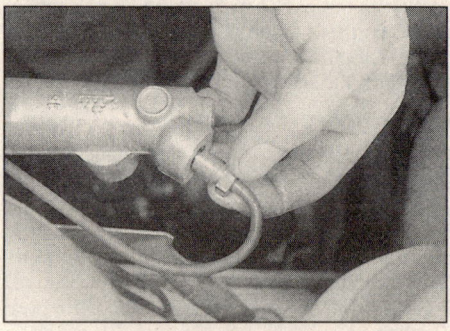

10.5 A master cylinder hydraulic union

10 Brake master cylinder - removal, overhaul and refitting

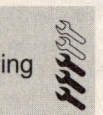

Note: *Before starting work, refer to the warning at the beginning of Section 2.*

Removal

1 Syphon as much fluid as possible from the master cylinder reservoir, using a hydrometer or old poultry baster.

⚠ **Warning: Do not syphon the fluid by mouth, it is poisonous.**

2 Where applicable, disconnect the low fluid level sensor wiring connector from the reservoir.
3 Unbolt the heat shield (when fitted) from around the master cylinder **(see illustration)**.
4 Disconnect the clutch master cylinder feed pipe from the side of the reservoir (when applicable). Be prepared for fluid spillage. Plug the open end of the pipe.
5 Disconnect the hydraulic unions from the master cylinder. Expect fluid spillage. Cap the open unions to keep dirt out **(see illustration)**.
6 Remove the nuts which secure the master cylinder to the servo. Pull the master cylinder off the servo studs and remove it **(see illustration)**. Be careful not to spill hydraulic fluid on the paintwork.

Overhaul

Note: *Master cylinder overhaul is only possible on pre-1992 models without ABS. If overhaul is necessary on models from 1992 onward, or on all models with ABS, the master cylinder must be renewed as a complete assembly.*

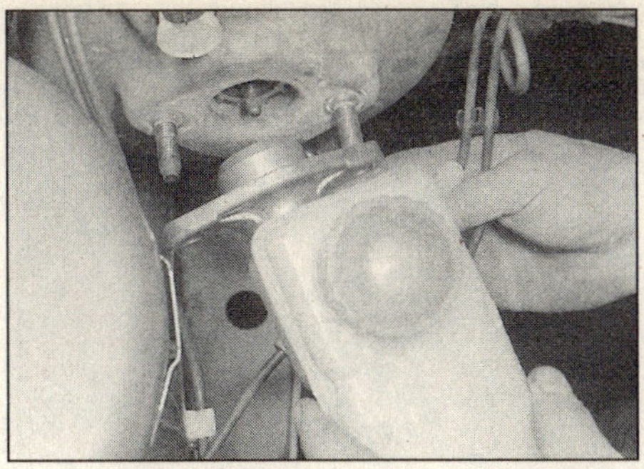

Braking system 9•7

10.6 Removing the master cylinder

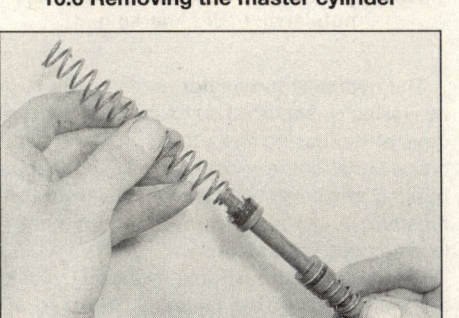

10.9 Remove circlip to release the pistons

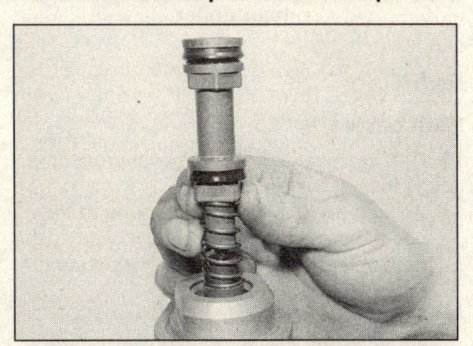

10.15a Fitting the spring seat . . .

10.15b . . . and the spring

10.15c Fitting pistons into master cylinder

7 Empty the fluid out of the master cylinder by pumping the pistons with a screwdriver. Clean the cylinder externally.
8 Pull the reservoir off the master cylinder and recover the seals.
9 Depress the pistons and extract the circlip from the mouth of the cylinder **(see illustration)**.
10 Shake the pistons, spring seat and spring out of the cylinder.
11 Inspect the master cylinder bore. If it is badly corroded or scratched, renew the cylinder complete. Light scoring or surface rust may be removed with steel wool and methylated spirit.
12 Obtain a repair kit, which will contain new pistons with seals already fitted.
13 Clean all parts not being renewed with methylated spirit. Blow through fluid passages with an air line or foot pump.
14 Lubricate the cylinder bore with clean hydraulic fluid. Apply more fluid to the pistons and seals, or smear them with assembly lubricant if this is supplied in the kit.
15 Assemble the spring, spring seat and pistons. Make sure that all components are perfectly clean, then insert the spring and pistons into the master cylinder. Depress the pistons and insert the circlip **(see illustrations)**.
16 Refit the reservoir and seals; renew the seals if necessary. Make sure the reservoir cap breather hole is clear.

Refitting

17 Refit by reversing the removal operations. Bleed the complete brake hydraulic system (Section 2), and if necessary the clutch hydraulic system (Chapter 6), on completion.

11 Brake pedal - removal and refitting

The procedure for removal and refitting of the brake pedal is the same as for the clutch pedal. Refer to Chapter 6, Section 3.

12 Brake servo - removal and refitting

Removal

1 Remove the brake master cylinder (see Section 10). If care is taken, the master cylinder can be moved away from the servo without disconnecting the hydraulic unions. It will be necessary to disconnect the clutch master cylinder feed pipe, however.
2 Disconnect the servo vacuum feed, either

13.4a Front of handbrake shoes, showing strut

by disconnecting the hose or by levering out the check valve.
3 Inside the vehicle, remove the steering column/pedal trim. Disconnect the servo clevis from the brake pedal.
4 Remove the four servo securing nuts.
5 Withdraw the servo from the engine bay.

Refitting

6 Refit by reversing the removal operations. If a new servo is being fitted, adjust the pushrod if necessary to give small clearance between the servo pushrod and the master cylinder piston in the resting position.
7 Bleed the hydraulic system on completion if necessary (Section 2).

13 Handbrake shoes - inspection and renewal

Inspection

1 Slacken the handbrake cable adjuster (Chapter 1).
2 Remove the rear brake disc (Section 7).
3 Inspect the shoes for wear, damage or oil contamination. Renew them if necessary and rectify the source of any contamination. As with the brake pads, the shoes must be renewed in axle sets.

Renewal

4 Prise the shoes apart and displace the operating mechanism from them at the rear end, and the strut from them at the front **(see illustrations)**.

13.4b Disengaging the rear of the shoes from the operating mechanism

9•8 Braking system

13.6 Handbrake shoe engaged in U-clip

14.4 Handbrake cable showing rubber gaiter

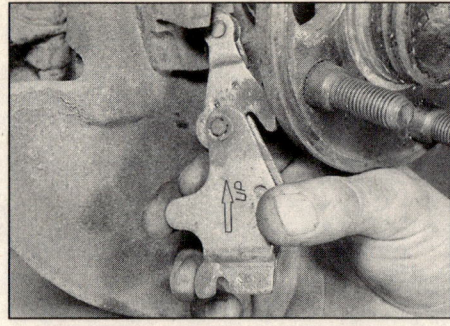

14.12 Refitting the handbrake mechanism - note arrow "UP" marking

5 Unhook one of the coil return springs from one of the shoes, working through the hole in the halfshaft flange.
6 Free the shoes from the U-clips on the backplate and remove them complete with springs **(see illustration)**.
7 Refit the shoes by reversing the removal operations. Adjust the handbrake on completion (Chapter 1).

14 Handbrake cables - removal and refitting

Removal

Short (right-hand) cable

1 Remove the handbrake shoes on the right-hand side (Section 13).
2 Free the cable from the operating mechanism by pushing out the clevis pin.
3 Remove the clevis pin from the other end of the cable. Free the cable from the guides or retaining clips and remove it.
4 Check the condition of the rubber gaiter and renew it if necessary **(see illustration)**.

Long (left-hand) cable

5 Inside the vehicle, slacken off the handbrake adjustment as far as possible (Chapter 1).
6 Remove the centre console and the rear seat cushion (Chapter 11). Lift up the carpets as necessary to expose the cable exit point in the floor pan.
7 Bend up the locking tab and release the cable from the handbrake lever.
8 Remove the handbrake shoes on the left-hand side (Section 13).
9 Free the cable from the operating mechanism by pressing out the clevis pin.
10 Release the cable from the brake backplate and from the rear axle.
11 Release the cable from the under-floor clamps and grommets and remove it. Transfer the grommets etc to the new cable. Renew the rubber gaiter if necessary.

Refitting

Both cables

12 Refit by reversing the removal procedure, noting the following points:
a) Apply brake anti-seize compound to the operating mechanism and backplate rubbing surfaces. Keep the compound off brake friction surfaces.
b) Fit the operating mechanism with the arrow visible and pointing upwards **(see illustration)**.
c) Adjust the handbrake on completion (Chapter 1).

15 Anti-lock braking system (ABS) - general information

When fitted, the anti-lock braking system monitors the rotational speed of the wheels under braking. Sudden deceleration of one wheel, indicating that lock-up is occurring, causes the hydraulic pressure to that wheel's brake to be reduced or interrupted momentarily. Monitoring and correction take place several times per second, giving rise to a "pulsing" effect at the brake pedal when correction is taking place. The system gives inexperienced drivers a good chance of retaining control when braking hard on slippery surfaces.

The main components are the sensors, the control unit and the hydraulic modulator.

One sensor is fitted to each front wheel, picking up speed information from a pulse wheel carried on the wheel hub. Rear wheel speed information is picked up from the speedometer sensor in the differential housing. For ABS purposes the rear wheels are treated as one unit.

Information from the sensors is fed to the control unit which is located in the driver's footwell area. The control unit operates solenoid valves in the hydraulic modulator, located in the engine compartment, to restrict if necessary the supply to either front caliper or both rear calipers. The control unit also illuminates a warning light in the event of system malfunction.

The hydraulic modulator contains a pump as well as solenoid valves. It is a semi-active device, increasing the effort applied at the brake pedal. If the modulator fails, adequate braking effort will still be available from the master cylinder and servo, though the anti-lock function will be lost.

On models with ABS, the hydraulic circuits are split front to rear (axle-split) instead of triangularly.

To avoid damage to the ABS control unit, do not subject it to voltage surges in excess of 16V, nor to temperatures in excess of 80°C.

16 Anti-lock Braking System (ABS) components - removal and refitting

Removal

Front wheel sensor

1 Follow the sensor wiring back to the suspension turret. Separate the connector, push the wires out of it and feed them back into the wheel arch.
2 Remove the Allen screw which secures the sensor to the steering knuckle. Withdraw the sensor and its wiring.

Front disc pulse wheel

3 The front pulse wheel is a press fit on the front wheel hub and special tools are required for removal. This work should be entrusted to a Volvo dealer.

Rear wheel sensor

4 This is the same as the speedometer sender, refer to Chapter 12, Section 7 for details.

Control unit

5 Disconnect the battery negative lead.
6 Remove the trim from below the instrument panel and around the right-hand side of the driver's footwell.
7 Identify the control unit, free it from its strap and withdraw it **(see illustration)**. Disconnect the wiring plug from the unit and remove it.

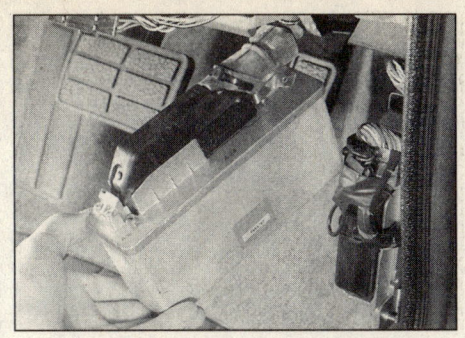

16.7 ABS control unit removal

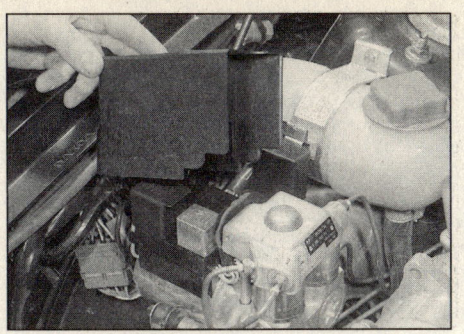

16.8 Removing the hydraulic modulator cover

16.10 Hydraulic pipe connections at the ABS hydraulic modulator fitted to later models

Hydraulic modulator

Note: *Before starting work, refer to the warning at the beginning of Section 2 concerning the dangers of hydraulic fluid.*

8 Disconnect the battery negative lead. Remove the securing screw and lift the cover off the hydraulic modulator **(see illustration)**.
9 Remove both relays from the modulator. Undo the cable clamp screw and disconnect the multi-plug. Also disconnect the earth strap.
10 Inspect the hydraulic pipes for identification marks. Mark the pipes if necessary, following the identification letters on the modulator **(see illustration)**:

Early units:
V - front Inlet
H - rear Inlet
l - outlet, left front
r - outlet, right front
h - outlet, rear

Later units:
LF - outlet, left front
RF - outlet, right front
RR - outlet, rear
F - front inlet
R - rear inlet

11 Place rags under the modulator to catch spilt fluid. Disconnect the hydraulic unions.
12 Remove the two nuts and one bolt which secure the modulator. Remove the modulator, being careful not to spill hydraulic fluid on the paintwork.

Refitting

13 In all cases, refit by reversing the removal operations but noting the following points:

a) When refitting the front wheel sensor, apply a little of the special grease (Volvo No 1 161 037-5, or equivalent) to the body of the sensor.
b) Bleed the complete hydraulic system after refitting the hydraulic modulator.

Notes

Chapter 10
Suspension and steering

Contents

Accessory drivebelts check and renewal ....See Chapter 1
Front anti-roll bar - removal and refitting 6
Front control arm - removal and refitting 3
Front control arm balljoint - removal and refitting 4
Front radius rod - removal and refitting 5
Front suspension strut - dismantling and reassembly 8
Front suspension strut - removal and refitting 7
Front wheel bearings - checking and renewal 2
General information 1
Panhard rod - removal and refitting 16
Power steering fluid level check ....See "Weekly checks"
Power steering gear - removal and refitting 20
Power steering pump - removal and refitting 23
Power steering system - bleeding 22
Rear anti-roll bar - removal and refitting 15
Rear shock absorber - removal, testing and refitting 14
Rear spring - removal and refitting 13
Rear subframe and mountings - removal and refitting 11
Rear torque rods - removal and refitting 10
Rear trailing arm - removal and refitting 12
Steering column - removal and refitting 18
Steering column lock/ignition switch - removal and refitting ...19
Steering rack bellows - renewal 21
Steering and suspension check ....See Chapter 1
Steering wheel - removal and refitting 17
Suspension rubber bushes - renewal 9
Track rod end - removal and refitting 24
Tyre condition and pressure checks ....See "Weekly checks"
Wheel alignment and steering angles - general information ...25

Degrees of difficulty

| **Easy,** suitable for novice with little experience | **Fairly easy,** suitable for beginner with some experience | **Fairly difficult,** suitable for competent DIY mechanic | **Difficult,** suitable for experienced DIY mechanic | **Very difficult,** suitable for expert DIY or professional |

Specifications

Steering
Power steering fluid type .... See "Weekly checks"

Front wheel alignment and steering angles
Castor .... 5.0° ± 1.0°
Camber .... 0.1° ± 1.0°
Toe setting (measured at wheel rims) .... 2.2 ± 1.0 mm toe-in

Roadwheels
Lateral run-out:
  Aluminium .... 0.8 mm maximum
  Steel .... 1.0 mm maximum
Radial run-out:
  Aluminium .... 0.6 mm maximum
  Steel .... 0.8 mm maximum

Torque wrench settings   Nm

Front suspension
Front wheel hub nut:
  Stage 1 100
  Stage 2 .... Angle tighten 45° further
Control arm ballpin nut 70
Balljoint to strut:
  Stage 1 30
  Stage 2 .... Angle tighten 90° further
Control arm to crossmember* 85
Radius rod to control arm* 100
Radius rod to subframe* 120
Strut top mounting (to body) 50
Strut piston rod nut 70
Crossmember to body 95
*Use new fastenings every time

10•2 Suspension and steering

Rear suspension
Trailing arm to axle	45
Trailing arm bracket bolts	45
Trailing arm bracket nuts	85
Rear spring upper mounting	48
Shock absorber mountings	85
Panhard rod bolts	85
Torque rods	140
Subframe front mounting	85
Subframe rear bush bracket	48

Steering
Steering wheel bolt	32
Steering column universal joints	21
Steering gear to crossmember:	
Stage 1	35
Stage 2	Angle tighten 150° further
Track rod end balljoint nut	60
Track rod end locknut	70
Steering column mountings	24
Hydraulic union banjo bolts:	
Pressure unions	30
Return unions	25

Roadwheels
Wheel nuts	See Chapter 1

1 General information

The independent front suspension is of the MacPherson strut type incorporating coil springs and integral telescopic shock absorbers. The struts are located at their lower ends by control arms, each carrying a balljoint. The control arms are attached to the front crossmember, to a radius rod each, and to the front anti-roll bar.

Rear suspension is of the non-independent live rear axle type. The axle is supported by two trailing arms, two torque rods and a Panhard rod. The torque rods are attached to a central subframe, and a coil spring and a telescopic shock absorber are attached to each trailing arm. An anti-roll bar may also be fitted.

Steering is by power-assisted rack and pinion on all models. Power assistance is derived from a hydraulic pump, belt-driven from the crankshaft pulley.

2 Front wheel bearings - checking and renewal

Checking

1 Raise and support the front of the vehicle with the wheels free (see "*Jacking and vehicle support*").
2 Hold the wheel at top and bottom and try to rock it. Spin the wheel and listen for rumbling or grinding noises. Play should be barely perceptible and noise should be absent.
3 No adjustment is possible and if play or noise is evident, renewal is the only course of action.

Renewal

Note: *A new hub retaining nut will be required for refitting.*

4 The hub and wheel bearings are a single assembly. If the bearings are worn, the complete hub must be renewed.
5 Remove the front brake caliper and bracket (see Chapter 9, Section 8), but do not disconnect the hydraulic hoses. Tie the caliper up so that the hoses are not strained.
6 Remove the spigot pin which holds the disc to the hub. Lift off the disc **(see illustrations)**.
7 Prise or chisel off the bearing dust cap. Obtain a new cap for reassembly.
8 Undo the hub nut now exposed. This nut is very tight so make sure the car is well supported. Use a new nut on reassembly.
9 Pull the hub and bearings off the stub axle **(see illustration)**. The inner race of the inboard bearing may remain on the stub axle; if so pull it off.

2.6a Remove the spigot pin . . .

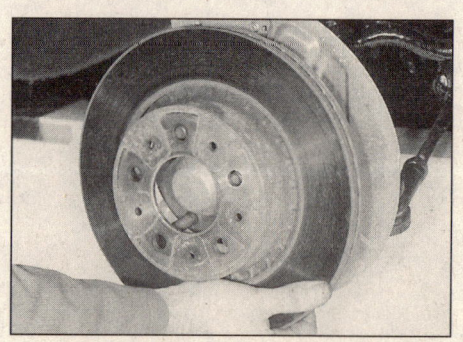

2.6b . . . and lift off the brake disc

2.9 Removing the hub (with ABS pulse wheel) from the stub axle

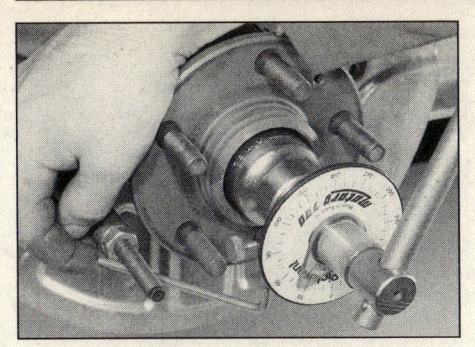

Suspension and steering 10•3

2.11 Angle-tightening the front hub nut

3.2 Control arm balljoint - split pin partly withdrawn

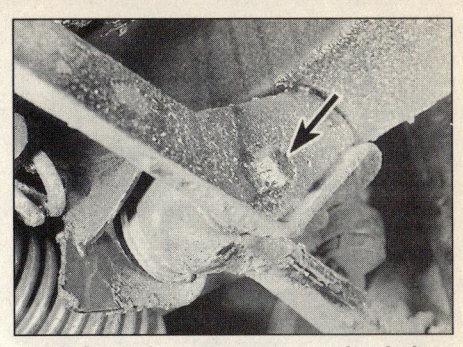

3.5 Control arm-to-crossmember bolt (arrowed)

10 Clean the stub axle and lightly grease it before fitting the new hub and bearing assembly.
11 Fit the nut and tighten it to the stage one specified torque. Tighten the nut further through the angle specified for stage two **(see illustration)**.
12 Refit the remaining components in the reverse order to removal.

3 Front control arm - removal and refitting

Note: All nuts and bolts which are angled tightened on reassembly (see Specifications) must be renewed.

Removal
1 Slacken the front wheel nuts, raise and support the front of the car and remove the front wheel (see "*Jacking and vehicle support*").
2 Remove the split pin and nut from the ballpin nut **(see illustration)**. Obtain a new split pin for reassembly.
3 Unbolt the anti-roll bar link and the radius rod from the control arm. Obtain a new bolt for reassembly.
4 Separate the control arm from the balljoint, using a proprietary balljoint separator if necessary. Be careful not to damage the balljoint.
5 Remove the control arm-to-crossmember nut and bolt **(see illustration)**. Remove the control arm from the crossmember. Obtain a new nut and bolt for reassembly.

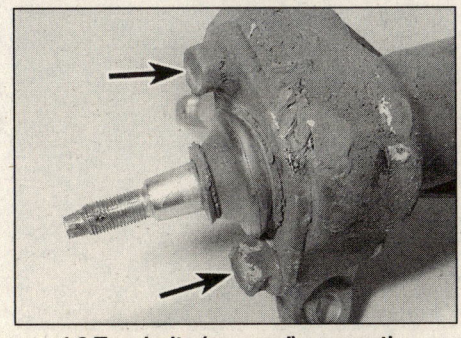

Refitting
6 Refit by reversing the removal operations, but do not fully tighten the control arm-to-crossmember nut and bolt until the weight of the vehicle is back on its wheels. Rock the vehicle to settle the suspension, then tighten the nut and bolt to the specified torque.

4 Front control arm balljoint - removal and refitting

Removal
Note: All nuts and bolts which are angled tightened on reassembly (see Specifications) must be renewed.

1 Proceed as for control arm removal (Section 3, paragraphs 1 to 4) but without unbolting the radius rod.
2 Remove the two bolts which secure the balljoint to the strut **(see illustration)**. Remove the balljoint.

Refitting
3 When refitting, use new bolts to secure the balljoint and apply thread locking compound to them. Tighten the bolts in the specified stages, making sure that the balljoint is properly seated.
4 The remainder of refitting is a reversal of the removal procedure.

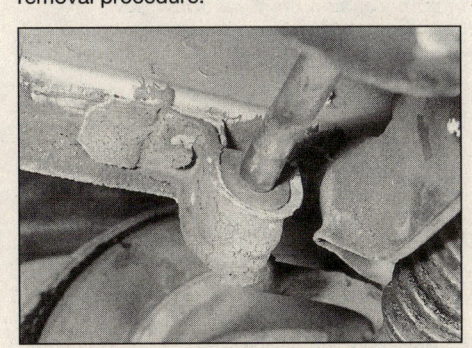

5 Front radius rod - removal and refitting

Removal
Note: All nuts and bolts which are angled tightened on reassembly (see Specifications) must be renewed.

1 Slacken the front wheel nuts, raise and support the car and remove the front wheel.
2 Unbolt the radius rod from the control arm and from the subframe. Remove the radius rod.

Refitting
3 Refitting is a reversal of removal, using new nuts and bolts to secure the radius rod. Do not fully tighten the radius rod-to-subframe nut and bolt until the car is back on its wheels and it has been rocked a few times.

6 Front anti-roll bar - removal and refitting

Removal
1 Raise the front of the vehicle on ramps, or drive it over a pit.
2 Unbolt the two saddle brackets which secure the anti-roll bar **(see illustration)**.
3 Unbolt the anti-roll bar from its end links, or unbolt the end links from the control arms, as preferred **(see illustration)**.

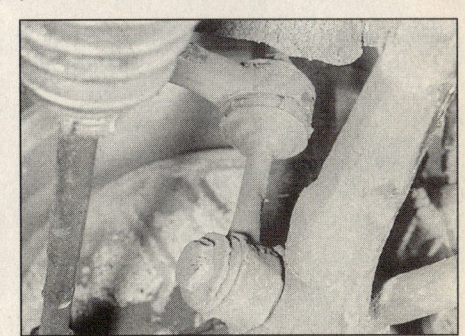

4.2 Two bolts (arrowed) secure the balljoint to the strut (strut removed)

6.2 An anti-roll bar saddle bracket

6.3 An anti-roll bar link

10

10•4 Suspension and steering

6.5 Tighten the anti-roll bar link nut (arrowed) to achieve the dimension shown

7.9 Releasing the piston rod nut (strut removed)

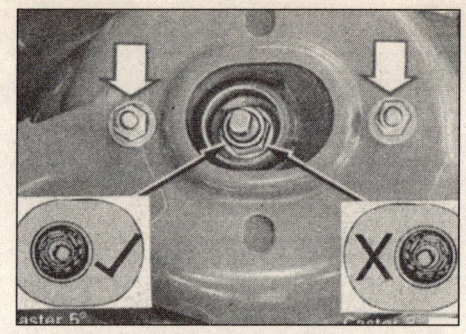

7.11 Correct fitting of strut gives correct castor (inset, left). Top mounting nuts arrowed; right-hand strut shown

Refitting

4 Refit by reversing the removal operations. Renew the mounting rubbers as necessary. (The saddle bracket rubbers are split and may be renewed without removing the anti-roll bar.)
5 Tighten the link upper nuts to achieve the correct dimension between the washers **(see illustration)**.

7 Front suspension strut - removal and refitting

Removal

1 Slacken the front wheel nuts, raise and support the front of the vehicle and remove the front wheel.
2 Remove the brake caliper (see Chapter 9, Section 8), but do not disconnect the hydraulic hoses. Tie the caliper up so that the hoses are not strained.
3 On models with ABS, disconnect or remove the wheel sensor.
4 If the strut is to be renewed, remove the front hub assembly (see Section 2) then remove the brake backplate.
5 Remove the split pin from the suspension bottom balljoint nut. Unscrew the nut to the end of the threads. Free the ballpin from the control arm using a proprietary balljoint separator, then remove the nut.
6 Similarly separate the track rod end balljoint from the steering arm.

7 Lever the control arm downwards and free it from the bottom balljoint. If there is not enough movement to allow this, unbolt the anti-roll bar link.
8 Remove the cover from the strut top mounting. Note which way round the mounting is fitted: it is not symmetrical.
9 If the strut is to be dismantled, slacken the piston rod nut, at the same time counter-holding the piston rod **(see illustration)**.
Caution: Do not remove the nut, just slacken it a turn or two.
10 Have an assistant support the strut. Check that all attachments have been removed, then remove the two top mounting nuts. Remove the strut through the wheel arch.

Refitting

11 Refit by reversing the removal operations, noting the following points:

a) Observe the correct fitted direction of the top mounting **(see illustration)**.
b) Tighten all fastenings to their specified torques.

8 Front suspension strut - dismantling and reassembly

Warning: Before attempting to dismantle the shock absorber and coil spring assembly, a suitable tool to hold the spring in compression must be obtained.

Adjustable coil spring compressors are readily available, and are recommended for this operation. Any attempt at dismantling without such a tool is likely to result in damage or personal injury.

Dismantling

1 Remove the strut from the vehicle (see Section 7).
2 Fit spring compressors to catch at least three coils of the spring. Tighten the compressors until the load is taken off the spring seats. Make sure that the compressors are secure.
3 Remove the piston rod nut (which should already have been slackened) and the strut top mounting. Note the position of any washers **(see illustrations)**.
4 Remove the spring upper seat, the spring itself, the washer, bump stop and bellows. (With gas-filled shock absorbers there is no bump stop.) Do not drop or jar the compressed spring.
5 Recover the rubber ring (when fitted) from the spring lower seat.
6 Using a C-spanner or similar tool, unscrew the shock absorber retaining nut **(see illustration)**.
7 Pull the shock absorber out of its tube.
8 Dismantling of the strut is now complete. Renew components as necessary, remembering that it is good practice to renew springs and shock absorbers in pairs.
9 If the spring is to be renewed, carefully remove the compressors from the old spring and fit them to the new one.

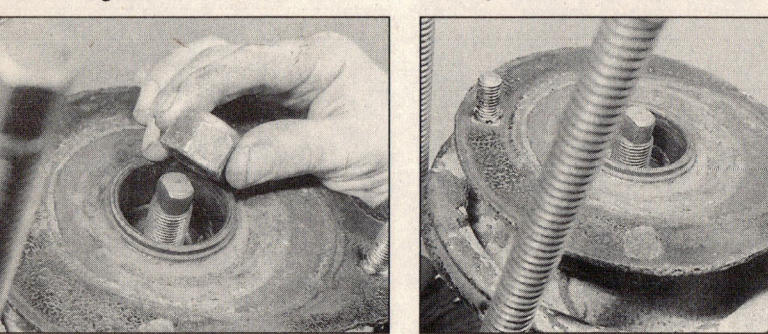

8.3a Removing the piston rod nut . . .

8.3b . . . and the strut top mounting

8.6 Unscrewing the shock absorber nut with a C-spanner

Suspension and steering 10•5

11.2 Rear subframe and torque rods
1 Front mounting
2 Subframe
3 X-link
4 Lower torque rod
5 Upper torque rod
6 Rear mounting

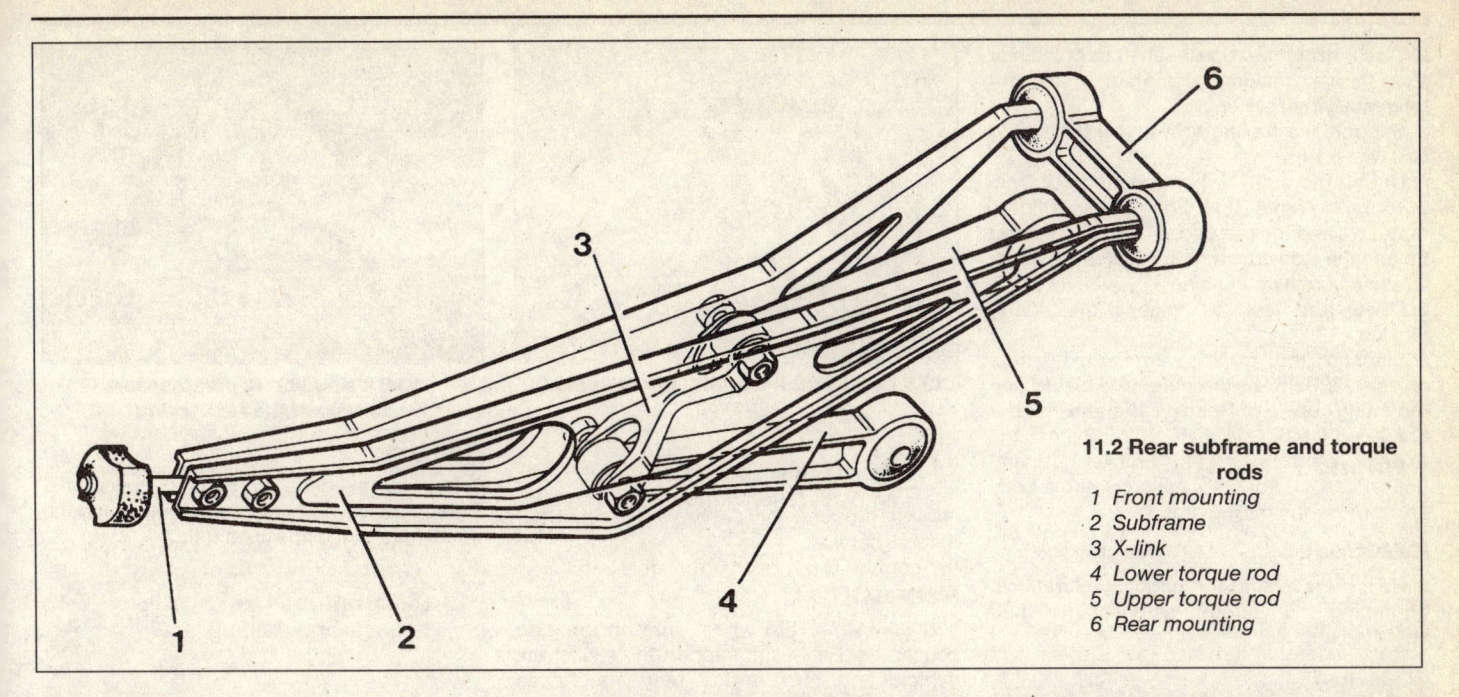

Reassembly

10 Reassemble by reversing the dismantling operations. Note the relationship of the disc to the bellows on models with gas-filled shock absorbers **(see illustration)**. Do not fully tighten the piston rod nut until the top mounting has been secured to the vehicle.

11 Ensure that the axial ball-bearing in the top mounting is fitted with the yellow side up, and the grey or orange side down. Incorrect fitting will result in the bearing being too tightly clamped, with consequent problems of stiff steering and noise.

9 Suspension rubber bushes - renewal

1 The principle of bush renewal is simple enough: the old bush is pressed out and the new one is pressed in. The reality is slightly more difficult.

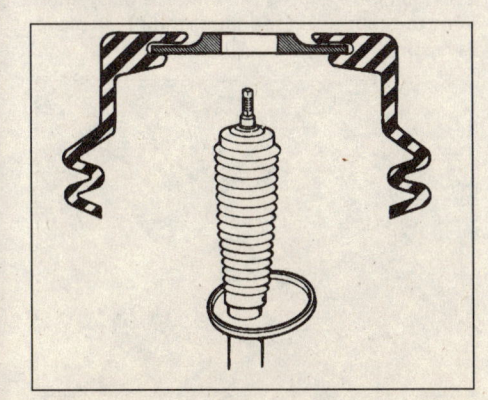

8.10 Bellows and disc fitted with gas-filled shock absorbers

2 Various special tools are specified by the makers for bush renewal. They are basically mandrels and tubes of different sizes which are used with a suitable press and sometimes with V-blocks. The amateur may experiment with a bench vice and socket spanners or pieces of tubing, using liquid soap or petroleum jelly as a lubricant. If this is unsuccessful it will be necessary to have the bush renewed by a workshop having press facilities.

3 Bush renewal *in situ* is not recommended.

10 Rear torque rods - removal and refitting

Removal

1 Raise and support the rear of the vehicle (see "Jacking and vehicle support").
2 Remove the front mounting bolts from both torque rods, even if only one is to be removed.
3 Unbolt and remove the torque rods. Recover the X-link.

Refitting

4 When refitting, unbolt the subframe front mounting to allow movement of the subframe. Fit the torque rods to the rear axle first without tightening the mountings, then attach them and the X-link to the subframe.
5 Tighten the torque rod-to-subframe mountings to the specified torque.
6 Tighten the subframe front mounting to the specified torque.
7 With the weight of the vehicle back on the rear wheels, tighten the torque rod-to-axle mountings to the specified torque.

11 Rear subframe and mountings - removal and refitting

Removal

1 Raise and support the rear of the vehicle (see "Jacking and vehicle support").
2 Remove the subframe front mounting nuts and bolts **(see illustration)**.
3 The front mounting rubber and mounting bracket may now be removed if wished, using a chisel and some lubricant around the rubber. Note the orientation of the rubber.
4 To remove the subframe completely, unbolt the torque rods and X-link from it. Also release the handbrake cable from the subframe bracket.
5 Refit one of the front mounting bolts. Hook a G-clamp behind the bolt and use the clamp to pull the subframe out of the rear mountings.
6 The rear mounting bracket can now be unbolted if required.

Refitting

7 Refit by reversing the removal operations, noting the following points:
a) Use petroleum jelly as a lubricant for the mounting rubbers.
b) Carry out the final tightening of the front mounting before that of the torque rods.

12 Rear trailing arm - removal and refitting

Removal

1 Proceed as if for rear spring removal (see Section 13, paragraphs 1 to 3).

10•6 Suspension and steering

2 Disconnect the propeller shaft from the rear axle flange, making alignment marks for reference when refitting.
3 Support the trailing arm below the spring pan with a jack.
4 Unbolt the anti-roll bar (when fitted) from both trailing arms. If no anti-roll bar is fitted, remove the shock absorber lower mounting bolt on the side concerned. Slacken the lower mounting on the other side.
5 Lower the jack to release the spring tension.
6 Slacken the trailing arm-to-axle nuts crosswise. Remove the nuts, axle clamp and mounting rubbers. Recover the anti-roll bar bracket, if fitted.
7 Remove the trailing arm bracket nuts and bolts. Prise the front mounting out of the body and remove the trailing arm.

Refitting

8 Refit by reversing the removal operations, tightening the various fastenings to their specified torques.

13 Rear spring - removal and refitting

Removal

Note: *New rear brake caliper retaining bolts will be required for refitting.*

1 Slacken the rear wheel nuts on the side concerned. Raise and support the rear of the vehicle so that both rear wheels hang free. Remove the rear wheel.
2 Remove the two bolts which secure the rear brake caliper. Slide the caliper off the disc and tie it up so that the flexible hose is not strained. Obtain new bolts for reassembly.
3 If the exhaust system will be in the way, unhook it from its mountings and lower it or move it aside.
4 Jack up the trailing arm slightly to take the load off the shock absorber. Remove the shock absorber lower mounting nut and bolt. Lower the jack.
5 Remove the nut which secures the spring upper seat **(see illustration)**.
6 Pull the trailing arm downwards as far as possible. Pull the top of the spring downwards until the upper seat is clear of the mounting stud, then remove the spring and seat rearwards. If difficulty is experienced, either use spring compressors to unload the spring, or disconnect the rear anti-roll bar to allow the trailing arm more downward movement **(see illustration)**.
7 Inspect the spring seat rubbers and renew them if necessary.

Refitting

8 Refitting is a reversal of removal, tightening the fastenings to their specified torques. Use new bolts to secure the brake caliper.
9 Refit the roadwheel, lower the vehicle and tighten the wheel nuts.

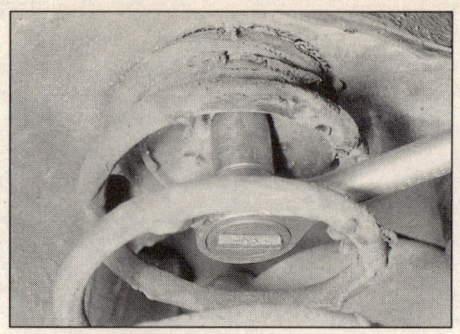

13.5 Removing the spring upper seat nut

14 Rear shock absorber - removal, testing and refitting

Removal

1 Slacken the rear wheel nuts on the side concerned. Raise and support the rear of the vehicle and remove the rear wheel (see "*Jacking and vehicle support*").
2 Jack up the trailing arm slightly to take the load off the shock absorber. Remove the shock absorber lower mounting nut and bolt **(see illustration)**. Lower the jack.
3 In the wheel arch, remove the rubber bung covering the shock absorber upper mounting bolt **(see illustration)**. Remove the bolt.
4 Pull the shock absorber downwards and remove it.

Testing

5 Examine the shock absorber for fluid leakage. Check the spindle for signs of wear or pitting along its entire length, and check the shock absorber body for signs of damage or corrosion. Test the operation of the shock absorber, while holding it in an upright position, by moving the spindle through a full stroke, and then through short strokes of 50 to 100 mm. In both cases, the resistance felt should be smooth and continuous. If the resistance is jerky or uneven, or if there is any visible sign of wear, damage or fluid leakage, renewal is necessary. Also check the condition of the upper and lower mountings, and renew any components as necessary.

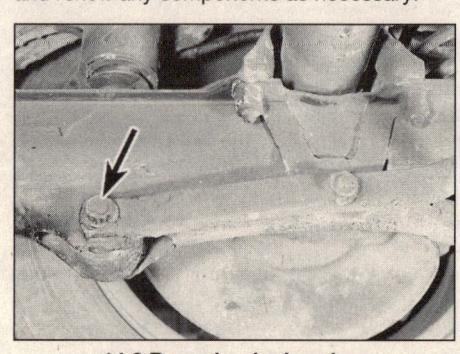

14.2 Rear shock absorber lower mounting bolt (arrowed)

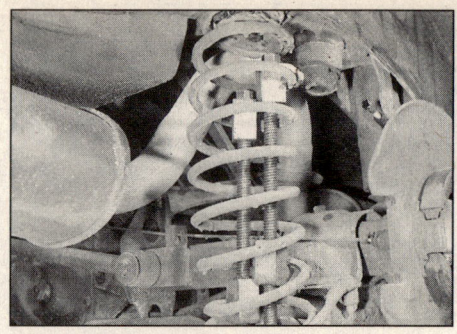

13.6 Using spring compressors to unload the rear spring

Refitting

6 Refit by reversing the removal operations. Tighten the shock absorber mounting and the wheel nuts to the specified torque.

15 Rear anti-roll bar - removal and refitting

Removal

1 Raise the rear of the vehicle on ramps or drive it over a pit.
2 Remove the two nuts and bolts on each side which secure the anti-roll bar. The forward bolts also secure the rear shock absorber lower mountings: it may be necessary to jack up under the trailing arms to take the load off these bolts.
3 Remove the anti-roll bar.

Refitting

4 Refit by reversing the removal operations.

16 Panhard rod - removal and refitting

Removal

1 Raise and support the car with the rear wheels free (see "*Jacking and vehicle support*").
2 Unbolt the Panhard rod from the body, then from the rear axle **(see illustration)**. Remove the rod.

14.3 Exposing the shock absorber upper mounting bolt

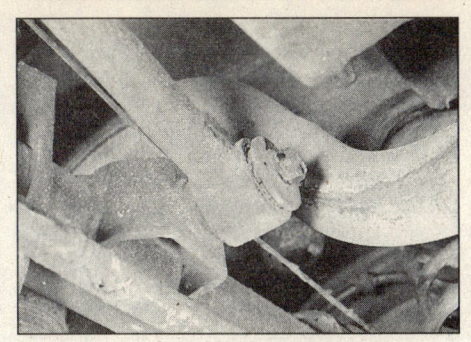

Suspension and steering 10•7

16.2 Panhard rod attachment to the rear axle

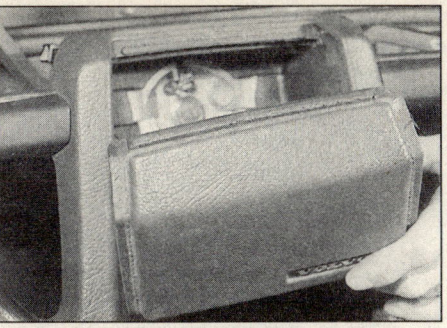

17.3 Removing the steering wheel centre pad

17.4 Undoing the steering wheel centre bolt

3 If the rod bushes need renewing, have the old ones pressed out and new ones pressed in by a Volvo dealer or other specialist.

Refitting

4 Refit the rod and tighten the bolts to the specified torque, axle end first. Lower the vehicle.

17 Steering wheel - removal and refitting

⚠ **Warning: On vehicles equipped with a Supplementary Restraint System (air bag), DO NOT attempt to remove the steering wheel. Have any work involving steering wheel removal carried out by a Volvo dealer. Refer to Chapter 12, Section 23 for further information.**

Removal

1 Disconnect the battery negative lead.
2 Bring the steering wheel to the straight-ahead position.
3 Prise off the steering wheel centre pad **(see illustration)**.
4 Undo the steering wheel centre bolt **(see illustration)**.
5 Make alignment marks between the steering wheel and column, then pull the steering wheel off its splines. If the wheel is tight, tap it up near the centre, using the palm of your hand, or twist it from side to side whilst pulling, to release it from the column splines.

Refitting

6 Refit by reversing the removal operations, observing the alignment marks or the straight-ahead position of the wheel.

18 Steering column - removal and refitting

⚠ **Warning: On vehicles equipped with a Supplementary Restraint System (air bag), DO NOT attempt to remove the steering** wheel. **Have any work involving steering wheel removal carried out by a Volvo dealer. Refer to Chapter 12, Section 23 for further information.**

Removal

1 Disconnect the battery negative lead.
2 Still under the bonnet, remove the clamp nut and bolt from the top universal joint of the intermediate steering shaft. The nut is secured by a spring clip **(see illustration)**.
3 Remove the steering wheel (see Section 17) and the steering column switches, complete with baseplate and horn contact ring **(see illustration)**.
4 Remove the trim panel from below the steering column. It is secured by two screws and two clips. Disconnect the heater duct as the panel is withdrawn.
5 Where necessary, remove the switch panel adjacent to the steering lock.

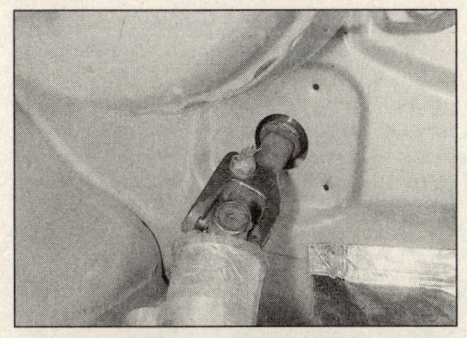

18.2 Intermediate shaft upper universal joint

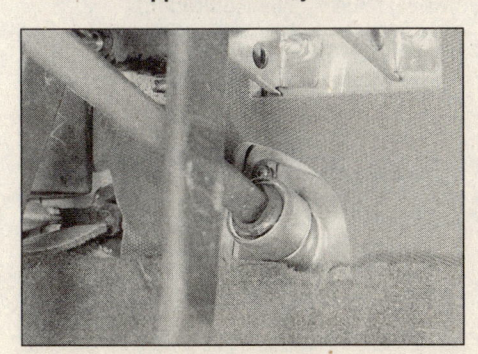

18.7 Steering column bottom bearing plate

6 Disconnect the multi-plug from the ignition/starter switch.
7 Remove the three screws which secure the column bottom bearing plate to the bulkhead **(see illustration)**.
8 Remove the two bolts which secure the column top bearing to the support crossmember **(see illustration)**. In some vehicles shear-head bolts will be found here: remove them by drilling and inserting a stud extractor, or by driving their heads round with a punch.
9 Remove the third bolt securing the top bearing. Recover the spacer tube **(see illustration)**.
10 Remove the three bolts which secure the column support crossmember. To gain access to the right-hand bolts it may be necessary to remove the right-hand lower trim panel, and move the wiring harnesses aside.

18.3 Removing the horn contact ring

18.8 The three bolts which secure the column top bearing to the crossmember

10

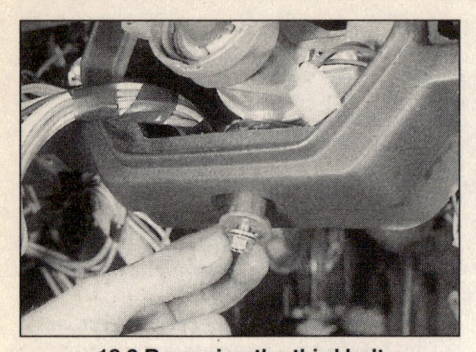

10•8 Suspension and steering

18.9 Removing the third bolt and spacer tube

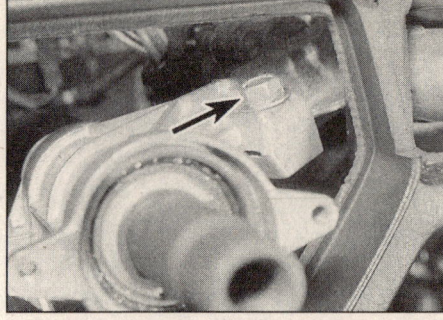

19.3 Steering lock pinch-bolt (arrowed)

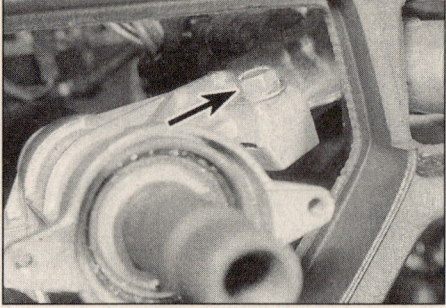

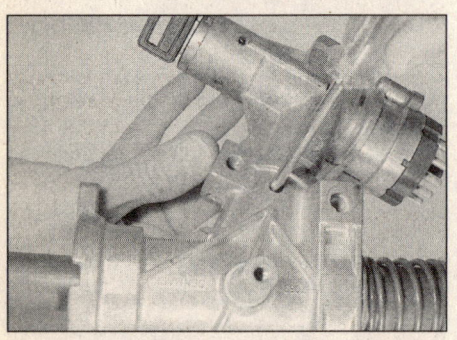

19.4 Depressing the locking button (column removed)

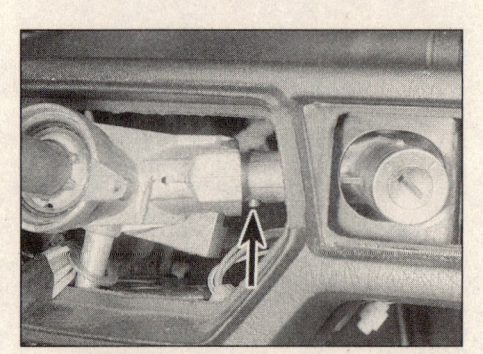

19.5 Withdrawing the steering lock - column fitted. Locking button (arrowed) has just emerged

11 Remove the steering column lock/ignition switch (see Section 19).
12 Free the column and withdraw it into the vehicle. Recover the washer from the top bearing spigot.
13 The column bearings may now be removed if necessary. Be careful not to collapse the coupling in the upper section. The overall length of the column must be 727.2 ± 1 mm.

Refitting

14 Refit by reversing the removal operations, noting the following points:
 a) Tighten nuts and bolts to the specified torque (where given).
 b) When shear-head bolts are used, only tighten them lightly at first. When satisfied that installation is correct tighten the bolts until their heads break off.

19 Steering column lock/ignition switch - removal and refitting

⚠️ **Warning: On vehicles equipped with a Supplementary Restraint System (air bag), DO NOT attempt to remove the steering wheel. Have any work involving steering wheel removal carried out by a Volvo dealer. Refer to Chapter 12, Section 23 for further information.**

Removal

1 Disconnect the battery negative lead.
2 Carry out the operations described in Section 18, paragraphs 3 to 10.
3 Remove the lock pinch-bolt from the top bearing housing (see illustration).
4 Insert the ignition key and turn it to position II. Depress the locking button and begin to withdraw the lock from the bearing housing (see illustration).
5 The ignition key and lock barrel will obstruct removal by fouling the surrounding trim. Therefore remove the key and free the top bearing housing from the crossmember; do not lose the washer from the spigot. By moving the bearing housing enough clearance can be gained to withdraw the steering lock complete with ignition/starter switch (see illustration).
6 Remove the switch from the lock by undoing the two screws.

Refitting

7 Refit by reversing the removal operations.

20 Power steering gear - removal and refitting

Removal

Note: *New copper sealing washers must be used on the fluid unions when refitting.*

1 Raise and support the front of the vehicle (see "Jacking and vehicle support"). Remove the engine undertray.
2 Remove the cover panel from the middle of the front crossmember.
3 Remove the spring clips and slacken the pinch-bolts and nuts on the lower universal joint (see illustration). Slide the universal joint up the intermediate shaft to free it from the pinion.
4 Disconnect the track rod ends from the steering arms (See Section 24).
5 Clean around the fluid supply and return unions, then disconnect them (see illustration). Be prepared for fluid spillage. Plug or cap open unions to keep dirt out.
6 Remove the two mounting bolts and nuts. Remove the steering gear from the crossmember (see illustration). It may be necessary to displace the front anti-roll bar.

Refitting

7 Refit by reversing the removal operations, noting the following points:
 a) Tighten all fastenings to the specified torque.

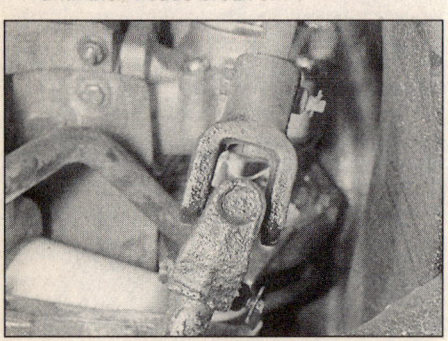

20.3 Intermediate shaft lower universal joint

20.5 Steering gear fluid supply and return unions (arrowed)

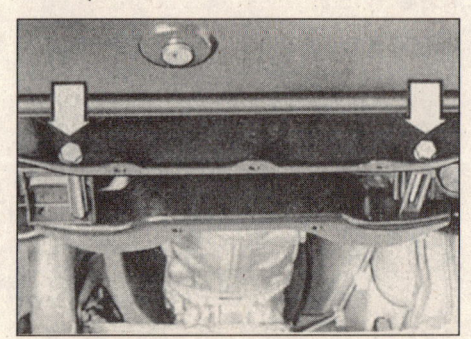

20.6 Steering gear mounting bolts (arrowed)

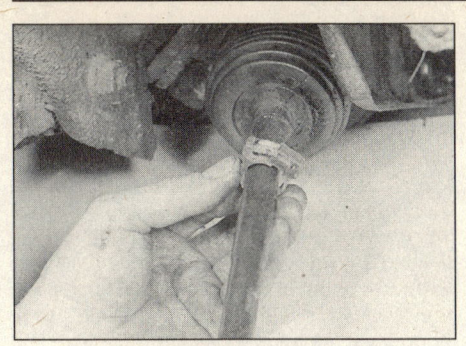

Suspension and steering 10•9

21.2a Removing a steering rack bellows clip . . .

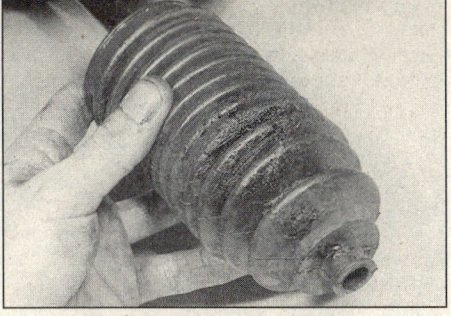

21.2b . . . and the bellows

b) Use new copper washers on the fluid unions.
c) Bleed the power steering system (Section 22).
d) Check the front wheel toe setting (Section 25).

21 Steering rack bellows - renewal

Removal
1 Remove the track rod end on the side concerned (see Section 24). Also remove the rod end locknut.
2 Release the two clips which secure the bellows. Peel off the bellows **(see illustrations)**.

Refitting
3 Clean out any dirt and grit from the inner end of the track rod and (when accessible) the rack. Apply fresh grease to these components.
4 Fit and secure the new bellows, then refit the track rod end.

22 Power steering system - bleeding

1 The steering fluid reservoir is remotely mounted on the inner wing panel. It may have a dipstick, or there may simply be level markings on a translucent container.
2 Fluid level should not exceed the "MAX" mark, nor drop below the "LOW" or "ADD" mark. Some dipsticks are calibrated both for hot and for cold fluid: use the correct markings.
3 If topping-up is necessary, use clean fluid of the specified type (see "Weekly checks"). Check for leaks if frequent topping-up is required. Do not run the pump without fluid in it - remove the drivebelt if necessary.
4 After component renewal, or if the fluid level has been allowed to fall so low that air has entered the hydraulic system, bleeding must be carried out as follows.
5 Referring to "Weekly checks", fill the reservoir to the "MAX" mark. Start the engine and allow it to idle.

6 Turn the steering wheel from lock to lock a couple of times. Do not hold it on full lock.
7 Top-up the fluid if necessary.
8 Repeat paragraphs 6 and 7 until the fluid level ceases to fall. Stop the engine and refit the reservoir cap.

23 Power steering pump - removal and refitting

Removal
Note: *New copper sealing washers must be used on the fluid unions when refitting.*
1 Slacken the pump pivot and adjuster retaining nuts and bolts. Slacken the drivebelt adjuster and slip the drivebelt off the pulley **(see illustration)**.
2 Disconnect the pump hydraulic pipes, either from below (remove the undertray) or from the back of the pump. Be prepared for fluid spillage.
3 Remove the pivot and adjuster nuts and bolts.
4 Lift away the pump. Remove the remote fluid reservoir with the pump, or disconnect the fluid hose from it.
5 If a new pump is to be fitted, transfer the pulley and mounting brackets to it.

Refitting
6 Refit by reversing the removal operations, using new copper washers on disturbed banjo unions.
7 Tension the drivebelt (Chapter 1).

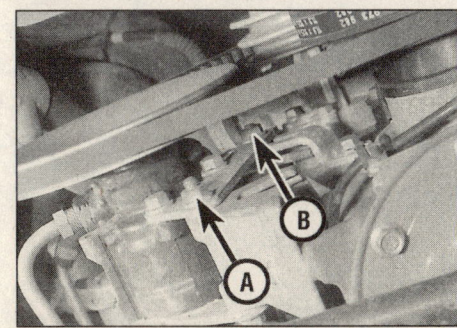

23.1 Steering pump pivot bolt nut (A) and adjuster retaining bolt (B)

8 Refill the pump reservoir and bleed the system (Section 22).

24 Track rod end - removal and refitting

Removal
1 Raise and support the front of the vehicle (see "*Jacking and vehicle support*"). Remove the front wheel on the side concerned.
2 Counterhold the track rod and slacken the rod end locknut by half a turn.
3 Unscrew the rod end ballpin nut to the end of its threads. Separate the ballpin from the steering arm with a proprietary balljoint separator, then remove the nut and disengage the ballpin from the arm **(see illustration)**.
4 Unscrew the track rod end from the track rod, counting the number of turns needed to remove it. Record this number.

Refitting
5 Screw the track rod end onto the track rod by the same number of turns noted during removal.
6 Engage the ballpin in the steering arm. Fit the nut and tighten it to the specified torque.
7 Counterhold the track rod and tighten the locknut.
8 Refit the front wheel, lower the vehicle and tighten the wheel nuts.
9 Have the front wheel toe setting checked at the first opportunity (Section 25), especially if new components have been fitted.

25 Wheel alignment and steering angles - general information

General
1 A car's steering and suspension geometry is defined in four basic settings - all angles are expressed in degrees (toe settings are also expressed as a measurement); the relevant settings are camber, castor, steering axis inclination, and toe setting. With the exception of vehicles with independent rear suspension, only the front wheel toe setting is adjustable. On

24.3 Using a balljoint separator on the track rod end

10

10•10 Suspension and steering

vehicles with independent rear suspension, the rear suspension geometry is fully adjustable.

Front wheel toe setting - checking and adjustment

2 Due to the special measuring equipment necessary to accurately check the wheel alignment, and the skill required to use it properly, checking and adjustment is best left to a Volvo dealer or similar expert. Note that most tyre fitting shops now posses sophisticated checking equipment. The following is provided as a guide should the owner decide to carry out a DIY check.

3 The front wheel toe setting is checked by measuring the distance between the front and rear inside edges of the roadwheel rims. Proprietary toe measuring gauges are available from accessory shops. Adjustment is made by screwing the track rod ends in or out of their track rods to alter the effective length of the track rod assemblies.

4 For **accurate** checking, the vehicle **must** be at kerb weight, ie unladen and with a full tank of fuel.

5 Before starting work, check first that the tyre sizes and types are as specified, then check the tyre pressures and tread wear, the roadwheel run-out, the condition of the wheel bearings, the steering wheel free play, and the condition of the front suspension components (see "*Weekly checks*" and Chapter 1). Correct any faults found.

6 Park the vehicle on level ground, check that the front roadwheels are in the straight-ahead position, then rock the rear and front ends to settle the suspension. Release the handbrake and roll the vehicle backwards 1 metre, then forwards again, to relieve any stresses in the steering and suspension components.

7 Measure the distance between the front edges of the wheel rims and the rear edges of the rims. Subtract the front measurement from the rear measurement, and check that the result is within the specified range.

8 If adjustment is necessary, apply the handbrake, then jack up and securely support the front of the car (see "*Jacking and vehicle support*"). Turn the steering wheel onto full-left lock and record the number of exposed threads on the right-hand track rod. Now turn the steering onto full-right lock, and record the number of threads on the left-hand side. If there are the same number of threads visible on both sides, then subsequent adjustment should be made equally on both sides. If there are more threads visible on one side than the other, it will be necessary to compensate for this during adjustment. **Note:** *It is most important that after adjustment, the same number of threads are visible on each track rod.*

9 First clean the track rod threads; If they are corroded, apply penetrating fluid before starting adjustment. Release the steering rack bellows outer retaining clips and peel back the bellows; apply a smear of grease to the inside of the bellows, so that both are free and will not be twisted or strained as their respective track rods are rotated.

10 Use a straight-edge and a scriber or similar to mark the relationship of each track rod to its track rod end then, holding each track rod in turn, unscrew its locknut.

11 Alter the lengths of the track rods, bearing in mind the note made in paragraph 8. Screw them into or out of the track rod ends, rotating the track rods with grips or a similar tool. Shortening the track rods (screwing them into their track rod ends) will increase toe-in/reduce toe-out.

12 When the setting is correct, hold the track rods and securely tighten the track rod end locknuts. Count the number of exposed threads to check the length of both track rods. If they are not the same, then the adjustment has not been made equally, and problems will be encountered with tyre scrubbing in turns; also, the steering wheel spokes will no longer be horizontal when the wheels are in the straight-ahead position.

13 If the track rod lengths are the same, lower the vehicle to the ground and re-check the toe setting; re-adjust if necessary. When the setting is correct, securely tighten the track rod end locknuts. Ensure that the rubber bellows are seated correctly, and are not twisted or strained, and secure them in position with their retaining clips.

Chapter 11
Bodywork and fittings

Contents

Bodywork, paint and exterior trim check . . . . .See Chapter 1	General information 1
Bonnet - removal and refitting 6	Glovebox - removal and refitting 32
Bonnet release cable - removal and refitting 10	Head restraints - removal and refitting 27
Boot lid - removal and refitting 8	Maintenance - bodywork and underframe 2
Boot lock - removal and refitting 19	Maintenance - upholstery and carpets 3
Bumpers - removal and refitting 37	Major body damage - repair 5
Central locking components - removal and refitting 21	Minor body damage - repair 4
Centre console - removal and refitting 33	Rear console - removal and refitting 34
Door, boot, tailgate and bonnet check and lubrication . . .See Chapter 1	Rear door interior trim - removal and refitting 12
Door handles, locks and latches - removal and refitting 18	Rear door windows - removal and refitting 16
Door mirror - removal and refitting 22	Rear seat - removal and refitting 26
Door mirror glass and motor - removal and refitting 23	Seat belt check . . . . .See Chapter 1
Doors - removal and refitting 7	Seat belts - removal and refitting 30
Door surround weatherstrip - removal and refitting 24	Seat heating elements - removal and refitting 29
Facia - removal and refitting 35	Steering column/pedal trim panel - removal and refitting 31
Front door interior trim - removal and refitting 11	Sunroof - general information 39
Front door window - removal and refitting 15	Tailgate - removal and refitting 9
Front grille panel - removal and refitting 38	Tailgate interior trim - removal and refitting 13
Front seat - removal and refitting 25	Tailgate lock - removal and refitting 20
Front seat position adjusters - removal and refitting 28	Window lift mechanism - removal and refitting 17
Front spoiler - removal and refitting 36	Windscreen and other fixed glass - removal and refitting 14

Degrees of difficulty

Easy, suitable for novice with little experience	**Fairly easy,** suitable for beginner with some experience	**Fairly difficult,** suitable for competent DIY mechanic	**Difficult,** suitable for experienced DIY mechanic	**Very difficult,** suitable for expert DIY or professional

1 General information

Body styles available are 4-door Saloon and 5-door Estate. The body and floorpan are of welded steel construction and form a very strong unit, with crumple zones at front and rear which will deform progressively in case of accident. The doors are also reinforced against side impacts. The tailgate on Estate models is made of aluminium.

Stout bumpers are fitted front and rear, with energy-absorbing buffers to protect against damage in low-speed collisions.

The front wings bolt on for easy renewal. The bonnet has two opening positions: partly open for normal work, and fully open for major work.

Interior trim and fittings are of the high standard expected in a vehicle of this class.

2 Maintenance - bodywork and underframe

The general condition of a vehicle's bodywork is the one thing that significantly affects its value. Maintenance is easy but needs to be regular. Neglect, particularly after minor damage, can lead quickly to further deterioration and costly repair bills. It is important also to keep watch on those parts of the vehicle not immediately visible, for instance the underside, inside all the wheel arches and the lower part of the engine compartment.

The basic maintenance routine for the bodywork is washing preferably with a lot of water, from a hose. This will remove all the loose solids which may have stuck to the vehicle. It is important to flush these off in such a way as to prevent any grit from scratching the finish. The wheel arches and underframe need washing in the same way to remove any accumulated mud which will retain moisture and tend to encourage rust. Oddly enough, the best time to clean the underframe and wheel arches is in wet weather when the mud is thoroughly wet and soft. In very wet weather the underframe is usually cleaned of large accumulations automatically and this is a good time for inspection.

Periodically, except on vehicles with a wax-based underbody protective coating, it is a good idea to have the whole of the underframe of the vehicle steam cleaned, engine compartment included, so that a thorough inspection can be carried out to see what minor repairs and renovations are necessary. Steam cleaning is available at many garages and is necessary for removal of the accumulation of oily grime which sometimes is allowed to become thick in certain areas. If steam cleaning facilities are not available, there are one or two excellent grease solvents available which can be brush applied; the dirt can then be simply hosed off. Note that these methods should not be used on vehicles with wax-based underbody protective coating or the coating will be removed. Such vehicles should be inspected annually, preferably just prior to winter, when the underbody should be washed down and any damage to the wax coating repaired using underseal. Ideally, a completely fresh coat should be applied. It would also be worth considering the use of such wax-based protection for injection into door panels, sills, box sections, etc, as an additional safeguard against rust damage where such protection is not provided by the vehicle manufacturer.

After washing paintwork, wipe off with a chamois leather to give an unspotted clear finish. A coat of clear protective wax polish will give added protection against chemical pollutants in the air. If the paintwork sheen

11•2 Bodywork and fittings

has dulled or oxidised, use a cleaner/polisher combination to restore the brilliance of the shine. This requires a little effort, but such dulling is usually caused because regular washing has been neglected. Care needs to be taken with metallic paintwork as special non-abrasive cleaner/polisher is required to avoid damage to the finish.

Always check that the door and ventilator opening drain holes and pipes are completely clear so that water can be drained out. Bright work should be treated in the same way as paint work. Windscreens and windows can be kept clear of the smeary film which often appears by the use of a proprietary glass cleaner. Never use any form of wax or other body or chromium polish on glass.

3 Maintenance - upholstery and carpets

Mats and carpets should be brushed or vacuum cleaned regularly to keep them free of grit. If they are badly stained remove them from the vehicle for scrubbing or sponging and make quite sure they are dry before refitting. Seats and interior trim panels can be kept clean by wiping with a damp cloth and a proprietary upholstery cleaner. If they do become stained (which can be more apparent on light coloured upholstery) use a little liquid detergent and a soft nail brush to scour the grime out of the grain of the material. Do not forget to keep the headlining clean in the same way as the upholstery. When using liquid cleaners inside the vehicle do not over-wet the surfaces being cleaned. Excessive damp could get into the seams and padded interior causing stains, offensive odours or even rot. If the inside of the vehicle gets wet accidentally it is worthwhile taking some trouble to dry it out properly, particularly where carpets are involved. *Do not leave oil or electric heaters inside the vehicle for this purpose.*

4 Minor body damage - repair

Repair of minor scratches in bodywork

If the scratch is very superficial, and does not penetrate to the metal of the bodywork, repair is very simple. Lightly rub the area of the scratch with a paintwork renovator, or a very fine cutting paste, to remove loose paint from the scratch, and to clear the surrounding bodywork of wax polish. Rinse the area with clean water.

Apply touch-up paint to the scratch using a fine paint brush; continue to apply fine layers of paint until the surface of the paint in the scratch is level with the surrounding paintwork. Allow the new paint at least two weeks to harden: then blend it into the surrounding paintwork by rubbing the scratch area with a paintwork renovator or a very fine cutting paste. Finally, apply wax polish.

Where the scratch has penetrated right through to the metal of the bodywork, causing the metal to rust, a different repair technique is required. Remove any loose rust from the bottom of the scratch with a penknife, then apply rust-inhibiting paint, to prevent the formation of rust in the future. Using a rubber or nylon applicator fill the scratch with bodystopper paste. If required, this paste can be mixed with cellulose thinners, to provide a very thin paste which is ideal for filling narrow scratches. Before the stopper-paste in the scratch hardens, wrap a piece of smooth cotton rag around the top of a finger. Dip the finger in cellulose thinners, and then quickly sweep it across the surface of the stopper-paste in the scratch; this will ensure that the surface of the stopper-paste is slightly hollowed. The scratch can now be painted over as described earlier in this Section.

Repair of dents in bodywork

When deep denting of the vehicle's bodywork has taken place, the first task is to pull the dent out, until the affected bodywork almost attains its original shape. There is little point in trying to restore the original shape completely, as the metal in the damaged area will have stretched on impact and cannot be reshaped fully to its original contour. It is better to bring the level of the dent up to a point which is about 3 mm below the level of the surrounding bodywork. In cases where the dent is very shallow anyway, it is not worth trying to pull it out at all. If the underside of the dent is accessible, it can be hammered out gently from behind, using a mallet with a wooden or plastic head. Whilst doing this, hold a suitable block of wood firmly against the outside of the panel to absorb the impact from the hammer blows and thus prevent a large area of the bodywork from being "belled-out".

Should the dent be in a section of the bodywork which has a double skin or some other factor making it inaccessible from behind, a different technique is called for. Drill several small holes through the metal inside the area - particularly in the deeper section. Then screw long self-tapping screws into the holes just sufficiently for them to gain a good purchase in the metal. Now the dent can be pulled out by pulling on the protruding heads of the screws with a pair of pliers.

The next stage of the repair is the removal of the paint from the damaged area, and from an inch or so of the surrounding "sound" bodywork. This is accomplished most easily by using a wire brush or abrasive pad on a power drill, although it can be done just as effectively by hand using sheets of abrasive paper. To complete the preparation for filling, score the surface of the bare metal with a screwdriver or the tang of a file, or alternatively, drill small holes in the affected area. This will provide a really good "key" for the filler paste.

To complete the repair see the Section on filling and re-spraying.

Repair of rust holes or gashes in bodywork

Remove all paint from the affected area and from an inch or so of the surrounding "sound" bodywork, using an abrasive pad or a wire brush on a power drill. If these are not available a few sheets of abrasive paper will do the job just as effectively. With the paint removed you will be able to gauge the severity of the corrosion and therefore decide whether to renew the whole panel (if this is possible) or to repair the affected area. New body panels are not as expensive as most people think and it is often quicker and more satisfactory to fit a new panel than to attempt to repair large areas of corrosion.

Remove all fittings from the affected area except those which will act as a guide to the original shape of the damaged bodywork (eg headlight shells etc). Then, using tin snips or a hacksaw blade, remove all loose metal and any other metal badly affected by corrosion. Hammer the edges of the hole inwards in order to create a slight depression for the filler paste.

Wire brush the affected area to remove the powdery rust from the surface of the remaining metal. Paint the affected area with rust inhibiting paint; if the back of the rusted area is accessible treat this also.

Before filling can take place it will be necessary to block the hole in some way. This can be achieved by the use of aluminium or plastic mesh, or aluminium tape.

Aluminium or plastic mesh or glass fibre matting is probably the best material to use for a large hole. Cut a piece to the approximate size and shape of the hole to be filled, then position it in the hole so that its edges are below the level of the surrounding bodywork. It can be retained in position by several blobs of filler paste around its periphery.

Aluminium tape should be used for small or very narrow holes. Pull a piece off the roll and trim it to the approximate size and shape required, then pull off the backing paper (if used) and stick the tape over the hole; it can be overlapped if the thickness of one piece is insufficient. Burnish down the edges of the tape with the handle of a screwdriver or similar, to ensure that the tape is securely attached to the metal underneath.

Bodywork repairs - filling and re-spraying

Before using this Section, see the Sections on dent, deep scratch, rust holes and gash repairs.

Many types of bodyfiller are available, but generally speaking those proprietary kits which contain a tin of filler paste and a tube of resin hardener are best for this type of repair; some can be used directly from the tube. A wide, flexible plastic or nylon applicator will be found invaluable for imparting a smooth and well contoured finish to the surface of the filler.

Mix up a little filler on a clean piece of card or board - measure the hardener carefully (follow the maker's instructions on the pack) otherwise the filler will set too rapidly or too slowly. Using the applicator, apply the filler paste to the prepared area; draw the applicator across the surface of the filler to achieve the correct contour and to level the filler surface. As soon as a contour that approximates to the correct one is achieved, stop working the paste - if you carry on too long the paste will become sticky and begin to "pick up" on the applicator. Continue to add thin layers of filler paste at twenty-minute intervals until the level of the filler is just proud of the surrounding bodywork.

Once the filler has hardened, excess can be removed using a metal plane or file. From then on, progressively finer grades of abrasive paper should be used, starting with a 40 grade production paper and finishing with 400 grade wet-and-dry paper. Always wrap the abrasive paper around a flat rubber, cork, or wooden block - otherwise the surface of the filler will not be completely flat. During the smoothing of the filler surface the wet-and-dry paper should be periodically rinsed in water. This will ensure that a very smooth finish is imparted to the filler at the final stage.

At this stage the "dent" should be surrounded by a ring of bare metal, which in turn should be encircled by the finely "feathered" edge of the good paintwork. Rinse the repair area with clean water, until all of the dust produced by the rubbing-down operation has gone.

Spray the whole repair area with a light coat of primer - this will show up any imperfections in the surface of the filler. Repair these imperfections with fresh filler paste or bodystopper, and once more smooth the surface with abrasive paper. If bodystopper is used, it can be mixed with cellulose thinners to form a really thin paste which is ideal for filling small holes. Repeat this spray and repair procedure until you are satisfied that the surface of the filler, and the feathered edge of the paintwork are perfect. Clean the repair area with clean water and allow to dry fully.

The repair area is now ready for final spraying. Paint spraying must be carried out in a warm, dry, windless and dust free atmosphere. This condition can be created artificially if you have access to a large indoor working area, but if you are forced to work in the open, you will have to pick your day very carefully. If you are working indoors, dousing the floor in the work area with water will help to settle the dust which would otherwise be in the atmosphere. If the repair area is confined to one body panel, mask off the surrounding panels; this will help to minimise the effects of a slight mis-match in paint colours. Bodywork fittings (eg chrome strips, door handles etc) will also need to be masked off. Use genuine masking tape and several thicknesses of newspaper for the masking operations.

Before commencing to spray, agitate the aerosol can thoroughly, then spray a test area (an old tin, or similar) until the technique is mastered. Cover the repair area with a thick coat of primer; the thickness should be built up using several thin layers of paint rather than one thick one. Using 400 grade wet-and-dry paper, rub down the surface of the primer until it is really smooth. While doing this, the work area should be thoroughly doused with water, and the wet-and-dry paper periodically rinsed in water. Allow to dry before spraying on more paint.

Spray on the top coat, again building up the thickness by using several thin layers of paint. Start spraying in the centre of the repair area and then, with a single side-to-side motion, work outwards until the whole repair area and about 50 mm of the surrounding original paintwork is covered. Remove all masking material 10 to 15 minutes after spraying on the final coat of paint.

Allow the new paint at least two weeks to harden, then, using a paintwork renovator or a very fine cutting paste, blend the edges of the paint into the existing paintwork. Finally, apply wax polish.

Plastic components

With the use of more and more plastic body components by the vehicle manufacturers (eg bumpers, spoilers, and in some cases major body panels), rectification of more serious damage to such items has become a matter of either entrusting repair work to a specialist in this field, or renewing complete components. Repair of such damage by the DIY owner is not really feasible owing to the cost of the equipment and materials required for effecting such repairs. The basic technique involves making a groove along the line of the crack in the plastic using a rotary burr in a power drill. The damaged part is then welded back together by using a hot air gun to heat up and fuse a plastic filler rod into the groove. Any excess plastic is then removed and the area rubbed down to a smooth finish. It is important that a filler rod of the correct plastic is used, as body components can be made of a variety of different types (eg polycarbonate, ABS, polypropylene).

Damage of a less serious nature (abrasions, minor cracks etc) can be repaired by the DIY owner using a two-part epoxy filler repair material. Once mixed in equal proportions, this is used in similar fashion to the bodywork filler used on metal panels. The filler is usually cured in twenty to thirty minutes, ready for sanding and painting.

If the owner is renewing a complete component himself, or if he has repaired it with epoxy filler, he will be left with the problem of finding a suitable paint for finishing which is compatible with the type of plastic used. At one time the use of a universal paint was not possible owing to the complex range of plastics encountered in body component applications. Standard paints, generally speaking, will not bond to plastic or rubber satisfactorily. However, it is now possible to obtain a plastic body parts finishing kit which consists of a pre-primer treatment, a primer and coloured top coat. Full instructions are normally supplied with a kit, but basically the method of use is to first apply the pre-primer to the component concerned and allow it to dry for up to 30 minutes. Then the primer is applied and left to dry for about an hour before finally applying the special coloured top coat. The result is a correctly coloured component where the paint will flex with the plastic or rubber, a property that standard paint does not normally possess.

Aluminium components

The tailgate on Estate models is made of aluminium. Be careful when hammering out dents in an aluminium panel as the material is easily work-hardened and may crack. Abrasives should be used with great caution on aluminium as it is much softer than steel.

5 Major body damage - repair

Where serious damage has occurred or large areas need renewal due to neglect, completely new sections or panels will need welding in - this is best left to professionals. If the damage is due to impact, it will also be necessary to check completely the alignment of the body shell structure. Due to the principle of construction, the strength and shape of the whole can be affected by damage to a part. In such instances, the services of a Volvo agent with specialist checking jigs are essential. If a body is left misaligned, it is first of all dangerous as the car will not handle properly and secondly uneven stresses will be imposed on the steering, engine and transmission, causing abnormal wear or complete failure. Tyre wear may also be excessive.

6 Bonnet - removal and refitting

Removal

1 Disconnect the battery negative lead.
2 Disconnect the washer tube from the bonnet at the T-piece. Unclip the tube from the bulkhead.
3 Remove the under-bonnet light (when fitted) and disconnect the wire from it. Tie a piece of string to the wire, draw the wire

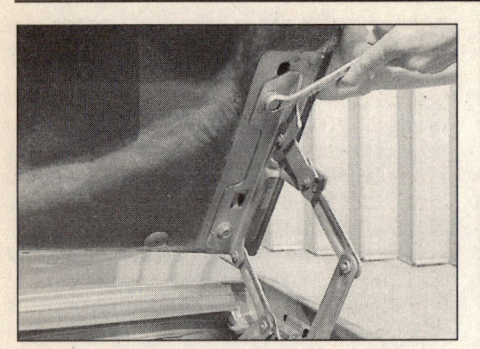

11•4 Bodywork and fittings

6.5 Undoing a bonnet hinge bolt

7.3a Guide pin (arrowed) determines hinge position

7.3b Door hinge details

through the bonnet cavity into the engine bay, then untie the string and leave it in the bonnet. This will make refitting easier.
4 Mark around the hinge bolts with a soft lead pencil for reference when refitting.
5 With the aid of an assistant, support the bonnet and remove the hinge bolts **(see illustration)**. Lift off the bonnet.

Refitting

6 Before refitting, place pads of rags under the corners of the bonnet rear the hinges to protect the paintwork from damage.
7 Fit the bonnet and insert the hinge bolts. Just nip the bolts up in their previously marked positions.
8 Draw the light lead through with the string. Reconnect and refit the light.
9 Reconnect the washer tube and clip it to the bulkhead.
10 Shut the bonnet and check its fit. The hinge-to-bonnet bolt holes control the fore-and-aft and left-right adjustment. Front height is adjusted by screwing the rubber buffers in or out. Rear height is adjusted at the hinge mounting bolts near the wheel arch.
11 Tighten the hinge bolts when adjustment is correct, and reconnect the battery.

7 Doors - removal and refitting

Removal

1 Open the door. Support it with a jack or axle stand, using rags to protect the paintwork.
2 Disconnect the door electrical wiring, either by removing the door trim panel or the adjacent pillar trim. Feed the wiring through so that it hangs free.
3 Although a guide pin in the hinge is used to ensure correct alignment, it is a good idea to mark around the hinge bolts for reference when refitting. With the lid of an assistant, remove the hinge bolts and lift away the door **(see illustrations)**. Recover any hinge shims.

Refitting

4 Refit by reversing the removal operations.

8 Boot lid - removal and refitting

Removal

1 Open the boot. Disconnect the central locking system and/or boot light wiring so that the boot lid is free to be removed.
2 Mark around the hinge bolts. With the aid of an assistant, disconnect the boot lid strut at the hinge end, remove the hinge bolts and lift away the lid **(see illustrations)**.

Refitting

3 Refit by reversing the removal operations. If height adjustment is necessary, this is carried out at the rear by adjusting the lock bracket, and at the front by adjusting the hinges. Access to the hinge front bolts is via the covers in the rear window pillar trim.

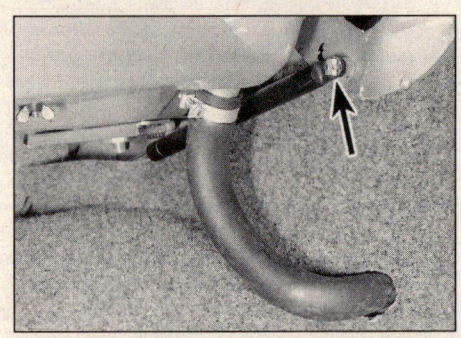

8.2a Boot lid strut - remove spring clip (arrowed) at hinge end

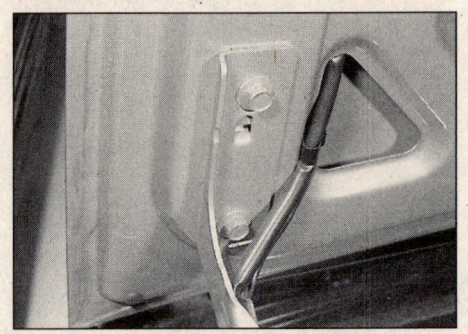

8.2b Boot hinge bolts

9 Tailgate - removal and refitting

Removal

1 Disconnect the battery negative lead.
2 Open the tailgate. Disconnect the washer tube at the junction next to the right-hand hinge.
3 Prise out the bungs which conceal two hinge bolts. Slacken the hinge bolts but do not remove them yet **(see illustration)**.
4 Remove the trim panel from around the load area light. Besides the visible fasteners, there is one concealed behind the light itself **(see illustration)**.
5 Separate the wiring connectors exposed by removal of the trim panel, making notes for refitting if necessary. Feed the wiring through to the tailgate.

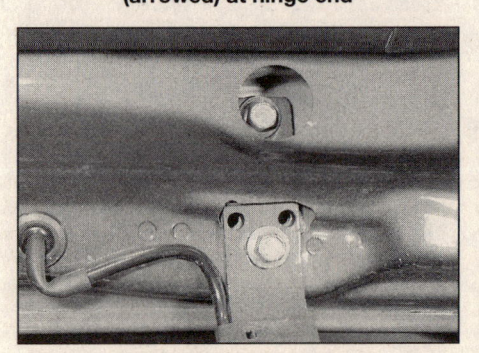

9.3 Tailgate hinge bolts

9.4 Trim panel fastener (arrowed) behind load area light

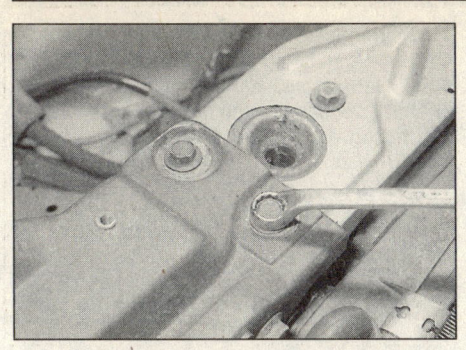

Bodywork and fittings 11•5

10.2 Unbolt the upper support panel in front of the radiator for access to the bonnet catches

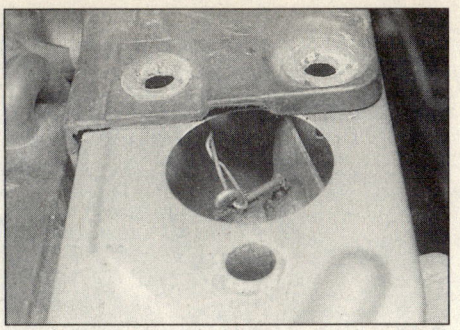

10.3 Disconnect the cable inner from the bonnet catch

6 Have an assistant support the tailgate. Disconnect the gas struts by removing the wire clips and separating the balljoints.
7 Remove the hinge bolts and lift away the tailgate.

Refitting

8 Refit by reversing the removal operations. Only provisionally tighten the hinge bolts until satisfied with the fit of the tailgate. Adjust the lock striker and side guide pieces if necessary for a good fit.

10 Bonnet release cable - removal and refitting

Removal

1 Open the bonnet. If the cable is broken, the catches must be released from below, or access can be gained by the destructive removal of the headlights.
2 Unbolt the upper support panel in front of the radiator for access to the bonnet catches **(see illustration)**.
3 Unbolt the release catch which is furthest from the release handle. Disconnect the cable inner from it **(see illustration)**.
4 Release the cable outer from the other catch. Pull the cable free of the catches.
5 Inside the vehicle, release the cable from the lever by unhooking the inner and removing the slide clip from the outer.
6 Feed the cable into the engine bay and remove it.

Refitting

7 Refit by reversing the removal operations. Adjust the threaded section of the cable at the release lever end to take most of the slack out of the inner in the resting position.

11 Front door interior trim - removal and refitting

Removal

1 Disconnect the battery negative lead.
2 Prise out the control switches from the armrest and disconnect them **(see illustration)**.
3 Remove the loudspeaker trim by sliding it forwards **(see illustration)**.

4 Remove the clip from the well behind the interior handle by turning the clip a quarter-turn with a screwdriver **(see illustration)**.
5 Unclip the edge marker light lens.
6 Prise out the three clips from the bottom edge of the trim panel.
7 Unclip the panel by tugging it firmly. Disconnect the loudspeaker and edge marker light connectors and remove it.
8 To remove the armrest frame, first prise the plug out of the end of the interior handle cap **(see illustration)**. Remove the exposed screw and remove the cap.
9 Unclip any wiring from the armrest frame. Remove the two securing screws and lift off the frame **(see illustration)**.

Refitting

10 In all cases, refit by reversing the removal operations.

12 Rear door interior trim - removal and refitting

The removal and refitting procedures are virtually identical to those for the front door (Section 11) except that both doors have a pull handle, and there are no clips securing the door panel base.

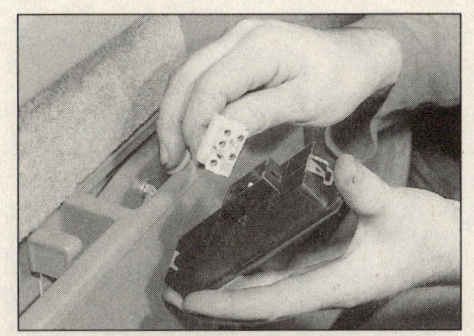

11.2 Disconnecting a control switch from the armrest

11.3 Removing the loudspeaker trim

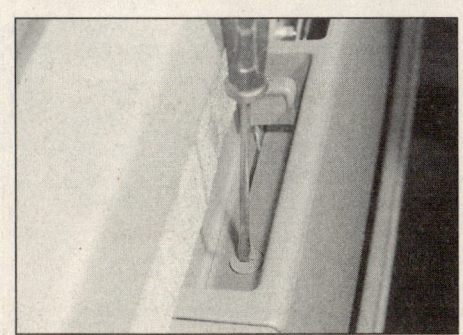

11.4 Turn the clip through a quarter turn to release it

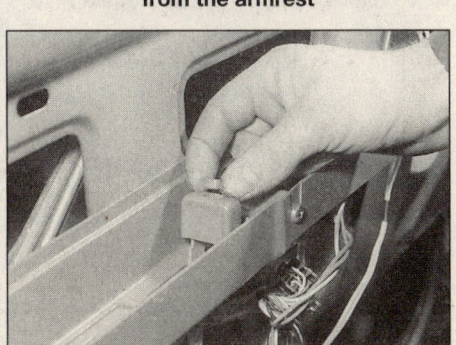

11.8 Remove the plug for access to the screw

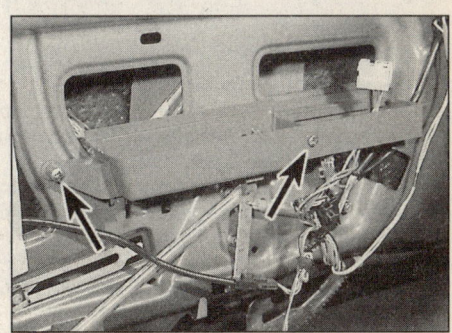

11.9 Two screws (arrowed) securing the armrest

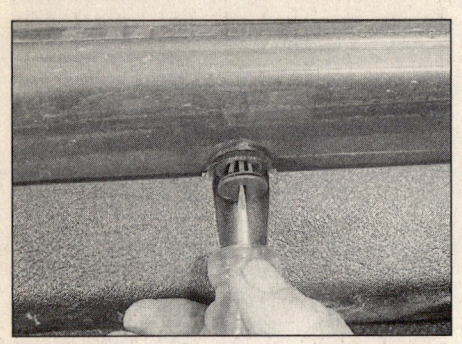

11•6 Bodywork and fittings

13.1 Removing a tailgate trim fastener

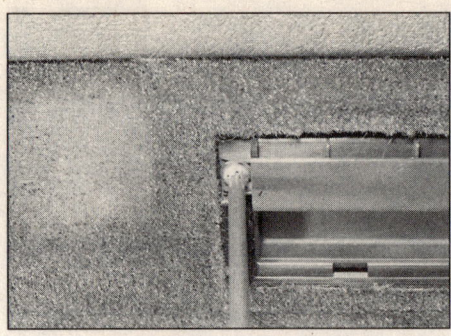

13.2 Removing the tailgate interior handle trim

13 Tailgate interior trim - removal and refitting

Removal
1 Open the tailgate. From the bottom of the trim panel remove the four fasteners by turning them through 90° **(see illustration)**.
2 Unclip the plastic surround from the interior handle. Remove the two screws now exposed, and the handle trim piece which they also secure **(see illustration)**.
3 Slide the trim upwards (relative to the closed position of the tailgate) to free the "keyhole" fasteners along the top edge. Remove the trim panel.

Refitting
4 Refit by reversing the removal operations.

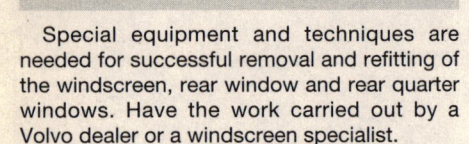

14 Windscreen and other fixed glass - removal and refitting

Special equipment and techniques are needed for successful removal and refitting of the windscreen, rear window and rear quarter windows. Have the work carried out by a Volvo dealer or a windscreen specialist.

15 Front door window - removal and refitting

Removal
1 Remove the door interior trim (Section 11).
2 Raise or lower the window so that the lift arms are accessible. Remove each lift arm-to-lift channel clip **(see illustration)**.
3 Have an assistant support the window, or wedge or tape it in position. Disengage the lift arms from the channel and lift the glass out of the door.
4 If new glass is being fitted; check whether or not it is supplied with the lift channel attached. If not, it will be necessary to transfer the old channel. Where possible, note the fitted position of the channel relative to the trailing edge of the glass. The channel is removed by judicious use of a rubber mallet. If the fitted position of the channel is not known, position it as shown **(see illustration)**.

Refitting
5 Refit by reversing the removal operations.

16 Rear door windows - removal and refitting

Removal
1 Remove the door interior trim (Section 12).
2 Remove the drop glass as described for the front window (Section 15).
3 The fixed glass may now be removed after drilling out the blind rivets which secure the guide channel. Remove the guide channel and slide out the glass.

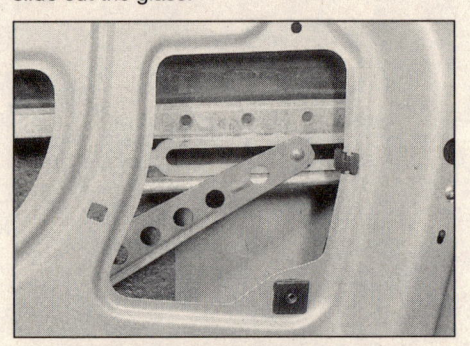

15.2 Window lift arm in the channel. Clip is behind the end of the arm

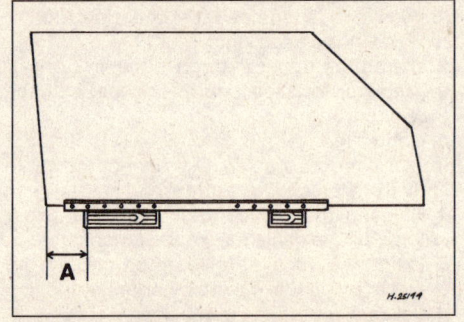

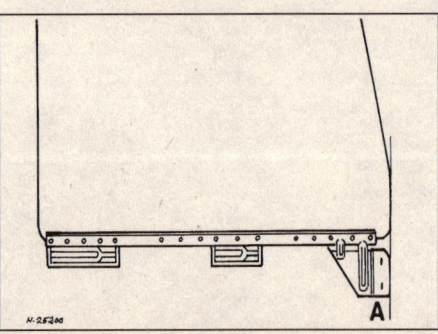

16.6 Correct position of rear window channel
A = 0 to 1 mm (0 to 0.04 in)

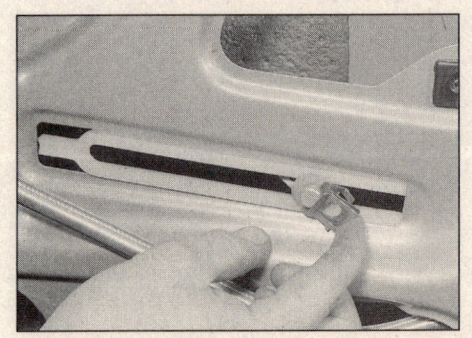

4 When refitting the fixed glass, lubricate the surround with liquid soap.
5 Press the glass home and refit the guide channel, securing it with new blind rivets.
6 If fitting a lift channel to the drop glass, position it as shown **(see illustration)**.

Refitting
7 Refit the drop glass and the interior trim.

17 Window lift mechanism - removal and refitting

Removal
1 Proceed as for door window glass removal (Section 15 or 16), but do not remove the glass completely. Tape or wedge it in the fully raised position.
2 Remove the clip which secures the slide arm in its channel **(see illustration)**.
3 In the case of electrically-operated windows, remove the motor connectors from the multi-plug, prising them out with a small screwdriver or scriber **(see illustration)**. It is difficult to do this without damaging the connectors, but if a new motor is to be fitted this does not matter. On later models an additional multi-plug is fitted in the harness which simplifies disconnection.
4 Remove the nuts which secure the mechanism to the door skin. On later models, rivets are used instead of nuts which must be removed by drilling them out.
5 Push the mechanism into the door cavity and

15.4 Position of front window channel
A = 70 mm (2.75 in) approx

17.2 The clip which secures the slide arm in the channel

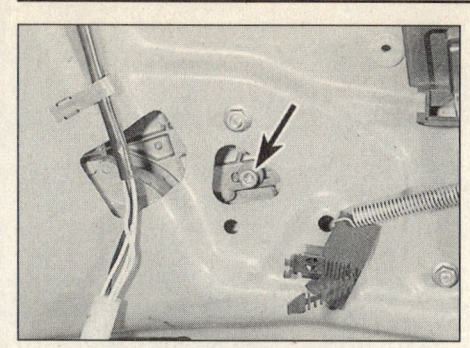

Bodywork and fittings 11•7

17.7 Window mechanism stop screw (arrowed)

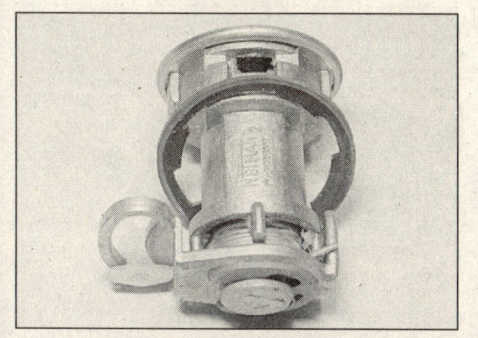

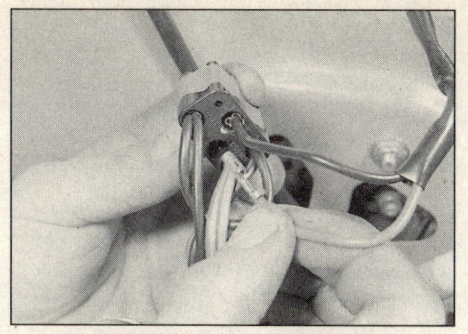

17.3 Removing the window motor connectors from the multi-plug

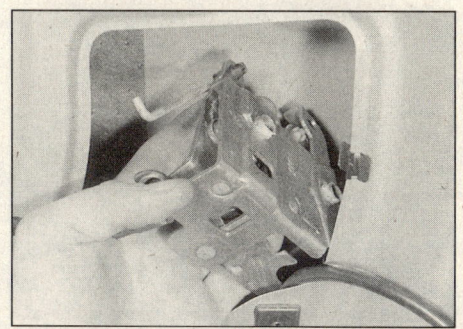

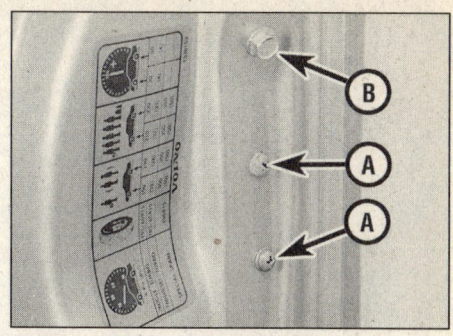

18.2 Lock barrel clip screws (A). Screw B secures one end of the exterior handle

18.3 Door lock barrel removed

18.8 Removing the latch mechanism

remove it through the large hole at the bottom. It may be necessary to alter the position of the mechanism to allow it to pass through the hole; with electrically-operated windows, do this by carefully connecting a battery to the connectors using jump leads. Do not allow the connectors or the jump lead clips to touch.
6 The motor may be unbolted from the mechanism if wished. Take great care that as the motor is removed, spring pressure does not cause a sudden movement of the toothed quadrant, which could result in injury.

Refitting

7 Refit by reversing the removal operations. Before refitting the door trim, adjust the stop screw as follows **(see illustration)**.
8 Slacken the stop screw and press it forwards. Wind the window fully up, press the stop screw rearwards and tighten it.

18 Door handles, locks and latches - removal and refitting

Removal

1 Remove the door interior trim (Section 11 or 12).

Lock barrel

2 Remove the two screws in the door shut face which secure the lock barrel clip **(see illustration)**.
3 Unhook the lock-to-latch rod, noting which way round it is fitted. Slide the clip off the lock and remove the lock and clip **(see illustration)**.

Exterior handle

4 Remove the two screws which secure the handle. Unhook the link rod and remove the handle.

Latch mechanism

5 Disconnect the lock barrel and exterior handle link rods from the latch.
6 Remove the catch from the door. It is secured by two Allen screws.
7 Remove the single securing screw exposed by removal of the catch.
8 Unclip the interior handle link and remove the latch mechanism **(see illustration)**.

Refitting

9 In all cases, refit by reversing the removal operations. Check for correct operation before refitting the door trim.
10 Note that the exterior handle link rod contains an adjustable section. The length of the rod should be set so that the latch stop contacts its base, and the handle tongue protrudes at least 22 mm.

19 Boot lock - removal and refitting

Removal

1 Release the inner trim panel plastic retaining screws, one each side, at the lower corners of the boot lid by turning them a quarter turn. Remove the ten retaining clips and withdraw the trim panel.
2 Release the latch link rod at the exterior handle by bending up the locking clip and pulling out the rod **(see illustration)**.
3 Separate the two halves of the lock barrel link rod by opening the locking tab on the connector/adjuster midway between the latch and lock barrel.
4 Disconnect the central locking motor wiring connector at the latch assembly.
5 Undo the three screws, lift off the cover plate and withdraw the latch and central locking motor as a unit.
6 To remove the lock barrel, undo the screw which secures the lock barrel clip, slide off the clip and withdraw the lock barrel.

Refitting

7 Refitting is a reversal of removal. When reconnecting the two halves of the lock barrel link rod, first turn the lock barrel to the "private" position. Push the two link rod halves toward each other, locate them in the connector/adjuster and secure with the locking tab. Check the operation of the lock components before refitting the trim panel.

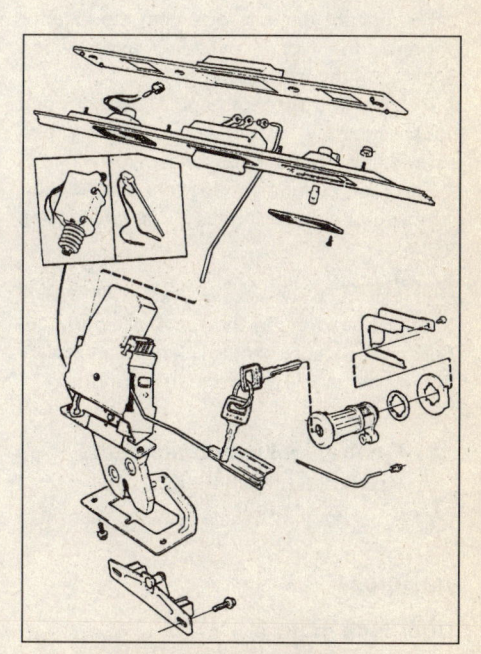

19.2 Boot lock components and attachments

11•8 Bodywork and fittings

21.2a Removing the two screws below the catch

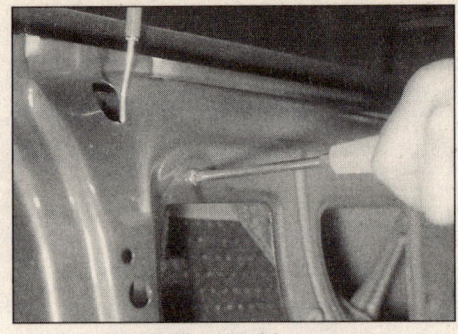

21.2b Glass guide screw near the lock button

21.3 The single screw hidden by the catch

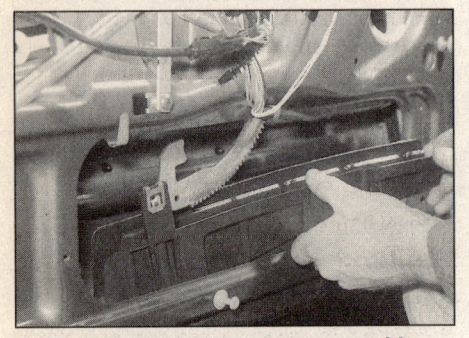

21.4 Removing the glass rear guide

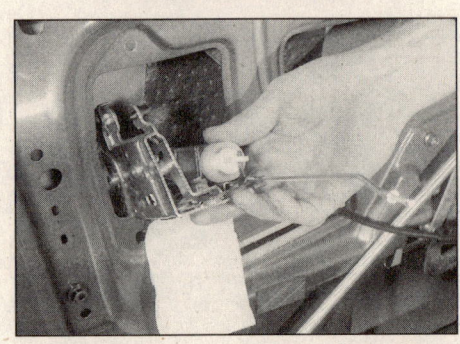

21.5 Removing the door lock motor

21.6 Lock motor showing securing screws

20 Tailgate lock - removal and refitting

Removal

1 Remove the tailgate interior trim panel (Section 13).
2 Disconnect the link rods from the exterior handle, the lock cylinder and (when applicable) the lock motor.
3 Remove the exterior handle/number plate light assembly, which is secured by two screws and two nuts. Disconnect the wiring.
4 The lock cylinder and levers can now be removed after releasing the E-clip and locking plate.

Refitting

5 Refit by reversing the removal operation. Adjust the exterior handle link rod if necessary to give the handle approximately 3 mm.

21 Central locking components - removal and refitting

Removal

Door lock motors

1 Remove the interior trim from the door (Section 11 or 12).
2 Remove the two screws from below the catch, and the single screw near the interior lock button, to release the glass rear guide **(see illustrations)**.
3 Remove the two Torx screws which secure the catch. Remove the catch, and the single screw thus exposed **(see illustration)**.
4 Remove the glass rear guide **(see illustration)**.
5 Unclip the handle operating levers. Unhook the motor and remove it complete with interior lock button rod **(see illustration)**.
6 The motor itself can be removed from the locking mechanism by undoing the two securing screws **(see illustration)**.

Driver's door switch

7 Proceed as for door lock motor removal. The driver's door switch looks the same as a door lock motor, but the casing only contains a switch.

Boot lock motor

8 Remove the latch assembly as described in Section 19.
9 Remove the securing nuts or screws and remove the motor.

Tailgate lock motor

10 Remove the tailgate interior trim (see Section 13).
11 The lock motor may now be removed in a similar way to the boot lock motor.

Refitting

12 In all cases, refit by reversing the removal operations.

22 Door mirror - removal and refitting

Removal

Electrically-operated

1 Remove the door interior trim (Section 11).
2 Prise free the trim plate which covers the mirror mounting.
3 Disconnect the mirror wiring plug. Free the wiring harness from the door **(see illustration)**.

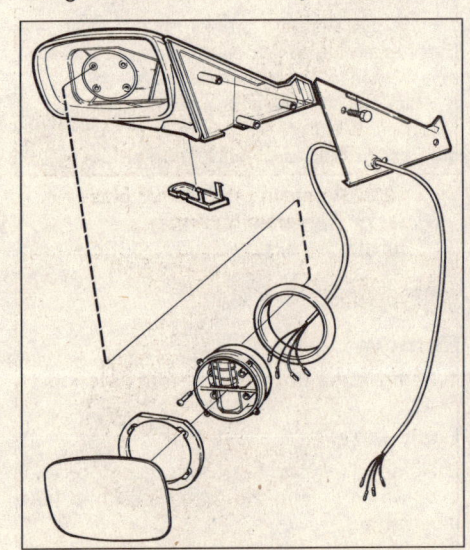

22.3 Electrically operated door mirror components

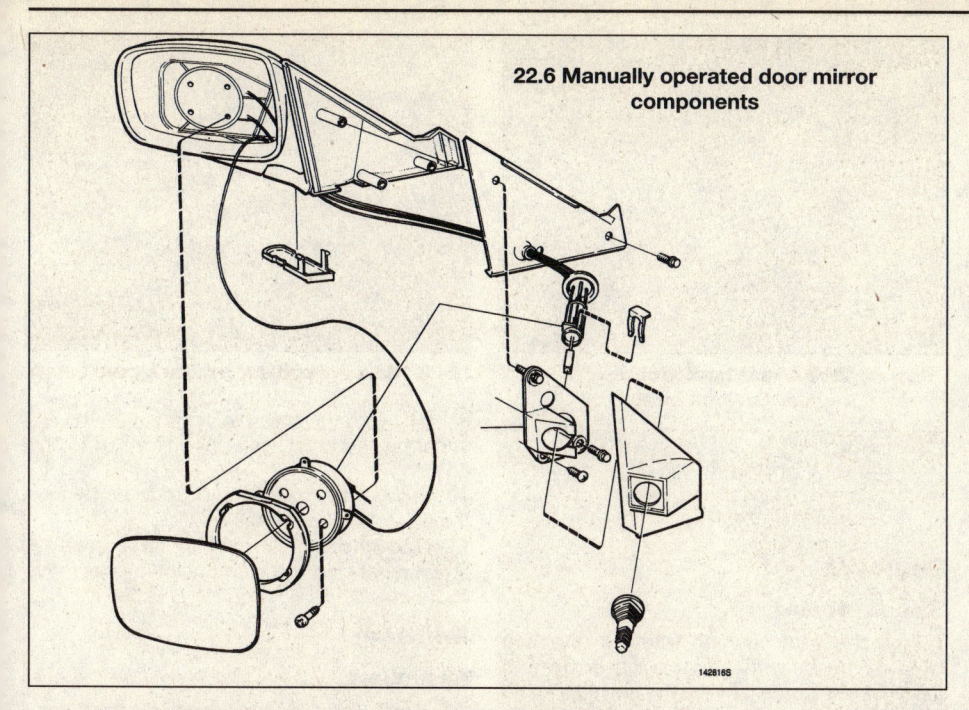

Bodywork and fittings 11•9

22.6 Manually operated door mirror components

4 Support the mirror and remove the mounting screws. Lift the mirror off the door.

Manually-operated

5 Remove the door interior trim.
6 Release the trim panel and adjustment stalk from the mirror and door (see illustration).
7 Undo the three retaining bolts and one screw, release the retaining clip and withdraw the mirror from the door.

Refitting

8 Refit by reversing the removal operations.

23 Door mirror glass and motor
- removal and refitting

Note: *There is no need to remove the mirror from the door for the following operations.*

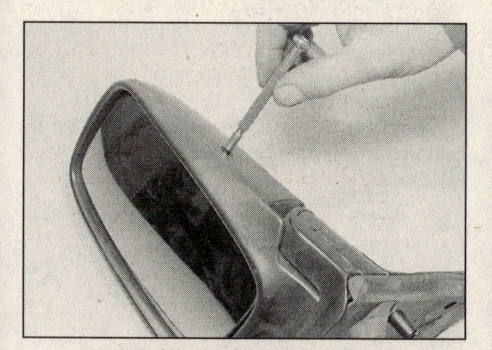

23.2 Releasing the mirror glass retaining ring

23.3 Mirror motor, showing the retaining screws

23.5a Mirror motor is marked "TOP" . . .

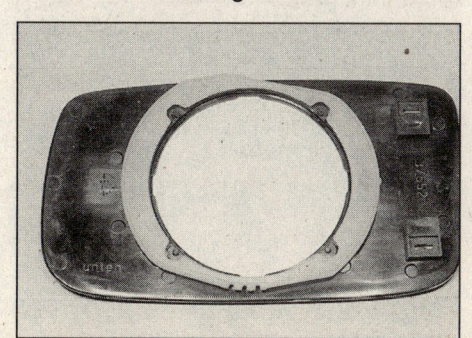

23.5b . . . and glass is marked "unten"

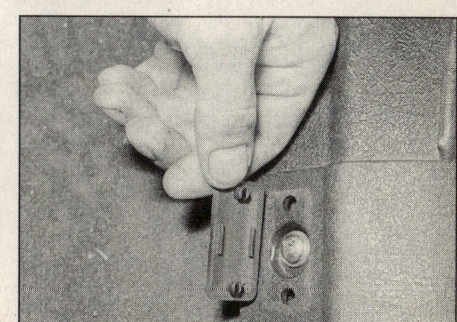

Removal

Pre-1992 models

1 Press the mirror glass inwards at the bottom until the retaining ring teeth are visible through the access hole.
2 Prise the teeth with a screwdriver to move the ring anti-clockwise (looking at the glass). This will release the retaining ring from the mounting plate (see illustration). Remove the glass and retaining ring. When applicable, disconnect the heating element wires.
3 The motor may now be removed after undoing the four retaining screws and disconnecting the wires from it. If the wires cannot be separated from the motor, remove the door interior trim and disconnect the mirror multi-plug (see illustration).

1992 models onward

4 Place your fingers behind the mirror glass edge nearest the door and pull the glass straight out. Where applicable disconnect the heating element wiring.

Refitting

Pre-1992 models

5 Refit by reversing the removal operations. Observe the "TOP" marking on the motor, and the "UNTEN" (bottom) marking on the mirror glass (see illustration).

1992 models onward

6 Where applicable, reconnect the heating element wiring.
7 Locate the mirror glass connecting pins on the adjustment unit and press the glass firmly into position.

24 Door surround weatherstrip
- removal and refitting

Removal

1 Remove the kick panel from the door sill (see illustration).
2 Prise the weatherstrip free, starting at the bottom. Use a wide-bladed screwdriver and protect the paintwork by prising against a piece of wood.

24.1 Sill kick panel screw and cover

11

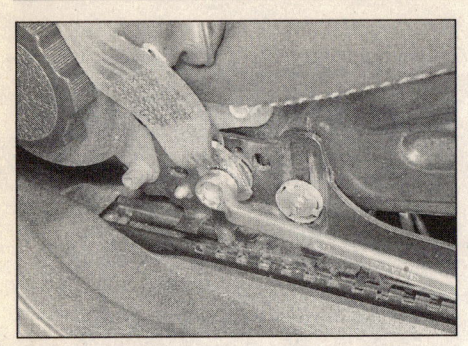

25.1 Unbolting the seat belt anchorage

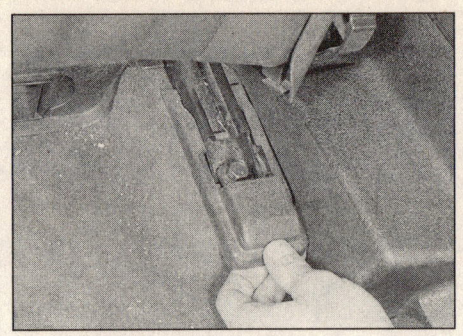

25.2 A rear track bolt . . .

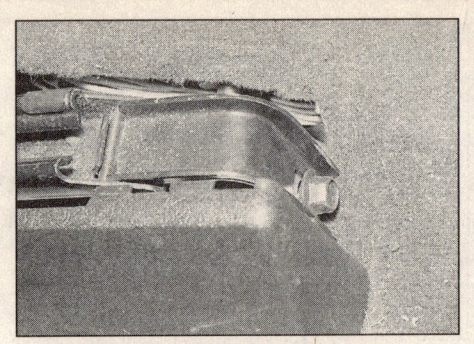

25.3 . . . and a front track bolt

Refitting

3 Refit the weatherstrip starting at the uppermost corner. Tap it home with a rubber mallet.
4 Refit the kick panel.

25 Front seat - removal and refitting

Removal

1 Remove the trim or storage pocket from the outboard side of the seat base. Unbolt the seat belt anchorage thus exposed **(see illustration)**.
2 Move the seat forwards. Remove the single screw from the rear of each track - these may be concealed by trim covers **(see illustration)**.
3 Move the seat rearwards. Remove any trim covers, then remove the single screw from the front of each track **(see illustration)**.
4 Disconnect the seat heater, seat belt switch and adjustment motor multi-plugs (as applicable).
5 Lift the front of the seat, pushing it rearwards at the same time, to free the tracks from their "keyhole" fixings in the floor. Remove the seat and tracks together.

Refitting

6 Refit by reversing the removal operations.

26 Rear seat - removal and refitting

Removal

Saloon models

1 Free the seat cushion from its retaining clips by pushing the front edge down and pulling it rearwards. Lift out the cushion.
2 Fold down the centre armrest and pull up the centre head restraint as far as it will go.
3 Lift up the panel under the head restraint, slacken the three bolts and remove the restraint.
4 Straighten the tongues of the clips which secure the base of the seat back. Thump the seat back upwards to free it from the top clips and remove it.
5 The armrest may now be unbolted and removed if wished.

Estate models

Pre-1993 models

6 Fold the seat cushions forwards. Remove the hinge retaining nuts and lift out the cushions **(see illustration)**.
7 Fold down the seat backs. Pull the pins out of the centre mounting **(see illustration)** and release the side mounting pins by turning them with pliers. Lift out the seat backs.

1993 models onward

8 Free the seat cushion from its retaining clips by pushing the front edge down and pulling it rearwards. Lift out the cushion.

9 Fold down the seat backs and undo the nut securing the head restraint link strap to the floor.
10 Pull out the locking clip from the peg on the side of the seat back.
11 Disconnect the tension spring at the floor attachment, pull the seat back sideways and lift it out.

Refitting

All models

12 Refit by reversing the removal operations.

27 Head restraints - removal and refitting

Removal

1 Press on the rear of the seat backrest, just below the frame and at the same time pull the head restraint upwards to free it.
2 Pull the head restraint out of the guides and remove it.

Refitting

3 Refit by pushing the head restraint firmly into place until it latches.

28 Front seat position adjusters - removal and refitting

Removal

1 Remove the seat and cushion (Sections 25 and 29).

Mechanical height adjusters

2 Raise the adjuster to its highest position. Remove the Allen screws which secure it to the seat.
3 Press the height adjuster lever towards the front of the seat and push downwards on the seat. Separate the seat from the rods.
4 The height adjuster components may now be renewed as necessary.

Mechanical reclining adjuster

5 Proceed as for backrest heater renewal (Section 29), but also unbolt the reclining mechanism from the seat base frame. The

26.6 Two seat cushion hinges (Estate)

26.7 Seat back centre mounting (Estate) - pins arrowed

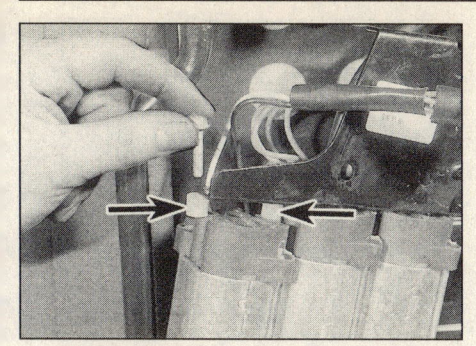

Bodywork and fittings 11•11

28.8 Removing a front height adjuster motor bolt. Note spacers (arrowed)

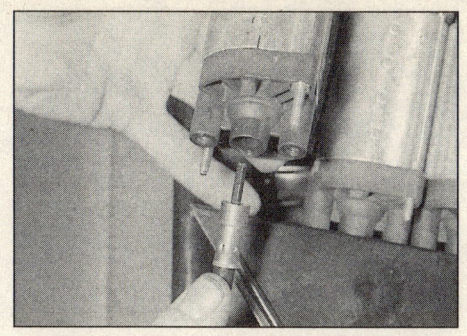

28.9 Separating the motor from the cable

complete backrest frame and reclining mechanism must be renewed together.

Fore-and-aft and height adjuster motor

6 Invert the seat on a clean bench or floor so that the base is accessible.
7 Remove the four small bolts which secure the motor mounting plate.
8 Ease the mounting plate away from the seat. Remove the four bolts which secure the motor in question; note the spacers fitted to the front height adjuster motor **(see illustration)**.
9 Remove the motor from the bracket and withdraw the cable from it **(see illustration)**.
10 Disconnect the motor multi-plug. This plug is shared by all three motors to remove one motor it will be necessary to prise its connectors out of the plug, or to cut the wires and make new connections for a new motor.

Backrest motor

11 Remove the lumbar support adjustment knob. Also remove the covers at the base of the backrest on both sides.
12 Recline the backrest as far as possible, using a screwdriver or similar tool inserted in the hole in the reclining gear mechanism at the base of the backrest.
13 On the underside of the seat disconnect the multi-plugs which feed the heater pads and the backrest motor. It will also be necessary to free or cut the black wire from the three-pole connector. Cut cable-ties as necessary.
14 Remove the four bolts which secure the backrest. Lift the backrest off the seat base.
15 Cut the rings which secure the upholstery to the base of the backrest. Peel back the upholstery and unhook the clips inside to gain access to the motor.
16 Remove the nut which secures the motor bracket to the backrest frame. Withdraw the motor with cables and bracket still attached.
17 Unbolt the bracket from the motor and free it from the cables. Disconnect its wiring plug and remove it.

Seat adjuster motor control panel

18 Cut the cable-tie which secures the wiring harness to the motor mounting plate.
19 Disconnect the motor multi-plugs.
20 Remove the two screws which secure the control panel.

21 Withdraw the control panel, feeding the cables and connectors through the side of the seat.

Refitting

22 In all cases, refit by reversing the removal operations using new cable-ties, upholstery rings etc, as necessary.

29 Seat heating elements - removal and refitting

Removal

1 Remove the front seat (Section 25).
2 Recline the backrest as far as it will go. Invert the seat and free the wiring from the cable-ties.

Backrest heater

3 Remove the head restraint (Section 27).
4 Remove the backrest adjuster knob, and the lumbar support adjuster knob and guide.
5 Remove the upholstery retaining rod. Cut the clamp rings which secure the bottom edge of the upholstery. Peel off the upholstery, freeing the centre attachment clamps.
6 The heating element can now be removed.

Cushion heater

7 Remove the upholstery retaining rods. Unhook the side springs and remove the cushion.
8 Cut the clamp rings which secure the upholstery. Peel off the upholstery, unhooking the centre attachments.
9 The heating element and thermostat can now be removed.

Seat heater control unit

10 Each seat has a control unit which varies the seat heater output according to temperature. Maximum output is only provided at under-seat temperatures below 10°C. Low output is provided at temperatures between 10 and 18°C. No output is provided at higher temperatures, apart from a burst of a few seconds when the ignition is first switched on.
11 If the seat heater does not behave as described, the control unit may be at fault.

Access is obtained by removing the seat, cutting the mounting strap and unplugging the control unit.
12 Testing of the control unit is by substitution of a known good unit. Assuming that only one control unit will fail at a time, a good unit may be borrowed from the other seat to confirm the fault.

Refitting

13 In all cases, refit by reversing the removal operations, using new clamp rings when necessary.

30 Seat belts - removal and refitting

⚠ *Warning: Vehicles for certain markets may be equipped with mechanical front seat belt tensioners, and vehicles equipped with a Supplementary Restraint System (air bag), may be fitted with pyrotechnical seat belt tensioners. DO NOT attempt to remove the front seat belts on vehicles so equipped. Have any work involving front seat belt removal carried out by a Volvo dealer. Refer to Chapter 12, Section 23 for further information.*

Removal

Front seat belts

1 Move the front seat forwards. Remove the trim or storage pocket from the outboard side of the seat base. Unbolt the seat belt anchorage.
2 Remove the B-pillar trim panel, which is secured by two screws concealed by plugs **(see illustration)**. Free the belt guide from the slot in the trim.
3 Remove the reel cover/sill trim panel, which is secured by seven concealed screws.

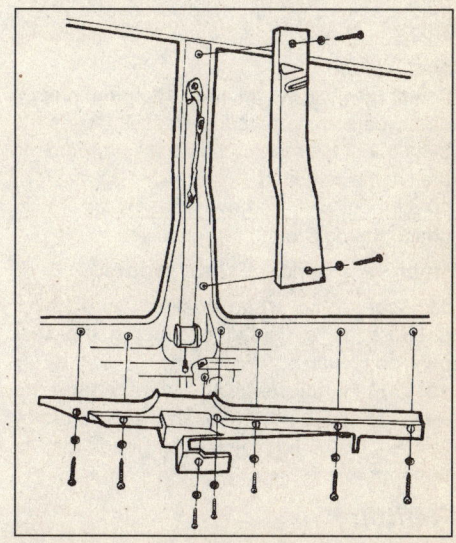

30.2 Remove the trim panels for access to the front seat belt

11•12 Bodywork and fittings

32.1 Removing a glovebox screw trim pad

32.3 Glovebox base nut (arrowed)

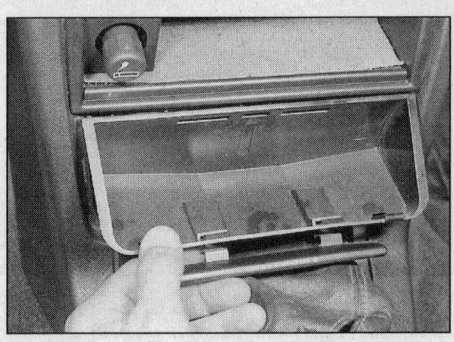

33.4 Removing the ashtray carrier

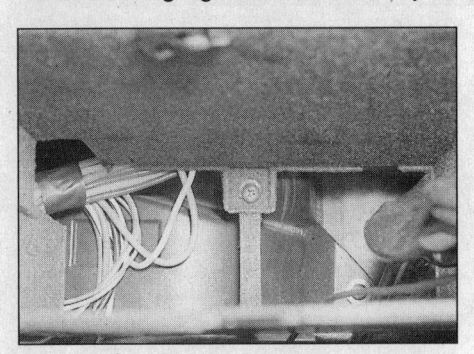

33.6 Radio tray securing screw

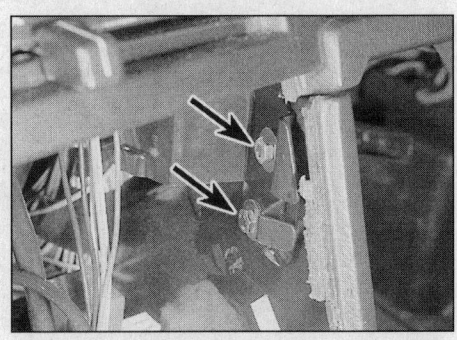

33.7 Side panel screws (arrowed) below the heater controls

33.8 Side panel rear edge screws

4 Unbolt the belt upper guide and the inertia reel unit, noting the location of any washers and spacers. Remove the belt and reel.
5 To remove the buckle, it is first necessary to remove the seat (Section 25).

Rear seat belts - Saloon models

6 Remove the rear seat (Section 26).
7 The buckles and floor anchorages can now be unbolted from the seat pan.
8 To gain access to the inertia reels it will first be necessary to remove the parcel shelf loudspeakers (when fitted). Access to their connectors and fastenings is from inside the boot.
9 Remove the parcel shelf securing screws and clips and the parcel shelf itself. Tease the belts out of the slots in the plastic protector as the shelf is removed.
10 Unbolt and remove the inertia reels, noting the position of any spacers.

Rear seat belts - Estate models

11 Access to the buckles and floor anchorages is gained by tipping the seat cushion forwards.
12 The inertia reels are accessible after removing the C-pillar trim. This is attached by a screw at the top, by the seat back stop at the bottom and by a clip at the rear.

Refitting

13 In all cases, refit by reversing the removal operations

31 Steering column/pedal trim panel - removal and refitting

Removal

1 The large trim panel below the steering column is secured by two screws and two clips. Remove the screws and turn the clips 90° to release them.
2 Lower the trim panel and disconnect the heater duct from it. Remove the panel.

Refitting

3 Refit by reversing the removal operations.

32 Glovebox - removal and refitting

Removal

1 Open the glovebox. Prise out the two trim pads from the edges of the glovebox and remove the two screws exposed **(see illustration)**.
2 Remove the trim panel from below the glovebox. This is secured by three clips which must be turned 90°.
3 Remove the nut at the base of the glovebox (towards the centre of the vehicle) **(see illustration)**.
4 Lower the glovebox, disconnect the wires from it and remove it.

Refitting

5 Refit by reversing the removal operations.

33 Centre console - removal and refitting

Removal

1 Disconnect the battery negative lead.
2 Remove the steering column/pedal trim (Section 31) and the glovebox (Section 32). This may not be essential but will improve access.
3 Remove the radio (Chapter 12).
4 Remove the ashtray and its carrier **(see illustration)**.
5 Remove the cigarette lighter tray. This is secured by one or two screws, exposed by removing the lighter element and cover plate. Disconnect the lighter feed and withdraw the bulb holder as the tray is withdrawn. (On some models the tray may contain audio equipment.)
6 Remove the radio tray, which is secured by a single screw at the back **(see illustration)**.
7 Remove the side panel screws from below the heater controls **(see illustration)**.
8 Remove the screws (two on each side) which secure the rear edge of the centre console side panels. It will be necessary to release the rear console and move it rearwards to gain access to these screws **(see illustration)**.

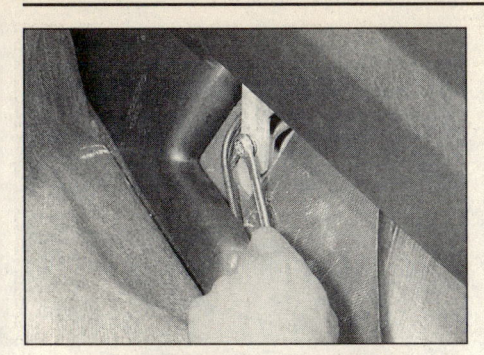

Bodywork and fittings 11•13

33.9 Removing a side panel forward end screw

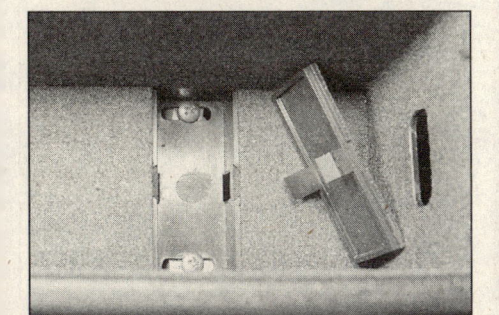

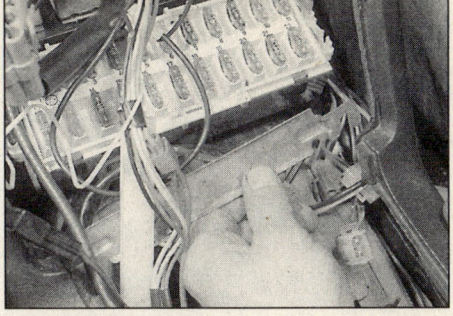

33.10 Removing the side panel connecting strut

35.4 Footwell side trim panel screws (arrowed)

34.1 Two screws in the bottom of the storage box

35.7 Removing the central air vent

9 Peel back the carpet from the forward end of the transmission tunnel and remove the two screws (one each side) securing the forward ends of the side panels **(see illustration)**.
10 Slacken the screws which secure the side panel connecting strut. Release the strut, which has slotted fixing holes **(see illustration)**.
11 Remove the centre console side panels.

Refitting
12 Refit by reversing the removal operations.

34 Rear console - removal and refitting

Removal
1 Lift the armrest, empty the storage box and prise out the cover plate from the bottom of the box. Remove the two screws thus exposed **(see illustration)**.
2 On manual transmission models, remove the gear lever/handbrake trim. This is retained by two screws. Disconnect any switches.
3 On automatic transmission models, remove the selector lever trim.
4 Lift the rear console. Separate the rear ashtray/cigarette lighter/seat belt warning light panel from the console. Remove the console, leaving the panel behind.

Refitting
5 Refit by reversing the removal operations.

35 Facia - removal and refitting

⚠ **Warning: On vehicles equipped with a Supplementary Restraint System (air bag), some of the following operations will entail disturbing some of the SRS components. Have any work involving removal of the SRS components carried out by a Volvo dealer. Refer to Chapter 12, Section 23 for further information.**

Removal
1 Disconnect the battery negative lead.
2 Remove the steering wheel, the steering column switches and the instrument panel. See Chapters 10 and 12.
3 Remove the steering column/pedal trim, the glovebox, the centre console and the rear console. See Sections 31 to 34.
4 Remove the footwell side trim panels **(see illustration)**. Also remove the A-pillar trim.
5 Disconnect the switch and lighting multi-plugs.
6 Remove the screw which secures the steering column top bearing to the facia. Recover the spacer tube.
7 Remove the central air vents **(see illustration)**. Remove the air mix box retaining screw and disconnect the air ducts.
8 Unclip the wiring harness from the facia.
9 On vehicles with automatic climate control, remove the inner temperature sensor.

10 Remove the facia panel complete with switchgear, demister vents etc. Transfer components as necessary if a new panel is to be fitted.

Refitting
11 Refit by reversing the removal operations.

36 Front spoiler - removal and refitting

Removal
1 Have an assistant support the spoiler. Remove the screws and side retaining clips which secure it to the bumper.
2 Free the spoiler from the bumper and remove it.

Refitting
3 Refit by reversing the removal operations.

37 Bumpers - removal and refitting

Removal

Front bumper
1 Remove the front spoiler as described in the previous Section.
2 Release the upper trim moulding from the retaining clips along the bumper top edge **(see illustration)**.
3 Undo the lower retaining screws and nuts securing the bumper to the body and the upper bolts securing it to the buffers. The location of these varies according to model.
4 Pull the bumper forward to release it from the guide channels on each side and remove it from the car.

Rear bumper
5 This is removed in a similar way to the front bumper but the location of the screws and clips varies **(see illustration)**.

Refitting
6 Refit by reversing the removal operations.

11

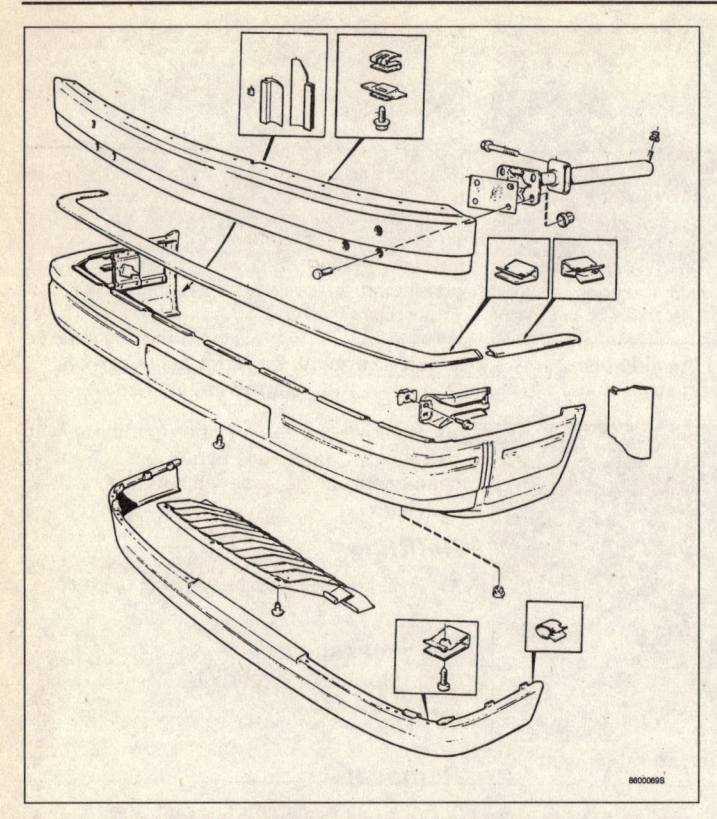

11•14 Bodywork and fittings

37.2 Front bumper components and attachments

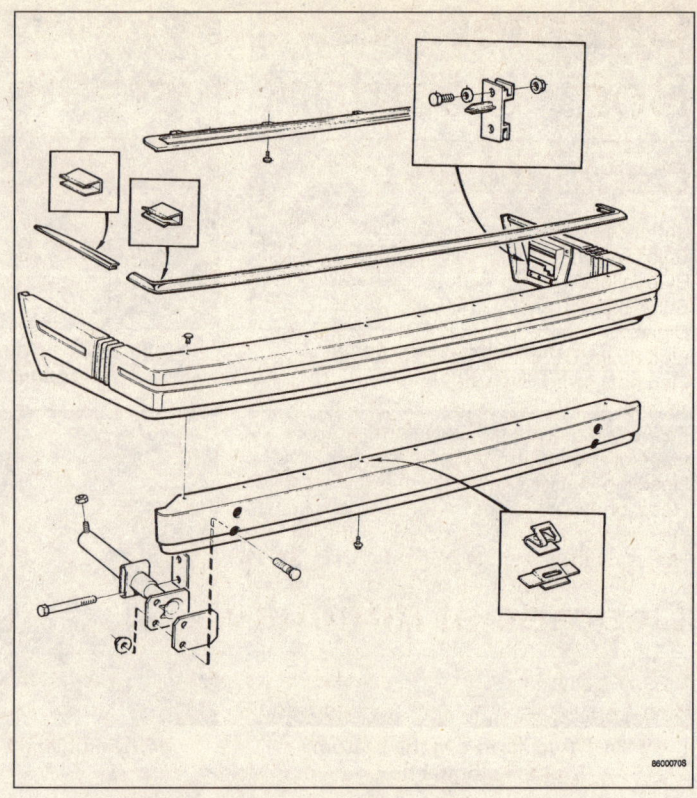

37.5 Rear bumper components and attachments

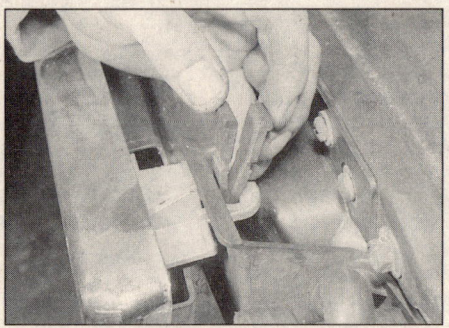

38.1 Removing a grille panel clip

38.2 Grille panel bottom mounting

38 Front grille panel - removal and refitting

Removal

1 Open the bonnet. Squeeze the grille panel top clips and remove them **(see illustration)**.
2 Release the panel from its bottom mountings and remove it **(see illustration)**.

Refitting

3 Refit by reversing the removal operations.

39 Sunroof - general information

A mechanically or electrically operated sunroof is available as standard or optional equipment according to model.

The sunroof is maintenance-free, but any adjustment or removal and refitting of the component parts should be entrusted to a dealer, due to the complexity of the unit and the need to remove much of the interior trim and headlining to gain access. The latter operation is involved, and requires care and specialist knowledge to avoid damage.

Chapter 12
Body electrical systems

Contents

Battery check	See "Weekly checks"
Bulbs (exterior lights) - renewal	8
Bulb failure warning system - general information	12
Bulbs (interior lights) - renewal	9
Cigarette lighter - removal and refitting	19
Electrical fault finding - general information	2
Electrical systems check	See "Weekly checks"
Exterior light units - removal and refitting	10
Fuses and relays - general information	3
General information and precautions	1
Headlight beam alignment - checking and adjusting	11
Headlight wiper motor - removal and refitting	17
Heated rear window - general information	20
Horn - removal and refitting	13
Instrument cluster - dismantling and reassembly	6
Instrument cluster - removal and refitting	5
Radio aerial - removal and refitting	22
Radio/cassette player - removal and refitting	21
Screen washer fluid level check	See "Weekly checks"
Speedometer sender unit - removal and refitting	7
Supplementary Restraint System (SRS) - general information and precautions	23
Switches - removal and refitting	4
Tailgate wiper motor - removal and refitting	18
Windscreen/headlight/tailgate washers - general information	14
Windscreen wiper motor and linkage - removal and refitting	16
Wiper arms - removal and refitting	15
Wiper blade check	See "Weekly checks"

Degrees of difficulty

Easy, suitable for novice with little experience

Fairly easy, suitable for beginner with some experience

Fairly difficult, suitable for competent DIY mechanic

Difficult, suitable for experienced DIY mechanic

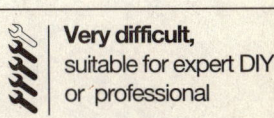

Very difficult, suitable for expert DIY or professional

Specifications

Fuses - all models (except 1991, 940 SE)

No	Rating (amps)	Circuit(s) protected
1	25	Fuel pump, fuel injection system, heated oxygen sensor
2	25	Hazard warning, headlight flasher, central locking
3	15	Power-operated seats
4	15	Stop-lights, automatic transmission shift-lock solenoid
5	15	Clock, interior lighting, power aerial, radio (full-time), door edge marker lights
6	30	Air conditioning electronic climate control, ECC heater blower
7	15	Front and rear foglights
8	30	Window motors
9	15	Direction indicators, seat belt reminder, seat heater relay, window motor relay, air conditioning relay, cooling fan relay, automatic transmission shift-lock supply
10	30	Heated rear window, sunroof motor, heated mirrors
11	15	Fuel pump (auxiliary)
12	15	Reversing lights, overdrive relay, bulb failure monitor, cruise control
13	15	Fuel injection systems (depending on model/territory)
14	15	Mirror motors, cigarette lighter, radio (ignition-controlled), rear window wiper/washer
15	25	Horn, windscreen wash/wipe, headlight wash/wipe, power-operated seat relay
16	30	Heater blower, air conditioning
17	15	Main beam (LH) and main beam warning light
18	15	Main beam (RH)
19	15	Dipped beam (LH), front foglight relay
20	15	Dipped beam (RH)
21	15	Instrument lighting, tail/parking lights (LH), number plate lights
22	15	Rear ashtray light, transmission tunnel switch light, tail/parking lights (RH), front foglight relay
23	25	Seat heater supply
24	-	Spare
25	15	Day running lights
26	15	Radio amplifier

12•2 Body electrical systems

Fuses - 1991, 940 SE models

No	Rating (amps)	Circuit(s) protected
1	10	Tail/parking lights (LH), number plate lights
2	10	Tail/parking lights (RH)
3	15	Main beam (LH)
4	15	Main beam (RH)
5	-	Spare
6	15	Dipped beam (LH)
7	10	Dipped beam (RH)
8	15	Foglights front
9	10	Foglights rear
10	5	Instrument and control lighting
11	15	Reversing lights, direction indicators, cruise control
12	15	Dim-dip system, automatic transmission shift-lock
13	25	Heated rear window, heated mirrors
14	10	Bulb failure warning, overdrive relay, power window relay, sunroof motor relay, seat belt warning, heated seats
15	-	Spare
16	-	Spare
17	-	Spare
18	5	Radio
19	15	Electronic climate control, mirror motors, rear window wiper motor relay, cigarette lighter, power seats
20	25	Horn, windscreen wipers, headlight wipers
21	-	Spare
22	5	ABS
23	-	Spare
24	-	Spare
25	25	Hazard warning lights, central locking
26	10	Clock, interior lights, door markers
27	15	Stop-lights switch, automatic transmission shift-lock supply
28	30	Heater blower, electronic climate control
29	30	Radio aerial, trailer lighting
30	10	Auxiliary fuel pump
31	25	Main fuel pump, heated oxygen sensor
32	15	Radio amplifier
33	10	Radio
34	30	Window motors, sunroof motor
35	30	Seat heaters, seat motors

Light bulbs (typical)

	Wattage	Pattern
Headlights	60/55	P43t-38 (H4)
Day running/parking lights	5	BA 15s
Direction indicators	21	BA 15s
Direction indicator side repeaters	5	W2.1x9.5d
Front foglights/spotlights	55	PK 22s (H3)
Tail lights	5	BA 15s
Stop-lights	21	BA 15s
High-level stop light	21	BA 15s
Combined stop and tail	21/5	BAY 15d
Rear foglights/reversing lights	21	BA 15s
Number plate light:		
Saloon models	5	W2.1x9.5d
Estate models	4	BA 9s
Interior (courtesy) lights	10	SV 8.5
Reading lights	5	W 2.1x9.5d
Engine bay/load area lights	10	SV 8.5
Glovebox light	2	BA 9s
Vanity mirror light	3	SV 7
Door edge marker light	3	W 2.1x9.5d
Indicator and warning lights	1.2	Integral holder
Instrument illumination	3	W 2.1x9.5d
Control illumination	1.2	W 2x4.6d

1 General information and precautions

General information

The electrical system is of 12-volt negative earth type. Power for the lights and all electrical accessories is supplied by a lead/acid battery which is charged by the alternator.

This Chapter covers repair and service procedures for the various electrical components and systems not associated with the engine. Information on the battery, ignition system, alternator, and starter motor can be found in Chapter 5.

Precautions

Warning: Before carrying out any work on the electrical system, read through the precautions given in "Safety first!" at the beginning of this manual and in Chapter 5.

Prior to working on any component in the electrical system, the battery negative lead should first be disconnected, to prevent the possibility of electrical short-circuits and/or fires. If a radio/cassette player with anti-theft security code is fitted, refer to the information given in the reference sections of this manual before disconnecting the battery.

2 Electrical fault finding - general information

Note: *Refer to the precautions given in "Safety first!" and in Section 1 of this Chapter before starting work. The following tests relate to testing of the main electrical circuits, and should not be used to test delicate electronic circuits, particularly where an electronic control module is used.*

General

1 A typical electrical circuit consists of an electrical component, any switches, relays, motors, fuses, fusible links or circuit breakers related to that component, and the wiring and connectors which link the component to both the battery and the chassis. To help to pinpoint a problem in an electrical circuit, wiring diagrams are included at the end of this manual.

2 Before attempting to diagnose an electrical fault, first study the appropriate wiring diagram, to obtain a complete understanding of the components included in the particular circuit concerned. The possible sources of a fault can be narrowed down by noting if other components related to the circuit are operating properly. If several components or circuits fail at one time, the problem is likely to be related to a shared fuse or earth connection.

3 Electrical problems usually stem from simple causes, such as loose or corroded connections, a faulty earth connection, a blown fuse, a melted fusible link, or a faulty relay. Visually inspect the condition of all fuses, wires and connections in a problem circuit before testing the components. Use the wiring diagrams to determine which terminal connections will need to be checked in order to pinpoint the trouble-spot.

4 The basic tools required for electrical fault-finding include a circuit tester or voltmeter (a 12-volt bulb with a set of test leads can also be used for certain tests); an ohmmeter (to measure resistance and check for continuity); a battery and set of test leads; and a jumper wire, preferably with a circuit breaker or fuse incorporated, which can be used to bypass suspect wires or electrical components. Before attempting to locate a problem with test instruments, use the wiring diagram to determine where to make the connections.

5 To find the source of an intermittent wiring fault (usually due to a poor or dirty connection, or damaged wiring insulation), a "wiggle" test can be performed on the wiring. This involves wiggling the wiring by hand to see if the fault occurs as the wiring is moved. It should be possible to narrow down the source of the fault to a particular section of wiring. This method of testing can be used in conjunction with any of the tests described in the following sub-Sections.

6 Apart from problems due to poor connections, two basic types of fault can occur in an electrical circuit - open-circuit, or short-circuit.

7 Open-circuit faults are caused by a break somewhere in the circuit, which prevents current from flowing. An open-circuit fault will prevent a component from working.

8 Short-circuit faults are caused by a "short" somewhere in the circuit, which allows the current flowing in the circuit to "escape" along an alternative route, usually to earth. Short-circuit faults are normally caused by a breakdown in wiring insulation, which allows a feed wire to touch either another wire, or an earthed component such as the bodyshell. A short-circuit fault will normally cause the relevant circuit fuse to blow.

Finding an open-circuit

9 To check for an open-circuit, connect one lead of a circuit tester or the negative lead of a voltmeter either to the battery negative terminal or to a known good earth.

10 Connect the other lead to a connector in the circuit being tested, preferably nearest to the battery or fuse. At this point, battery voltage should be present, unless the lead from the battery or the fuse itself is faulty (bearing in mind that some circuits are live only when the ignition switch is moved to a particular position).

11 Switch on the circuit, then connect the tester lead to the connector nearest the circuit switch on the component side.

12 If voltage is present (indicated either by the tester bulb lighting or a voltmeter reading, as applicable), this means that the section of the circuit between the relevant connector and the switch is problem-free.

13 Continue to check the remainder of the circuit in the same fashion.

14 When a point is reached at which no voltage is present, the problem must lie between that point and the previous test point with voltage. Most problems can be traced to a broken, corroded or loose connection.

Finding a short-circuit

15 To check for a short-circuit, first disconnect the load(s) from the circuit (loads are the components which draw current from a circuit, such as bulbs, motors, heating elements, etc).

16 Remove the relevant fuse from the circuit, and connect a circuit tester or voltmeter to the fuse connections.

17 Switch on the circuit, bearing in mind that some circuits are live only when the ignition switch is moved to a particular position.

18 If voltage is present (indicated either by the tester bulb lighting or a voltmeter reading, as applicable), this means that there is a short-circuit.

19 If no voltage is present during this test, but the fuse still blows with the load(s) reconnected, this indicates an internal fault in the load(s).

Finding an earth fault

20 The battery negative terminal is connected to "earth" - the metal of the engine/transmission and the vehicle body - and many systems are wired so that they only receive a positive feed, the current returning via the metal of the car body. This means that the component mounting and the body form part of that circuit. Loose or corroded mountings can therefore cause a range of electrical faults, ranging from total failure of a circuit, to a puzzling partial failure. In particular, lights may shine dimly (especially when another circuit sharing the same earth point is in operation), motors (eg wiper motors or the radiator cooling fan motor) may run slowly, and the operation of one circuit may have an apparently-unrelated effect on another. Note that on many vehicles, earth straps are used between certain components, such as the engine/transmission and the body, usually where there is no metal-to-metal contact between components, due to flexible rubber mountings, etc.

21 To check whether a component is properly earthed, disconnect the battery and connect one lead of an ohmmeter to a known good earth point. Connect the other lead to the wire or earth connection being tested. The resistance reading should be zero; if not, check the connection as follows.

22 If an earth connection is thought to be faulty, dismantle the connection, and clean both the bodyshell and the wire terminal (or

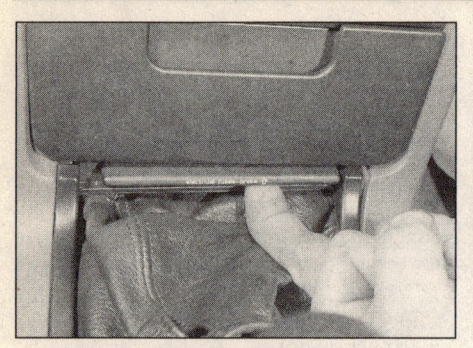

12•4 Body electrical systems

3.1 Unclip the ashtray carrier for access to the fuses

3.2 A sticker behind the ashtray gives fuse details for the particular vehicle

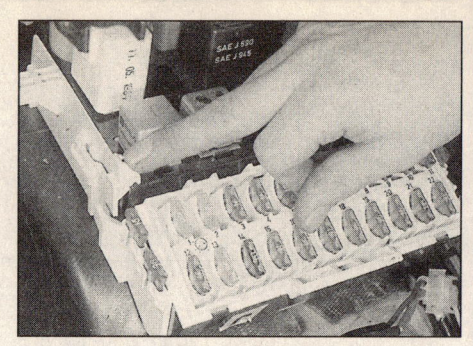

3.10a Release the clips . . .

the component earth connection mating surface) back to bare metal. Be careful to remove all traces of dirt and corrosion, then use a knife to trim away any paint, so that a clean metal-to-metal joint is made. On reassembly, tighten the joint fasteners securely; if a wire terminal is being refitted, use serrated washers between the terminal and the bodyshell, to ensure a clean and secure connection. When the connection is remade, prevent the onset of corrosion in the future by applying a coat of petroleum jelly or silicone-based grease, or by spraying on (at regular intervals) a proprietary ignition sealer, or a water-dispersant lubricant.

3 Fuses and relays - general information

Fuses

1 The fuses are located on the sloping face of the central electric unit, behind the front ashtray. Access is gained by removing the ashtray, then unclipping the ashtray carrier by pressing up the section marked "electrical fuses - press" **(see illustration)**.
2 If a fuse blows, the electrical circuit(s) protected by that fuse will cease to operate. Lists of the circuits protected are given in the Specifications; a sticker behind the ashtray gives details for the particular vehicle **(see illustration)**.
3 To check for a blown fuse, either remove the fuse and inspect its wire link, or (with the power on) connect a 12 volt test light between earth and each of the fuse pegs. If the test light comes on at both pegs, the fuse is OK; if it comes on at one peg only, the fuse is blown.
4 To renew a blown fuse, pull out the old fuse either with the fingers or with the special tool provided. Press in a new fuse of the correct rating (indicated by colour and by a number on the fuse). Spare fuses are provided at each side of the central electrical unit.
5 Never fit a fuse of a higher rating than that specified, nor bypass a blown fuse with wire or metal foil. Serious damage or fire could result.
6 Persistent blowing of a particular fuse indicates a fault in the circuit(s) protected. Where more than one circuit is involved, switch on one item at a time until the fuse blows, so showing in which circuit the fault lies.
7 Besides a fault in the electrical component concerned, a blown fuse can also be caused by a short-circuit in the wiring to the component. Look for trapped or frayed wires allowing a live wire to touch vehicle metal, and for loose or damaged connectors.

Relays - general

8 A relay is an electrically-operated switch, which is used for the following reasons:
a) *A relay can switch a heavy current remotely from the circuit in which the current is flowing, allowing the use of lighter gauge wiring and switch contacts.*
b) *A relay can receive more than one control input, unlike a mechanical switch.*
c) *A relay can have a timer function - for example an intermittent wiper delay.*
9 If a circuit which includes a relay develops a fault, remember that the relay itself could be faulty. Testing is by substitution of a known good relay. Do not assume that relays which look similar are necessarily identical for purposes of substitution.
10 Most relays are located on the central electrical unit, in front of the fuses. For access, remove the ashtray and ashtray holder, then release the clips and draw the unit into the vehicle **(see illustrations)**.
11 Additional relays relating to the fuel and ignition systems are located in the engine compartment, and two air conditioning system relays are located behind the facia panel.

4 Switches - removal and refitting

Steering column switches

1 Disconnect the battery negative lead.
2 Remove the steering wheel (Chapter 10).
3 Remove the screws and lift off the column shrouds.
4 Remove the switch in question. Each switch is secured by two screws. Remove the screws, pull the switch out and disconnect the multi-plug **(see illustrations)**.
5 Refit by reversing the removal operations.

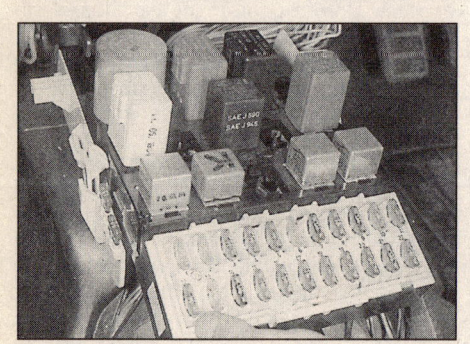

3.10b . . . and withdraw the central electrical unit (centre console removed)

4.4a Removing a column switch screw

4.4b Disconnecting a column switch multi-plug

Body electrical systems 12•5

4.11 Removing a horn push switch

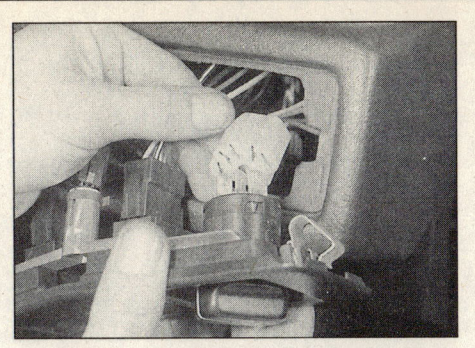

4.13 Disconnecting a switch multi-plug

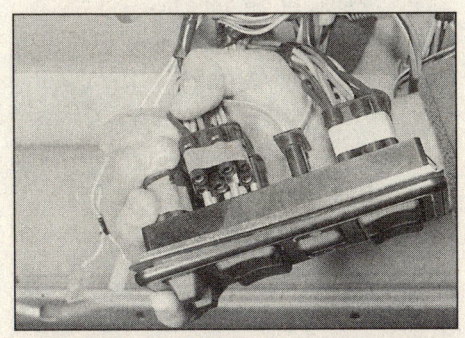

4.14 Removing a switch from the panel

4.18 Disconnecting a window switch

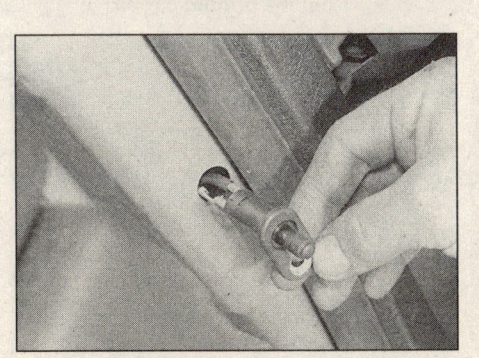

4.21 Removing a door switch

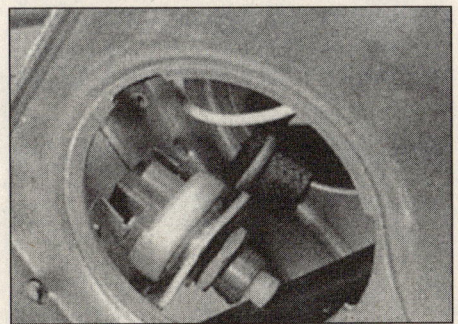

4.25 Stop-light switch seen through a hole in the brake pedal bracket

4.29 Handbrake warning switch - securing screw arrowed

Ignition/starter switch

6 Disconnect the battery negative lead.
7 Remove the trim panel from below the steering column.
8 Disconnect the multi-plug from the switch.
9 Remove the two screws which secure the switch to the steering lock. Withdraw the switch.
10 Refit by reversing the removal operations. Note that the hole in the centre of the switch is shaped so that it will only engage with the driving spindle in one position.

Horn push switches

11 These are removed by prising them out of the steering wheel. They are difficult to remove without damage **(see illustration)**.

Facia panel switches

12 Unclip the switch panel (and its surround, if applicable) and withdraw it from the facia.
13 Disconnect the switch multi-plugs, making identifying marks or notes if necessary **(see illustration)**.
14 Remove the switch concerned by depressing its retaining lugs **(see illustration)**. Where rotary switches are used, pull off the switch knob and remove the switch by unscrewing the retaining nut.
15 Refit by reversing the removal operations.

Rear console switches

16 See Chapter 11, Section 34.

Window/mirror control switches

17 Remove the door armrest and separate the switch panel from it. See Chapter 11, Section 11.
18 Disconnect the multi-plug from the switch in question **(see illustration)**.
19 Carefully prise free the retaining lugs and remove the switch from the underside of the switch plate.
20 Refit by reversing the removal operations.

Door/tailgate switches

21 Open the door or tailgate. Remove the screw and withdraw the switch **(see illustration)**.
22 Secure the wires with a clothes peg before disconnecting them so that they are not lost in the door pillar.
23 Refit by reversing the removal operations.

Brake stop light switch

24 Remove the steering column/pedal trim.
25 Disconnect the wiring from the switch. Undo the locknut and unscrew the switch **(see illustration)**.
26 When refitting, screw the switch in so that it operates after 8 to 14 mm movement of the brake pedal. Reconnect the wires and tighten the locknut.
27 Check for correct operation, then refit the disturbed trim.

Handbrake warning switch

28 Remove the rear console (Chapter 11, Section 34).
29 Remove the switch securing screw **(see illustration)**. Lift out the switch, disconnect the lead from it and remove it.
30 Refit by reversing the removal operations. Check for correct operation of the switch before refitting the rear console.

Other switches

31 Some switches will be found in the Chapter dealing with their system or equipment - for example, temperature-operated switches in Chapter 3, and transmission-operated switches in Chapter 7.

5 Instrument cluster - removal and refitting

Removal

1 Disconnect the battery negative lead.
2 Prise out the bright trim strip to the right of the cluster.
3 Remove the screw which secures the left-hand bright trim strip. This screw is accessible from inside the glovebox. Prise out the trim strip.

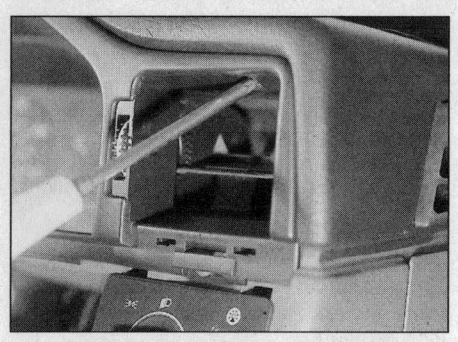

12•6 Body electrical systems

5.6a Removing a screw from within an air grille housing

5.6b Removing a screw cover below an air grille housing

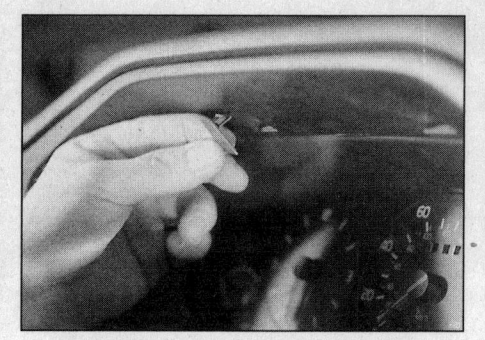

5.6c Removing an instrument hood screw cover

5.7a Removing an instrument cluster screw

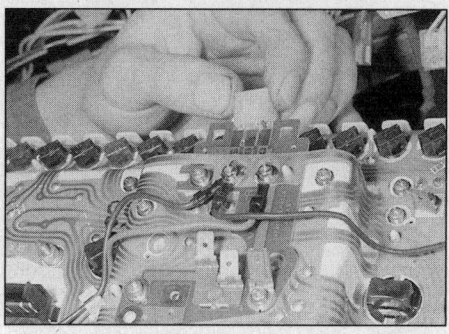

5.7b Disconnecting an instrument cluster multi-plug

4 Unclip the switch panels, disconnect the multi-plugs and remove the panels. (The main lighting switch can be left in position.)

5 Remove the air direction grilles by turning them upwards as far as possible, then unclipping them from their pivots using firm hand pressure.

6 Remove the seven screws which secure the cluster surround. These are located as follows: one in each air grille housing, two (under covers) below the air grille housings, and two (under covers) on the underside of the instrument hood **(see illustrations)**. Remove the surround.

7 Remove the four screws, one in each corner, which secure the instrument cluster itself **(see illustration)**. Carefully draw the cluster out of its recess and disconnect the multi-plugs from it **(see illustration)**. Remove the cluster.

Refitting

8 Refit by reversing the removal operations.

6 Instrument cluster - dismantling and reassembly

Dismantling

1 Remove the screws which secure the instrument cluster to the transparent panel and surround. Carefully remove the cluster.

2 Individual instruments can now be removed after undoing their securing nuts or screws

(see illustration). Note that the screws are not identical: those which secure conductors are plated.

3 Bulb holders are removed by twisting them

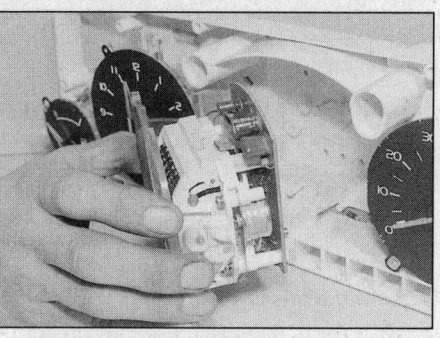

6.2 Removing the speedometer

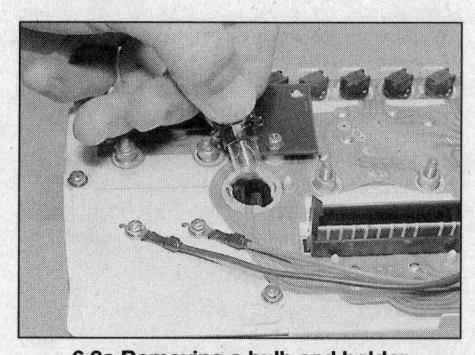

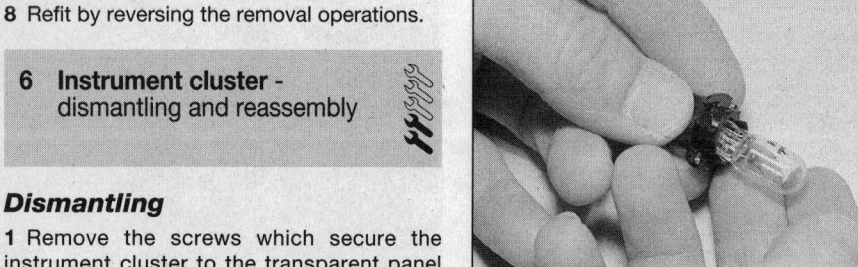

6.3b Separating the capless bulb and holder

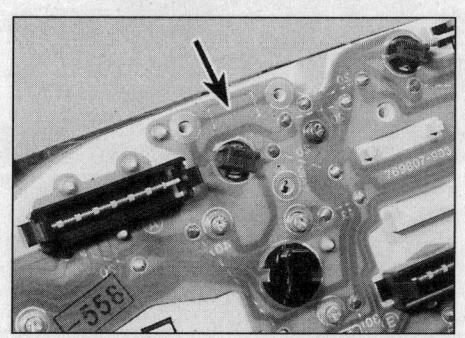

through 90° and pulling. Some bulbs can be separated from their holders for renewal; others must be renewed complete with holder **(see illustrations)**.

4 The printed circuit can be renewed after removing all the instruments, bulbs and connectors. Be careful when handling the printed circuit, it is fragile.

5 Some makes of instrument cluster incorporate a fusible link in the printed circuit **(see illustration)**. If this link blows, a repair strip or portion of circuit card should be obtained and secured in the same position. The fault which caused the original link to blow must also be rectified.

Reassembly

6 Reassembly is the reversal of the dismantling sequence.

6.3a Removing a bulb and holder from the printed circuit

6.5 Fusible link (arrowed) in the printed circuit

Body electrical systems 12•7

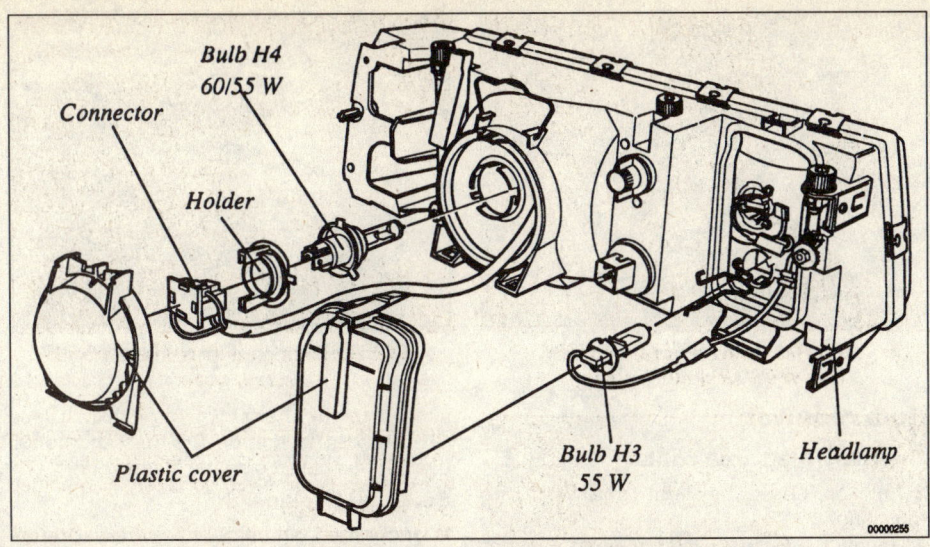

8.4 Bulb location and layout at the rear of the headlight unit

7 Speedometer sender unit - removal and refitting

Removal

1 The sender unit is located in the rear axle differential cover plate. On cars with ABS, the sender performs a dual function and acts as the ABS system rear wheel speed sensor.
2 Raise the rear of the vehicle on ramps (see "Jacking and vehicle support").
3 Unplug the sender connector.
4 Undo the retaining bolt and withdraw the sender from the cover plate.

Refitting

5 Refit by reversing the removal operations.

8 Bulbs (exterior lights) - renewal

General

1 With all light bulbs, remember that if they have just been in use, they may be very hot. Switch off the power before renewing a bulb.
2 With quartz halogen bulbs (headlights and similar applications), do not touch the bulb glass with the fingers. Even small quantities of grease from the fingers will cause blackening and premature failure. If a bulb is accidentally touched, clean it with methylated spirit and a clean rag.
3 Unless otherwise stated, fit the new bulb by reversing the removal operations.

Bulb renewal

Headlight

4 Open the bonnet. Unclip the plastic cover from the rear of the headlight unit (see illustration).
5 Unplug the connector from the bulb. Release the retainer by pushing it and twisting it anti-clockwise. Remove the retainer, spring and bulb.
6 When fitting the new bulb, do not touch the glass (paragraph 2). Make sure that the lugs on the bulb flange engage with the slots in the holder.

Auxiliary front light

7 Open the bonnet. Depress the clip on the plastic cover and remove the cover from the rear of the headlight unit.
8 Release the spring clip and withdraw the bulb.
9 Fit the new bulb, being careful not to touch it with the fingers (paragraph 2). Secure with the spring clip.
10 Refit the cover to the headlight unit.

Front direction indicator/day running/parking lights

11 Open the bonnet. Turn the appropriate bulb holder anti-clockwise (without disconnecting it) and withdraw it.
12 Remove the bulb from the holder.
13 When refitting, note that one of the bulbholder lugs is wider than the others so it will only fit one way round.

Direction indicator side repeater

14 Insert a thin feeler blade (wrapped with adhesive tape to avoid scratching the paintwork) under the front edge of the lens unit and depress the internal lug.
15 When the lug releases, free the lens from the rear and withdraw it from the wing. Disconnect the wiring and withdraw the bulbholder.
16 Pull the bulb from the holder, fit a new bulb and reassemble.

Rear light cluster (Saloon models)

17 Open the boot. To gain access to the bulbs in the wing, undo the knurled screw on the light unit cover and pivot the cover downwards. To gain access to the bulbs in the boot lid, lift the catch and withdraw the cover panel (see illustration).
18 Remove the bulb holder from the light unit and remove the relevant bayonet fitting bulb from the holder.

Rear light cluster (Estate models)

19 Open the tailgate and remove the light unit cover with the aid of a screwdriver (see illustration).
20 Withdraw the relevant bulbholder by turning it anticlockwise, then remove the bayonet fitting bulb from the holder.

High level stop light

21 Pull off the stop light cover.
22 Squeeze the catches on each side of the reflector/bulbholder and withdraw it.

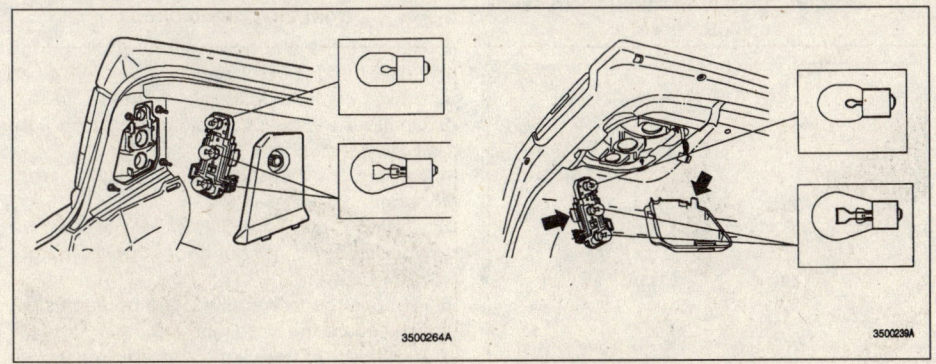

8.17 Bulb arrangement in the rear light cluster on Saloon models. Wing mounted bulbs (left), boot lid mounted bulbs (right)

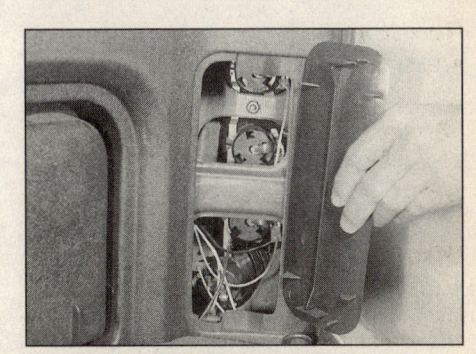

8.19 Rear light unit and cover - Estate models

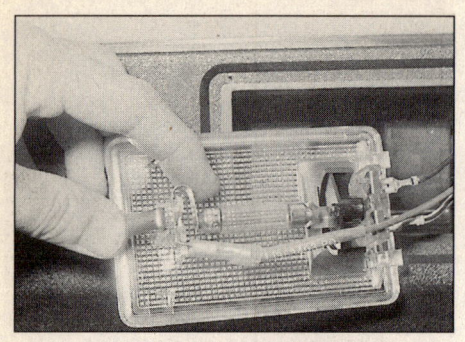

12•8 Body electrical systems

9.4 A load area light with an end clip fitting bulb

9.5 Glovebox light and switch (seen in a mirror)

9.6 Vanity mirror light bulbs exposed

23 Remove the old bulb and fit a new one.
24 Fit the reflector and press it home until the catches engage. Check for correct operation, then refit the cover.

Number plate light
25 Unclip the light unit by sliding it rearwards (Saloon models) or undoing the retaining screws (Estate models).
26 Release the bulb from the holder, fit a new bulb and reassemble.

9 Bulbs (interior lights) - renewal

General
1 See Section 8, paragraphs 1 and 3.
2 Some switch illumination/pilot bulbs are integral with their switches and cannot be renewed separately.

9.7 Fitting a door edge marker bulb

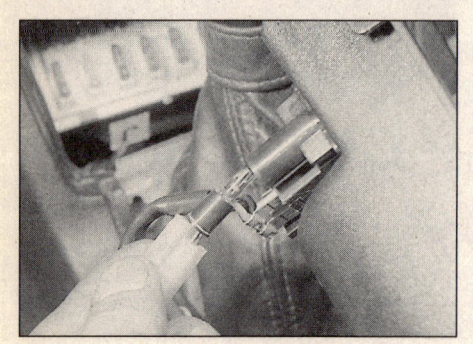

9.10 Removing a rear console switch light

Bulb renewal

Courtesy/load area lights
3 Pull or prise the light unit from its mountings.
4 Renew the bulb(s), which may be bayonet or end clip fitting (see illustration).

Glovebox lights
5 Unclip the combined bulb holder/switch unit from the top of the glovebox for access to the bulb (see illustration).
6 When vanity mirror bulbs are fitted, these are accessible after prising out the light diffuser strip (see illustration).

Door edge marker lights
7 Prise off the lens for access to the bulb. The bulb is of the capless type, so it is a push fit (see illustration).

Automatic transmission selector light
8 Remove the selector quadrant as if for

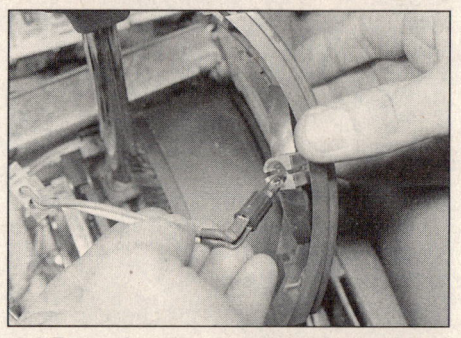

9.8 Extracting the automatic transmission selector light

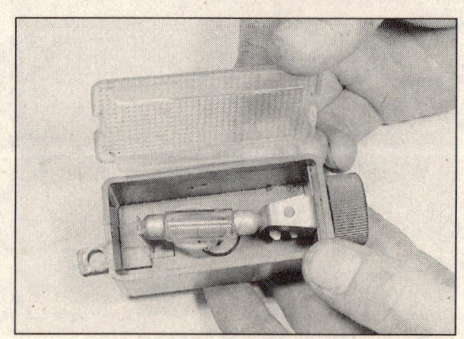

9.12 Under-bonnet light unit (removed)

access to the starter inhibitor switch (see Chapter 7B, Section 6). The bulb and holder can then be pulled out (see illustration).

Seat belt buckle light
9 Unclip the bulb holder from the buckle for access to the bulb.

Switch illumination bulbs
10 When these are separable from the switch, they simply pull out (see illustration).

Instrument panel bulbs
11 See Sections 5 and 6. (The reader with small hands and deft fingers may manage to renew bulbs *in situ* after removing the steering column/pedal trim.)

Under-bonnet light
12 Prise off the lens with a screwdriver. The bulb is of the end clip fitting type (see illustration).

Cigarette lighter/ashtray light
13 See Section 19.

10 Exterior light units - removal and refitting

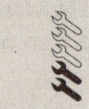

Note: *Ensure that all lights are switched off before disconnecting any wiring connectors.*

Headlight unit
1 Remove the front grille. Depending on model, it may also be beneficial to remove the battery or air cleaner unit (according to side) if clearance is insufficient.
2 Remove the bulbholders, with bulbs, from the direction indicator/parking light unit. Push and twist the holders to release them.
3 Unclip the direction indicator/parking light unit and remove it.
4 Unplug the headlight and auxiliary front light connector.
5 Unplug the headlight wiper motor connector and disconnect the headlight washer tube.
6 Remove the four screws, two on each side, which secure the headlight unit.
7 Remove the headlight unit complete with wiper motor, arm and blade.
8 To dismantle the unit, remove the two

screws which secure the headlight wiper motor. Unclip the front trim strip and remove the wiper motor complete with arm, blade and trim strip.
9 Remove the four wiper blade stops, which are secured by one screw each.
10 Remove the eight clips which secure the lens to the reflector.
11 Remove the lens and extract the seal.
12 Remove the bulb covers from the rear of the unit. Disconnect and remove the bulbs, being careful not to touch the glass with the fingers.
13 Renew components as necessary and reassemble by reversing the dismantling procedure. Pay particular attention to the condition and fit of the lens-to-reflector seal.
14 Refit the unit to the car by reversing the removal operations. Note that the securing screws allow the headlight unit to be moved to align it relative to the body, then bumper and the other headlight; do not tighten the screws until satisfied with the position of the unit. If the headlight is fitted too high, the bonnet will strike it.
15 Have the headlight beam alignment checked on completion. The adjustment screws are on top of the unit.

Auxiliary front light

16 Follow the wiring back from the light unit and unplug the connector.
17 Remove the nut which secures the light unit to the bracket, or unbolt the bracket complete with the light unit, as wished.
18 Refit by reversing the removal operations.

Direction indicator/ parking light unit

19 Open the bonnet. Disconnect the two multi-plugs from the bulb holders on the rear of the unit.
20 Unclip the direction indicator/parking light unit and remove it.

Rear light cluster (Saloon models)

21 Remove the bulbholder from the rear of the light cluster as described in Section 8.
22 Remove the retaining nuts securing the cluster to the wing or boot lid.
23 Remove the cluster from the vehicle.
24 Refit by reversing the removal operations.

Rear light cluster (Estate models)

25 Proceed as described for Saloon models, making allowances for the detail differences which will be found.

11 Headlight beam alignment - checking and adjusting

Beam alignment should be carried out by a Volvo dealer or other specialist having the necessary optical alignment equipment.

In an emergency, adjustment may be carried out on a trial and error basis, using the two adjustment screws on the rear, or on the top, of each headlight unit.

12 Bulb failure warning system - general information

1 The bulb failure warning sensor is a special kind of relay. It is mounted on the central electrical unit.
2 The sensor contains a number of reed switches surrounded by coils of wire. Current to each bulb covered by the system travels through one coil. The coils are arranged in pairs, one pair carrying the current for one pair of bulbs.
3 When both bulbs of a pair are lit, the magnetic fields produced by the two coils cancel each other out. If one bulb fails, the coil remaining in circuit will produce an uncancelled magnetic field. The magnetic field operates the reed switch, which illuminates the warning light.
4 From the above it will be realised that no warning will be given if a pair of bulbs fails simultaneously. False alarms may result if bulbs of different wattage, or even of different make, are fitted.
5 Wiring for trailer lighting must be connected upstream of the bulb failure warning sensor, otherwise it may be damaged by excessive current flow. Consult a Volvo dealer or an auto-electrician.

13 Horn - removal and refitting

Removal

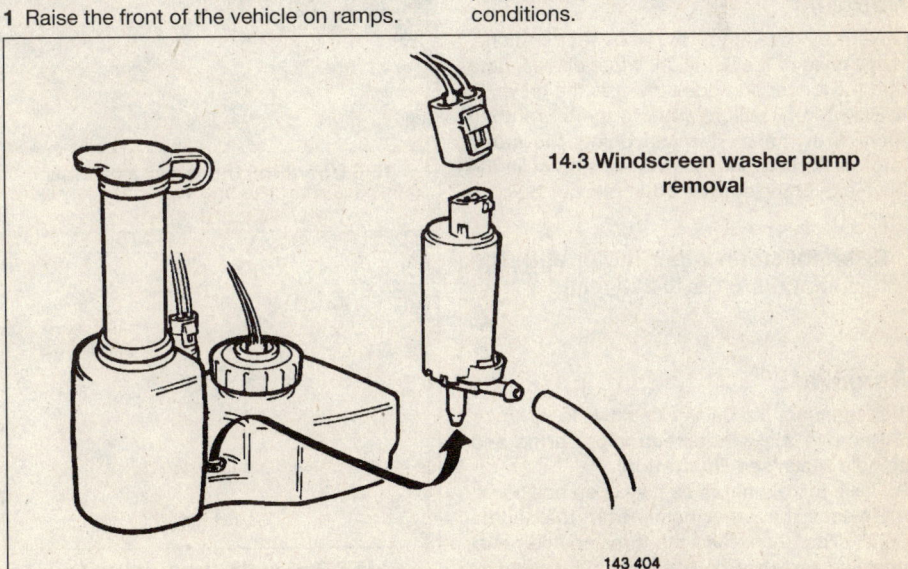

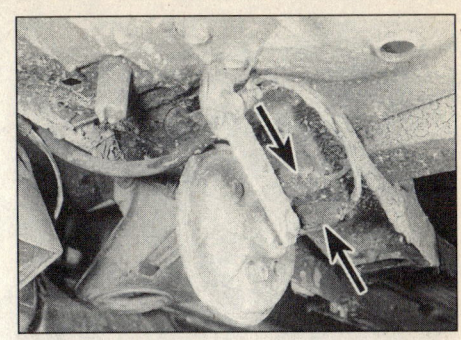

1 Raise the front of the vehicle on ramps.

13.2 Horn wiring connectors (arrowed)

2 Working under the front bumper, disconnect the wires from the horn (see illustration).
3 Unbolt the horn from its bracket and remove it.

Refitting

4 Refit by reversing the removal operations.

14 Windscreen/headlight/ tailgate washers - general information

1 The washer systems share a common reservoir, located under the bonnet. For access to the pump(s) and level indicator it will be necessary to remove the air cleaner unit or battery (as applicable).
2 The level indicator is a float-operated switch which can be removed after unscrewing its retaining ring.
3 To remove a washer pump, unplug its electrical connector, disconnect the hose from it and pull the pump out of its locating spigot (see illustration). Be prepared for fluid spillage.
4 If a pump malfunctions it must be renewed.
5 Only use clean water, and an approved screen wash additive if wished, in the washer reservoir. Use an additive with antifreeze properties (not engine antifreeze) in freezing conditions.

14.3 Windscreen washer pump removal

12•10 Body electrical systems

15.2 Removing a wiper arm nut

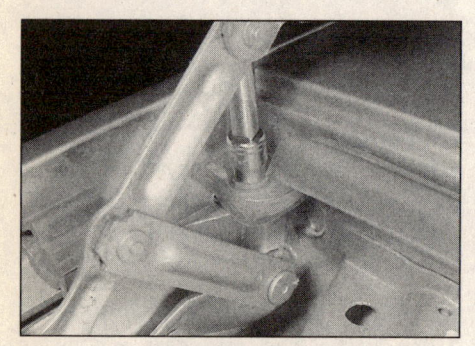

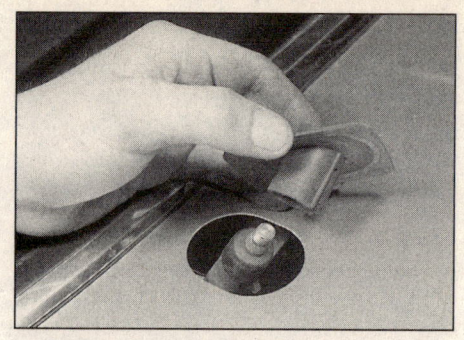

16.2 Removing a wiper arm spindle seal

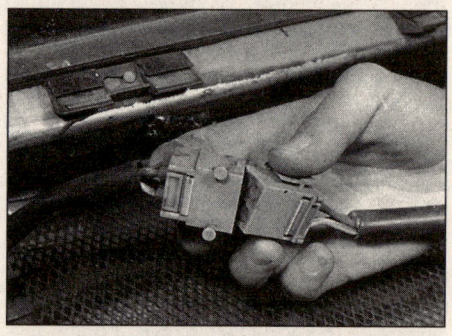

16.4 Removing one of the scuttle panel bolts

16.5 Disconnecting the wiper motor multi-plug

16.6 Unbolting the wiper assembly

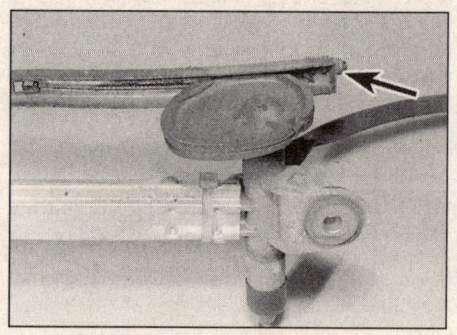

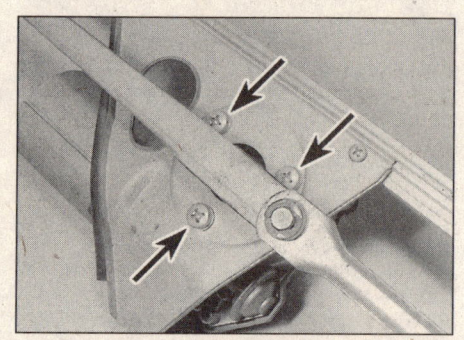

16.7 Wiper motor securing screws (arrowed)

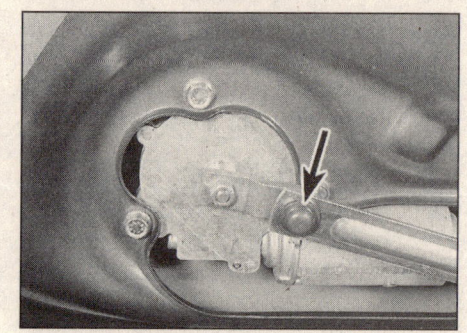

16.8 Part of the wiper linkage - cable tensioning nut is arrowed

18.2 Rear wiper motor showing crank arm balljoint (arrowed) and securing bolts

15 Wiper arms - removal and refitting

Removal
1 Remove the wiper blades as described in "Weekly checks".
2 Remove the nut at the base of the wiper arm and pull the arm off the splines **(see illustration)**. Release the washer hose on the headlight wiper arms.

Refitting
3 Refit by reversing the removal operations. In the case of the headlight wiper blades, note that the longer end goes towards the grille.
4 Bias the headlight wiper arms by refitting them with the blades just below the stops (motors parked). Secure the arms, then lift the blades over the stops.

16 Windscreen wiper motor and linkage - removal and refitting

Removal
1 Disconnect the battery negative lead.
2 Remove the windscreen wiper arms and spindle seals **(see illustration)**.
3 Raise the bonnet to its fully open position.
4 Release the water hoses from the scuttle panel clips, then undo the three scuttle panel retaining screws. Remove the scuttle panel by pulling it forward slightly and lifting it up at the rear **(see illustration)**. Close the bonnet.
5 Remove the wiper motor cover and disconnect the wiper motor multi-plug **(see illustration)**.
6 Remove the two bolts and lift out the wiper motor and linkage **(see illustration)**.
7 The motor may be removed from the linkage by undoing the spindle nut and the three securing screws **(see illustration)**. Do not attempt to dismantle the motor except out of curiosity; spares are unlikely to be available.
8 Other components of the linkage, including the cable, may be renewed as necessary. There is a tensioning nut at one end of the cable **(see illustration)**.

Refitting
9 Refit by reversing the removal operations. Before refitting the wiper arms, switch the wipers on and off to bring the motor into the parked position.

17 Headlight wiper motor - removal and refitting

The wiper motor is removed complete with the headlight unit then separated after removal. Refer to Section 10.

18 Tailgate wiper motor - removal and refitting

Removal
1 Remove the tailgate interior trim (see Chapter 11).
2 Prise the link balljoint off the wiper motor crank arm **(see illustration)**.

Body electrical systems 12•11

19.3 Undoing a cigarette lighter screw

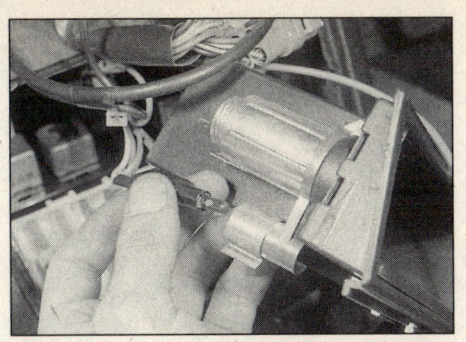

19.4 Removing the lighter bulb and holder. This also serves the ashtray

22.3 Removing the aerial tube nut and cover

3 Remove the three bolts which secure the motor. Withdraw the motor (it may be necessary to rotate the crank arm) and disconnect the wiring from it **(see illustration)**.

Refitting

4 Refit by reversing the removal operations. Check the operation of the motor before refitting the trim.

19 Cigarette lighter - removal and refitting

Removal

Front lighter

1 Make sure that the ignition is switched off.
2 Remove the lighter element and unclip the trim from around the aperture.
3 Remove the screws now exposed **(see illustration)**.
4 Remove the lighter and tray, disconnecting the wiring feed and bulb holder from the rear **(see illustration)**. Also disconnect any audio equipment which may be occupying the tray.
5 The lighter may now be removed from the tray if wished.

Rear lighter

6 This is covered in removal of the rear console (Chapter 11).

Refitting

7 Refit by reversing the removal operations.

20 Heated rear window - general information

1 All models are equipped with a heated rear window. Heating is achieved by passing current through a resistive grid bonded to the inside of the rear window.
2 Do not allow hard or sharp items of luggage to rub against the heating grid. Use a soft cloth or chamois to clean the inside of the window, working along the lines of the grid.

HAYNES HiNT *Small breaks in the heated rear window grid can be repaired using special conductive paint, obtainable from motor accessory shops. Use the paint as directed by its manufacturer.*

3 The heated rear window draws a high current, so it should not be left switched on longer than necessary. On some models a so-called "delay relay" is incorporated into the circuit in order to switch the window off after a few minutes.
4 When heated door mirrors are fitted, their heaters are controlled by the heated rear window switch.

21 Radio/cassette player - removal and refitting

Note: *Radio/cassette players of various designs may be fitted, according to model, territory and optional equipment. The removal and refitting procedures for one of the common types are as follows.*

Removal

1 Disconnect the battery negative lead. If the radio/cassette player is equipped with an anti-theft security code, refer to the information given in the reference sections of this manual before disconnecting the battery.
2 In order to release the radio retaining clips, two U-shaped rods must be inserted into the special holes on each side of the radio. If possible, it is preferable to obtain purpose made rods from an audio specialist as these have cut-outs which snap firmly into the clips so that the radio can be pulled out. Note that on some models, it will be necessary to remove the two side bezels first, to allow access to the holes for insertion of the U-shaped removal tools.
3 Insert the removal tools into each pair of holes at the edge of the unit, and push the tools fully home to engage the radio retaining clips.
4 Move the tools outward to depress the retaining clips, and withdraw the radio from the facia sufficiently to gain access to the wiring at the rear.
5 Note the location of the speaker wiring by recording the cable colours and their positions, then disconnect the speaker leads, aerial lead and wiring multiplug(s). Remove the unit from the car.
6 Disengage the removal tools from the retaining clips on the side of the radio, and remove the tools.

Refitting

7 Refitting is a reversal of removal.

22 Radio aerial - removal and refitting

Note: *Two types of original equipment aerial are shown in the accompanying illustrations. Others may be encountered. On later models, the aerial is in the form of a thin element incorporated in the rear side window.*

Removal

Saloon models (automatic aerial, in boot)

1 Disconnect the battery negative lead.
2 Open the boot and remove the left-hand side trim.
3 Remove the nut and cover which secure the aerial tube to the rear wing **(see illustration)**.
4 Disconnect the aerial signal and power leads **(see illustrations)**.
5 Remove the tube and drive securing nuts and bolts. Withdraw the aerial into the boot.

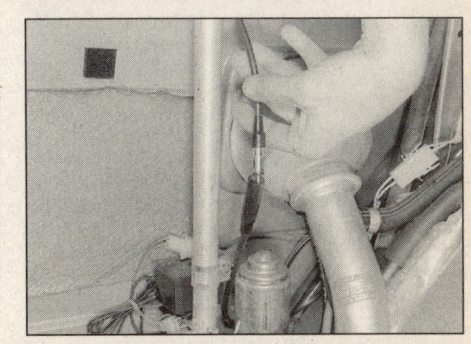

22.4a Disconnect the signal lead . . .

12•12 Body electrical systems

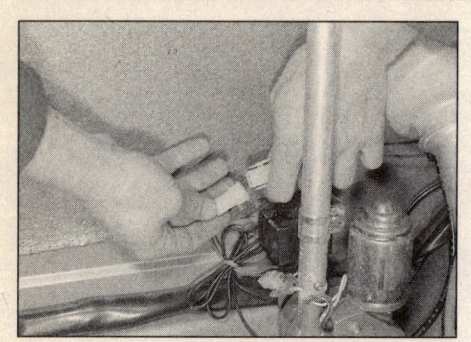

22.4b . . . and the power lead

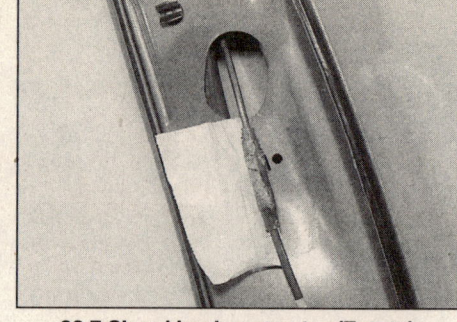

22.7 Signal lead connector (Estate) wrapped in sticky tape

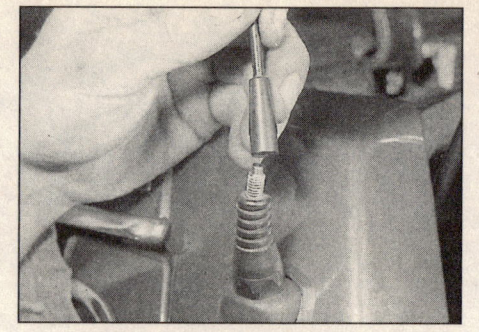

22.8 Unscrewing the aerial rod from the stub

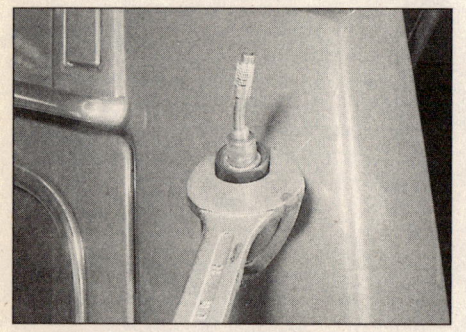

22.9a Remove the aerial tube nut . . .

22.9b . . . and withdraw the aerial into the vehicle

Estate models
(fixed aerial, on rear pillar)

6 Open the tailgate. Unclip the trim panel which covers the aerial mounting and wiring.
7 Disconnect the aerial signal lead **(see illustration)**.
8 Outside the vehicle, unscrew the aerial rod from the stub **(see illustration)**. Recover the spacer.
9 Unscrew the tube securing nut. Recover the lower spacer and seal and withdraw the aerial into the vehicle **(see illustrations)**.

Refitting

10 On all types, refit by reversing the removal operations, but check for correct operation before refitting disturbed trim.

23 Supplementary Restraint System (SRS) - general information and precautions

A supplementary restraint system is available as standard or optional equipment depending on model and territory.
The system consists of a driver's airbag, which is designed to prevent serious chest and head injuries to the driver during an accident. A similar bag for the front seat passenger is also available on certain models. A crash sensor, which detects frontal impact, is located under the driver's seat, with a standby power unit mounted alongside. The crash sensor incorporates a deceleration sensor, a mercury switch and a microprocessor, to monitor the severity of the impact and trigger the airbag where necessary. The airbag is inflated by a gas generator, which forces the bag out of the module cover in the centre of the steering wheel, or out of a cover on the passenger's side of the facia. A contact reel behind the steering wheel at the top of the steering column, ensures that a good electrical connection is maintained with the airbag at all times, as the steering wheel is turned in each direction.

In addition to the airbag units, the supplementary restraint system may also incorporate mechanical seat belt tensioners, or pyrotechnical seat belt tensioners operated by gas cartridges in the belt inertia reel assembly. These units are also triggered by the crash sensor, in conjunction with the air bag, to tighten the seat belts and provide additional collision protection.

⚠ *Warning: The safe removal and refitting of the SRS components requires the use of Volvo special equipment. Any attempt to remove or dismantle the airbag module, crash sensor, contact reel, seat belt tensioners or any associated wiring or components without this equipment, and the specialist knowledge needed to use it correctly, could result in severe personal injury and/or malfunction of the system. For this reason it is imperative that any work involving the SRS components is entrusted*

Wiring diagrams 12•13

Key to wiring diagram

No	Description	Location
1	Battery (12V)	D3
2	Ignition switch	E3
3	Instrument connector, 4-pin	T5
4	Ignition coil (12V)	E5, N5, P5
5	Distributor	E5, R5
6	Spark plugs	E5
8	Instrument connector, 8-pin	T5
9	Starter motor (800W/1.7 kW)	D3
10	Alternator and regulator	D4
11	Fusebox	C1-K1
12	Instrument connector, 12-pin	T5
13	High beam (max 60W)	A1, A6
14	Low beam (max 55W)	A1, A6
15	Busbar 15, electrical distribution unit	T4
16	Parking lights (4CP/5W) (also rear lights in USA)	A1, A6, L1, L6
18	Instrument connector, 18-pin	T6
21	Rear light (4CP/5W)	L1, L6
22	Brake lights (32CP/21W)	L1, L5, L6
23	Foglight (55W)	A1, A6, L1, L6
24	Number plate lighting (4CP/5W)	L4
25	Courtesy light	W4
26	Reading light, front (5W)	W5
27	Interior lighting (10W)	W5
28	Reading light, rear (5W)	V5, W5
29	Direction indicators (32CP/21W)	A1, A6, B1, B6, L2, L6
30	Busbar 30, electrical distribution unit	T4
31	Busbar 31, electrical distribution unit	T4
32	Glove compartment lighting (2W)	W3
33	Ashtray lighting, front (1.2W)	I3
33	Ashtray lighting, rear (1.2W)	I3
35	Sunroof switch light (1.2W)	H3
36	Seat heater switch light, passenger side (1.2W)	I3
37	Gear selector light (automatic) (1.2W)	I3
38	Control panel lighting (1.2W)	H3
40	Luggage compartment lighting	V5
41	Door open warning light	V4, V5, X4, X5
42	Heater control panel lighting	H3
43	Sun visor lighting	W4
44	Glove compartment lighting switch	W4
45	Seat belt lock light, driver's side (1.2W)	J4
46	Seat belt lock light, passenger side (1.2W)	J3
47	Windscreen wiper/washer switch	B4
48	Light switch	C2
49	Direction indicator, hazard warning and high/low beam switch	C4
50	Horn	A4
51	Rear window heater switch	J2
52	Heater switch, driver's seat	J4
53	Seat heater switch, passenger side	J3
54	Overdrive switch, M46	N6, P6
56	Window winder switch, driver's side, front	X3
57	Window winder switch, passenger side, front	Y4
58	Window winder switch, driver's side, rear	X4
59	Window winder switch passenger side, rear	X4
60	Rear-view mirror switch, driver's side	X5
61	Rear-view mirror switch, passenger side	X5
62	Central locking linkage switch	W6
63	Mode selector	CC4
64	Sunroof switch	T6
65	Foglight switch, front/rear	B3
66	Brake light switch	J6, R5, R6, CC4
67	Gear selector switch	AA4
68	Handbrake switch	G5
70	Reversing light switch	J6, AA3
71	Starter inhibitor switch (automatic)	E3, AA4
72	Door switch, driver's door	V3
73	Door switch, passenger door	X3
74	Door switch, rear doors	V3, X3
75	Shift lock relay	R6
76	Shift lock solenoid	R6
77	Overdrive switch, M46	P6
78	Positive terminal board	D2
79	Fusebox lighting	W4
80	Thermal time switch	D4
81	AC pressure switch	P2, U3, BB1
82	Low-speed pressure switch radiator fan	P1, Q2, BB5
83	Safety and high-speed pressure switch, radiator fan	P2, BB6
84	Coolant temperature sensor	H4, P3, P5, Q2, Q6, R3, V1, AA1, AA4
85	Speedometer	G4
86	Tachometer	H4
87	Clock	F4
88	Temperature gauge	H4
89	Fuel gauge	F4
90	Indicating light, rear foglight	F5
91	'Service' warning light	F5
92	'Diagnostics' indicating light	F5
93	Speed warning (chime)	G4
94	Instrument and control lighting rheostat	H4
95	Instrument lighting	G4
96	Temperature warning light	F5
97	Indicating light, oil pressure	G5
98	Turbo pressure warning light	H5
99	Handbrake warning light	G5
100	Brake failure warning	G5
101	Washer reservoir warning light	F5
102	Overdrive indicator light, AW 70/71	H5
103	Bulb failure warning light	F5
104	Glow plug warning light (diesel)	H5
105	Ignition light	G5
106	Trailer indicator light	F5
107	ABS warning light	G5
108	LH direction indicator light	G4
109	High beam warning light	G5
110	RH direction indicator light	G4
112	Overdrive indicating light, M46	G5
113	Indicating light, front seat belts	H5
114	Indicating light, rear seat belts	I4
115	Bulb failure warning sensor, 14-pin	K5
116	Seat belt reminder	I4
117	Intermittent relay, windscreen wipers	B5
118	Intermittent relay, rear window wiper	U6
120	Bulb failure warning sensor, 9-pin	C2
121	Flasher unit/switch, hazard warning lights	C4
122	Exhaust gas temperature relay (Japan)	R5
123	Overdrive relay, M46	N6
124	Window winder + radiator fan	Y5
125	Central locking relay	X6
127	Spotlight relay	C3
129	AC blocking relay	N2
130	Glow plug relay (diesel)	S5
131	Radiator fan relay	P1, V2, BB5
134	Ignition coil relay	AA3
135	LH-2.2 and LH-2.4 relay	N2, Q3, CC1
136	Overdrive relay, AW 70/71	Q6
137	Main lighting relay	C3
138	Heating element, driver's seat (30/130W)	K4
	Heating element, passenger seat (30/130W)	K3

12

Key to wiring diagram (continued)

No	Description	Location
139	Heating element, driver's seat backrest	K4
	Heating element, passenger seat backrest	K3
140	Loudspeaker, instrument panel, LH side	U2
141	Loudspeaker, instrument panel, RH side	U2
142	Seat heater thermostat driver's seat	J4
	Seat heater thermostat, passenger seat	J3
143	Loudspeaker, passenger door (4 ohm)	U1
144	Loudspeaker, driver's door (4 ohm)	U2
145	Loudspeaker, left rear (4 ohm)	U2
146	Loudspeaker, right rear (4 ohm)	U1
147	Aerial	T2
148	Electric aerial (3A)	U3
149	Radio	T2
150	Window winder motor, driver's door (5A)	Y4
151	Window winder motor, passenger door (5A)	Y5
152	Window winder motor, rear door, driver's side (5A)	X5
153	Window winder motor, rear door, passenger side (5A)	X5
154	Electric rear-view mirror driver's side	W5
155	Electric rear-view mirror passenger side	Y5
156	Electric radiator fan motor (13A)	P1, W2, CC6
157	Headlight wiper motor (1A)	A2, A5
158	Sunroof motor	T6
159	Central locking motor, passenger door	Y6
160	Central locking motor, rear door, driver's side	W6
161	Central locking motor, rear door, passenger side	Y6
162	Central locking motor, boot	Y6
163	Windscreen wiper motor (3.5A)	B4
164	Windscreen washer motor (2.6A)	A2
166	Capacitor	D4
167	Suppressor resistor	E5
170	Catalytic converter thermocouple	R5
171	Temperature switch (diesel)	S5
178	Washer reservoir level sensor	F5
182	Fuel level transmitter	F3
187	Oxygen sensor (Lambdasond)	N2, Q3, AA1
188	Cold-start injector	E4, N4
189	Lock-up solenoid	AA4
190	Linear solenoid	AA5
191	Shift solenoid 1	AA5
192	Shift solenoid 2	AA5
194	EGR valve	Q5
195	Solenoid valve, carburettor or fuel injector (diesel)	S6
196	Idling (CIS) valve	N3, Q4, BB2
197	Oil pressure switch	G6
198	Throttle switch	P2, P5, R3, R5, AA1
199	Throttle position sensor	R1
200	AC compressor (3.9A)	N1, U3, AA5
201	Overdrive solenoid	P6, R6
207	Horn (5A + 5A)	A4
208	Glow plug	S5
210	Tank pump	F3
211	Main fuel pump (6.5A)	N4, Q4, CC1
212	Service socket	E4, N3, AA2, AA4
214	Position sensor	AA1
215	Speed pick-up	BB3
216	Motronic control unit	BB1
217	LH-2.2 control unit	R3
218	Knock sensor	N6, P6, R6, AA2
219	Oxygen sensor test terminal	Q4
220	Idling test terminal	R4
221	Rear window heater (150W)	J2
222	Light, cigarette lighter	I3
223	Cigarette lighter	I2
224	Radiator fan thermostat	W2
225	Cruise control switch	S4
226	Control unit, cruise control	T4
227	Vacuum pump, cruise control	S5
228	Clutch switch	S5
229	Brake switch	S4
231	Relay rear foglight	C3
233	Pressure switch turbo diesel	S6
235	PTC resistor	N4
238	Rear window washer motor (2.6A)	U6
240	Rear window wiper/washer switch	U5
241	Rear window wiper motor	U5
242	Stop button electrically-operated seat	V6
243	Relay, electrically operated seat	V6
244	Control unit, electrically-operated seat	V5
245	Seat motor, forward-backward	W6
246	Seat motor, front raise-lower	W5
247	Seat motor, rear raise-lower	W5
248	Seat motor backrest	W6
251	Kickdown inhibitor	R6, AA4
252	ABS control unit	T1
253	ABS modulator	S3
254	ABS transient surge protector	S2
256	ABS sensor, left front	S1
257	ABS sensor, right front	S1
260	EZ-K ignition system control unit	N5, Q5
265	Time relay, rear window heater	K2
266	Time relay, rear window and rear-view mirror heaters	K3
267	TCV solenoid valve	R1
268	EGTC sensor	R2
269	TCU control unit	Q1
270	Speedometer pick-up	S1
284	Air mass meter	Q3, R3, CC1
290	Motronic power stage 1	AA2
291	Motronic power stage 2	AA3
296	DIM-DIP control unit	T3
300	Headlight adjuster control	V3
301	Headlight beam adjuster, RH actuator	U3
302	Headlight beam adjuster, LH actuator	U4
346	Boot light	W5
347	Rear door switch	W5
361	Injector No1	Q4, R4, CC3
362	Injector No2	Q4, R4, CC3
363	Injector No3	Q4, R4, CC2
364	Injector No4	Q4, R4, CC3
365	Injector No5	R4, CC2
366	Injector No6	R4, CC2
371	Ignition coil, No1 cylinder	AA2
372	Ignition coil, No2 cylinder	AA3
373	Ignition coil, No3 cylinder	AA2
374	Ignition coil, No4 cylinder	AA3
375	Ignition coil, No5 cylinder	AA2
376	Ignition coil, No6 cylinder	AA2
377	Ballast resistor	P4
378	ABS ground terminal	S1
384	Brake fluid level switch	G5
412	Motronic pulse generator	AA1
413	EZ-K pulse generator	P5
414	Transmission control unit A	BB3
415	Transmission control unit B	BB3
416	Timing pick-up	N6
417	EZ-K service terminal	P5
419	EZ-K power stage	N5, Q5
424	Solenoid valve, boost pressure limiter	S6
456	Busbar 30, electrical distribution unit	J4
457	Busbar in fusebox	W3
458	Busbar 30 in fusebox	W4

Wiring diagrams 12•15

Key to wiring diagram (continued)

No	Description	Location
464	Injector relay	N4, Q4, BB3
472	LH-2.4 control unit	P2
482	Diagnostic unit	S3, U4
490	Electric aerial switch	U2
491	Dimmer switch	B3
495	ECC controls (1/30)	Y1
496	ECC control sensor	W1
497	ECC solenoid valve	W1
498	ECC servomotor	Y3
499	ECC power unit	X2
501	ECC fan motor	X2
502	ECC outside temperature sensor	V1
503	ECC solar sensor	W1
504	ECC interior temperature sensor	V1
870	Clock adjuster	H3
886	Transfer box 1234705	P3, R4, AA1
900	Accessories	H3
901	Radio amplifier	T1
928	SRS	C5
929	SRS ignition module	C5
930	SRS indicating light	H5
931	SRS safety circuit	H4

Wire colour code

P	Pink	BL	Blue
OR	Orange	Y	Yellow
VO	Lilac	GN	Green
SB	Black	GR	Grey
W	White	BN	Brown
R	Red		

12•16 Wiring diagrams

Wiring diagram – models from 1991

Wiring diagrams 12•17

Wiring diagram - models from 1991

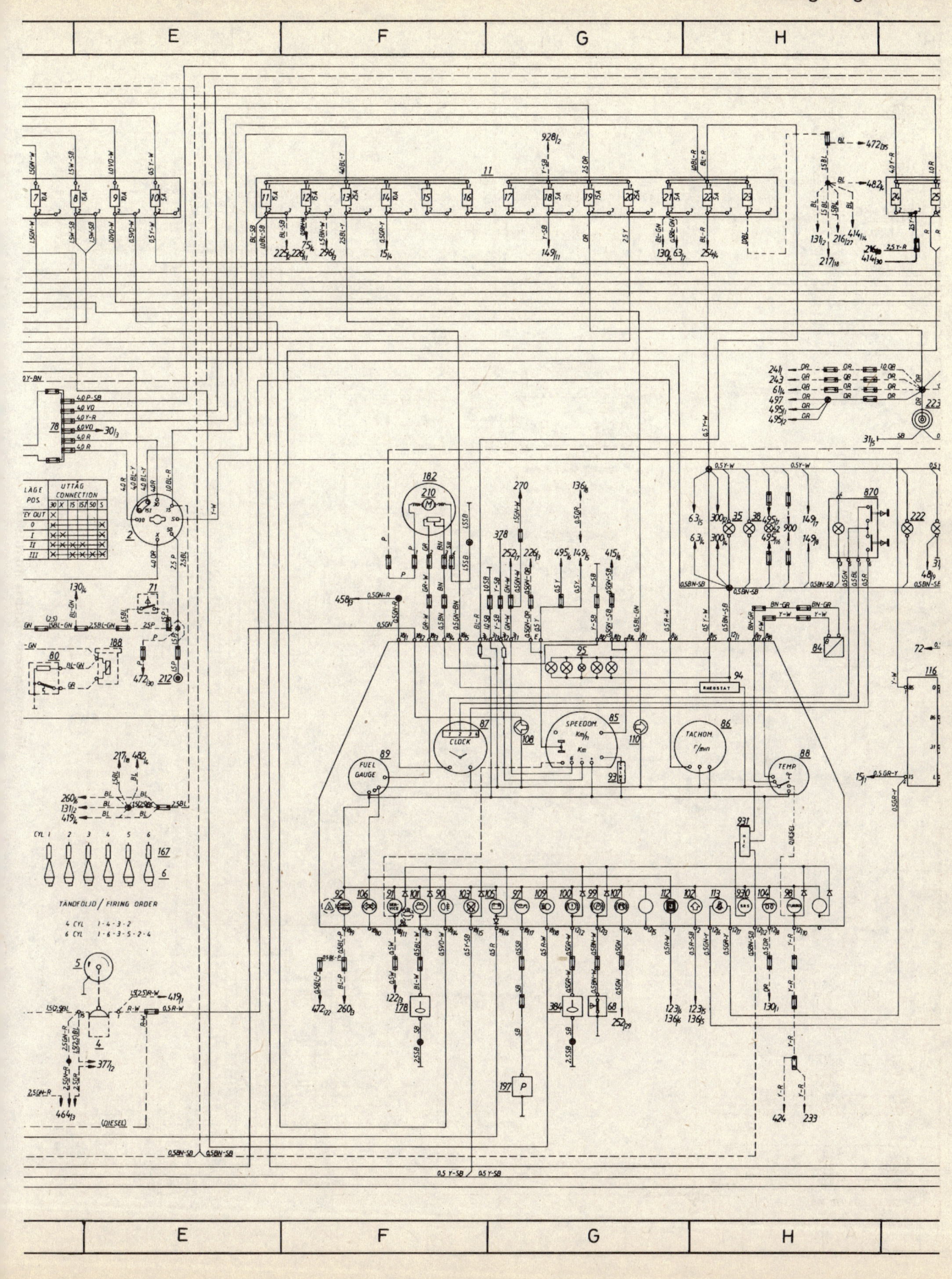

12•18 Wiring diagrams

Wiring diagram - models from 1991

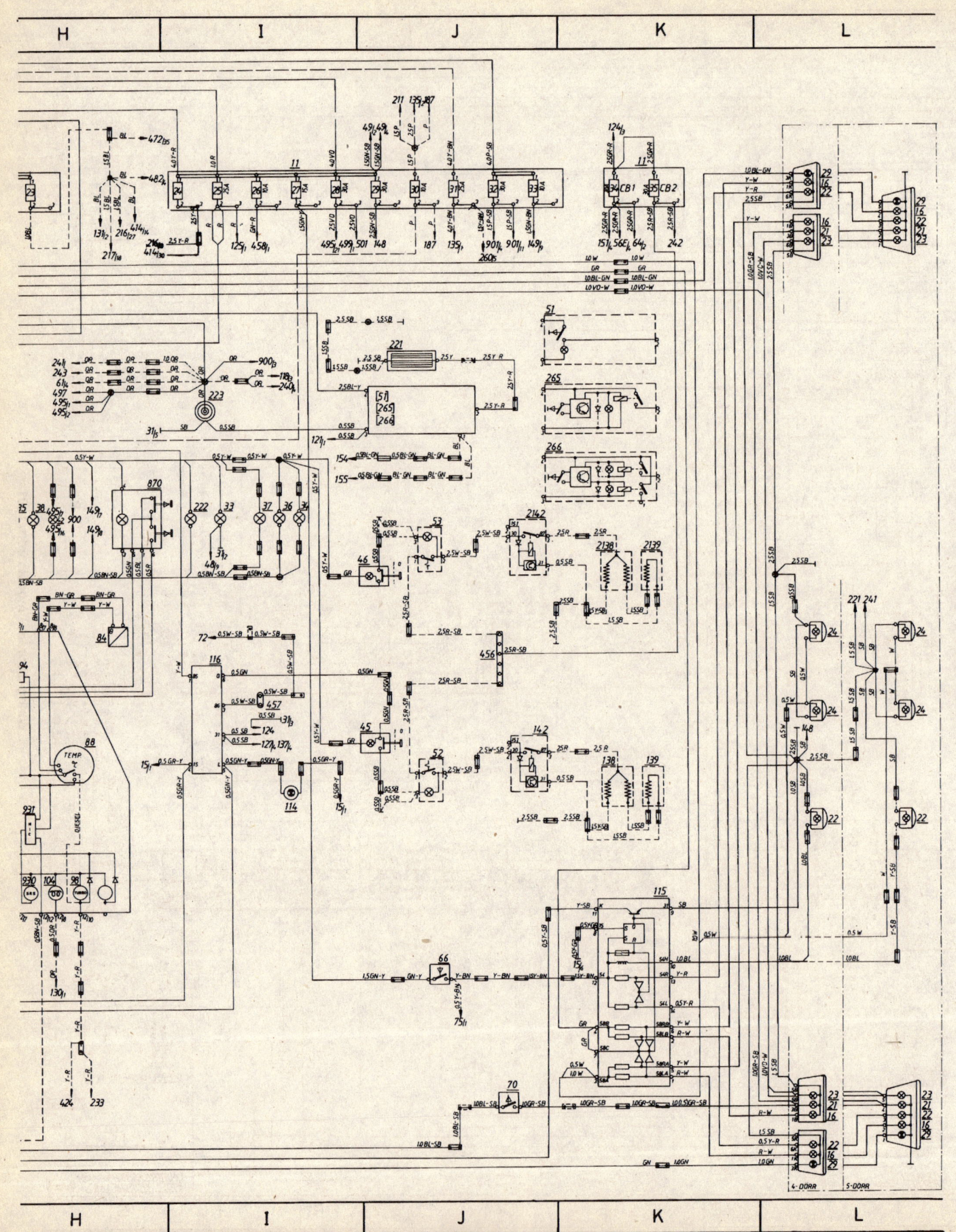

Wiring diagrams 12•19

Wiring diagram - models from 1991

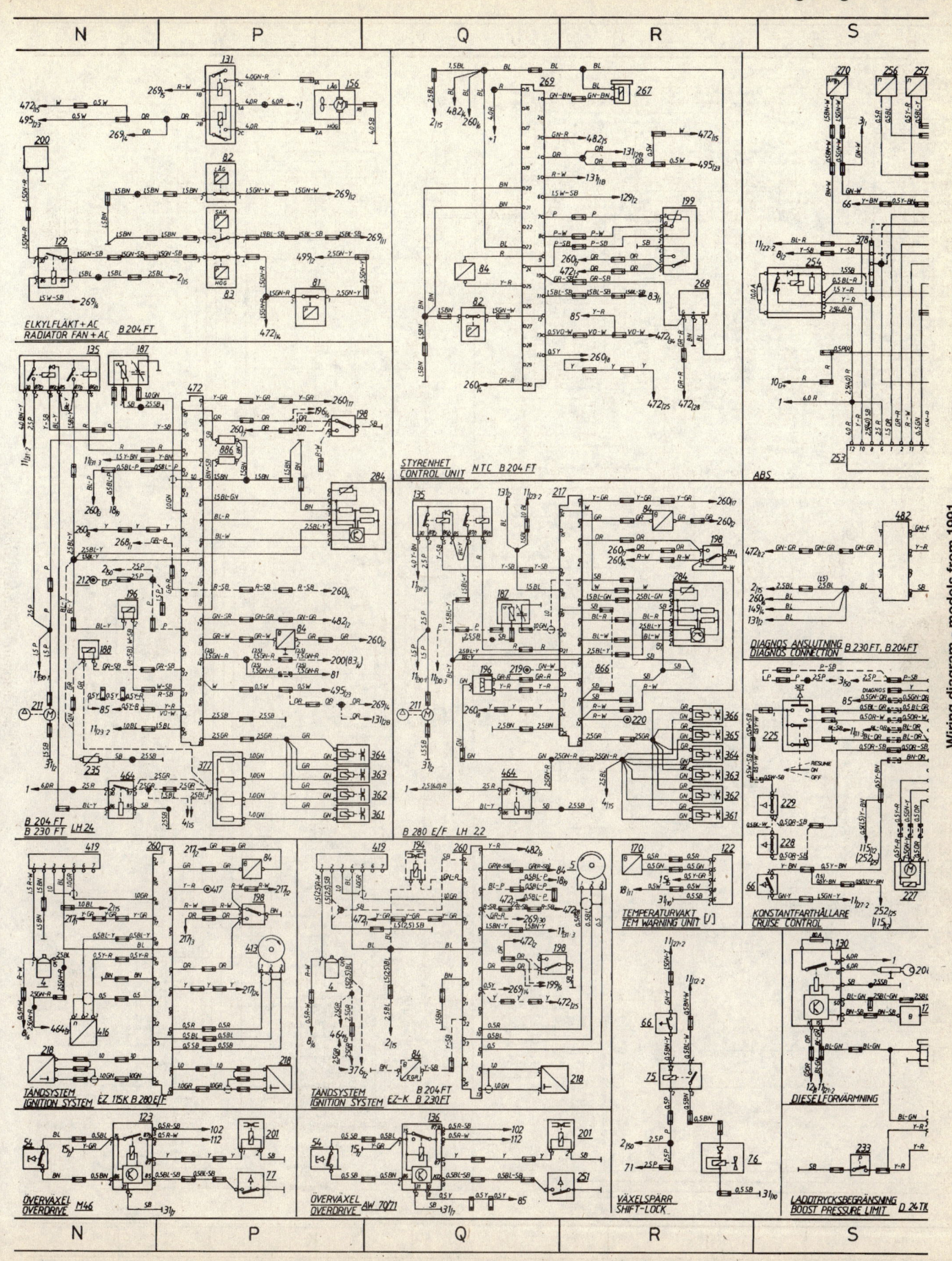

12•20 Wiring diagrams

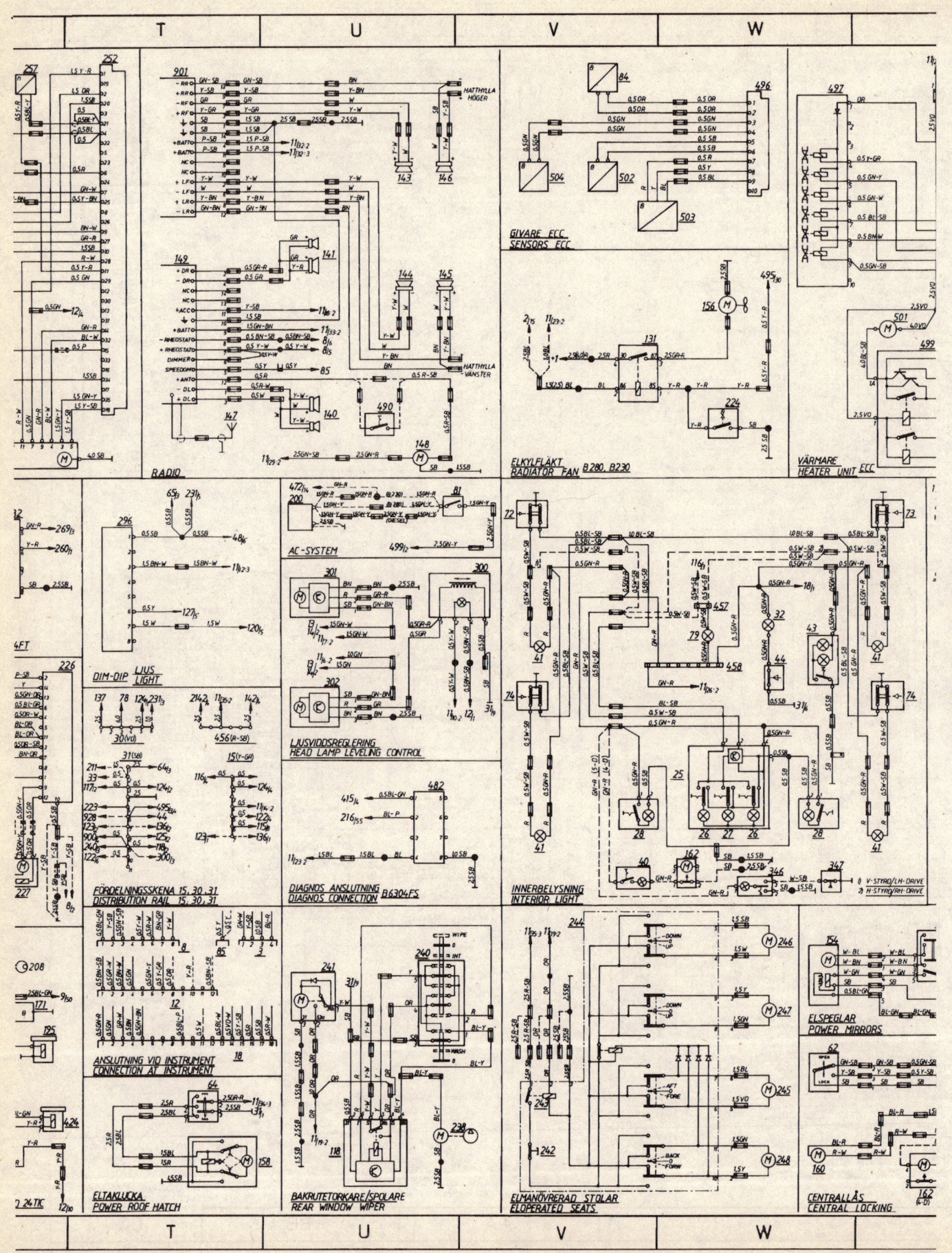

Wiring diagrams 12•21

Wiring diagram - models from 1991

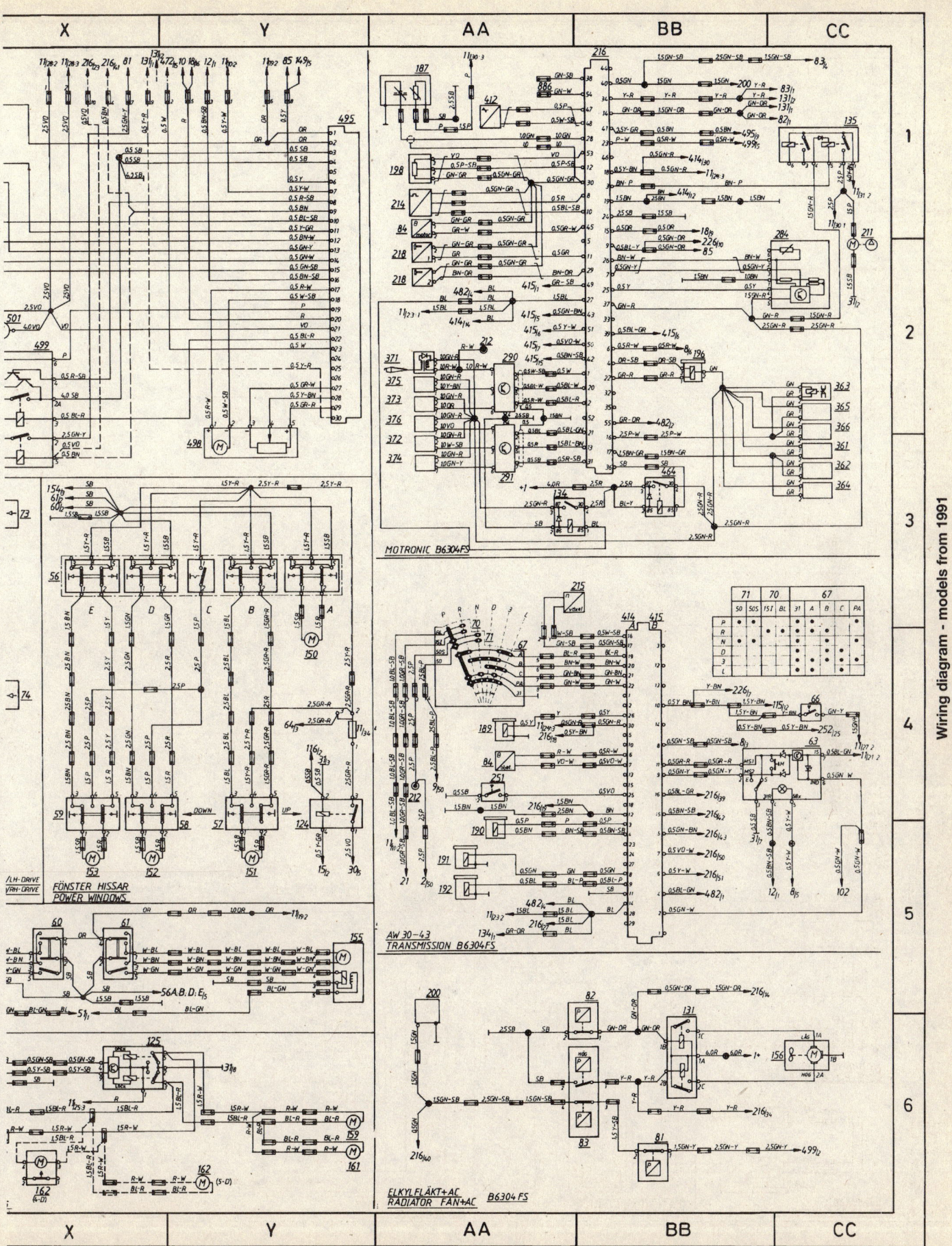

Reference REF•1

Dimensions and weights . . . . **REF•1**	Radio/cassette anti-theft system - precaution . . . **REF•5**
Conversion factors . . . . **REF•2**	Tools and working facilities . . . . **REF•6**
Buying spare parts . . . . **REF•3**	MOT test checks . . . . **REF•8**
Vehicle identification . . . . **REF•3**	Fault finding . . . . **REF•12**
General repair procedures . . . . **REF•4**	Glossary of technical terms . . . . **REF•20**
Jacking and vehicle support . . . . **REF•5**	Index . . . . **REF•25**

Dimensions and weights

Dimensions
Overall length:
- Saloon . . . . 4871 mm
- Estate . . . . 4844 mm

Overall width . . . . 1750 mm
Overall height . . . . 1410 to 1460 mm
Wheelbase . . . . 2770 mm

Weights
Kerb weight (depending on equipment) . . . . 1327 to 1496 kg
Gross vehicle weight . . . . (see type designation plate in engine compartment)

Conversion factors

Length (distance)
Inches (in)	x 25.4	= Millimetres (mm)	x 0.0394	= Inches (in)
Feet (ft)	x 0.305	= Metres (m)	x 3.281	= Feet (ft)
Miles	x 1.609	= Kilometres (km)	x 0.621	= Miles

Volume (capacity)
Cubic inches (cu in; in^3)	x 16.387	= Cubic centimetres (cc; cm^3)	x 0.061	= Cubic inches (cu in; in^3)
Imperial pints (Imp pt)	x 0.568	= Litres (l)	x 1.76	= Imperial pints (Imp pt)
Imperial quarts (Imp qt)	x 1.137	= Litres (l)	x 0.88	= Imperial quarts (Imp qt)
Imperial quarts (Imp qt)	x 1.201	= US quarts (US qt)	x 0.833	= Imperial quarts (Imp qt)
US quarts (US qt)	x 0.946	= Litres (l)	x 1.057	= US quarts (US qt)
Imperial gallons (Imp gal)	x 4.546	= Litres (l)	x 0.22	= Imperial gallons (Imp gal)
Imperial gallons (Imp gal)	x 1.201	= US gallons (US gal)	x 0.833	= Imperial gallons (Imp gal)
US gallons (US gal)	x 3.785	= Litres (l)	x 0.264	= US gallons (US gal)

Mass (weight)
Ounces (oz)	x 28.35	= Grams (g)	x 0.035	= Ounces (oz)
Pounds (lb)	x 0.454	= Kilograms (kg)	x 2.205	= Pounds (lb)

Force
Ounces-force (ozf; oz)	x 0.278	= Newtons (N)	x 3.6	= Ounces-force (ozf; oz)
Pounds-force (lbf; lb)	x 4.448	= Newtons (N)	x 0.225	= Pounds-force (lbf; lb)
Newtons (N)	x 0.1	= Kilograms-force (kgf; kg)	x 9.81	= Newtons (N)

Pressure
Pounds-force per square inch (psi; lbf/in^2; lb/in^2)	x 0.070	= Kilograms-force per square centimetre (kgf/cm^2; kg/cm^2)	x 14.223	= Pounds-force per square inch (psi; lbf/in^2; lb/in^2)
Pounds-force per square inch (psi; lbf/in^2; lb/in^2)	x 0.068	= Atmospheres (atm)	x 14.696	= Pounds-force per square inch (psi; lbf/in^2; lb/in^2)
Pounds-force per square inch (psi; lbf/in^2; lb/in^2)	x 0.069	= Bars	x 14.5	= Pounds-force per square inch (psi; lbf/in^2; lb/in^2)
Pounds-force per square inch (psi; lbf/in^2; lb/in^2)	x 6.895	= Kilopascals (kPa)	x 0.145	= Pounds-force per square inch (psi; lbf/in^2; lb/in^2)
Kilopascals (kPa)	x 0.01	= Kilograms-force per square centimetre (kgf/cm^2; kg/cm^2)	x 98.1	= Kilopascals (kPa)
Millibar (mbar)	x 100	= Pascals (Pa)	x 0.01	= Millibar (mbar)
Millibar (mbar)	x 0.0145	= Pounds-force per square inch (psi; lbf/in^2; lb/in^2)	x 68.947	= Millibar (mbar)
Millibar (mbar)	x 0.75	= Millimetres of mercury (mmHg)	x 1.333	= Millibar (mbar)
Millibar (mbar)	x 0.401	= Inches of water (inH$_2$O)	x 2.491	= Millibar (mbar)
Millimetres of mercury (mmHg)	x 0.535	= Inches of water (inH$_2$O)	x 1.868	= Millimetres of mercury (mmHg)
Inches of water (inH$_2$O)	x 0.036	= Pounds-force per square inch (psi; lbf/in^2; lb/in^2)	x 27.68	= Inches of water (inH$_2$O)

Torque (moment of force)
Pounds-force inches (lbf in; lb in)	x 1.152	= Kilograms-force centimetre (kgf cm; kg cm)	x 0.868	= Pounds-force inches (lbf in; lb in)
Pounds-force inches (lbf in; lb in)	x 0.113	= Newton metres (Nm)	x 8.85	= Pounds-force inches (lbf in; lb in)
Pounds-force inches (lbf in; lb in)	x 0.083	= Pounds-force feet (lbf ft; lb ft)	x 12	= Pounds-force inches (lbf in; lb in)
Pounds-force feet (lbf ft; lb ft)	x 0.138	= Kilograms-force metres (kgf m; kg m)	x 7.233	= Pounds-force feet (lbf ft; lb ft)
Pounds-force feet (lbf ft; lb ft)	x 1.356	= Newton metres (Nm)	x 0.738	= Pounds-force feet (lbf ft; lb ft)
Newton metres (Nm)	x 0.102	= Kilograms-force metres (kgf m; kg m)	x 9.804	= Newton metres (Nm)

Power
Horsepower (hp)	x 745.7	= Watts (W)	x 0.0013	= Horsepower (hp)

Velocity (speed)
Miles per hour (miles/hr; mph)	x 1.609	= Kilometres per hour (km/hr; kph)	x 0.621	= Miles per hour (miles/hr; mph)

Fuel consumption*
Miles per gallon (mpg)	x 0.354	= Kilometres per litre (km/l)	x 2.825	= Miles per gallon (mpg)

Temperature
Degrees Fahrenheit = (°C x 1.8) + 32   Degrees Celsius (Degrees Centigrade; °C) = (°F - 32) x 0.56

* It is common practice to convert from miles per gallon (mpg) to litres/100 kilometres (l/100km), where mpg x l/100 km = 282

Buying spare parts   REF•3

Spare parts are available from many sources, including maker's appointed garages, accessory shops, and motor factors. To be sure of obtaining the correct parts, it may sometimes be necessary to quote the vehicle identification number.

Our advice regarding spare part sources is:

Officially-appointed garages

This is the best source of parts which are peculiar to your car, and are not otherwise generally available (e.g. badges, interior trim, certain body panels, etc.). It is also the only place at which you should buy parts if the vehicle is still under warranty.

Accessory shops

These are very good places to buy materials and components needed for the maintenance of your car (oil, air and fuel filters, spark plugs, light bulbs, drivebelts, oils and greases, brake pads, touch-up paint, etc.). Components of this nature sold by a reputable shop are of the same standard as those used by the car manufacturer.

Motor factors

Good factors will stock all the more important components which wear out comparatively quickly and can sometimes supply individual components needed for the overhaul of a larger assembly. They may also handle work such as cylinder block reboring, crankshaft regrinding and balancing, etc.

Tyre and exhaust specialists

These outlets may be independent or members of a local or national chain. They frequently offer competitive prices when compared with a main dealer or local garage, but it will pay to obtain several quotes before making a decision. Also ask what "extras" may be added to the quote - for instance, fitting a new valve and balancing the wheel are both often charged on top of the price of a new tyre.

Other sources

Beware of parts or materials obtained from market stalls, car boot sales or similar outlets. Such items are not invariably sub-standard, but there is little chance of compensation if they do prove unsatisfactory. In the case of safety-critical components such as brake pads there is the risk not only of financial loss but also of an accident causing injury or death.

Vehicle identification

Modifications are a continuing and unpublicised process in vehicle manufacture, quite apart from major model changes. Spare parts manuals and lists are compiled upon a numerical basis, the individual vehicle identification numbers being absolutely essential to correct identification of the part concerned.

When ordering spare parts, always quote as much information as possible. Quote the car model, year of manufacture, body and engine numbers as appropriate.

The **vehicle identification number** is shown on a plate located above the right-hand headlight. In addition to many other details, it carries the Vehicle Identification Number, maximum vehicle weight information, and codes for interior trim and body colours. The vehicle type, model year designation and chassis number are also stamped on the right-hand centre door pillar **(see illustration)**.

The **body number and paint code numbers** are located on the plate with the vehicle identification number.

The **engine number** is stamped onto the left-hand side of the cylinder block, and also shown on a decal on the front of the camshaft drivebelt upper cover.

The **transmission number** is beneath the transmission on manual transmission models, and on the left-hand side of the transmission on automatic transmission models.

The **rear axle number**, including final drive ratio, and part number is on a plate attached to the left-hand side of the axle casing.

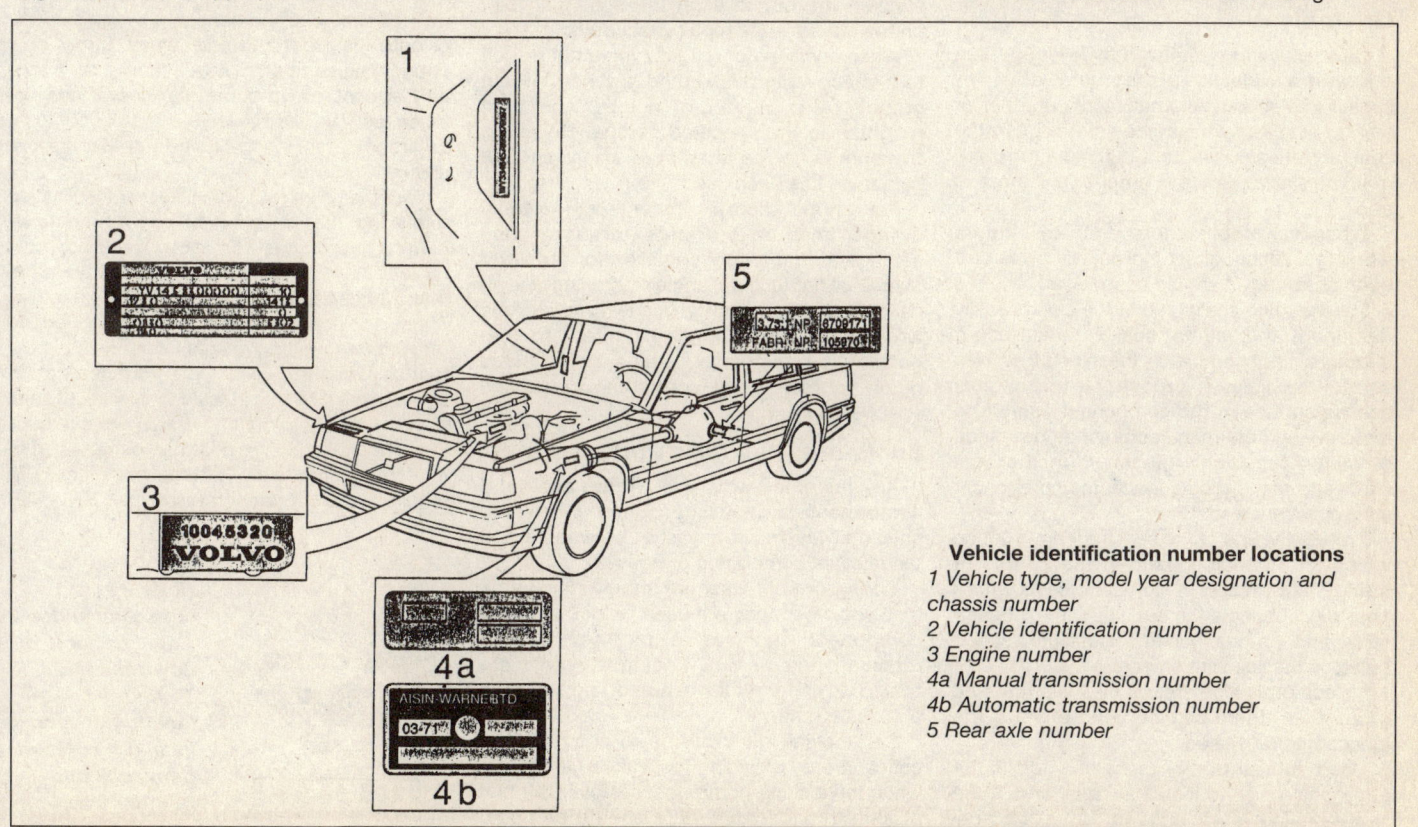

Vehicle identification number locations
1 Vehicle type, model year designation and chassis number
2 Vehicle identification number
3 Engine number
4a Manual transmission number
4b Automatic transmission number
5 Rear axle number

General repair procedures

Whenever servicing, repair or overhaul work is carried out on the car or its components, observe the following procedures and instructions. This will assist in carrying out the operation efficiently and to a professional standard of workmanship.

Joint mating faces and gaskets

When separating components at their mating faces, never insert screwdrivers or similar implements into the joint between the faces in order to prise them apart. This can cause severe damage which results in oil leaks, coolant leaks, etc. upon reassembly. Separation is usually achieved by tapping along the joint with a soft-faced hammer in order to break the seal. However, note that this method may not be suitable where dowels are used for component location.

Where a gasket is used between the mating faces of two components, a new one must be fitted on reassembly; fit it dry unless otherwise stated in the repair procedure. Make sure that the mating faces are clean and dry, with all traces of old gasket removed. When cleaning a joint face, use a tool which is unlikely to score or damage the face, and remove any burrs or nicks with an oilstone or fine file.

Make sure that tapped holes are cleaned with a pipe cleaner, and keep them free of jointing compound, if this is being used, unless specifically instructed otherwise.

Ensure that all orifices, channels or pipes are clear, and blow through them, preferably using compressed air.

Oil seals

Oil seals can be removed by levering them out with a wide flat-bladed screwdriver or similar implement. Alternatively, a number of self-tapping screws may be screwed into the seal, and these used as a purchase for pliers or some similar device in order to pull the seal free.

Whenever an oil seal is removed from its working location, either individually or as part of an assembly, it should be renewed.

The very fine sealing lip of the seal is easily damaged, and will not seal if the surface it contacts is not completely clean and free from scratches, nicks or grooves. If the original sealing surface of the component cannot be restored, and the manufacturer has not made provision for slight relocation of the seal relative to the sealing surface, the component should be renewed.

Protect the lips of the seal from any surface which may damage them in the course of fitting. Use tape or a conical sleeve where possible. Lubricate the seal lips with oil before fitting and, on dual-lipped seals, fill the space between the lips with grease.

Unless otherwise stated, oil seals must be fitted with their sealing lips toward the lubricant to be sealed.

Use a tubular drift or block of wood of the appropriate size to install the seal and, if the seal housing is shouldered, drive the seal down to the shoulder. If the seal housing is unshouldered, the seal should be fitted with its face flush with the housing top face (unless otherwise instructed).

Screw threads and fastenings

Seized nuts, bolts and screws are quite a common occurrence where corrosion has set in, and the use of penetrating oil or releasing fluid will often overcome this problem if the offending item is soaked for a while before attempting to release it. The use of an impact driver may also provide a means of releasing such stubborn fastening devices, when used in conjunction with the appropriate screwdriver bit or socket. If none of these methods works, it may be necessary to resort to the careful application of heat, or the use of a hacksaw or nut splitter device.

Studs are usually removed by locking two nuts together on the threaded part, and then using a spanner on the lower nut to unscrew the stud. Studs or bolts which have broken off below the surface of the component in which they are mounted can sometimes be removed using a stud extractor. Always ensure that a blind tapped hole is completely free from oil, grease, water or other fluid before installing the bolt or stud. Failure to do this could cause the housing to crack due to the hydraulic action of the bolt or stud as it is screwed in.

When tightening a castellated nut to accept a split pin, tighten the nut to the specified torque, where applicable, and then tighten further to the next split pin hole. Never slacken the nut to align the split pin hole, unless stated in the repair procedure.

When checking or retightening a nut or bolt to a specified torque setting, slacken the nut or bolt by a quarter of a turn, and then retighten to the specified setting. However, this should not be attempted where angular tightening has been used.

For some screw fastenings, notably cylinder head bolts or nuts, torque wrench settings are no longer specified for the latter stages of tightening, "angle-tightening" being called up instead. Typically, a fairly low torque wrench setting will be applied to the bolts/nuts in the correct sequence, followed by one or more stages of tightening through specified angles.

Locknuts, locktabs and washers

Any fastening which will rotate against a component or housing during tightening should always have a washer between it and the relevant component or housing.

Spring or split washers should always be renewed when they are used to lock a critical component such as a big-end bearing retaining bolt or nut. Locktabs which are folded over to retain a nut or bolt should always be renewed.

Self-locking nuts can be re-used in non-critical areas, providing resistance can be felt when the locking portion passes over the bolt or stud thread. However, it should be noted that self-locking "stiffnuts" tend to lose their effectiveness after long periods of use, and should then be renewed as a matter of course.

Split pins must always be replaced with new ones of the correct size for the hole.

When thread-locking compound is found on the threads of a fastener which is to be re-used, it should be cleaned off with a wire brush and solvent, and fresh compound applied on reassembly.

Special tools

Some repair procedures in this manual entail the use of special tools such as a press, two or three-legged pullers, spring compressors, etc. Wherever possible, suitable readily-available alternatives to the manufacturer's special tools are described, and are shown in use. In some instances, where no alternative is possible, it has been necessary to resort to the use of a manufacturer's tool, and this has been done for reasons of safety as well as the efficient completion of the repair operation. Unless you are highly-skilled and have a thorough understanding of the procedures described, never attempt to bypass the use of any special tool when the procedure described specifies its use. Not only is there a very great risk of personal injury, but expensive damage could be caused to the components involved.

Environmental considerations

When disposing of used engine oil, brake fluid, antifreeze, etc., give due consideration to any detrimental environmental effects. Do not, for instance, pour any of the above liquids down drains into the general sewage system, or onto the ground to soak away. Many local council refuse tips provide a facility for waste oil disposal, as do some garages. If none of these facilities are available, consult your local Environmental Health Department for further advice.

With the universal tightening-up of legislation regarding the emission of environmentally-harmful substances from motor vehicles, most vehicles have tamperproof devices fitted to the main adjustment points of the fuel system. These devices are primarily designed to prevent unqualified persons from adjusting the fuel/air mixture, with the chance of a consequent increase in toxic emissions. If such devices are found during servicing or overhaul, they should, wherever possible, be renewed or refitted in accordance with the manufacturer's requirements or current legislation.

Note: It is antisocial and illegal to dump oil down the drain. To find the location of your local oil recycling bank, call this number free.

OIL CARE — FOLLOW THE CODE
OIL BANK LINE
0800 66 33 66
www.oilbankline.org.uk

Jacking and vehicle support   REF•5

The jack supplied with the vehicle tool kit should only be used for changing the roadwheels - see *"Wheel changing"* at the front of this manual. When carrying out any other kind of work, raise the vehicle using a hydraulic (or "trolley") jack, and always supplement the jack with axle stands positioned under the vehicle jacking points **(see illustration)**.

When using a hydraulic jack or axle stands, always position the jack head or axle stand head under one of the relevant jacking points.

To raise the front of the vehicle, remove the engine undertray and position the jack head below the centre of the front axle crossmember. Do not jack the vehicle under the sump or any of the steering or suspension components.

To raise the rear of the vehicle, position the jack head under the rear axle final drive casing, but use a block of wood between the jack head and the casing.

The jack supplied with the vehicle locates in the jacking points on the underside of the sills. Ensure that the jack head is correctly engaged before attempting to raise the vehicle.

Never work under, around or near a raised vehicle unless it is adequately supported in at least two places.

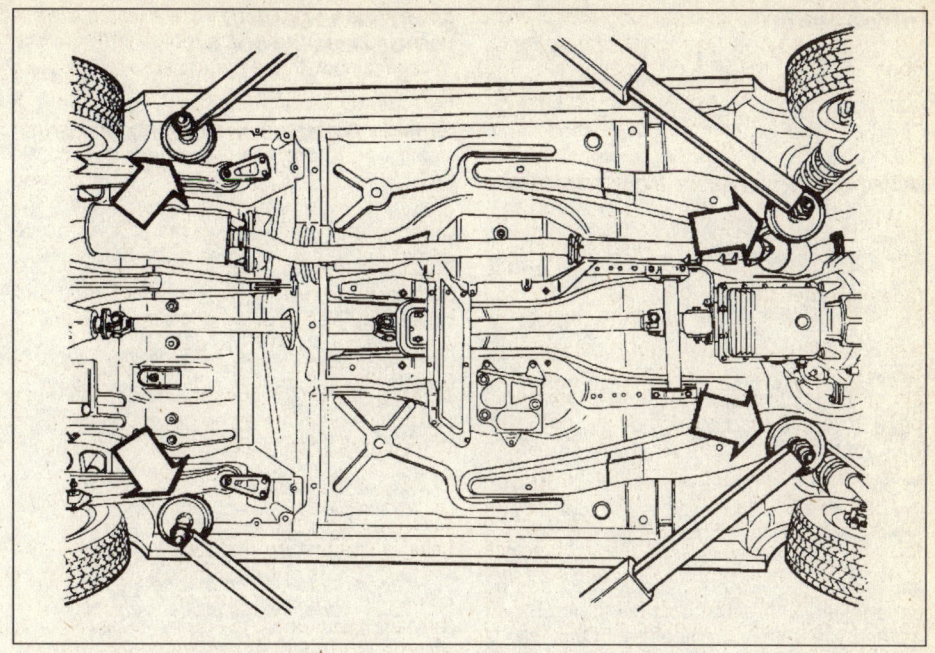

Support points (arrowed) for a four-point lift, or when using four axle stands

Radio/cassette anti-theft system - precaution

The radio/cassette unit fitted as standard equipment by Volvo may be equipped with a built-in security code, to deter thieves. If the power source to the unit is cut, the anti-theft system will activate. Even if the power source is immediately reconnected, the unit will not function until the correct security code has been entered. Therefore, if you do not know the correct security code for the radio/cassette unit **do not** disconnect either of the battery terminals, or remove the radio/cassette unit from the vehicle.

To enter the correct security code, follow the instructions in the radio/cassette handbook.

If an incorrect code is entered, the unit will become locked, and cannot be operated.

If this happens, or if the code is lost or forgotten, seek the advice of your Volvo dealer.

REF•6 Tools and working facilities

Introduction

A selection of good tools is a fundamental requirement for anyone contemplating the maintenance and repair of a motor vehicle. For the owner who does not possess any, their purchase will prove a considerable expense, offsetting some of the savings made by doing-it-yourself. However, provided that the tools purchased meet the relevant national safety standards and are of good quality, they will last for many years and prove an extremely worthwhile investment.

To help the average owner to decide which tools are needed to carry out the various tasks detailed in this manual, we have compiled three lists of tools under the following headings: *Maintenance and minor repair*, *Repair and overhaul*, and *Special*. Newcomers to practical mechanics should start off with the *Maintenance and minor repair* tool kit, and confine themselves to the simpler jobs around the vehicle. Then, as confidence and experience grow, more difficult tasks can be undertaken, with extra tools being purchased as, and when, they are needed. In this way, a *Maintenance and minor repair* tool kit can be built up into a *Repair and overhaul* tool kit over a considerable period of time, without any major cash outlays. The experienced do-it-yourselfer will have a tool kit good enough for most repair and overhaul procedures, and will add tools from the *Special* category when it is felt that the expense is justified by the amount of use to which these tools will be put.

Maintenance and minor repair tool kit

The tools given in this list should be considered as a minimum requirement if routine maintenance, servicing and minor repair operations are to be undertaken. We recommend the purchase of combination spanners (ring one end, open-ended the other); although more expensive than open-ended ones, they do give the advantages of both types of spanner.

- ☐ *Combination spanners:*
  Metric - 8 to 19 mm inclusive
- ☐ *Adjustable spanner - 35 mm jaw (approx.)*
- ☐ *Spark plug spanner (with rubber insert) - petrol models*
- ☐ *Spark plug gap adjustment tool - petrol models*
- ☐ *Set of feeler gauges*
- ☐ *Brake bleed nipple spanner*
- ☐ *Screwdrivers:*
  Flat blade - 100 mm long x 6 mm dia
  Cross blade - 100 mm long x 6 mm dia
  Torx - various sizes (not all vehicles)
- ☐ *Combination pliers*
- ☐ *Hacksaw (junior)*
- ☐ *Tyre pump*
- ☐ *Tyre pressure gauge*
- ☐ *Oil can*
- ☐ *Oil filter removal tool*
- ☐ *Fine emery cloth*
- ☐ *Wire brush (small)*
- ☐ *Funnel (medium size)*
- ☐ *Sump drain plug key (not all vehicles)*

Repair and overhaul tool kit

These tools are virtually essential for anyone undertaking any major repairs to a motor vehicle, and are additional to those given in the *Maintenance and minor repair* list. Included in this list is a comprehensive set of sockets. Although these are expensive, they will be found invaluable as they are so versatile - particularly if various drives are included in the set. We recommend the half-inch square-drive type, as this can be used with most proprietary torque wrenches.

The tools in this list will sometimes need to be supplemented by tools from the *Special* list:

- ☐ *Sockets (or box spanners) to cover range in previous list (including Torx sockets)*
- ☐ *Reversible ratchet drive (for use with sockets)*
- ☐ *Extension piece, 250 mm (for use with sockets)*
- ☐ *Universal joint (for use with sockets)*
- ☐ *Flexible handle or sliding T "breaker bar" (for use with sockets)*
- ☐ *Torque wrench (for use with sockets)*
- ☐ *Self-locking grips*
- ☐ *Ball pein hammer*
- ☐ *Soft-faced mallet (plastic or rubber)*
- ☐ *Screwdrivers:*
  Flat blade - long & sturdy, short (chubby), and narrow (electrician's) types
  Cross blade – long & sturdy, and short (chubby) types
- ☐ *Pliers:*
  Long-nosed
  Side cutters (electrician's)
  Circlip (internal and external)
- ☐ *Cold chisel - 25 mm*
- ☐ *Scriber*
- ☐ *Scraper*
- ☐ *Centre-punch*
- ☐ *Pin punch*
- ☐ *Hacksaw*
- ☐ *Brake hose clamp*
- ☐ *Brake/clutch bleeding kit*
- ☐ *Selection of twist drills*
- ☐ *Steel rule/straight-edge*
- ☐ *Allen keys (inc. splined/Torx type)*
- ☐ *Selection of files*
- ☐ *Wire brush*
- ☐ *Axle stands*
- ☐ *Jack (strong trolley or hydraulic type)*
- ☐ *Light with extension lead*
- ☐ *Universal electrical multi-meter*

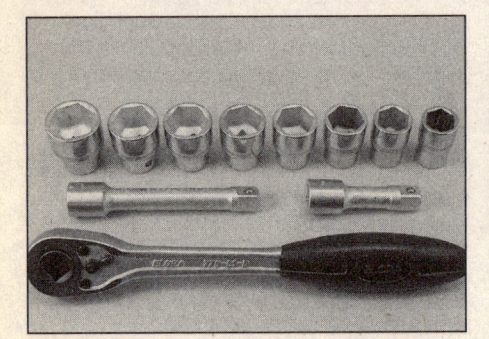

Sockets and reversible ratchet drive

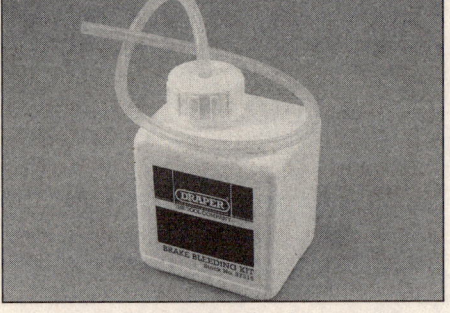

Brake bleeding kit

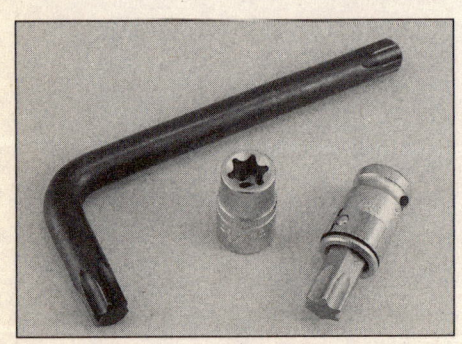

Torx key, socket and bit

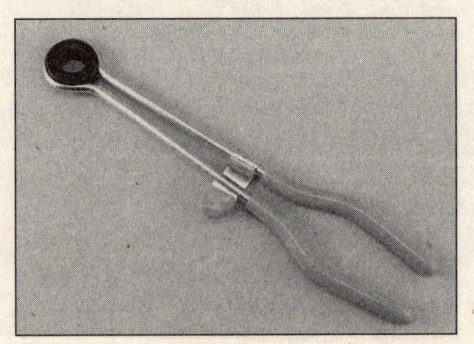

Hose clamp

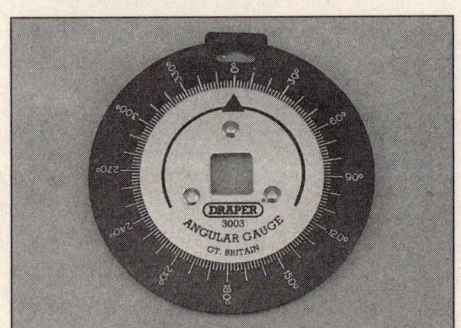

Angular-tightening gauge

Tools and working facilities

Special tools

The tools in this list are those which are not used regularly, are expensive to buy, or which need to be used in accordance with their manufacturers' instructions. Unless relatively difficult mechanical jobs are undertaken frequently, it will not be economic to buy many of these tools. Where this is the case, you could consider clubbing together with friends (or joining a motorists' club) to make a joint purchase, or borrowing the tools against a deposit from a local garage or tool hire specialist. It is worth noting that many of the larger DIY superstores now carry a large range of special tools for hire at modest rates.

The following list contains only those tools and instruments freely available to the public, and not those special tools produced by the vehicle manufacturer specifically for its dealer network. You will find occasional references to these manufacturers' special tools in the text of this manual. Generally, an alternative method of doing the job without the vehicle manufacturers' special tool is given. However, sometimes there is no alternative to using them. Where this is the case and the relevant tool cannot be bought or borrowed, you will have to entrust the work to a dealer.

- [ ] *Angular-tightening gauge*
- [ ] *Valve spring compressor*
- [ ] *Valve grinding tool*
- [ ] *Piston ring compressor*
- [ ] *Piston ring removal/installation tool*
- [ ] *Cylinder bore hone*
- [ ] *Balljoint separator*
- [ ] *Coil spring compressors (where applicable)*
- [ ] *Two/three-legged hub and bearing puller*
- [ ] *Impact screwdriver*
- [ ] *Micrometer and/or vernier calipers*
- [ ] *Dial gauge*
- [ ] *Stroboscopic timing light*
- [ ] *Dwell angle meter/tachometer*
- [ ] *Fault code reader*
- [ ] *Cylinder compression gauge*
- [ ] *Hand-operated vacuum pump and gauge*
- [ ] *Clutch plate alignment set*
- [ ] *Brake shoe steady spring cup removal tool*
- [ ] *Bush and bearing removal/installation set*
- [ ] *Stud extractors*
- [ ] *Tap and die set*
- [ ] *Lifting tackle*
- [ ] *Trolley jack*

Buying tools

Reputable motor accessory shops and superstores often offer excellent quality tools at discount prices, so it pays to shop around.

Remember, you don't have to buy the most expensive items on the shelf, but it is always advisable to steer clear of the very cheap tools. Beware of 'bargains' offered on market stalls or at car boot sales. There are plenty of good tools around at reasonable prices, but always aim to purchase items which meet the relevant national safety standards. If in doubt, ask the proprietor or manager of the shop for advice before making a purchase.

Care and maintenance of tools

Having purchased a reasonable tool kit, it is necessary to keep the tools in a clean and serviceable condition. After use, always wipe off any dirt, grease and metal particles using a clean, dry cloth, before putting the tools away. Never leave them lying around after they have been used. A simple tool rack on the garage or workshop wall for items such as screwdrivers and pliers is a good idea. Store all normal spanners and sockets in a metal box. Any measuring instruments, gauges, meters, etc, must be carefully stored where they cannot be damaged or become rusty.

Take a little care when tools are used. Hammer heads inevitably become marked, and screwdrivers lose the keen edge on their blades from time to time. A little timely attention with emery cloth or a file will soon restore items like this to a good finish.

Working facilities

Not to be forgotten when discussing tools is the workshop itself. If anything more than routine maintenance is to be carried out, a suitable working area becomes essential.

It is appreciated that many an owner-mechanic is forced by circumstances to remove an engine or similar item without the benefit of a garage or workshop. Having done this, any repairs should always be done under the cover of a roof.

Wherever possible, any dismantling should be done on a clean, flat workbench or table at a suitable working height.

Any workbench needs a vice; one with a jaw opening of 100 mm is suitable for most jobs. As mentioned previously, some clean dry storage space is also required for tools, as well as for any lubricants, cleaning fluids, touch-up paints etc, which become necessary.

Another item which may be required, and which has a much more general usage, is an electric drill with a chuck capacity of at least 8 mm. This, together with a good range of twist drills, is virtually essential for fitting accessories.

Last, but not least, always keep a supply of old newspapers and clean, lint-free rags available, and try to keep any working area as clean as possible.

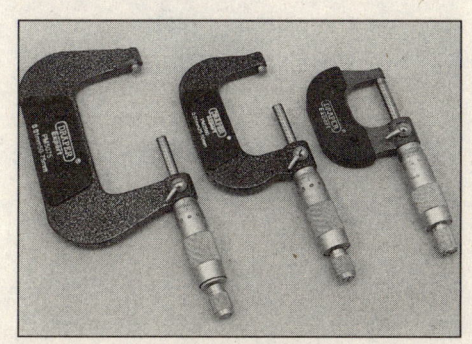

Micrometers

Dial test indicator ("dial gauge")

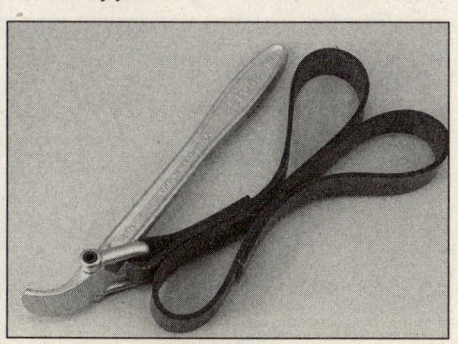

Strap wrench

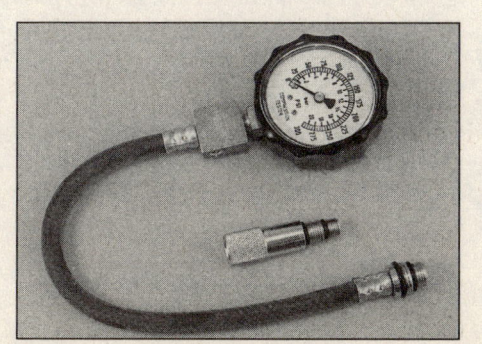

Compression tester

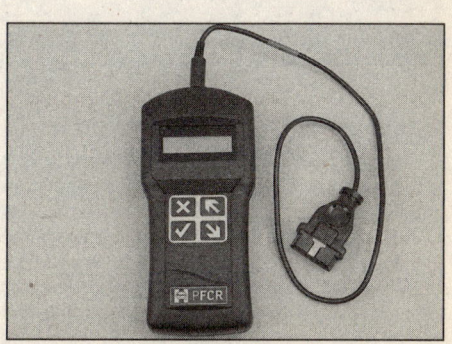

Fault code reader

REF•8 MOT test checks

This is a guide to getting your vehicle through the MOT test. Obviously it will not be possible to examine the vehicle to the same standard as the professional MOT tester. However, working through the following checks will enable you to identify any problem areas before submitting the vehicle for the test.

Where a testable component is in borderline condition, the tester has discretion in deciding whether to pass or fail it. The basis of such discretion is whether the tester would be happy for a close relative or friend to use the vehicle with the component in that condition. If the vehicle presented is clean and evidently well cared for, the tester may be more inclined to pass a borderline component than if the vehicle is scruffy and apparently neglected.

It has only been possible to summarise the test requirements here, based on the regulations in force at the time of printing. Test standards are becoming increasingly stringent, although there are some exemptions for older vehicles.

An assistant will be needed to help carry out some of these checks.

The checks have been sub-divided into four categories, as follows:

1 Checks carried out **FROM THE DRIVER'S SEAT**

2 Checks carried out **WITH THE VEHICLE ON THE GROUND**

3 Checks carried out **WITH THE VEHICLE RAISED AND THE WHEELS FREE TO TURN**

4 Checks carried out on **YOUR VEHICLE'S EXHAUST EMISSION SYSTEM**

---

1 Checks carried out **FROM THE DRIVER'S SEAT**

Handbrake

☐ Test the operation of the handbrake. Excessive travel (too many clicks) indicates incorrect brake or cable adjustment.

☐ Check that the handbrake cannot be released by tapping the lever sideways. Check the security of the lever mountings.

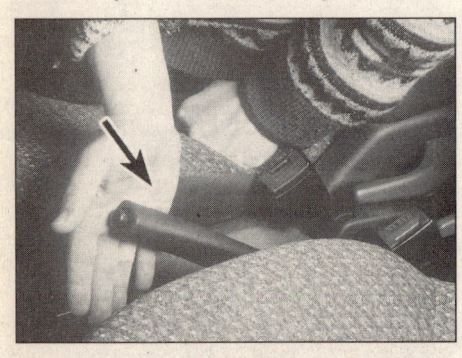

Footbrake

☐ Depress the brake pedal and check that it does not creep down to the floor, indicating a master cylinder fault. Release the pedal, wait a few seconds, then depress it again. If the pedal travels nearly to the floor before firm resistance is felt, brake adjustment or repair is necessary. If the pedal feels spongy, there is air in the hydraulic system which must be removed by bleeding.

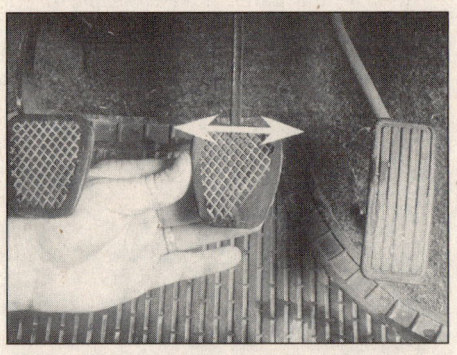

☐ Check that the brake pedal is secure and in good condition. Check also for signs of fluid leaks on the pedal, floor or carpets, which would indicate failed seals in the brake master cylinder.

☐ Check the servo unit (when applicable) by operating the brake pedal several times, then keeping the pedal depressed and starting the engine. As the engine starts, the pedal will move down slightly. If not, the vacuum hose or the servo itself may be faulty.

Steering wheel and column

☐ Examine the steering wheel for fractures or looseness of the hub, spokes or rim.

☐ Move the steering wheel from side to side and then up and down. Check that the steering wheel is not loose on the column, indicating wear or a loose retaining nut. Continue moving the steering wheel as before, but also turn it slightly from left to right.

☐ Check that the steering wheel is not loose on the column, and that there is no abnormal movement of the steering wheel, indicating wear in the column support bearings or couplings.

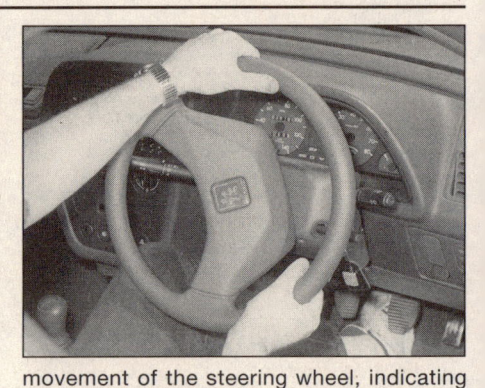

Windscreen, mirrors and sunvisor

☐ The windscreen must be free of cracks or other significant damage within the driver's field of view. (Small stone chips are acceptable.) Rear view mirrors must be secure, intact, and capable of being adjusted.

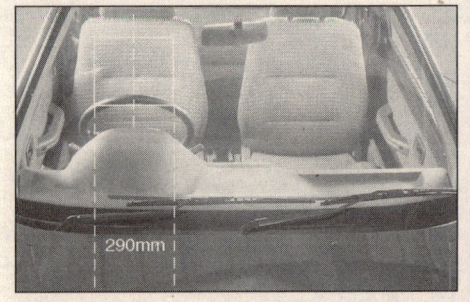

☐ The driver's sunvisor must be capable of being stored in the "up" position.

MOT test checks   REF•9

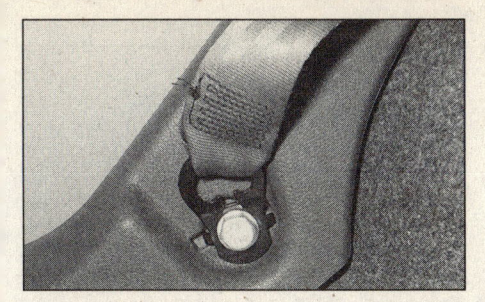

Seat belts and seats

Note: *The following checks are applicable to all seat belts, front and rear.*

☐ Examine the webbing of all the belts (including rear belts if fitted) for cuts, serious fraying or deterioration. Fasten and unfasten each belt to check the buckles. If applicable, check the retracting mechanism. Check the security of all seat belt mountings accessible from inside the vehicle.

☐ Seat belts with pre-tensioners, once activated, have a "flag" or similar showing on the seat belt stalk. This, in itself, is not a reason for test failure.

☐ The front seats themselves must be securely attached and the backrests must lock in the upright position.

Doors

☐ Both front doors must be able to be opened and closed from outside and inside, and must latch securely when closed.

2 Checks carried out WITH THE VEHICLE ON THE GROUND

Vehicle identification

☐ Number plates must be in good condition, secure and legible, with letters and numbers correctly spaced – spacing at (A) should be at least twice that at (B).

☐ The VIN plate and/or homologation plate must be legible.

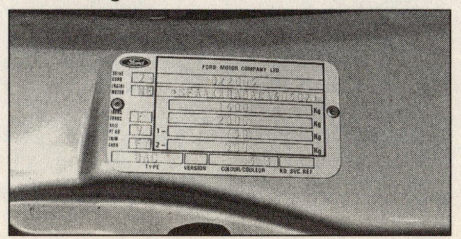

Electrical equipment

☐ Switch on the ignition and check the operation of the horn.

☐ Check the windscreen washers and wipers, examining the wiper blades; renew damaged or perished blades. Also check the operation of the stop-lights.

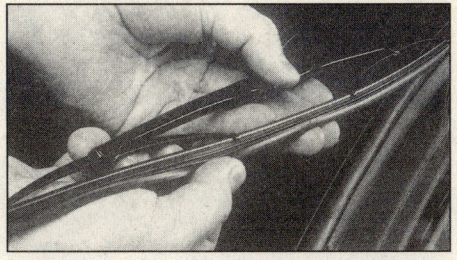

☐ Check the operation of the sidelights and number plate lights. The lenses and reflectors must be secure, clean and undamaged.

☐ Check the operation and alignment of the headlights. The headlight reflectors must not be tarnished and the lenses must be undamaged.

☐ Switch on the ignition and check the operation of the direction indicators (including the instrument panel tell-tale) and the hazard warning lights. Operation of the sidelights and stop-lights must not affect the indicators - if it does, the cause is usually a bad earth at the rear light cluster.

☐ Check the operation of the rear foglight(s), including the warning light on the instrument panel or in the switch.

☐ The ABS warning light must illuminate in accordance with the manufacturers' design. For most vehicles, the ABS warning light should illuminate when the ignition is switched on, and (if the system is operating properly) extinguish after a few seconds. Refer to the owner's handbook.

Footbrake

☐ Examine the master cylinder, brake pipes and servo unit for leaks, loose mountings, corrosion or other damage.

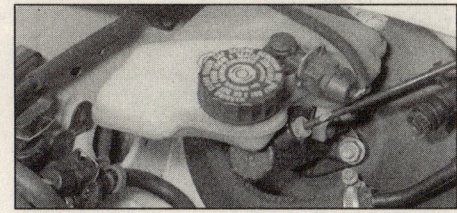

☐ The fluid reservoir must be secure and the fluid level must be between the upper (A) and lower (B) markings.

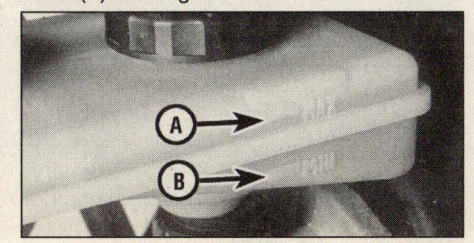

☐ Inspect both front brake flexible hoses for cracks or deterioration of the rubber. Turn the steering from lock to lock, and ensure that the hoses do not contact the wheel, tyre, or any part of the steering or suspension mechanism. With the brake pedal firmly depressed, check the hoses for bulges or leaks under pressure.

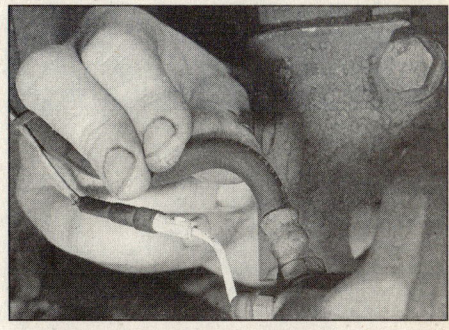

Steering and suspension

☐ Have your assistant turn the steering wheel from side to side slightly, up to the point where the steering gear just begins to transmit this movement to the roadwheels. Check for excessive free play between the steering wheel and the steering gear, indicating wear or insecurity of the steering column joints, the column-to-steering gear coupling, or the steering gear itself.

☐ Have your assistant turn the steering wheel more vigorously in each direction, so that the roadwheels just begin to turn. As this is done, examine all the steering joints, linkages, fittings and attachments. Renew any component that shows signs of wear or damage. On vehicles with power steering, check the security and condition of the steering pump, drivebelt and hoses.

☐ Check that the vehicle is standing level, and at approximately the correct ride height.

Shock absorbers

☐ Depress each corner of the vehicle in turn, then release it. The vehicle should rise and then settle in its normal position. If the vehicle continues to rise and fall, the shock absorber is defective. A shock absorber which has seized will also cause the vehicle to fail.

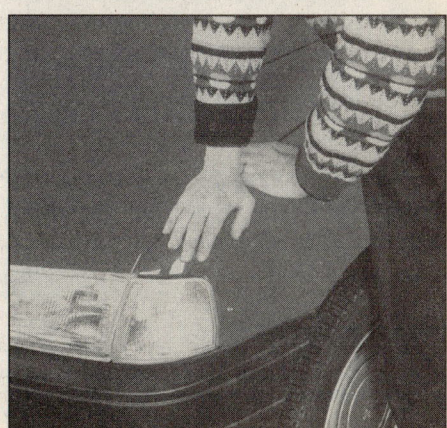

REF•10 MOT test checks

Exhaust system
☐ Start the engine. With your assistant holding a rag over the tailpipe, check the entire system for leaks. Repair or renew leaking sections.

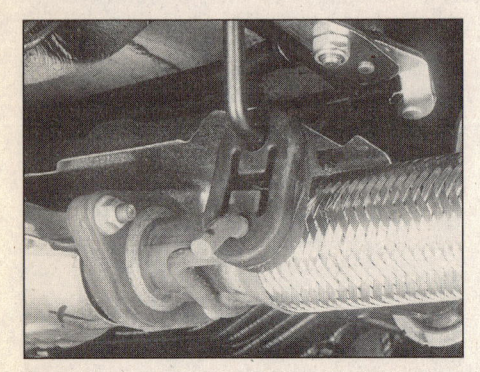

3 Checks carried out WITH THE VEHICLE RAISED AND THE WHEELS FREE TO TURN

Jack up the front and rear of the vehicle, and securely support it on axle stands. Position the stands clear of the suspension assemblies. Ensure that the wheels are clear of the ground and that the steering can be turned from lock to lock.

Steering mechanism
☐ Have your assistant turn the steering from lock to lock. Check that the steering turns smoothly, and that no part of the steering mechanism, including a wheel or tyre, fouls any brake hose or pipe or any part of the body structure.
☐ Examine the steering rack rubber gaiters for damage or insecurity of the retaining clips. If power steering is fitted, check for signs of damage or leakage of the fluid hoses, pipes or connections. Also check for excessive stiffness or binding of the steering, a missing split pin or locking device, or severe corrosion of the body structure within 30 cm of any steering component attachment point.

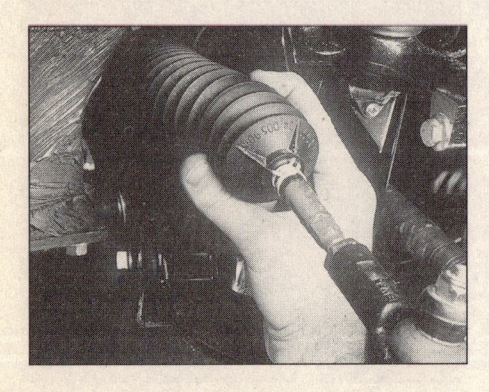

Front and rear suspension and wheel bearings
☐ Starting at the front right-hand side, grasp the roadwheel at the 3 o'clock and 9 o'clock positions and rock gently but firmly. Check for free play or insecurity at the wheel bearings, suspension balljoints, or suspension mountings, pivots and attachments.
☐ Now grasp the wheel at the 12 o'clock and 6 o'clock positions and repeat the previous inspection. Spin the wheel, and check for roughness or tightness of the front wheel bearing.

☐ If excess free play is suspected at a component pivot point, this can be confirmed by using a large screwdriver or similar tool and levering between the mounting and the component attachment. This will confirm whether the wear is in the pivot bush, its retaining bolt, or in the mounting itself (the bolt holes can often become elongated).

☐ Carry out all the above checks at the other front wheel, and then at both rear wheels.

Springs and shock absorbers
☐ Examine the suspension struts (when applicable) for serious fluid leakage, corrosion, or damage to the casing. Also check the security of the mounting points.
☐ If coil springs are fitted, check that the spring ends locate in their seats, and that the spring is not corroded, cracked or broken.
☐ If leaf springs are fitted, check that all leaves are intact, that the axle is securely attached to each spring, and that there is no deterioration of the spring eye mountings, bushes, and shackles.

☐ The same general checks apply to vehicles fitted with other suspension types, such as torsion bars, hydraulic displacer units, etc. Ensure that all mountings and attachments are secure, that there are no signs of excessive wear, corrosion or damage, and (on hydraulic types) that there are no fluid leaks or damaged pipes.
☐ Inspect the shock absorbers for signs of serious fluid leakage. Check for wear of the mounting bushes or attachments, or damage to the body of the unit.

Driveshafts (fwd vehicles only)
☐ Rotate each front wheel in turn and inspect the constant velocity joint gaiters for splits or damage. Also check that each driveshaft is straight and undamaged.

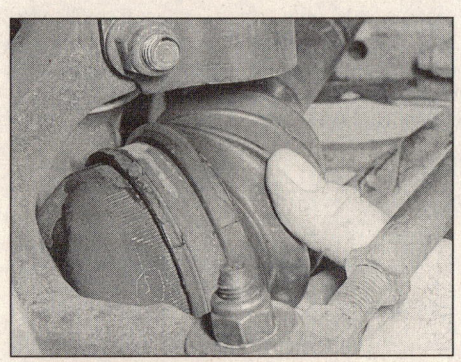

Braking system
☐ If possible without dismantling, check brake pad wear and disc condition. Ensure that the friction lining material has not worn excessively, (A) and that the discs are not fractured, pitted, scored or badly worn (B).

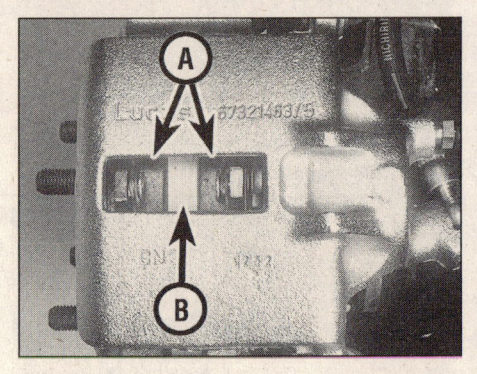

☐ Examine all the rigid brake pipes underneath the vehicle, and the flexible hose(s) at the rear. Look for corrosion, chafing or insecurity of the pipes, and for signs of bulging under pressure, chafing, splits or deterioration of the flexible hoses.
☐ Look for signs of fluid leaks at the brake calipers or on the brake backplates. Repair or renew leaking components.
☐ Slowly spin each wheel, while your assistant depresses and releases the footbrake. Ensure that each brake is operating and does not bind when the pedal is released.

MOT test checks   REF•11

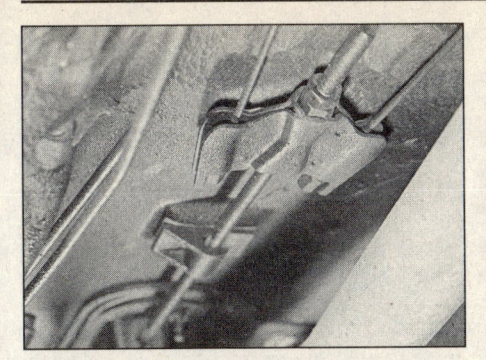

☐ Examine the handbrake mechanism, checking for frayed or broken cables, excessive corrosion, or wear or insecurity of the linkage. Check that the mechanism works on each relevant wheel, and releases fully, without binding.
☐ It is not possible to test brake efficiency without special equipment, but a road test can be carried out later to check that the vehicle pulls up in a straight line.

Fuel and exhaust systems

☐ Inspect the fuel tank (including the filler cap), fuel pipes, hoses and unions. All components must be secure and free from leaks.
☐ Examine the exhaust system over its entire length, checking for any damaged, broken or missing mountings, security of the retaining clamps and rust or corrosion.

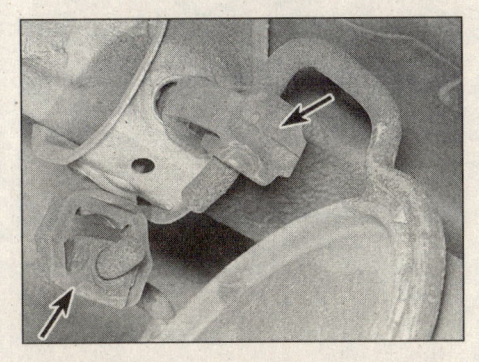

Wheels and tyres

☐ Examine the sidewalls and tread area of each tyre in turn. Check for cuts, tears, lumps, bulges, separation of the tread, and exposure of the ply or cord due to wear or damage. Check that the tyre bead is correctly seated on the wheel rim, that the valve is sound and properly seated, and that the wheel is not distorted or damaged.
☐ Check that the tyres are of the correct size for the vehicle, that they are of the same size and type on each axle, and that the pressures are correct.
☐ Check the tyre tread depth. The legal minimum at the time of writing is 1.6 mm over at least three-quarters of the tread width. Abnormal tread wear may indicate incorrect front wheel alignment.

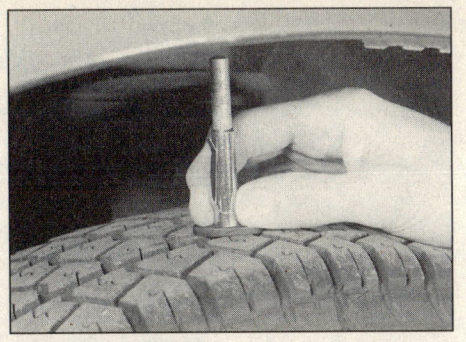

Body corrosion

☐ Check the condition of the entire vehicle structure for signs of corrosion in load-bearing areas. (These include chassis box sections, side sills, cross-members, pillars, and all suspension, steering, braking system and seat belt mountings and anchorages.) Any corrosion which has seriously reduced the thickness of a load-bearing area is likely to cause the vehicle to fail. In this case professional repairs are likely to be needed.
☐ Damage or corrosion which causes sharp or otherwise dangerous edges to be exposed will also cause the vehicle to fail.

4 Checks carried out on **YOUR VEHICLE'S EXHAUST EMISSION SYSTEM**

Petrol models

☐ Have the engine at normal operating temperature, and make sure that it is in good tune (ignition system in good order, air filter element clean, etc).
☐ Before any measurements are carried out, raise the engine speed to around 2500 rpm, and hold it at this speed for 20 seconds. Allow the engine speed to return to idle, and watch for smoke emissions from the exhaust tailpipe. If the idle speed is obviously much too high, or if dense blue or clearly-visible black smoke comes from the tailpipe for more than 5 seconds, the vehicle will fail. As a rule of thumb, blue smoke signifies oil being burnt (engine wear) while black smoke signifies unburnt fuel (dirty air cleaner element, or other carburettor or fuel system fault).
☐ An exhaust gas analyser capable of measuring carbon monoxide (CO) and hydrocarbons (HC) is now needed. If such an instrument cannot be hired or borrowed, a local garage may agree to perform the check for a small fee.

CO emissions (mixture)

☐ At the time of writing, for vehicles first used between 1st August 1975 and 31st July 1986 (P to C registration), the CO level must not exceed 4.5% by volume. For vehicles first used between 1st August 1986 and 31st July 1992 (D to J registration), the CO level must not exceed 3.5% by volume. Vehicles first used after 1st August 1992 (K registration) must conform to the manufacturer's specification. The MOT tester has access to a DOT database or emissions handbook, which lists the CO and HC limits for each make and model of vehicle. The CO level is measured with the engine at idle speed, and at "fast idle". The following limits are given as a general guide:
At idle speed -
   CO level no more than 0.5%
At "fast idle" (2500 to 3000 rpm) -
   CO level no more than 0.3%
   (Minimum oil temperature 60ºC)
☐ If the CO level cannot be reduced far enough to pass the test (and the fuel and ignition systems are otherwise in good condition) then the carburettor is badly worn, or there is some problem in the fuel injection system or catalytic converter (as applicable).

HC emissions

☐ With the CO within limits, HC emissions for vehicles first used between 1st August 1975 and 31st July 1992 (P to J registration) must not exceed 1200 ppm. Vehicles first used after 1st August 1992 (K registration) must conform to the manufacturer's specification. The MOT tester has access to a DOT database or emissions handbook, which lists the CO and HC limits for each make and model of vehicle. The HC level is measured with the engine at "fast idle". The following is given as a general guide:
At "fast idle" (2500 to 3000 rpm) -
   HC level no more than 200 ppm
   (Minimum oil temperature 60ºC)
☐ Excessive HC emissions are caused by incomplete combustion, the causes of which can include oil being burnt, mechanical wear and ignition/fuel system malfunction.

Diesel models

☐ The only emission test applicable to Diesel engines is the measuring of exhaust smoke density. The test involves accelerating the engine several times to its maximum unloaded speed.

Note: *It is of the utmost importance that the engine timing belt is in good condition before the test is carried out.*

☐ The limits for Diesel engine exhaust smoke, introduced in September 1995 are:
Vehicles first used before 1st August 1979:
   Exempt from metered smoke testing, but must not emit "dense blue or clearly visible black smoke for a period of more than 5 seconds at idle" or "dense blue or clearly visible black smoke during acceleration which would obscure the view of other road users".
Non-turbocharged vehicles first used after 1st August 1979: 2.5m^{-1}
Turbocharged vehicles first used after 1st August 1979: 3.0m^{-1}
☐ Excessive smoke can be caused by a dirty air cleaner element. Otherwise, professional advice may be needed to find the cause.

REF•12 Fault finding

Engine...1
- ☐ Engine backfires
- ☐ Engine difficult to start when cold
- ☐ Engine difficult to start when hot
- ☐ Engine fails to rotate when attempting to start
- ☐ Engine hesitates on acceleration
- ☐ Engine idles erratically
- ☐ Engine lacks power
- ☐ Engine misfires at idle speed
- ☐ Engine misfires throughout the driving speed range
- ☐ Engine noises
- ☐ Engine rotates but will not start
- ☐ Engine runs-on after switching off
- ☐ Engine stalls
- ☐ Engine starts but stops immediately
- ☐ Oil pressure warning light illuminated with engine running
- ☐ Starter motor noisy or excessively-rough in engagement

Cooling system..2
- ☐ Corrosion
- ☐ External coolant leakage
- ☐ Internal coolant leakage
- ☐ Overcooling
- ☐ Overheating

Fuel and exhaust systems...............................3
- ☐ Excessive fuel consumption
- ☐ Excessive noise or fumes from exhaust system
- ☐ Fuel leakage and/or fuel odour

Clutch..4
- ☐ Clutch fails to disengage (unable to select gears)
- ☐ Clutch slips (engine speed increases but no acceleration occurs)
- ☐ Judder as clutch is engaged
- ☐ Noise when depressing or releasing clutch pedal
- ☐ Pedal travels to floor - no pressure or very little resistance

Manual transmission..5
- ☐ Jumps out of gear
- ☐ Lubricant leaks
- ☐ Noisy in neutral with engine running
- ☐ Noisy in one particular gear
- ☐ Vibration

Automatic transmission....................................6
- ☐ Engine won't start in any gear, or starts in gears other than P or N
- ☐ Fluid leakage
- ☐ General gear selection problems
- ☐ Transmission fluid brown, or has burned smell
- ☐ Transmission slips, shifts roughly, is noisy, or has no drive in forward or reverse gears
- ☐ Transmission will not downshift (kickdown) with accelerator fully depressed

Propeller shaft..7
- ☐ Vibration when accelerating or decelerating
- ☐ Noise (grinding or high pitched squeak) when moving slowly
- ☐ Noise (knocking or clicking) when accelerating or decelerating

Braking system..8
- ☐ Brake pedal feels spongy when depressed
- ☐ Brakes binding
- ☐ Excessive brake pedal effort required to stop vehicle
- ☐ Excessive brake pedal travel
- ☐ Judder felt through brake pedal or steering wheel when braking
- ☐ Noise (grinding or high-pitched squeal) when brakes applied
- ☐ Rear wheels locking under normal braking
- ☐ Vehicle pulls to one side under braking

Rear axle..9
- ☐ Roughness or rumble from rear of vehicle (perhaps less with handbrake slightly applied)
- ☐ Noise (high pitched whine) increasing with road speed
- ☐ Noise (knocking or clicking) when accelerating or decelerating
- ☐ Lubricant leaks

Suspension and steering systems.....................10
- ☐ Excessive pitching and/or rolling around corners, or during braking
- ☐ Excessive play in steering
- ☐ Excessively-stiff steering
- ☐ Lack of power assistance
- ☐ Tyre wear excessive
- ☐ Vehicle pulls to one side
- ☐ Wandering or general instability
- ☐ Wheel wobble and vibration

Electrical system..11
- ☐ Battery will not hold a charge for more than a few days
- ☐ Central locking system inoperative, or unsatisfactory in operation
- ☐ Electric windows inoperative, or unsatisfactory in operation
- ☐ Horn inoperative, or unsatisfactory in operation
- ☐ Ignition warning light fails to come on
- ☐ Ignition warning light remains illuminated with engine running
- ☐ Instrument readings inaccurate or erratic
- ☐ Lights inoperative
- ☐ Windscreen/tailgate washers inoperative, or unsatisfactory in operation
- ☐ Windscreen/tailgate wipers inoperative, or unsatisfactory in operation

Introduction

The vehicle owner who does his or her own maintenance according to the recommended service schedules should not have to use this section of the manual very often. Modern component reliability is such that, provided those items subject to wear or deterioration are inspected or renewed at the specified intervals, sudden failure is comparatively rare. Faults do not usually just happen as a result of sudden failure, but develop over a period of time. Major mechanical failures in particular are usually preceded by characteristic symptoms over hundreds or even thousands of miles. Those components which do occasionally fail without warning are often small and easily carried in the vehicle.

With any fault-finding, the first step is to decide where to begin investigations. Sometimes this is obvious, but on other occasions, a little detective work will be necessary. The owner who makes half a dozen haphazard adjustments or replacements may be successful in curing a fault (or its symptoms), but will be none the wiser if the fault recurs, and ultimately may have spent more time and money than was necessary. A calm and logical approach will be found to be more satisfactory in the long run. Always take into account any warning signs or abnormalities that may have been noticed in the period preceding the fault - power loss, high or low gauge readings, unusual

Fault finding REF•13

smells, etc - and remember that failure of components such as fuses or spark plugs may only be pointers to some underlying fault.

The pages which follow provide an easy reference guide to the more common problems which may occur during the operation of the vehicle. These problems and their possible causes are grouped under headings denoting various components or systems, such as Engine, Cooling system, etc. The Chapter and/or Section which deals with the problem is also shown in brackets. Whatever the fault, certain basic principles apply. These are as follows:

Verify the fault. This is simply a matter of being sure that you know what the symptoms are before starting work. This is particularly important if you are investigating a fault for someone else, who may not have described it very accurately.

Don't overlook the obvious. For example, if the vehicle won't start, is there petrol in the tank? (Don't take anyone else's word on this particular point, and don't trust the fuel gauge either!) If an electrical fault is indicated, look for loose or broken wires before using the test gear.

Cure the disease, not the symptom. Substituting a flat battery with a fully-charged one will get you off the hard shoulder, but if the underlying cause is not attended to, the new battery will go the same way. Similarly, changing oil-fouled spark plugs for a new set will get you moving again, but remember that the reason for the fouling (if it wasn't simply an incorrect grade of plug) will have to be established and corrected.

Don't take anything for granted. Particularly, don't forget that a "new" component may itself be defective (especially if it's been rattling around in the boot for months), and don't leave components out of a fault diagnosis sequence just because they are new or recently fitted. When you do finally diagnose a difficult fault, you'll probably realise that all the evidence was there from the start.

1 Engine

Engine fails to rotate when attempting to start
- ☐ Battery terminal connections loose or corroded (*"Weekly checks"*).
- ☐ Battery discharged or faulty (Chapter 5A).
- ☐ Broken, loose or disconnected wiring in the starting circuit (Chapter 5A).
- ☐ Defective starter solenoid or switch (Chapter 5A).
- ☐ Defective starter motor (Chapter 5A).
- ☐ Starter pinion or flywheel ring gear teeth loose or broken (Chapter 2A, 2B, 2C and 5A).
- ☐ Engine earth strap broken or disconnected (Chapter 5A).
- ☐ Automatic transmission not in Park/Neutral position, or selector lever position sensor faulty (Chapter 7B).

Engine rotates but will not start
- ☐ Fuel tank empty.
- ☐ Battery discharged (engine rotates slowly) (Chapter 5A).
- ☐ Battery terminal connections loose or corroded (*"Weekly checks"*).
- ☐ Ignition components damp or damaged (Chapters 1 and 5B).
- ☐ Broken, loose or disconnected wiring in the ignition circuit (Chapters 1 and 5B).
- ☐ Worn, faulty or incorrectly-gapped spark plugs (Chapter 1).
- ☐ Low cylinder compressions (Chapter 2A).
- ☐ Major mechanical failure (eg camshaft drive) (Chapter 2A or 2B).

Engine difficult to start when cold
- ☐ Battery discharged (Chapter 5A).
- ☐ Battery terminal connections loose or corroded (*"Weekly checks"*).
- ☐ Worn, faulty or incorrectly-gapped spark plugs (Chapter 1).
- ☐ Other ignition system fault (Chapters 1 and 5B).
- ☐ Engine management system fault (Chapters 1, 4B and 5B).
- ☐ Incorrect valve clearance adjustment (Chapter 1).
- ☐ Low cylinder compressions (Chapter 2A).

Engine difficult to start when hot
- ☐ Air filter element dirty or clogged (Chapter 1).
- ☐ Engine management system fault (Chapters 1, 4B and 5B).
- ☐ Incorrect valve clearance adjustment (Chapter 1).
- ☐ Low cylinder compressions (Chapter 2A).

Starter motor noisy or excessively-rough in engagement
- ☐ Starter pinion or flywheel ring gear teeth loose or broken (Chapters 2A, 2B or 5A).
- ☐ Starter motor mounting bolts loose or missing (Chapter 5A).
- ☐ Starter motor internal components worn or damaged (Chapter 5A).

Engine starts but stops immediately
- ☐ Loose or faulty electrical connections in the ignition circuit (Chapters 1 and 5B).
- ☐ Engine management system fault (Chapters 1 and 4B).
- ☐ Vacuum leak at the inlet manifold (Chapters 1 and 4A or 4B).

Engine idles erratically
- ☐ Engine management system fault (Chapters 1, 4B and 5B).
- ☐ Air filter element clogged (Chapter 1).
- ☐ Vacuum leak at the inlet manifold or associated hoses (Chapters 1 and 4A or 4B).
- ☐ Worn, faulty or incorrectly-gapped spark plugs (Chapter 1).
- ☐ Incorrect valve clearance adjustment (Chapter 1).
- ☐ Uneven or low cylinder compressions (Chapter 2A).
- ☐ Camshaft lobes worn (Chapter 2A or 2B).
- ☐ Camshaft drivebelt incorrectly-tensioned (Chapter 2A).

Engine misfires at idle speed
- ☐ Worn, faulty or incorrectly-gapped spark plugs (Chapter 1).
- ☐ Faulty spark plug HT leads (Chapter 1).
- ☐ Engine management system fault (Chapters 1, 4B and 5B).
- ☐ Vacuum leak at the inlet manifold or associated hoses (Chapters 1, 4A or 4B).
- ☐ Incorrect valve clearance adjustment (Chapter 1).
- ☐ Uneven or low cylinder compressions (Chapter 2A).
- ☐ Disconnected, leaking or perished crankcase ventilation hoses (Chapters 1 and 4B).

Engine misfires throughout the driving speed range
- ☐ Fuel filter choked (Chapter 1).
- ☐ Fuel pump faulty (Chapter 4A).
- ☐ Fuel tank vent blocked or fuel pipes restricted (Chapter 4A or 4B).
- ☐ Vacuum leak at the inlet manifold or associated hoses (Chapters 1 and 4A or 4B).
- ☐ Worn, faulty or incorrectly-gapped spark plugs (Chapter 1).
- ☐ Faulty spark plug HT leads (Chapter 1).
- ☐ Engine management system fault (Chapters 1, 4B and 5B).
- ☐ Incorrect valve clearance adjustment (Chapter 1).
- ☐ Uneven or low cylinder compressions (Chapter 2A).

Engine hesitates on acceleration
- ☐ Worn, faulty or incorrectly-gapped spark plugs (Chapter 1).
- ☐ Engine management system fault (Chapters 1, 4B and 5B).
- ☐ Vacuum leak at the inlet manifold or associated hoses (Chapters 1 and 4A or 4B).

REF•14 Fault finding

1 Engine (continued)

Engine stalls
- [ ] Engine management system fault (Chapters 1, 4B and 5B).
- [ ] Vacuum leak at the inlet manifold or associated hoses (Chapters 1 and 4A or 4B).
- [ ] Fuel filter choked (Chapter 1).
- [ ] Fuel pump faulty (Chapter 4A or 4B).
- [ ] Fuel tank vent blocked or fuel pipes restricted (Chapter 4A or 4B).

Engine lacks power
- [ ] Engine management system fault (Chapters 1, 4B and 5B).
- [ ] Camshaft drivebelt incorrectly fitted or incorrectly tensioned (Chapter 2A).
- [ ] Fuel filter choked (Chapter 1).
- [ ] Fuel pump faulty (Chapter 4A or 4B).
- [ ] Incorrect valve clearance adjustment (Chapter 1).
- [ ] Uneven or low cylinder compressions (Chapter 2A).
- [ ] Worn, faulty or incorrectly-gapped spark plugs (Chapter 1).
- [ ] Vacuum leak at the inlet manifold or associated hoses (Chapters 1, 4A and 4B).
- [ ] Brakes binding (Chapters 1 and 9).
- [ ] Clutch slipping (Chapter 6).
- [ ] Automatic transmission fluid level incorrect (Chapter 1).

Engine backfires
- [ ] Engine management system fault (Chapters 1, 4B and 5B).
- [ ] Camshaft drivebelt incorrectly fitted or incorrectly tensioned (Chapter 2A).
- [ ] Vacuum leak at the inlet manifold or associated hoses (Chapters 1, and 4A or 4B).
- [ ] Emission control system fault (Chapter 4B).

Oil pressure warning light illuminated with engine running
- [ ] Low oil level or incorrect oil grade (Chapter 1).
- [ ] Faulty oil pressure warning light switch (Chapter 5A).
- [ ] Worn engine bearings and/or oil pump (Chapter 2B).
- [ ] High engine operating temperature (Chapter 3).
- [ ] Oil pressure relief valve defective (Chapter 2A or 2B).
- [ ] Oil pick-up strainer clogged (Chapter 2A or 2B).

Engine runs-on after switching off
- [ ] Engine management system fault (Chapters 1, 4B and 5B).
- [ ] Excessive carbon build-up in engine (Chapter 2A or 2B).
- [ ] High engine operating temperature (Chapter 3).

Engine noises

Pre-ignition (pinking) or knocking during acceleration or under load
- [ ] Incorrect grade of fuel (Chapter 4A).
- [ ] Vacuum leak at the inlet manifold or associated hoses (Chapters 1, 4A or 4B).
- [ ] Excessive carbon build-up in engine (Chapter 2A or 2B).

Whistling or wheezing noises
- [ ] Leaking inlet manifold gasket (Chapter 4A).
- [ ] Leaking exhaust manifold gasket or downpipe-to-manifold joint (Chapters 1, or 4A).
- [ ] Leaking vacuum hose (Chapters 1, 4A, 5B and 9).
- [ ] Blowing cylinder head gasket (Chapter 2A or 2B).

Tapping or rattling noises
- [ ] Incorrect valve clearance adjustment (Chapter 1).
- [ ] Worn valve gear or camshaft (Chapter 2A or 2B).
- [ ] Worn camshaft drivebelt or tensioner (Chapter 2A).
- [ ] Ancillary component fault (water pump, alternator, etc) (Chapters 3 and 5A).

Knocking or thumping noises
- [ ] Worn big-end bearings (regular heavy knocking, perhaps less under load) (Chapter 2B).
- [ ] Worn main bearings (rumbling and knocking, perhaps worsening under load) (Chapter 2B).
- [ ] Piston slap (most noticeable when cold) (Chapter 2B).
- [ ] Ancillary component fault (water pump, alternator, etc) (Chapters 3 and 5A).

2 Cooling system

Overheating
- [ ] Insufficient coolant in system (Chapter 1).
- [ ] Thermostat faulty (Chapter 3).
- [ ] Radiator core blocked or grille restricted (Chapter 3).
- [ ] Radiator electric cooling fan(s) or coolant temperature sensor faulty (Chapter 3).
- [ ] Engine management system fault (Chapters 1, 4B and 5B).
- [ ] Pressure cap faulty (Chapter 3).
- [ ] Accessory drivebelt(s) worn or slipping (Chapter 1).
- [ ] Inaccurate coolant temperature sensor (Chapter 3).
- [ ] Air-lock in cooling system (Chapter 1).

Overcooling
- [ ] Thermostat faulty (Chapter 3).
- [ ] Inaccurate coolant temperature sensor (Chapter 3).

External coolant leakage
- [ ] Deteriorated or damaged hoses or hose clips (Chapter 1).
- [ ] Radiator core or heater matrix leaking (Chapter 3).
- [ ] Pressure cap faulty (Chapter 3).
- [ ] Water pump seal leaking (Chapter 3).
- [ ] Boiling due to overheating (Chapter 3).
- [ ] Core plug leaking (Chapter 2B).

Internal coolant leakage
- [ ] Leaking cylinder head gasket (Chapter 2A or 2B).
- [ ] Cracked cylinder head or cylinder bore (Chapter 2B).

Corrosion
- [ ] Infrequent draining and flushing (Chapter 1).
- [ ] Incorrect antifreeze mixture, or inappropriate antifreeze type (Chapters 1 and 3).

Fault finding   REF•15

3 Fuel and exhaust system

Excessive fuel consumption
- [ ] Unsympathetic driving style, or adverse conditions.
- [ ] Air filter element dirty or clogged (Chapter 1).
- [ ] Engine management system fault (Chapter 1, 4B and 5B).
- [ ] Tyres under-inflated (Chapter 1).

Fuel leakage and/or fuel odour
- [ ] Damaged or corroded fuel tank, pipes or connections (Chapter 1).

Excessive noise or fumes from exhaust system
- [ ] Leaking exhaust system or manifold joints (Chapters 1, 4A or 4B).
- [ ] Leaking, corroded or damaged silencers or pipe (Chapter 1).
- [ ] Broken mountings, causing body or suspension contact (Chapters 1, 4A and 4B).

4 Clutch

Pedal travels to floor - no pressure or very little resistance
- [ ] Air in clutch hydraulic system (Chapter 6).
- [ ] Faulty clutch slave cylinder (Chapter 6).
- [ ] Faulty clutch master cylinder (Chapter 6).
- [ ] Broken clutch cable (Chapter 6).
- [ ] Incorrect adjustment (Chapter 6).
- [ ] Broken diaphragm spring in clutch pressure plate (Chapter 6).

Clutch fails to disengage (unable to select gears)
- [ ] Air in clutch hydraulic system (Chapter 6).
- [ ] Faulty clutch slave cylinder (Chapter 6).
- [ ] Faulty clutch master cylinder (Chapter 6).
- [ ] Broken clutch cable (Chapter 6).
- [ ] Incorrect adjustment (Chapter 6).
- [ ] Clutch disc sticking on transmission mainshaft splines (Chapter 6).
- [ ] Clutch disc sticking to flywheel or pressure plate (Chapter 6).
- [ ] Faulty pressure plate assembly (Chapter 6).
- [ ] Clutch release mechanism worn or poorly assembled (Chapter 6).

Clutch slips (engine speed increases with no increase in vehicle speed)
- [ ] Clutch disc linings excessively worn (Chapter 6).
- [ ] Clutch disc linings contaminated with oil or grease (Chapter 6).
- [ ] Faulty pressure plate or weak diaphragm spring (Chapter 6).

Judder as clutch is engaged
- [ ] Clutch disc linings contaminated with oil or grease (Chapter 6).
- [ ] Clutch disc linings excessively worn (Chapter 6).
- [ ] Faulty or distorted pressure plate or diaphragm spring (Chapter 6).
- [ ] Worn or loose engine/transmission mountings (Chapter 2A).
- [ ] Clutch disc hub or gearbox mainshaft splines worn (Chapter 6).

Noise when depressing or releasing clutch pedal
- [ ] Worn clutch release bearing (Chapter 6).
- [ ] Worn or dry clutch pedal bushes (Chapter 6).
- [ ] Faulty pressure plate assembly (Chapter 6).
- [ ] Pressure plate diaphragm spring broken (Chapter 6).
- [ ] Broken clutch disc cushioning springs (Chapter 6).

5 Manual transmission

Noisy in neutral with engine running
- [ ] Mainshaft bearings worn (noise apparent with clutch pedal released, but not when depressed) (Chapter 7A).*
- [ ] Clutch release bearing worn (noise apparent with clutch pedal depressed, possibly less when released) (Chapter 6).

Noisy in one particular gear
- [ ] Worn, damaged or chipped gear teeth (Chapter 7A).*
- [ ] Worn bearings (Chapter 7A).*

Difficulty engaging gears
- [ ] Clutch fault (Chapter 6).
- [ ] Worn or damaged gear linkage (Chapter 7A).
- [ ] Worn synchroniser assemblies (Chapter 7A).*

Jumps out of gear
- [ ] Worn or damaged gear linkage (Chapter 7A).
- [ ] Worn synchroniser assemblies (Chapter 7A).*
- [ ] Worn selector forks (Chapter 7A).*

Vibration
- [ ] Lack of oil (Chapter 1).
- [ ] Worn bearings (Chapter 7A).*

Lubricant leaks
- [ ] Leaking differential side gear oil seal (Chapter 7A).
- [ ] Leaking gearchange shaft or speedometer pinion oil seals (Chapter 7A).
- [ ] Leaking housing joint (Chapter 7A).*
- [ ] Leaking mainshaft oil seal (Chapter 7A).*

Although the corrective action necessary to remedy the symptoms described is beyond the scope of the home mechanic, the above information should be helpful in isolating the cause of the condition, so that the owner can communicate clearly with a professional mechanic.

6 Automatic transmission

Note: *Due to the complexity of the automatic transmission, it is difficult for the home mechanic to properly diagnose and service this unit. For problems other than the following, the vehicle should be taken to a dealer service department or automatic transmission specialist.*

Fluid leakage
- [ ] Automatic transmission fluid is usually dark in colour. Fluid leaks should not be confused with engine oil, which can easily be blown onto the transmission by airflow.
- [ ] To determine the source of a leak, first remove all built-up dirt and grime from the transmission housing and surrounding areas, using

REF•16 Fault finding

6 Automatic transmission (continued)

a degreasing agent, or by steam-cleaning. Drive the vehicle at low speed, so airflow will not blow the leak far from its source. Raise and support the vehicle, and determine where the leak is coming from. The following are common areas of leakage:
a) Transmission oil sump (Chapters 1 and 7B).
b) Dipstick tube (Chapters 1 and 7B).
c) Transmission-to-fluid cooler pipes/unions (Chapter 1 and 7B).
d) Transmission oil seals (Chapter 7B).

Transmission fluid brown, or has burned smell
☐ Transmission fluid level low, or fluid in need of renewal (Chapter 1).

General gear selection problems
☐ Chapter 7B, deals with checking and adjusting the selector cable on automatic transmissions. The following are common problems which may be caused by a poorly-adjusted cable:
a) Engine starting in gears other than Park or Neutral.
b) Indicator on gear selector lever pointing to a gear other than the one actually being used.
c) Vehicle moves when in Park or Neutral.
d) Poor gear shift quality or erratic gear changes.
☐ Refer to Chapter 7B for the selector cable adjustment procedure.

Transmission will not downshift (kickdown) with accelerator pedal fully depressed
☐ Low transmission fluid level (Chapter 1).
☐ Incorrect kickdown cable adjustment (Chapter 7B).
☐ Incorrect selector cable adjustment (Chapter 7B).

Engine will not start in any gear, or starts in gears other than Park or Neutral
☐ Incorrect selector cable adjustment (Chapter 7B).
☐ Incorrect starter inhibitor switch adjustment (Chapter 7B).

Transmission slips, is noisy, or has no drive in forward or reverse gears
☐ There are many probable causes for the above problems, but the home mechanic should be concerned with only one possibility - fluid level. Before taking the vehicle to a dealer or transmission specialist, check the fluid level and condition of the fluid as described in Chapter 1. Correct the fluid level as necessary, or change the fluid if needed. If the problem persists, professional help will be necessary.

7 Propeller shaft

Vibration when accelerating or decelerating
☐ Propeller shaft out of balance or incorrectly fitted (Chapter 8).
☐ Propeller shaft flange bolts loose (Chapter 8).
☐ Excessive wear in universal joints (Chapter 8).

Noise (grinding or high-pitched squeak) when moving slowly
☐ Excessive wear in universal joints (Chapter 8).
☐ Excessive wear in centre bearing (Chapter 8).

Noise (knocking or clicking) when accelerating or decelerating
☐ Propeller shaft flange bolts loose (Chapter 8).
☐ Excessive wear in universal joints (Chapter 8).

8 Rear axle

Roughness or rumble from rear of vehicle (perhaps less with handbrake slightly applied)
☐ Rear hub bearings worn (Chapter 8).

Noise (high-pitched whine) increasing with road speed
☐ Differential crownwheel and pinion gear teeth worn (Chapter 8).
☐ Incorrect crownwheel and pinion mesh (Chapter 8).
☐ Differential bearings worn (Chapter 8).

Noise (knocking or clicking) when accelerating or decelerating
☐ Worn halfshaft splines (Chapter 8).
☐ Differential pinion flange bolts loose (Chapter 8).
☐ Incorrect crownwheel and pinion mesh (Chapter 8).
☐ Roadwheel nuts loose (Chapters 1 and 10).

Lubricant leaks
☐ Leaking oil seal (Chapter 8).
☐ Leaking differential housing or cover joint (Chapter 8).

9 Braking system

Note: *Before assuming that a brake problem exists, make sure that the tyres are in good condition and correctly inflated, that the front wheel alignment is correct, and that the vehicle is not loaded with weight in an unequal manner. Apart from checking the condition of all pipe and hose connections, any faults occurring on the Anti-lock Braking System (ABS) should be referred to a Volvo dealer for diagnosis.*

Vehicle pulls to one side under braking
☐ Worn, defective, damaged or contaminated front or rear brake pads on one side (Chapter 9).
☐ Seized or partially-seized front or rear brake caliper piston (Chapter 9).
☐ A mixture of brake pad lining materials fitted between sides (Chapter 9).
☐ Brake caliper mounting bolts loose (Chapter 9).
☐ Worn or damaged steering or suspension components (Chapter 10).

Noise (grinding or high-pitched squeal) when brakes applied
☐ Brake pad friction lining material worn down to metal backing (Chapter 9).
☐ Excessive corrosion of brake disc (may be apparent after the vehicle has been standing for some time) (Chapter 9).

Fault finding

9 Braking system (continued)

Excessive brake pedal travel
- [ ] Faulty master cylinder (Chapter 9).
- [ ] Air in hydraulic system (Chapter 9).

Brake pedal feels spongy when depressed
- [ ] Air in hydraulic system (Chapter 9).
- [ ] Deteriorated flexible rubber brake hoses (Chapter 9).
- [ ] Master cylinder mounting nuts loose (Chapter 9).
- [ ] Faulty master cylinder (Chapter 9).

Excessive brake pedal effort required to stop vehicle
- [ ] Faulty vacuum servo unit (Chapter 9).
- [ ] Disconnected or damaged brake servo vacuum hose (Chapter 9).
- [ ] Primary or secondary hydraulic circuit failure (Chapter 9).
- [ ] Seized brake caliper piston(s) (Chapter 9).
- [ ] Brake pads incorrectly fitted (Chapter 9).
- [ ] Incorrect grade of brake pads fitted (Chapter 9).
- [ ] Brake pad linings contaminated (Chapter 9).

Judder felt through brake pedal or steering wheel when braking
- [ ] Excessive run-out or distortion of front or rear discs (Chapter 9).
- [ ] Brake pad linings worn (Chapter 9).
- [ ] Brake caliper mounting bolts loose (Chapter 9).
- [ ] Wear in suspension or steering components or mountings (Chapter 10).

Brakes binding
- [ ] Seized brake caliper piston(s) (Chapter 9).
- [ ] Faulty handbrake mechanism (Chapter 9).
- [ ] Faulty master cylinder (Chapter 9).

Rear wheels locking under normal braking
- [ ] Rear brake pad linings contaminated (Chapter 1).

10 Suspension and steering systems

Note: *Before diagnosing suspension or steering faults, be sure that the trouble is not due to incorrect tyre pressures, mixtures of tyre types, or binding brakes.*

Vehicle pulls to one side
- [ ] Defective tyre (*"Weekly checks"*).
- [ ] Excessive wear in suspension or steering components (Chapter 10).
- [ ] Incorrect front or rear wheel alignment (Chapter 10).
- [ ] Damage to steering or suspension components (Chapter 10).

Wheel wobble and vibration
- [ ] Front roadwheels out of balance (vibration felt mainly through the steering wheel).
- [ ] Rear roadwheels out of balance (vibration felt throughout the vehicle) (Chapter 1).
- [ ] Roadwheels damaged or distorted (Chapter 1).
- [ ] Faulty or damaged tyre (*"Weekly checks"*).
- [ ] Worn steering or suspension joints, bushes or components (Chapter 10).
- [ ] Roadwheel nuts loose (Chapter 1).

Excessive pitching and/or rolling around corners, or during braking
- [ ] Defective shock absorbers (Chapter 10).
- [ ] Broken or weak coil spring and/or suspension component (Chapter 10).
- [ ] Worn or damaged anti-roll bar or mountings (Chapter 10).

Wandering or general instability
- [ ] Incorrect wheel alignment (Chapter 10).
- [ ] Worn steering or suspension joints, bushes or components (Chapter 10).
- [ ] Roadwheels out of balance (Chapter 1).
- [ ] Faulty or damaged tyre (*"Weekly checks"*).
- [ ] Roadwheel nuts loose (Chapter 1).
- [ ] Defective shock absorbers (Chapter 10).

Excessively-stiff steering
- [ ] Broken or incorrectly adjusted power steering pump (accessory) drivebelt (Chapter 1).
- [ ] Power steering pump faulty (Chapter 10).
- [ ] Seized track rod end balljoint or suspension balljoint (Chapter 10).
- [ ] Incorrect front wheel alignment (Chapter 10).
- [ ] Steering rack or column bent or damaged (Chapter 10).

Excessive play in steering
- [ ] Worn steering column universal joint(s) (Chapter 10).
- [ ] Worn steering track rod end balljoints (Chapter 10).
- [ ] Worn rack-and-pinion steering gear (Chapter 10).
- [ ] Worn steering or suspension joints, bushes or components (Chapter 10).

Lack of power assistance
- [ ] Broken or slipping power steering pump (accessory) drivebelt (Chapter 1).
- [ ] Incorrect power steering fluid level (Chapter 1).
- [ ] Restriction in power steering fluid hoses (Chapter 10).
- [ ] Faulty power steering pump (Chapter 10).
- [ ] Faulty rack-and-pinion steering gear (Chapter 10).

Tyre wear excessive

Tyres worn on inside or outside edges
- [ ] Tyres under-inflated (*"Weekly checks"*).
- [ ] Incorrect camber or castor angles (wear on one edge only) (Chapter 10).
- [ ] Worn steering or suspension joints, bushes or components (Chapter 10).
- [ ] Excessively-hard cornering.
- [ ] Accident damage.

Tyre treads exhibit feathered edges
- [ ] Incorrect toe setting (Chapter 10).

Tyres worn in centre of tread
- [ ] Tyres over-inflated (*"Weekly checks"*).

Tyres worn on inside and outside edges
- [ ] Tyres under-inflated (*"Weekly checks"*).

Tyres worn unevenly
- [ ] Tyres out of balance (*"Weekly checks"*).
- [ ] Excessive wheel or tyre run-out (Chapter 1).
- [ ] Worn shock absorbers (Chapter 10).
- [ ] Faulty tyre (*"Weekly checks"*).

REF•18 Fault finding

11 Electrical system

Note: *For problems associated with the starting system, refer to the faults listed under **"Engine"** earlier in this Section.*

Battery will not hold a charge for more than a few days

- [ ] Battery defective internally (Chapter 5A).
- [ ] Battery electrolyte level low (Chapter 5A).
- [ ] Battery terminal connections loose or corroded (Chapters 1 and 5A).
- [ ] Accessory drivebelt worn or incorrectly-adjusted (Chapter 1).
- [ ] Alternator not charging at correct output (Chapter 5A).
- [ ] Alternator or voltage regulator faulty (Chapter 5A).
- [ ] Short-circuit causing continual battery drain (Chapters 5A and 12).

Ignition/no-charge warning light remains illuminated with engine running

- [ ] Accessory drivebelt broken, worn, or incorrectly-adjusted (Chapter 1).
- [ ] Alternator brushes worn, sticking, or dirty (Chapter 5A).
- [ ] Alternator brush springs weak or broken (Chapter 5A).
- [ ] Internal fault in alternator or voltage regulator (Chapter 5A).
- [ ] Broken, disconnected, or loose wiring in charging circuit (Chapter 5A).

Ignition/no-charge warning light fails to come on

- [ ] Warning light bulb blown (Chapter 12).
- [ ] Broken, disconnected, or loose wiring in warning light circuit (Chapter 12).
- [ ] Alternator faulty (Chapter 5A).

Lights inoperative

- [ ] Bulb blown (Chapter 12).
- [ ] Corrosion of bulb or bulbholder contacts (Chapter 12).
- [ ] Blown fuse (Chapter 12).
- [ ] Faulty relay (Chapter 12).
- [ ] Broken, loose, or disconnected wiring (Chapter 12).
- [ ] Faulty switch (Chapter 12).

Instrument readings inaccurate or erratic

Instrument readings increase with engine speed

- [ ] Faulty instrument voltage stabiliser (Chapter 12).

Fuel or temperature gauges give no reading

- [ ] Faulty instrument voltage stabiliser (Chapter 12).
- [ ] Faulty gauge sender unit (Chapters 3, 4A or 5B).
- [ ] Wiring open-circuit (Chapter 12).
- [ ] Faulty gauge (Chapter 12).

Fuel or temperature gauges give continuous maximum reading

- [ ] Faulty instrument voltage stabiliser (Chapter 12).
- [ ] Faulty gauge sender unit (Chapters 3, 4A or 5B).
- [ ] Wiring short-circuit (Chapter 12).
- [ ] Faulty gauge (Chapter 12).

Horn inoperative, or unsatisfactory in operation

Horn fails to operate

- [ ] Blown fuse (Chapter 12).
- [ ] Steering wheel cable connections loose, broken or disconnected (Chapter 10).
- [ ] Faulty horn (Chapter 12).

Horn emits intermittent or unsatisfactory sound

- [ ] Steering wheel cable connections loose, broken or disconnected (Chapter 10).
- [ ] Horn mountings loose (Chapter 12).
- [ ] Faulty horn (Chapter 12).

Horn operates all the time

- [ ] Horn push either earthed or stuck down (Chapter 10).
- [ ] Steering wheel cable connections earthed (Chapter 10).

Windscreen/tailgate wipers inoperative or unsatisfactory in operation

Wipers fail to operate, or operate very slowly

- [ ] Wiper blades stuck to screen, or linkage seized or binding (Chapter 12).
- [ ] Blown fuse (Chapter 12).
- [ ] Cable or cable connections loose, broken or disconnected (Chapter 12).
- [ ] Faulty relay (Chapter 12).
- [ ] Faulty wiper motor (Chapter 12).

Wiper blades sweep over too large or too small an area of the glass

- [ ] Wiper arms incorrectly-positioned on spindles (Chapter 12).
- [ ] Excessive wear of wiper linkage (Chapter 12).
- [ ] Wiper motor or linkage mountings loose or insecure (Chapter 12).

Wiper blades fail to clean the glass effectively

- [ ] Wiper blade rubbers worn or perished (*"Weekly checks"*).
- [ ] Wiper arm tension springs broken, or arm pivots seized (Chapter 12).
- [ ] Insufficient windscreen washer additive to adequately remove road film (*"Weekly checks"*).

Windscreen/tailgate washers inoperative, or unsatisfactory in operation

One or more washer jets inoperative

- [ ] Blocked washer jet (*"Weekly checks"*).
- [ ] Disconnected, kinked or restricted fluid hose (Chapter 1).
- [ ] Insufficient fluid in washer reservoir (*"Weekly checks"*).

Washer pump fails to operate

- [ ] Broken or disconnected wiring or connections (Chapter 12).
- [ ] Blown fuse (Chapter 12).
- [ ] Faulty washer switch (Chapter 12).
- [ ] Faulty washer pump (Chapter 12).

Washer pump runs for some time before fluid is emitted from jets

- [ ] Faulty one-way valve in fluid supply hose (Chapter 12).

Fault finding REF•19

11 Electrical system (continued)

Electric windows inoperative, or unsatisfactory in operation

Window glass will only move in one direction
- [ ] Faulty switch (Chapter 12).

Window glass slow to move
- [ ] Incorrectly-adjusted door glass guide channels (Chapter 11).
- [ ] Regulator seized or damaged, or in need of lubrication (Chapter 11).
- [ ] Door internal components or trim fouling regulator (Chapter 11).
- [ ] Faulty motor (Chapter 12).

Window glass fails to move
- [ ] Incorrectly-adjusted door glass guide channels (Chapter 11).
- [ ] Blown fuse (Chapter 12).
- [ ] Faulty relay (Chapter 12).
- [ ] Broken or disconnected wiring or connections (Chapter 12).
- [ ] Faulty motor (Chapter 12).

Central locking system inoperative, or unsatisfactory in operation

Complete system failure
- [ ] Blown fuse (Chapter 12).
- [ ] Faulty relay (Chapter 12).
- [ ] Broken or disconnected wiring or connections (Chapter 12).

Latch locks but will not unlock, or unlocks but will not lock
- [ ] Faulty master switch (Chapter 11).
- [ ] Broken or disconnected latch operating rods or levers (Chapter 11).
- [ ] Faulty relay (Chapter 12).

One lock motor fails to operate
- [ ] Broken or disconnected wiring or connections (Chapter 12).
- [ ] Faulty lock motor (Chapter 11).
- [ ] Broken, binding or disconnected latch operating rods or levers (Chapter 11).
- [ ] Fault in door latch (Chapter 11).

Glossary of technical terms

A

ABS (Anti-lock brake system) A system, usually electronically controlled, that senses incipient wheel lockup during braking and relieves hydraulic pressure at wheels that are about to skid.

Air bag An inflatable bag hidden in the steering wheel (driver's side) or the dash or glovebox (passenger side). In a head-on collision, the bags inflate, preventing the driver and front passenger from being thrown forward into the steering wheel or windscreen.

Air cleaner A metal or plastic housing, containing a filter element, which removes dust and dirt from the air being drawn into the engine.

Air filter element The actual filter in an air cleaner system, usually manufactured from pleated paper and requiring renewal at regular intervals.

Air filter

Allen key A hexagonal wrench which fits into a recessed hexagonal hole.

Alligator clip A long-nosed spring-loaded metal clip with meshing teeth. Used to make temporary electrical connections.

Alternator A component in the electrical system which converts mechanical energy from a drivebelt into electrical energy to charge the battery and to operate the starting system, ignition system and electrical accessories.

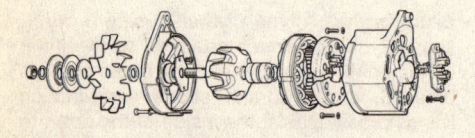

Alternator (exploded view)

Ampere (amp) A unit of measurement for the flow of electric current. One amp is the amount of current produced by one volt acting through a resistance of one ohm.

Anaerobic sealer A substance used to prevent bolts and screws from loosening. Anaerobic means that it does not require oxygen for activation. The Loctite brand is widely used.

Antifreeze A substance (usually ethylene glycol) mixed with water, and added to a vehicle's cooling system, to prevent freezing of the coolant in winter. Antifreeze also contains chemicals to inhibit corrosion and the formation of rust and other deposits that would tend to clog the radiator and coolant passages and reduce cooling efficiency.

Anti-seize compound A coating that reduces the risk of seizing on fasteners that are subjected to high temperatures, such as exhaust manifold bolts and nuts.

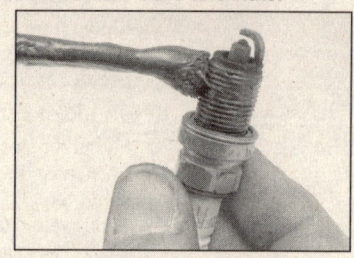

Anti-seize compound

Asbestos A natural fibrous mineral with great heat resistance, commonly used in the composition of brake friction materials. Asbestos is a health hazard and the dust created by brake systems should never be inhaled or ingested.

Axle A shaft on which a wheel revolves, or which revolves with a wheel. Also, a solid beam that connects the two wheels at one end of the vehicle. An axle which also transmits power to the wheels is known as a live axle.

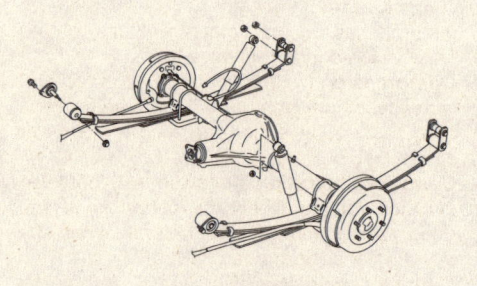

Axle assembly

Axleshaft A single rotating shaft, on either side of the differential, which delivers power from the final drive assembly to the drive wheels. Also called a driveshaft or a halfshaft.

B

Ball bearing An anti-friction bearing consisting of a hardened inner and outer race with hardened steel balls between two races.

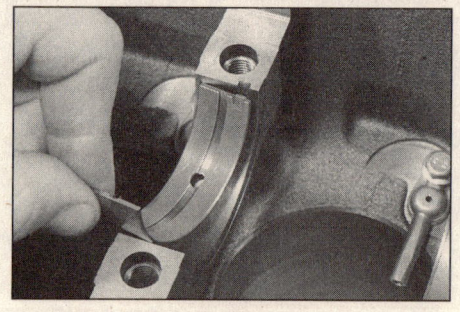

Bearing

Bearing The curved surface on a shaft or in a bore, or the part assembled into either, that permits relative motion between them with minimum wear and friction.

Big-end bearing The bearing in the end of the connecting rod that's attached to the crankshaft.

Bleed nipple A valve on a brake wheel cylinder, caliper or other hydraulic component that is opened to purge the hydraulic system of air. Also called a bleed screw.

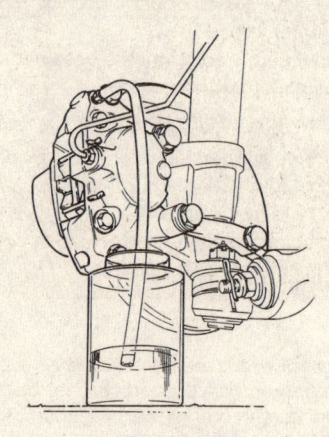

Brake bleeding

Brake bleeding Procedure for removing air from lines of a hydraulic brake system.

Brake disc The component of a disc brake that rotates with the wheels.

Brake drum The component of a drum brake that rotates with the wheels.

Brake linings The friction material which contacts the brake disc or drum to retard the vehicle's speed. The linings are bonded or riveted to the brake pads or shoes.

Brake pads The replaceable friction pads that pinch the brake disc when the brakes are applied. Brake pads consist of a friction material bonded or riveted to a rigid backing plate.

Brake shoe The crescent-shaped carrier to which the brake linings are mounted and which forces the lining against the rotating drum during braking.

Braking systems For more information on braking systems, consult the *Haynes Automotive Brake Manual*.

Breaker bar A long socket wrench handle providing greater leverage.

Bulkhead The insulated partition between the engine and the passenger compartment.

C

Caliper The non-rotating part of a disc-brake assembly that straddles the disc and carries the brake pads. The caliper also contains the hydraulic components that cause the pads to pinch the disc when the brakes are applied. A caliper is also a measuring tool that can be set to measure inside or outside dimensions of an object.

Glossary of technical terms REF•21

Camshaft A rotating shaft on which a series of cam lobes operate the valve mechanisms. The camshaft may be driven by gears, by sprockets and chain or by sprockets and a belt.

Canister A container in an evaporative emission control system; contains activated charcoal granules to trap vapours from the fuel system.

Canister

Carburettor A device which mixes fuel with air in the proper proportions to provide a desired power output from a spark ignition internal combustion engine.

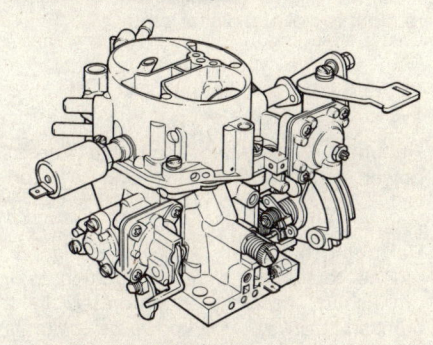

Carburettor

Castellated Resembling the parapets along the top of a castle wall. For example, a castellated balljoint stud nut.

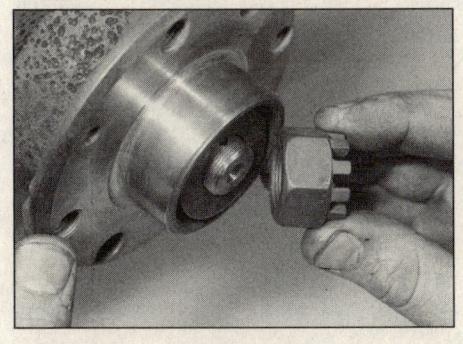

Castellated nut

Castor In wheel alignment, the backward or forward tilt of the steering axis. Castor is positive when the steering axis is inclined rearward at the top.

Catalytic converter A silencer-like device in the exhaust system which converts certain pollutants in the exhaust gases into less harmful substances.

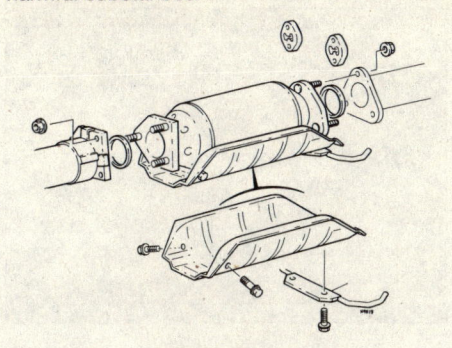

Catalytic converter

Circlip A ring-shaped clip used to prevent endwise movement of cylindrical parts and shafts. An internal circlip is installed in a groove in a housing; an external circlip fits into a groove on the outside of a cylindrical piece such as a shaft.

Clearance The amount of space between two parts. For example, between a piston and a cylinder, between a bearing and a journal, etc.

Coil spring A spiral of elastic steel found in various sizes throughout a vehicle, for example as a springing medium in the suspension and in the valve train.

Compression Reduction in volume, and increase in pressure and temperature, of a gas, caused by squeezing it into a smaller space.

Compression ratio The relationship between cylinder volume when the piston is at top dead centre and cylinder volume when the piston is at bottom dead centre.

Constant velocity (CV) joint A type of universal joint that cancels out vibrations caused by driving power being transmitted through an angle.

Core plug A disc or cup-shaped metal device inserted in a hole in a casting through which core was removed when the casting was formed. Also known as a freeze plug or expansion plug.

Crankcase The lower part of the engine block in which the crankshaft rotates.

Crankshaft The main rotating member, or shaft, running the length of the crankcase, with offset "throws" to which the connecting rods are attached.

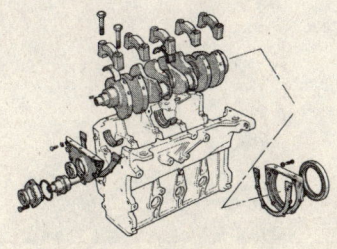

Crankshaft assembly

Crocodile clip See Alligator clip

D

Diagnostic code Code numbers obtained by accessing the diagnostic mode of an engine management computer. This code can be used to determine the area in the system where a malfunction may be located.

Disc brake A brake design incorporating a rotating disc onto which brake pads are squeezed. The resulting friction converts the energy of a moving vehicle into heat.

Double-overhead cam (DOHC) An engine that uses two overhead camshafts, usually one for the intake valves and one for the exhaust valves.

Drivebelt(s) The belt(s) used to drive accessories such as the alternator, water pump, power steering pump, air conditioning compressor, etc. off the crankshaft pulley.

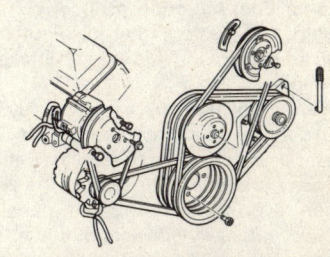

Accessory drivebelts

Driveshaft Any shaft used to transmit motion. Commonly used when referring to the axleshafts on a front wheel drive vehicle.

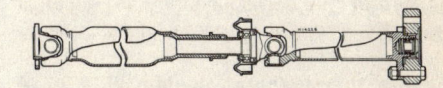

Driveshaft

Drum brake A type of brake using a drum-shaped metal cylinder attached to the inner surface of the wheel. When the brake pedal is pressed, curved brake shoes with friction linings press against the inside of the drum to slow or stop the vehicle.

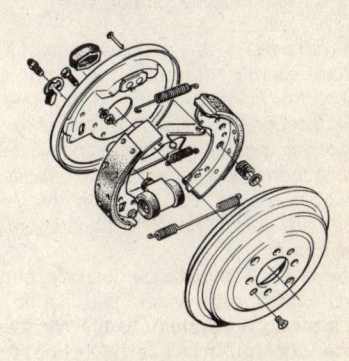

Drum brake assembly

REF•22 Glossary of technical terms

E

EGR valve A valve used to introduce exhaust gases into the intake air stream.

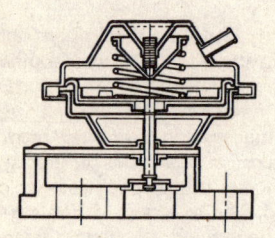

EGR valve

Electronic control unit (ECU) A computer which controls (for instance) ignition and fuel injection systems, or an anti-lock braking system. For more information refer to the *Haynes Automotive Electrical and Electronic Systems Manual*.

Electronic Fuel Injection (EFI) A computer controlled fuel system that distributes fuel through an injector located in each intake port of the engine.

Emergency brake A braking system, independent of the main hydraulic system, that can be used to slow or stop the vehicle if the primary brakes fail, or to hold the vehicle stationary even though the brake pedal isn't depressed. It usually consists of a hand lever that actuates either front or rear brakes mechanically through a series of cables and linkages. Also known as a handbrake or parking brake.

Endfloat The amount of lengthwise movement between two parts. As applied to a crankshaft, the distance that the crankshaft can move forward and back in the cylinder block.

Engine management system (EMS) A computer controlled system which manages the fuel injection and the ignition systems in an integrated fashion.

Exhaust manifold A part with several passages through which exhaust gases leave the engine combustion chambers and enter the exhaust pipe.

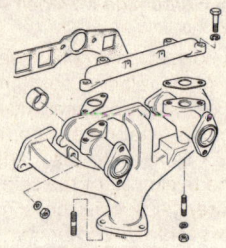

Exhaust manifold

F

Fan clutch A viscous (fluid) drive coupling device which permits variable engine fan speeds in relation to engine speeds.

Feeler blade A thin strip or blade of hardened steel, ground to an exact thickness, used to check or measure clearances between parts.

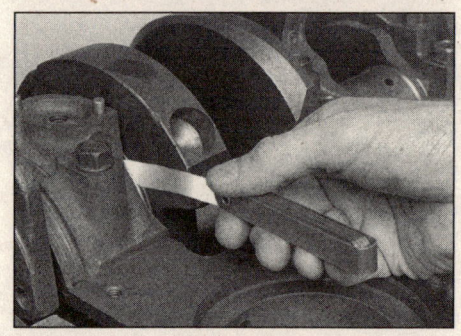

Feeler blade

Firing order The order in which the engine cylinders fire, or deliver their power strokes, beginning with the number one cylinder.

Flywheel A heavy spinning wheel in which energy is absorbed and stored by means of momentum. On cars, the flywheel is attached to the crankshaft to smooth out firing impulses.

Free play The amount of travel before any action takes place. The "looseness" in a linkage, or an assembly of parts, between the initial application of force and actual movement. For example, the distance the brake pedal moves before the pistons in the master cylinder are actuated.

Fuse An electrical device which protects a circuit against accidental overload. The typical fuse contains a soft piece of metal which is calibrated to melt at a predetermined current flow (expressed as amps) and break the circuit.

Fusible link A circuit protection device consisting of a conductor surrounded by heat-resistant insulation. The conductor is smaller than the wire it protects, so it acts as the weakest link in the circuit. Unlike a blown fuse, a failed fusible link must frequently be cut from the wire for replacement.

G

Gap The distance the spark must travel in jumping from the centre electrode to the side electrode in a spark plug. Also refers to the spacing between the points in a contact breaker assembly in a conventional points-type ignition, or to the distance between the reluctor or rotor and the pickup coil in an electronic ignition.

Gasket Any thin, soft material - usually cork, cardboard, asbestos or soft metal - installed between two metal surfaces to ensure a good seal. For instance, the cylinder head gasket seals the joint between the block and the cylinder head.

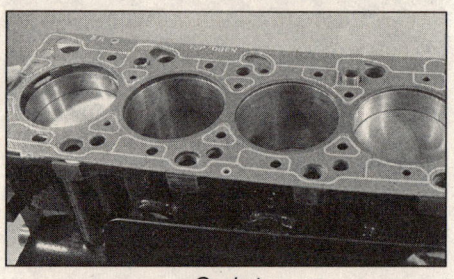

Gasket

Gauge An instrument panel display used to monitor engine conditions. A gauge with a movable pointer on a dial or a fixed scale is an analogue gauge. A gauge with a numerical readout is called a digital gauge.

H

Halfshaft A rotating shaft that transmits power from the final drive unit to a drive wheel, usually when referring to a live rear axle.

Harmonic balancer A device designed to reduce torsion or twisting vibration in the crankshaft. May be incorporated in the crankshaft pulley. Also known as a vibration damper.

Hone An abrasive tool for correcting small irregularities or differences in diameter in an engine cylinder, brake cylinder, etc.

Hydraulic tappet A tappet that utilises hydraulic pressure from the engine's lubrication system to maintain zero clearance (constant contact with both camshaft and valve stem). Automatically adjusts to variation in valve stem length. Hydraulic tappets also reduce valve noise.

I

Ignition timing The moment at which the spark plug fires, usually expressed in the number of crankshaft degrees before the piston reaches the top of its stroke.

Inlet manifold A tube or housing with passages through which flows the air-fuel mixture (carburettor vehicles and vehicles with throttle body injection) or air only (port fuel-injected vehicles) to the port openings in the cylinder head.

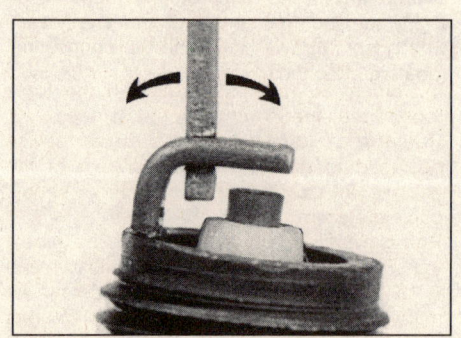

Adjusting spark plug gap

Glossary of technical terms

J
Jump start Starting the engine of a vehicle with a discharged or weak battery by attaching jump leads from the weak battery to a charged or helper battery.

L
Load Sensing Proportioning Valve (LSPV) A brake hydraulic system control valve that works like a proportioning valve, but also takes into consideration the amount of weight carried by the rear axle.
Locknut A nut used to lock an adjustment nut, or other threaded component, in place. For example, a locknut is employed to keep the adjusting nut on the rocker arm in position.
Lockwasher A form of washer designed to prevent an attaching nut from working loose.

M
MacPherson strut A type of front suspension system devised by Earle MacPherson at Ford of England. In its original form, a simple lateral link with the anti-roll bar creates the lower control arm. A long strut - an integral coil spring and shock absorber - is mounted between the body and the steering knuckle. Many modern so-called MacPherson strut systems use a conventional lower A-arm and don't rely on the anti-roll bar for location.
Multimeter An electrical test instrument with the capability to measure voltage, current and resistance.

N
NOx Oxides of Nitrogen. A common toxic pollutant emitted by petrol and diesel engines at higher temperatures.

O
Ohm The unit of electrical resistance. One volt applied to a resistance of one ohm will produce a current of one amp.
Ohmmeter An instrument for measuring electrical resistance.
O-ring A type of sealing ring made of a special rubber-like material; in use, the O-ring is compressed into a groove to provide the sealing action.

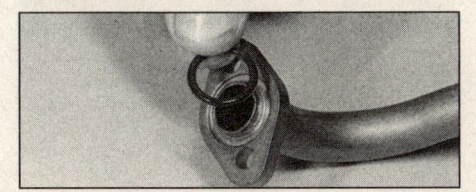

O-ring

Overhead cam (ohc) engine An engine with the camshaft(s) located on top of the cylinder head(s).
Overhead valve (ohv) engine An engine with the valves located in the cylinder head, but with the camshaft located in the engine block.
Oxygen sensor A device installed in the engine exhaust manifold, which senses the oxygen content in the exhaust and converts this information into an electric current. Also called a Lambda sensor.

P
Phillips screw A type of screw head having a cross instead of a slot for a corresponding type of screwdriver.
Plastigage A thin strip of plastic thread, available in different sizes, used for measuring clearances. For example, a strip of Plastigage is laid across a bearing journal. The parts are assembled and dismantled; the width of the crushed strip indicates the clearance between journal and bearing.

Plastigage

Propeller shaft The long hollow tube with universal joints at both ends that carries power from the transmission to the differential on front-engined rear wheel drive vehicles.
Proportioning valve A hydraulic control valve which limits the amount of pressure to the rear brakes during panic stops to prevent wheel lock-up.

R
Rack-and-pinion steering A steering system with a pinion gear on the end of the steering shaft that mates with a rack (think of a geared wheel opened up and laid flat). When the steering wheel is turned, the pinion turns, moving the rack to the left or right. This movement is transmitted through the track rods to the steering arms at the wheels.
Radiator A liquid-to-air heat transfer device designed to reduce the temperature of the coolant in an internal combustion engine cooling system.
Refrigerant Any substance used as a heat transfer agent in an air-conditioning system. R-12 has been the principle refrigerant for many years; recently, however, manufacturers have begun using R-134a, a non-CFC substance that is considered less harmful to the ozone in the upper atmosphere.
Rocker arm A lever arm that rocks on a shaft or pivots on a stud. In an overhead valve engine, the rocker arm converts the upward movement of the pushrod into a downward movement to open a valve.
Rotor In a distributor, the rotating device inside the cap that connects the centre electrode and the outer terminals as it turns, distributing the high voltage from the coil secondary winding to the proper spark plug. Also, that part of an alternator which rotates inside the stator. Also, the rotating assembly of a turbocharger, including the compressor wheel, shaft and turbine wheel.
Runout The amount of wobble (in-and-out movement) of a gear or wheel as it's rotated. The amount a shaft rotates "out-of-true." The out-of-round condition of a rotating part.

S
Sealant A liquid or paste used to prevent leakage at a joint. Sometimes used in conjunction with a gasket.
Sealed beam lamp An older headlight design which integrates the reflector, lens and filaments into a hermetically-sealed one-piece unit. When a filament burns out or the lens cracks, the entire unit is simply replaced.
Serpentine drivebelt A single, long, wide accessory drivebelt that's used on some newer vehicles to drive all the accessories, instead of a series of smaller, shorter belts. Serpentine drivebelts are usually tensioned by an automatic tensioner.

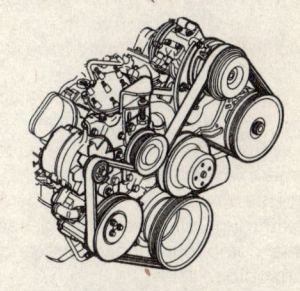

Serpentine drivebelt

Shim Thin spacer, commonly used to adjust the clearance or relative positions between two parts. For example, shims inserted into or under bucket tappets control valve clearances. Clearance is adjusted by changing the thickness of the shim.
Slide hammer A special puller that screws into or hooks onto a component such as a shaft or bearing; a heavy sliding handle on the shaft bottoms against the end of the shaft to knock the component free.
Sprocket A tooth or projection on the periphery of a wheel, shaped to engage with a chain or drivebelt. Commonly used to refer to the sprocket wheel itself.
Starter inhibitor switch On vehicles with an

REF•24 Glossary of technical terms

automatic transmission, a switch that prevents starting if the vehicle is not in Neutral or Park.
Strut See MacPherson strut.

T

Tappet A cylindrical component which transmits motion from the cam to the valve stem, either directly or via a pushrod and rocker arm. Also called a cam follower.
Thermostat A heat-controlled valve that regulates the flow of coolant between the cylinder block and the radiator, so maintaining optimum engine operating temperature. A thermostat is also used in some air cleaners in which the temperature is regulated.
Thrust bearing The bearing in the clutch assembly that is moved in to the release levers by clutch pedal action to disengage the clutch. Also referred to as a release bearing.
Timing belt A toothed belt which drives the camshaft. Serious engine damage may result if it breaks in service.
Timing chain A chain which drives the camshaft.
Toe-in The amount the front wheels are closer together at the front than at the rear. On rear wheel drive vehicles, a slight amount of toe-in is usually specified to keep the front wheels running parallel on the road by offsetting other forces that tend to spread the wheels apart.
Toe-out The amount the front wheels are closer together at the rear than at the front. On front wheel drive vehicles, a slight amount of toe-out is usually specified.
Tools For full information on choosing and using tools, refer to the *Haynes Automotive Tools Manual*.
Tracer A stripe of a second colour applied to a wire insulator to distinguish that wire from another one with the same colour insulator.
Tune-up A process of accurate and careful adjustments and parts replacement to obtain the best possible engine performance.
Turbocharger A centrifugal device, driven by exhaust gases, that pressurises the intake air. Normally used to increase the power output from a given engine displacement, but can also be used primarily to reduce exhaust emissions (as on VW's "Umwelt" Diesel engine).

U

Universal joint or U-joint A double-pivoted connection for transmitting power from a driving to a driven shaft through an angle. A U-joint consists of two Y-shaped yokes and a cross-shaped member called the spider.

V

Valve A device through which the flow of liquid, gas, vacuum, or loose material in bulk may be started, stopped, or regulated by a movable part that opens, shuts, or partially obstructs one or more ports or passageways. A valve is also the movable part of such a device.
Valve clearance The clearance between the valve tip (the end of the valve stem) and the rocker arm or tappet. The valve clearance is measured when the valve is closed.
Vernier caliper A precision measuring instrument that measures inside and outside dimensions. Not quite as accurate as a micrometer, but more convenient.
Viscosity The thickness of a liquid or its resistance to flow.
Volt A unit for expressing electrical "pressure" in a circuit. One volt that will produce a current of one ampere through a resistance of one ohm.

W

Welding Various processes used to join metal items by heating the areas to be joined to a molten state and fusing them together. For more information refer to the *Haynes Automotive Welding Manual*.
Wiring diagram A drawing portraying the components and wires in a vehicle's electrical system, using standardised symbols. For more information refer to the *Haynes Automotive Electrical and Electronic Systems Manual*.

Index

Note: *References throughout this index are in the form - "Chapter number" • "Page number"*

A

ABS - 9•8
Accelerator cable - 4A•3
Accelerator pedal - 4A•4
Acknowledgements - 0•4
Aerial - 12•11
Air cleaner - 1•15, 4A•1
Air conditioning control panel - 3•4
Air conditioning system - 3•6
Airbag - 12•12
Alternator - 5A•3
Anti-roll bar - 10•3, 10•6
Antifreeze - 0•11, 0•16, 1•11, 3•2
ATF - 0•16, 1•10, 1•14
Automatic transmission - 7B•1 et seq
    fault finding - REF•12, REF•15
    fluid - 0•16, 1•10, 1•14
    gear selector - 7B•2
    kickdown cable - 7B•2
    oil seals - 7B•4
    overdrive switch - 7B•3
    removal and refitting - 7B•4
    reversing light switch/inhibitor - 7B•3
Auxiliary shaft - 2B•7
Axle - 8•2, 8•3

B

Battery:
    booster - 0•7
    checks - 0•15
    connections - 0•6
    removal and refitting - 5A•2
    testing and charging - 5A•2
Bearings - 2B•10
Bleeding the brakes - 9•2
Bleeding the clutch - 6•3
Bleeding the power steering - 10•9
Body damage - 11•2
Body electrical systems - 12•1 et seq
Bodywork and fittings - 11•1 et seq
Bonnet - 11•3
Bonnet release cable - 11•5
Boot lid - 11•4
Boot lock - 11•7
Brake fluid - 0•12, 0•16, 1•12

Braking system - 9•1 et seq
    ABS general information - 9•8
    ABS components - 9•8
    bleeding - 9•2
    brake fluid - 0•12, 0•16, 1•12
    brake pads - 1•6
    brake line check - 1•9
    brake pads front - 9•3
    brake pads rear - 9•4
    brake disc front - 9•4
    brake disc rear - 9•5
    brake caliper front - 9•5
    brake caliper rear - 9•6
    brake pedal - 9•7
    brake stop light switch - 12•5
    fault finding - REF•12, REF•16
    handbrake check and adjustment - 1•7
    handbrake shoes - 9•7
    handbrake cables - 9•8
    handbrake warning switch - 12•5
    hydraulic pipes and hoses - 9•3
    master cylinder - 9•6
    road test - 1•10
    servo - 9•7
Bulbs - 0•15, 12•2
    failure warning system - 12•9
    renewal (exterior lights) - 12•7
    renewal (interior lights) - 12•8
Bumpers - 11•13

C

Cables:
    bonnet release - 11•5
    clutch - 6•1, 1•8
    handbrake - 9•8
    kickdown - 7B•2
    throttle - 4A•3
Caliper brake - 9•5, 9•6
Camshaft cover - 2A•3
Camshaft drivebelt - 2A•3
Camshaft oil seals - 2A•4
Capacities - 1•2
Carpets - 11•2
Catalytic converter - 4B•2
Central locking components - 11•8
Cigarette lighter - 12•11

Clutch - 6•1 et seq
    bleeding - 6•3
    cable - 1•8, 6•1
    fault finding - REF•12, REF•15
    fluid - 0•12, 0•16
    hydraulic check - 1•8
    inspection - 6•4
    master cylinder - 6•2
    pedal - 6•1
    refitting - 6•4
    release bearing - 6•4
    removal - 6•3
    road test - 1•10
    slave cylinder - 6•2
Coil - 5B•4
Compression test - 2A•3
Connecting rods - 2B•8, 2B•9, 2B•12
Console - 11•12, 11•13
Contents - 0•2
Conversion factors - REF•2
Coolant - 0•11, 0•16, 1•11, 3•2
Cooling, heating and air conditioning systems - 3•1 et seq
    air conditioning control panel - 3•4
    air conditioning system - 3•6
    antifreeze - 0•11, 0•16, 1•11, 3•2
    coolant draining - 1•11
    coolant flushing - 1•11
    coolant filling - 1•12
    fan - 3•2
    fault finding - REF•12, REF•14
    heater control panel - 3•4
    heater matrix - 3•5
    heater blower motor - 3•5
    heating and ventilation system - 3•4
    hoses - 3•1
    oil coolers - 3•4
    radiator - 3•2
    switches - 3•3
    thermostat - 3•3
    water pump - 3•3
Crankshaft - 2B•8, 2B•10, 2B•12
Crankshaft oil seals - 2A•7
Cruise control - 4A•7
Cylinder block - 2B•8
Cylinder head - 2A•6, 2B•5, 2B•6, 2B•7

D

Dents - 11•2
Diagnostic system - 5B•2
Dimensions - REF•1
Distributor - 1•12, 5B•5

Index

Doors - 11•4
  handles, locks and latches - 11•7
  interior trim - 11•5
  mirror - 11•8, 11•9
  weatherstrip - 11•9
  windows - 11•6
Drivebelts :
  air conditioning compressor - 1•11
  alternator - 1•11
  camshaft - 2A•3
  general - 1•11
  steering pump - 1•11

E

Earth fault - 12•3
Electrical fault finding - 12•3, REF•18
Electronic control module - 5B•5
Emission control equipment - 1•15
Emission control systems - *4B•1 et seq*
Engine removal and overhaul procedures - *2B•1 et seq*
Engine in-car repair procedures - *2A•1 et seq*
  auxiliary shaft - 2B•7
  bearings - 2B•10
  camshaft cover - 2A•3
  camshaft drivebelt - 2A•3
  camshaft oil seals - 2A•4
  compression test - 2A•3
  crankshaft - 2B•8, 2B•10, 2B•12
  crankshaft oil seals - 2A•7
  cylinder block - 2B•8
  cylinder head - 2A•6, 2B•5, 2B•6, 2B•7
  fault finding - REF•12, REF•13
  flywheel - 2A•8
  mountings - 2A•8
  oil - 0•11, 0•16, 1•6
  oil pump - 2A•7
  overhaul - 2B•3, 2B•5, 2B•11
  piston rings - 2B•11
  piston/connecting rods - 2B•8, 2B•9, 2B•12
  refitting - 2B•4
  removal - 2B•4
  separation - 2B•4
  sump - 2A•6
  tappets - 2A•5
  valves - 1•14, 2B•6
Exhaust manifold - 4A•8
Exhaust system - 1•9, 4A•9

F

Facia - 11•13
Fan - 3•2
Fault finding - *REF•12 et seq*
  automatic transmission - REF•12, REF•15
  braking system - REF•12, REF•16
  clutch - REF•12, REF•15
  cooling system - REF•12, REF•14
  electrical system - 12•3, REF•18
  engine - REF•12, REF•13
  fuel and exhaust systems - REF•12, REF•15
  manual transmission - REF•12, REF•15
  propeller shaft - REF•12, REF•16
  rear axle - REF•12, REF•16
  steering - REF•12, REF•17
  suspension - REF•12, REF•17

Fluid leaks - 0•9, 1•6
Fluids - 0•16
Flywheel - 2A•8
Fuel and exhaust systems - *4A•1 et seq*
  air cleaner - 1•15, 4A•1
  catalytic converter - 4B•2
  cruise control - 4A•7
  emission control equipment - 1•15
  exhaust system - 4A•9
  exhaust system check - 1•9
  fault finding - REF•12, REF•15
  fuel filter - 1•15
  fuel injection system
    general information - 4A•4
  fuel injection system testing - 4A•5
  fuel injection system components - 4A•6
  fuel line check - 1•9
  fuel tank - 4A•2
  fuel tank pump - 4A•2
  intercooler - 4A•9
  main fuel pump - 4A•3
  manifolds - 4A•8
  throttle cable - 4A•3
  throttle pedal - 4A•4
  turbocharger - 4A•8, 4A•9
Fuses - 0•15, 12•1, 12•4

G

Gear lever manual - 7A•2
Gear selector automatic - 7B•2
Gearbox - see Manual or Automatic transmission
Glass - 11•6, 11•9
Glossary of technical terms - REF•20
Glovebox - 11•12
Grille panel - 11•14

H

Handbrake:
  cables - 9•8
  check - 1•7
  shoes - 9•7
Head restraints - 11•10
Headlight beam alignment - 12•9
Headlight unit - 12•8
Headlight washers - 12•9
Heated rear window - 12•11
Heated seat elements - 11•11
Heater blower motor - 3•5
Heater matrix - 3•5
Heater control panel - 3•4
Heating and ventilation system - 3•4
Horn removal and refitting - 12•9
Hose check - 1•6
Hoses cooling system - 3•1
Hoses brake - 9•3
HT coil - 5B•4
HT lead - 1•12
Hydraulic pipes and hoses - 9•3
Hydraulic system brakes bleeding - 9•2
Hydraulic system clutch bleeding - 6•3

I

Ignition system - *5B•1 et seq*
  diagnostic system - 5B•2
  distributor - 5B•5
  distributor - 1•12, 5B•5
  ECU - 5B•5
  HT coil - 5B•4
  HT lead - 1•12
  sensors - 5B•5
  spark plugs - 1•13
  starter/switch - 10•8, 12•5
  testing - 5B•2
  timing - 5B•5
Indicator unit - 12•9
Inlet manifold - 4A•8
Instrument cluster - 12•5, 12•6
Intercooler - 4A•9
Introduction - 0•4

J

Jacking and vehicle support - REF•5
Jump starting - 0•7

K

Kickdown cable - 7B•2

L

Leaks - 0•9, 1•6
Light clusters rear - 12•9
Locks:
  boot - 11•7
  central locking components - 11•8
  door - 11•7
  steering column - 10•8
  tailgate - 11•8
Lubricants and fluids - 0•16

M

Maintenance schedule - 1•3
Manifolds - 4A•8
Manual transmission and overdrive - *7A•1 et seq*
  fault finding - REF•12, REF•15
  gear lever - 7A•2
  oil - 0•16, 1•8
  oil seals - 7A•3
  overdrive unit - 7A•4
  overdrive switches - 7A•4
  overhaul - 7A•4
  refitting - 7A•4
  removal - 7A•3
  reversing light switch - 7A•3
Master cylinder brake - 9•6
Master cylinder clutch - 6•2
Mirrors - 11•8, 11•9
MOT test checks - REF•8

O

Oil coolers - 3•4
Oil engine - 0•11, 0•16, 1•6
Oil manual transmission - 0•16, 1•8

Index

Oil pressure warning light switch - 5A•4
Oil pump - 2A•7
Oil seals general - REF•4
  automatic transmission - 7B•4
  camshaft - 2A•4
  crankshaft - 2A•7
  manual transmission - 7A•3
  pinion - 8•3
Overdrive switches - 7A•4, 7B•3
Overdrive unit - 7A•4

P

Painting - 11•2
Panhard rod - 10•6
Parts - REF•3
Pedals:
  brake - 9•7
  clutch - 6•1
  throttle - 4A•4
Piston rings - 2B•11
Piston/connecting rods - 2B•8, 2B•9, 2B•12
Power steering fluid - 0•13, 0•16
Power steering gear - 10•8
Power steering pump - 10•9
Power steering system bleeding - 10•9
Propeller shaft and rear axle - 8•1 et seq
  centre bearing - 8•2
  check - 1•9
  fault finding - REF•12, REF•16
  halfshaft, bearing & seals - 8•3
  pinion oil seal - 8•3
  rear axle - 8•2, 8•3
  removal and refitting - 8•2
  rubber coupling - 8•1
  universal joints - 1•9, 8•2

R

Radiator - 3•2
Radio/cassette anti-theft system - REF•5
Radio/cassette player - 12•11
Rear axle - 8•2, 8•3
Rear axle fault finding - REF•12, REF•16
Rear console - 11•13
Relays - 12•4
Repair procedures general - REF•4
Respraying - 11•2
Reversing light switch - 7A•3
**Reversing light switch/
  starter inhibitor** - 7B•3
Road test - 1•10
Routine maintenance and servicing - 1•1 et seq
Rust - 11•2

S

Safety first! - 0•5
Screen washer fluid - 0•12

Seats - 11•10
  adjusters - 11•10
  belt check - 1•9
  belts - 11•11
  head restraints - 11•10
  heating elements - 11•11
Servo brakes - 9•7
Shock absorber 10•6
Short circuit - 12•3
Slave cylinder clutch - 6•2
Spare parts - REF•3
Spark plugs - 1•13
Speedometer sender unit - 12•7
Spoiler - 11•13
Springs - 10•6
Starter motor - 5A•4
Starting problems - 0•6, 5B•2
Starting and charging systems - 5A•1 et seq
  alternator - 5A•3
  battery testing and charging - 5A•2
  battery removal and refitting - 5A•2
  starter motor - 5A•4
  testing - 5A•3
Steering - 10•1 et seq
  angles - 10•9
  anti-roll bar - 10•3, 10•6
  check - 1•7
  column - 10•7
  column lock/ignition switch - 10•8
  fault finding - REF•12, REF•17
  front control arm - 10•3
  front radius rod - 10•3
  power steering fluid - 0•13, 0•16
  power steering gear - 10•8
  power steering system bleeding - 10•9
  power steering pump - 10•9
  rack bellows - 10•9
  road test - 1•10
  track rod ends - 10•9
  wheel - 10•7
  wheel alignment - 10•9
  wheel bearings - 10•2
Subframe and mountings - 10•5
Sump - 2A•6
Sunroof - 11•14
**Supplementary Restraint System
  (SRS)** - 12•12
Suspension and steering - 10•1 et seq
  check - 1•7
  fault finding - REF•12, REF•17
  front strut - 10•4
  Panhard rod - 10•6
  rear shock absorber - 10•6
  rear spring - 10•6
  rear subframe and mountings - 10•5
  rear torque rods - 10•5
  rear trailing arm - 10•5
  road test - 1•10
  rubber bushes - 10•5

Switches:
  brake stop light - 12•5
  cooling system - 3•3
  door/tailgate - 12•5
  facia panel - 12•5
  handbrake warning - 12•5
  horn - 12•5
  ignition/starter - 10•8, 12•5
  oil pressure warning light - 5A•4
  overdrive - 7A•4, 7B•3
  rear console - 12•5
  reversing light - 7A•3
  starting inhibitor - 7B•3
  steering column - 12•4
  window/mirror control - 12•5

T

Tailgate - 11•4
  interior trim - 11•6
  lock - 11•8
  washers - 12•9
Tappets - 2A•5
Thermostat - 3•3
Throttle cable - 4A•3
Throttle pedal - 4A•4
Timing - 5B•5
Tools and working facilities - REF•6
Towing - 0•9
Track rod ends - 10•9
Turbocharger - 4A•8
Tyre condition - 0•14
Tyre pressures - 0•16

U

Underbody points - 1•4, 1•5
Underbonnet points - 0•10, 1•4
Universal joints - 1•9, 8•2
Upholstery - 11•2

V

Valves - 1•14, 2B•6
Vehicle identification - REF•3

W

Washer fluid - 0•12
Washers - 12•9
Water pump - 3•3
Weatherstrip - 11•9
Weekly checks - 0•10 et seq
Weights - REF•1
Wheel alignment - 10•9
Wheel bearings - 10•2
Wheel changing - 0•8
Window lift mechanism - 11•6
Windows - 11•6, 12•11
Windscreen - 11•6
Windscreen washers - 12•9
Wiper arms - 12•10
Wiper blades - 0•13
Wiper motors - 12•10
Wiring diagrams 12•13 et seq

Haynes Manuals – The Complete List

Title	Book No.
ALFA ROMEO	
Alfa Romeo Alfasud/Sprint (74 - 88) up to F	0292
Alfa Romeo Alfetta (73 - 87) up to E	0531
AUDI	
Audi 80, 90 (79 - Oct 86) up to D & Coupe (81 - Nov 88) up to F	0605
Audi 80, 90 (Oct 86 - 90) D to H & Coupe (Nov 88 - 90) F to H	1491
Audi 100 (Oct 82 - 90) up to H & 200 (Feb 84 - Oct 89) A to G	0907
Audi 100 & A6 Petrol & Diesel (May 91 - May 97) H to P	3504
Audi A4 (95 - Feb 00) M to V	3575
AUSTIN	
Austin A35 & A40 (56 - 67)*	0118
Austin Allegro 1100, 1300, 1.0, 1.1 & 1.3 (73 - 82)*	0164
Austin Healey 100/6 & 3000 (56 - 68)*	0049
Austin/MG/Rover Maestro 1.3 & 1.6 (83 - 95) up to M	0922
Austin Metro (80 - May 90) up to G	0718
Austin/Rover Montego 1.3 & 1.6 (84 - 94) A to L	1066
Austin/MG/Rover Montego 2.0 (84 - 95) A to M	1067
Mini (59 - 69) up to H	0527
Mini (69 - 01) up to X-reg	0646
Austin/Rover 2.0 litre Diesel Engine (86 - 93) C to L	1857
BEDFORD	
Bedford CF (69 - 87) up to E	0163
Bedford/Vauxhall Rascal & Suzuki Supercarry (86 - Oct 94) C to M	3015
BMW	
BMW 1500, 1502, 1600, 1602, 2000 & 2002 (59 - 77)*	0240
BMW 316, 320 & 320i (4-cyl) (75 - Feb 83) up to Y	0276
BMW 320, 320i, 323i & 325i (6-cyl) (Oct 77 - Sept 87) up to E	0815
BMW 3-Series (Apr 91 - 96) H to N	3210
BMW 3- & 5-Series (sohc) (81 - 91) up to J	1948
BMW 520i & 525e (Oct 81 - June 88) up to E	1560
BMW 525, 528 & 528i (73 - Sept 81) up to X*	0632
CHRYSLER	
Chrysler PT Cruiser (00 - 03) W-reg onwards	4058
CITROËN	
Citroën 2CV, Ami & Dyane (67 - 90) up to H	0196
Citroën AX Petrol & Diesel (87 - 97) D to P	3014
Citroën BX (83 - 94) A to L	0908
Citroën C15 Van Petrol & Diesel (89 - Oct 98) F to S	3509
Citroën CX (75 - 88) up to F	0528
Citroën Saxo Petrol & Diesel (96 - 01) N to X	3506
Citroën Visa (79 - 88) up to F	0620
Citroën Xantia Petrol & Diesel (93 - 98) K to S	3082
Citroën XM Petrol & Diesel (89 - 00) G to X	3451
Citroën Xsara Petrol & Diesel (97 - Sept 00) R to W	3751
Citroën Xsara Picasso Petrol & Diesel (00 - 02) W-reg. onwards	3944
Citroën ZX Diesel (91 - 98) J to S	1922
Citroën ZX Petrol (91 - 98) H to S	1881
Citroën 1.7 & 1.9 litre Diesel Engine (84 - 96) A to N	1379
FIAT	
Fiat 126 (73 - 87)*	0305
Fiat 500 (57 - 73) up to M	0090
Fiat Bravo & Brava (95 - 00) N to W	3572
Fiat Cinquecento (93 - 98) K to R	3501
Fiat Panda (81 - 95) up to M	0793
Fiat Punto Petrol & Diesel (94 - Oct 99) L to V	3251
Fiat Regata (84 - 88) A to F	1167
Fiat Tipo (88 - 91) E to J	1625
Fiat Uno (83 - 95) up to M	0923
Fiat X1/9 (74 - 89) up to G	0273

Title	Book No.
FORD	
Ford Anglia (59 - 68)*	0001
Ford Capri II (& III) 1.6 & 2.0 (74 - 87) up to E	0283
Ford Capri II (& III) 2.8 & 3.0 (74 - 87) up to E	1309
Ford Cortina Mk III 1300 & 1600 (70 - 76)*	0070
Ford Cortina Mk IV (& V) 1.6 & 2.0 (76 - 83)*	0343
Ford Cortina Mk IV (& V) 2.3 V6 (77 - 83)*	0426
Ford Escort Mk I 1100 & 1300 (68 - 74)*	0171
Ford Escort Mk I Mexico, RS 1600 & RS 2000 (70 - 74)*	0139
Ford Escort Mk II Mexico, RS 1800 & RS 2000 (75 - 80)*	0735
Ford Escort (75 - Aug 80)*	0280
Ford Escort (Sept 80 - Sept 90) up to H	0686
Ford Escort & Orion (Sept 90 - 00) H to X	1737
Ford Fiesta (76 - Aug 83) up to Y	0334
Ford Fiesta (Aug 83 - Feb 89) A to F	1030
Ford Fiesta (Feb 89 - Oct 95) F to N	1595
Ford Fiesta (Oct 95 - 01) N-reg. onwards	3397
Ford Focus (98 - 01) S to Y	3759
Ford Galaxy Petrol & Diesel (95 - Aug 00) M to W	3984
Ford Granada (Sept 77 - Feb 85) up to B	0481
Ford Granada & Scorpio (Mar 85 - 94) B to M	1245
Ford Ka (96 - 02) P-reg. onwards	3570
Ford Mondeo Petrol (93 - 99) K to T	1923
Ford Mondeo (Oct 00 - 03) X-reg. onwards	3990
Ford Mondeo Diesel (93 - 96) L to N	3465
Ford Orion (83 - Sept 90) up to H	1009
Ford Sierra 4 cyl. (82 - 93) up to K	0903
Ford Sierra V6 (82 - 91) up to J	0904
Ford Transit Petrol (Mk 2) (78 - Jan 86) up to C	0719
Ford Transit Petrol (Mk 3) (Feb 86 - 89) C to G	1468
Ford Transit Diesel (Feb 86 - 99) C to T	3019
Ford 1.6 & 1.8 litre Diesel Engine (84 - 96) A to N	1172
Ford 2.1, 2.3 & 2.5 litre Diesel Engine (77 - 90) up to H	1606
FREIGHT ROVER	
Freight Rover Sherpa (74 - 87) up to E	0463
HILLMAN	
Hillman Avenger (70 - 82) up to Y	0037
Hillman Imp (63 - 76) *	0022
HONDA	
Honda Accord (76 - Feb 84) up to A	0351
Honda Civic (Feb 84 - Oct 87) A to E	1226
Honda Civic (Nov 91 - 96) J to N	3199
Honda Civic (Mar 95 - 01) M to X	4050
HYUNDAI	
Hyundai Pony (85 - 94) C to M	3398
JAGUAR	
Jaguar E Type (61 - 72) up to L	0140
Jaguar MkI & II, 240 & 340 (55 - 69)*	0098
Jaguar XJ6, XJ & Sovereign; Daimler Sovereign (68 - Oct 86) up to D	0242
Jaguar XJ6 & Sovereign (Oct 86 - Sept 94) D to M	3261
Jaguar XJ12, XJS & Sovereign; Daimler Double Six (72 - 88) up to F	0478
JEEP	
Jeep Cherokee Petrol (93 - 96) K to N	1943
LADA	
Lada 1200, 1300, 1500 & 1600 (74 - 91) up to J	0413
Lada Samara (87 - 91) D to J	1610
LAND ROVER	
Land Rover 90, 110 & Defender Diesel (83 - 95) up to N	3017
Land Rover Discovery Petrol & Diesel (89 - 98) G to S	3016
Land Rover Freelander (97 - 02) R-reg. onwards	3929
Land Rover Series IIA & III Diesel (58 - 85) up to C	0529
Land Rover Series II, IIA & III Petrol (58 - 85) up to C	0314
MAZDA	
Mazda 323 (Mar 81 - Oct 89) up to G	1608

Title	Book No.
Mazda 323 (Oct 89 - 98) G to R	3455
Mazda 626 (May 83 - Sept 87) up to E	0929
Mazda B-1600, B-1800 & B-2000 Pick-up (72 - 88) up to F	0267
Mazda RX-7 (79 - 85)*	0460
MERCEDES-BENZ	
Mercedes-Benz 190, 190E & 190D Petrol & Diesel (83 - 93) A to L	3450
Mercedes-Benz 200, 240, 300 Diesel (Oct 76 - 85) up to C	1114
Mercedes-Benz 250 & 280 (68 - 72) up to L	0346
Mercedes-Benz 250 & 280 (123 Series) (Oct 76 - 84) up to B	0677
Mercedes-Benz 124 Series (85 - Aug 93) C to K	3253
Mercedes-Benz C-Class Petrol & Diesel (93 - Aug 00) L to W	3511
MG	
MGA (55 - 62)*	0475
MGB (62 - 80) up to W	0111
MG Midget & AH Sprite (58 - 80) up to W	0265
MITSUBISHI	
Mitsubishi Shogun & L200 Pick-Ups (83 - 94) up to M	1944
MORRIS	
Morris Ital 1.3 (80 - 84) up to B	0705
Morris Minor 1000 (56 - 71) up to K	0024
NISSAN	
Nissan Almera (Oct 95 - Feb 00) N - V reg	4053
Nissan Bluebird (May 84 - Mar 86) A to C	1223
Nissan Bluebird (Mar 86 - 90) C to H	1473
Nissan Cherry (Sept 82 - 86) up to D	1031
Nissan Micra (83 - Jan 93) up to K	0931
Nissan Micra (93 - 99) K to T	3254
Nissan Primera (90 - Aug 99) H to T	1851
Nissan Stanza (82 - 86) up to D	0824
Nissan Sunny (May 82 - Oct 86) up to D	0895
Nissan Sunny (Oct 86 - Mar 91) D to H	1378
Nissan Sunny (Apr 91 - 95) H to N	3219
OPEL	
Opel Ascona & Manta (B Series) (Sept 75 - 88) up to F	0316
Opel Ascona (81 - 88) *(Not available in UK see Vauxhall Cavalier 0812)*	3215
Opel Astra (Oct 91 - Feb 98) *(Not available in UK see Vauxhall Astra 1832)*	3156
Opel Astra & Zafira Diesel (Feb 98 - Sept 00) *(See Astra & Zafira Diesel Book No. 3797)*	
Opel Astra & Zafira Petrol (Feb 98 - Sept 00) *(See Vauxhall/Opel Astra & Zafira Petrol Book No. 3758)*	
Opel Calibra (90 - 98) *(See Vauxhall/Opel Calibra Book No. 3502)*	
Opel Corsa (83 - Mar 93) *(Not available in UK see Vauxhall Nova 0909)*	3160
Opel Corsa (Mar 93 - 97) *(Not available in UK see Vauxhall Corsa 1985)*	3159
Opel Frontera Petrol & Diesel (91 - 98) *(See Vauxhall/Opel Frontera Book No. 3454)*	
Opel Kadett (Nov 79 - Oct 84) up to B	0634
Opel Kadett (Oct 84 - Oct 91) *(Not available in UK see Vauxhall Astra & Belmont 1136)*	3196
Opel Omega & Senator (86 - 94) *(Not available in UK see Vauxhall Carlton & Senator 1469)*	3157
Opel Omega (94 - 99) *(See Vauxhall/Opel Omega Book No. 3510)*	
Opel Rekord (Feb 78 - Oct 86) up to D	0543
Opel Vectra (Oct 88 - Oct 95) *(Not available in UK see Vauxhall Cavalier 1570)*	3158
Opel Vectra Petrol & Diesel (95 - 98) *(Not available in UK see Vauxhall Vectra 3396)*	3523

* Classic reprint

Title	Book No.
PEUGEOT	
Peugeot 106 Petrol & Diesel (91 - 02) J-reg. onwards	1882
Peugeot 205 Petrol (83 - 97) A to P	0932
Peugeot 206 Petrol and Diesel (98 - 01) S to X	3757
Peugeot 305 (78 - 89) up to G*	0538
Peugeot 306 Petrol & Diesel (93 - 99) K to T	3073
Peugeot 309 (86 - 93) C to K	1266
Peugeot 405 Petrol (88 - 97) E to P	1559
Peugeot 405 Diesel (88 - 97) E to P	3198
Peugeot 406 Petrol & Diesel (96 - 97) N to R	3394
Peugeot 406 Petrol & Diesel (Mar 99 - 02) T-reg onwards	3982
Peugeot 505 (79 - 89) up to G	0762
Peugeot 1.7/1.8 & 1.9 litre Diesel Engine (82 - 96) up to N	0950
Peugeot 2.0, 2.1, 2.3 & 2.5 litre Diesel Engines (74 - 90) up to H	1607
PORSCHE	
Porsche 911 (65 - 85) up to C	0264
Porsche 924 & 924 Turbo (76 - 85) up to C	0397
PROTON	
Proton (89 - 97) F to P	3255
RANGE ROVER	
Range Rover V8 (70 - Oct 92) up to K	0606
RELIANT	
Reliant Robin & Kitten (73 - 83) up to A	0436
RENAULT	
Renault 4 (61 - 86)*	0072
Renault 5 (Feb 85 - 96) B to N	1219
Renault 9 & 11 (82 - 89) up to F	0822
Renault 18 (79 - 86) up to D	0598
Renault 19 Petrol (89 - 96) F to N	1646
Renault 19 Diesel (89 - 96) F to N	1946
Renault 21 (86 - 94) C to M	1397
Renault 25 (84 - 92) B to K	1228
Renault Clio Petrol (91 - May 98) H to R	1853
Renault Clio Diesel (91 - June 96) H to N	3031
Renault Clio Petrol & Diesel (May 98 - May 01) R to Y	3906
Renault Espace Petrol & Diesel (85 - 96) C to N	3197
Renault Fuego (80 - 86)*	0764
Renault Laguna Petrol & Diesel (94 - 00) L to W	3252
Renault Mégane & Scénic Petrol & Diesel (96 - 98) N to R	3395
Renault Mégane & Scénic Petrol & Diesel (Apr 99 - 02) T-reg onwards	3916
ROVER	
Rover 213 & 216 (84 - 89) A to G	1116
Rover 214 & 414 (89 - 96) G to N	1689
Rover 216 & 416 (89 - 96) G to N	1830
Rover 211, 214, 216, 218 & 220 Petrol & Diesel (Dec 95 - 98) N to R	3399
Rover 414, 416 & 420 Petrol & Diesel (May 95 - 98) M to R	3453
Rover 618, 620 & 623 (93 - 97) K to P	3257
Rover 820, 825 & 827 (86 - 95) D to N	1380
Rover 3500 (76 - 87) up to E	0365
Rover Metro, 111 & 114 (May 90 - 98) G to S	1711
SAAB	
Saab 90, 99 & 900 (79 - Oct 93) up to L	0765
Saab 95 & 96 (66 - 76)*	0198
Saab 99 (69 - 79)*	0247
Saab 900 (Oct 93 - 98) L to R	3512
Saab 9000 (4-cyl) (85 - 98) C to S	1686
SEAT	
Seat Ibiza & Cordoba Petrol & Diesel (Oct 93 - Oct 99) L to V	3571
Seat Ibiza & Malaga (85 - 92) B to K	1609

Title	Book No.
SKODA	
Skoda Estelle (77 - 89) up to G	0604
Skoda Favorit (89 - 96) F to N	1801
Skoda Felicia Petrol & Diesel (95 - 01) M to X	3505
SUBARU	
Subaru 1600 & 1800 (Nov 79 - 90) up to H	0995
SUNBEAM	
Sunbeam Alpine, Rapier & H120 (67 - 76)*	0051
SUZUKI	
Suzuki SJ Series, Samurai & Vitara (4-cyl) (82 - 97) up to P	1942
Suzuki Supercarry & Bedford/Vauxhall Rascal (86 - Oct 94) C to M	3015
TALBOT	
Talbot Alpine, Solara, Minx & Rapier (75 - 86) up to D	0337
Talbot Horizon (78 - 86) up to D	0473
Talbot Samba (82 - 86) up to D	0823
TOYOTA	
Toyota Carina E (May 92 - 97) J to P	3256
Toyota Corolla (Sept 83 - Sept 87) A to E	1024
Toyota Corolla (80 - 85) up to C	0683
Toyota Corolla (Sept 87 - Aug 92) E to K	1683
Toyota Corolla (Aug 92 - 97) K to P	3259
Toyota Hi-Ace & Hi-Lux (69 - Oct 83) up to A	0304
TRIUMPH	
Triumph Acclaim (81 - 84)*	0792
Triumph GT6 & Vitesse (62 - 74)*	0112
Triumph Herald (59 - 71)*	0010
Triumph Spitfire (62 - 81) up to X	0113
Triumph Stag (70 - 78) up to T	0441
Triumph TR2, TR3, TR3A, TR4 & TR4A (52 - 67)*	0028
Triumph TR5 & 6 (67 - 75)*	0031
Triumph TR7 (75 - 82)*	0322
VAUXHALL	
Vauxhall Astra (80 - Oct 84) up to B	0635
Vauxhall Astra & Belmont (Oct 84 - Oct 91) B to J	1136
Vauxhall Astra (Oct 91 - Feb 98) J to R	1832
Vauxhall/Opel Astra & Zafira Diesel (Feb 98 - Sept 00) R to W	3797
Vauxhall/Opel Astra & Zafira Petrol (Feb 98 - Sept 00) R to W	3758
Vauxhall/Opel Calibra (90 - 98) G to S	3502
Vauxhall Carlton (Oct 78 - Oct 86) up to D	0480
Vauxhall Carlton & Senator (Nov 86 - 94) D to L	1469
Vauxhall Cavalier 1300 (77 - July 81)*	0461
Vauxhall Cavalier 1600, 1900 & 2000 (75 - July 81) up to W	0315
Vauxhall Cavalier (81 - Oct 88) up to F	0812
Vauxhall Cavalier (Oct 88 - 95) F to N	1570
Vauxhall Chevette (75 - 84) up to B	0285
Vauxhall Corsa (Mar 93 - 97) K to R	1985
Vauxhall/Opel Corsa (Apr 97 - Oct 00) P to X	3921
Vauxhall/Opel Frontera Petrol & Diesel (91 - Sept 98) J to S	3454
Vauxhall Nova (83 - 93) up to K	0909
Vauxhall/Opel Omega (94 - 99) L to T	3510
Vauxhall/Opel Vectra Petrol & Diesel (95 - Feb 99) N to S	3396
Vauxhall/Opel Vectra (Mar 99 - May 02) T-reg. onwards	3930
Vauxhall/Opel 1.5, 1.6 & 1.7 litre Diesel Engine (82 - 96) up to N	1222
VOLKSWAGEN	
Volkswagen 411 & 412 (68 - 75)*	0091
Volkswagen Beetle 1200 (54 - 77) up to S	0036
Volkswagen Beetle 1300 & 1500 (65 - 75) up to P	0039

Title	Book No.
Volkswagen Beetle 1302 & 1302S (70 - 72) up to L	0110
Volkswagen Beetle 1303, 1303S & GT (72 - 75) up to P	0159
Volkswagen Beetle Petrol & Diesel (Apr 99 - 01) T-reg onwards	3798
Volkswagen Golf & Bora Petrol & Diesel (April 98 - 00) R to X	3727
Volkswagen Golf & Jetta Mk 1 1.1 & 1.3 (74 - 84) up to A	0716
Volkswagen Golf, Jetta & Scirocco Mk 1 1.5, 1.6 & 1.8 (74 - 84) up to A	0726
Volkswagen Golf & Jetta Mk 1 Diesel (78 - 84) up to A	0451
Volkswagen Golf & Jetta Mk 2 (Mar 84 - Feb 92) A to J	1081
Volkswagen Golf & Vento Petrol & Diesel (Feb 92 - Mar 98) J to R	3097
Volkswagen LT vans & light trucks (76 - 87) up to E	0637
Volkswagen Passat & Santana (Sept 81 - May 88) up to E	0814
Volkswagen Passat Petrol & Diesel (May 88 - 96) E to P	3498
Volkswagen Passat 4-cyl Petrol & Diesel (Dec 96 - Nov 00) P to X	3917
Volkswagen Polo & Derby (76 - Jan 82) up to X	0335
Volkswagen Polo (82 - Oct 90) up to H	0813
Volkswagen Polo (Nov 90 - Aug 94) H to L	3245
Volkswagen Polo Hatchback Petrol & Diesel (94 - 99) M to S	3500
Volkswagen Scirocco (82 - 90) up to H	1224
Volkswagen Transporter 1600 (68 - 79) up to V	0082
Volkswagen Transporter 1700, 1800 & 2000 (72 - 79) up to V	0226
Volkswagen Transporter (air-cooled) (79 - 82) up to Y	0638
Volkswagen Transporter (water-cooled) (82 - 90) up to H	3452
Volkswagen Type 3 (63 - 73)*	0084
VOLVO	
Volvo 120 & 130 Series (& P1800) (61 - 73)*	0203
Volvo 142, 144 & 145 (66 - 74) up to N	0129
Volvo 240 Series (74 - 93) up to K	0270
Volvo 262, 264 & 260/265 (75 - 85)*	0400
Volvo 340, 343, 345 & 360 (76 - 91) up to J	0715
Volvo 440, 460 & 480 (87 - 97) D to P	1691
Volvo 740 & 760 (82 - 91) up to J	1258
Volvo 850 (92 - 96) J to P	3260
Volvo 940 (90 - 96) H to N	3249
Volvo S40 & V40 (96 - 99) N to V	3569
Volvo S70, V70 & C70 (96 - 99) P to V	3573
AUTOMOTIVE TECHBOOKS	
Automotive Air Conditioning Systems	3740
Automotive Carburettor Manual	3288
Automotive Diagnostic Fault Codes Manual	3472
Automotive Diesel Engine Service Guide	3286
Automotive Electrical and Electronic Systems Manual	3049
Automotive Engine Management and Fuel Injection Systems Manual	3344
Automotive Gearbox Overhaul Manual	3473
Automotive Service Summaries Manual	3475
Automotive Timing Belts Manual – Austin/Rover	3549
Automotive Timing Belts Manual – Ford	3474
Automotive Timing Belts Manual – Peugeot/Citroën	3568
Automotive Timing Belts Manual – Vauxhall/Opel	3577
Automotive Welding Manual	3053
In-Car Entertainment Manual (3rd Edition)	3363

* Classic reprint

All the products featured on this page are available through most motor accessory shops, cycle shops and book stores. Our policy of continuous updating and development means that titles are being constantly added to the range. For up-to-date information on our complete list of titles, please telephone: (UK) +44 1963 442030 • (USA) +1 805 498 6703 • (France) +33 1 47 17 66 29 • (Sweden) +46 18 124016 • (Australia) +61 3 9763 8100

Notes